NP 54

ADMIRALTY SAILING DIRECTIONS

NORTH SEA (WEST) PILOT

East coasts of Scotland and England from Rattray Head to Southwold

EIGHTH EDITION
2009

IMPORTANT - SEE RELATED ADMIRALTY PUBLICATIONS

Notices to Mariners (Annual, permanent, temporary and preliminary), **Chart 5011** (Symbols and abbreviations), **The Mariner's Handbook** (especially Chapters 1 and 2 for important information on the use of UKHO products, their accuracy and limitations), **Sailing Directions** (Pilots), **List of Lights and Fog Signals**, **List of Radio Signals**, **Tide Tables** (or their digital equivalents).

Keep charts and publications up-to-date and use the largest scale chart appropriate.

PUBLISHED BY THE UNITED KINGDOM HYDROGRAPHIC OFFICE

DIRECTIONS FOR UPDATING THIS VOLUME

This volume is kept up to date in a "Continuous Revision" cycle. This means that it will be continuously revised by its Editor for a period of approximately three years using information received in the Hydrographic Office, and then republished. Publication is announced in Part 1 of *Admiralty Notices to Mariners,* and a listing of all current editions is updated and published quarterly in Part 1B of *Admiralty Notices to Mariners* and six-monthly in NP 234 *Cumulative List of Admiralty Notices to Mariners.* Additionally, this list is continuously updated and available on the UKHO website at www.ukho.gov.uk

During the life of the book, it is amended as necessary by notices published weekly in Section IV of *Admiralty Notices to Mariners.*

A check-list of all extant Notices, but not the text, is published quarterly at Section IB of *Admiralty Notices to Mariners.* The full text of all extant Section IV Notices are published annually in January in NP247(2) *Annual Summary of Admiralty Notices to Mariners - Amendments to Sailing Directions.*

These amendments will normally be restricted to those critical to the safety of navigation, and information required to be published as a result of changes to national legislation affecting shipping, and to port regulations.

It is recommended that amendments issued in this way are cut out and pasted into the book. Mariners may, however, prefer to keep amendments in a separate file, and annotate the text of the book in the margin to indicate the existence of an amendment. This latter method may be more appropriate in some volumes where significant numbers of amendments, sometimes overlapping, may make the cut-and-paste method unwieldy and confusing.

RECORD OF AMENDMENTS

The table below is to record Section IV Notices to Mariners amendments affecting this volume.

Sub-paragraph numbers in the margin of the body of the book are to assist the user when making amendments to this volume.

Weekly Notices to Mariners (Section IV)

2013 ~~2009~~	2010	2011	2012
WK5 – p.141	1/10 p.226	01/11 p.134,212,213,	WK6 – PAG. 204,224 PP
	11/10 – 220,221	225,227,223,221	WK7 – PAG 141,17,196 PP
	44/10 (216,218,219)	24/11 p.136	WK 21 – 174
	15/10 p.155	09/11 p.193	WK 36 – pg. 105
	38/10 p.221	26/11 p.89,91	
	39/10 p.213,215,217	34/11 p 233 TR.	
	12/10 p.156,169,170,193,194,199	36/11 p 59 TR.	
	25/10 154	42/11 p 201,202	
		45/11 p.83,107	
		47/11 p.106,108	

ii

CONTENTS

CHAPTER 1

CHAPTER 2

CHAPTER 3

CHAPTER 4

CHAPTER 5

CONTENTS

PREFACE

The Eighth Edition of the *North Sea (West) Pilot* has been prepared by Captain R S Coles, Master Mariner and Captain M Waight, Master Mariner based on the fully revised Third Edition (1995) compiled by Captain J H Gommersall, Master Mariner. The United Kingdom Hydrographic Office has used all reasonable endeavours to ensure that this Pilot contains all the information obtained by and assessed by it at the date shown below. Information received or assessed after that date will be included in *Admiralty Notices to Mariners* where appropriate. For details of *Admiralty Notices to Mariners* and guidance on their use; see *The Mariner's Handbook.*

This edition supersedes the Seventh Edition (2006), which is cancelled.

Information on climate and currents has been based on data provided by the Met Office, Exeter.

The following sources of information, other than UKHO Publications and Ministry of Defence papers, have been consulted:

Local Port Authorities
Port Handbooks produced by Port Authorities
Lloyd's Register Fairplay, Ports and Terminals Guide (2009)
Lloyds Shipping Information Services
Ports of Scotland (Graham Ogilvie) (2009)
The Statesman's Yearbook (2009)
Whitaker's Almanac (2009)
Port websites produced by Port Authorities

Mr M S Robinson
Chief Executive
United Kingdom Hydrographic Office

3rd September 2009

PURPOSE OF ADMIRALTY SAILING DIRECTIONS

Sailing Directions are intended for use by vessels of 150 gt or more. They amplify charted detail and contain information needed for safe navigation which is not available from charts or other hydrographic publications. They are written with the assumption that these are to hand and are intended to be read in conjunction with the charts quoted in the text which includes both charted and uncharted information.

They are normally arranged as follows:

Preface. Includes a list of publications and documents consulted in the writing of the volume.

Preliminary pages. Includes explanatory notes abbreviations and a glossary.

Chapter 1. Contains general information on navigation, regulations, countries, ports and natural conditions, pertaining to the whole book.

Chapter 2. Through-routing information where appropriate.

Chapter 3 and subsequent chapters. Geographical chapters containing coastal passage information, directions for waterways, and essential information on ports and anchorages.

Appendices. Transcripts or extracts of regulations.

Index.

Each volume has a book index diagram facing Page 1 which indicates the geographical coverage of each chapter. This will assist to identify which chapter contains the information required.

Each chapter has an index diagram facing its first page showing paragraph numbers against arrows or port names, which indicates the start of the appropriate text.

Chapters are divided into sections containing a number of sub-sections. Each sub-section is either a description of a waterway, offshore, coastal or inshore, with suitable cross-references to the texts in which the continuation of routes, or alternative routes, can be found. Otherwise it describes a major port. Smaller ports are described within the waterway sub-section.

General information relating to the whole book is contained in Chapter 1. General information at the start of the chapter is that relating to the chapter as a whole and includes material under the headings of topography, hazards, pilotage, VTS and traffic regulations, marine nature reserves, natural conditions and other topics. General information at the start of a section or sub-section only relates to that particular section.

Warning. This volume should only be used once fully amended by Section IV Notices to Mariners.

HOW TO REPORT NEW OR SUSPECTED DANGERS TO NAVIGATION OR CHANGES OBSERVED IN AIDS TO NAVIGATION

A Hydrographic Note, Form H.102, with instructions, is contained in the back of the Weekly Edition of Admiralty Notices to Mariners. This form can also be downloaded from the UKHO Website. The form should be used to report all observations, including new or suspected dangers to navigation or changes to aids to navigation.

FEEDBACK

In order to maintain and improve the accuracy of information contained within this volume, The United Kingdom Hydrographic Office welcomes general comments, new, additional or corroborative information and digital images from mariners and other users. Such information should be forwarded by post, fax or e-mail to the address below giving, where possible, the source for the information if this is not based on personal observation.

UKHO CONTACT DETAILS

Helpdesk
United Kingdom Hydrographic Office
Admiralty Way
TAUNTON
Somerset
TA1 2DN
United Kingdom
e-mail: helpdesk@ukho.gov.uk
Tel: +44 (0)1823 723366
Fax: +44 (0)1823 350561
Website: www.ukho.gov.uk

Admiralty Sailing Directions
e-mail: sailingdirections@ukho.gov.uk
Tel: +44 (0)1823 337900   extension 3518   (Book Support Unit)
                                              extension 3382   (Head of Sailing Directions)
Fax: +44 (0)1823 284077   (Book Support Unit)

HOW TO OBTAIN ADMIRALTY CHARTS AND PUBLICATIONS

A complete list of Admiralty Charts and Publications (both paper and digital), together with a list of authorised Admiralty Distributors for their purchase, is contained in the "Catalogue of Admiralty Charts and Publications" (NP131), which is published annually. The Admiralty Digital Catalogue is available to download free of charge from the UKHO Website.

Details of authorised Admiralty Distributors can also be obtained from the UKHO Helpdesk.

RELATED ADMIRALTY PUBLICATIONS AND THEIR CONTENTS

Admiralty Notices to Mariners (NMs):

Weekly Notices to Mariners

Navigationally significant changes to nautical charts, lights, fog signals, radio signals and Sailing Directions

Reprint of all Radio Navigational Warnings in force and a summary of of charts and publications being published.

Cumulative List of Notices to Mariners

Published in January and July of each year

A list of all nautical charts available and a complete list of all NMs affecting them during the previous two years.

Annual Summary of Notices to Mariners

Published at the beginning of the year in two parts

Annual Notices to Mariners, Temporary and Preliminary notices

Cumulative summary of amendments to Sailing Directions.

The Mariners Handbook:

Information on charts and their use

Operational information and regulation

Tides and currents

Characteristics of the sea

Basic meteorology

Navigation in ice

Hazards and restrictions to navigation

IALA Maritime Buoyage System.

Admiralty Sailing Directions (Pilots):

Waterway directions

Port facilities

Directions for port entry

Navigational hazards

Buoyage

Climatological data.

Admiralty List of Radio Signals:

Maritime Radio Stations

Radio Aids to Navigation

Time

Maritime Safety Information

Radio weather services

Global Maritime Distress and Safety System (GMDSS)

Pilot services

Vessel Traffic Services

Port operations.

Admiralty List of Lights:

Lighthouses, lightships, lit floating marks

Characteristics and intensity

Elevation

Range of light

Description of structure.

Admiralty Tidal Publications:

Tide Tables

  Daily predictions of time and height of high and low water at Standard Ports

  Time and height differences for Secondary Ports

  Harmonic constants where known

  Supplementary Tables including Land Levelling and Chart Datum corrections where known.

Tidal Stream Atlases

  Major tidal streams for selected waters of north west Europe

  Direction and rate of tidal streams at hourly intervals.

For more information, please visit www.ukho.gov.uk

GENERAL INFORMATION

Remarks on subject matter:

Buoys are generally described in detail only when they have special navigational significance, or where the scale of the chart is too small to show all the details clearly.

Chapter index diagrams in this volume show only those Admiralty charts of a suitable scale to give good coverage of the area. Mariners should consult NP 131 *Catalogue of Admiralty Charts and Publications* for details of larger scale charts.

Chart references in the text normally refer to the largest scale Admiralty chart but occasionally a smaller scale chart may be quoted where its use is more appropriate.

Firing, practice and exercise areas. Submarine exercise areas are mentioned in Sailing Directions. Other firing, practice and exercise areas may be mentioned with limited details. Signals and buoys used in connection with these areas may be mentioned if significant for navigation. Attention is invited to the Annual Notice to Mariners on this subject.

Names have been taken from the most authoritative source. When an obsolete name still appears on the chart, it is given in brackets following the proper name at the principal description of the feature in the text and where the name is first mentioned.

Port plans in this book are intended to assist the mariner in orientation and they are not to be used for navigation. The appropriate scale of chart should always be used.

Tidal information relating the daily vertical movements of the water is not given. For this information *Admiralty Tide Tables* or *Admiralty Total Tide* should be consulted. Changes in water level of an abnormal nature are mentioned.

Time difference used in the text when applied to the time of High Water found from the *Admiralty Tide Tables*, gives the time of the event being described in the Standard Time kept in the area of that event. Due allowance must be made for any seasonal daylight saving time which may be kept.

Wreck information is included where drying or below-water wrecks are relatively permanent features having significance for navigation or anchoring.

Units and terminology used in this volume:

Bands is the word used to indicate horizontal marking.

Bearings and directions are referred to the true compass and when given in degrees are reckoned clockwise from 000° (North) to 359°
Bearings used for positioning are given from the reference object.
Bearings of objects, alignments and light sectors are given as seen from the vessel.
Courses always refer to the course to be made good over the ground.

Conspicuous objects are natural and artificial marks which are outstanding, easily identifiable and clearly visible to the mariner over a large area of sea in varying conditions of light. If the scale is large enough they will normally be shown on the chart in bold capitals and may be marked "conspic".

Depths are given below chart datum, except where otherwise stated.

Distances are expressed in sea miles of 60 to a degree of latitude and sub-divided into cables of one tenth of a sea mile.

Elevations, as distinct from heights, are given above Mean High Water Springs or Mean Higher High Water whichever is quoted in *Admiralty Tide Tables*, and expressed as, "an elevation of ... m". However the elevation of natural features such as hills may alternatively be expressed as "... m high" since in this case there can be no confusion between elevation and height.

Heights of objects refer to the height of the object above the ground and are invariably expressed as "... m in height".

Latitude and Longitude given in brackets are approximate and are taken from the chart quoted.

Metric units are used for all measurements of depths, heights and short distances, but where feet/fathoms charts are referred to, these latter units are given in brackets after the metric values for depths and heights shown on the chart.

Principal marks are marks which qualify for inclusion and are outstanding and clearly visible throughout most of the waterway (or 15 to 20 miles of the waterway for particularly long waterways) as marks by day or lights by night; thereby being associated with the waterway as a whole, rather than being confined to any single set of Directions within it. In particular:
Landmarks comprise buildings and structures (including lighthouses, whether major lights or not), daymarks and natural features.
They may be on the coast or farther inland, provided they are distinctly visible from seaward.
Major lights is used in Sailing Directions to refer to all lights with a range of 15 miles or over.
Offshore marks include light vessels, light floats, LANBY, buoyant beacons, and oil production platforms.

Prominent objects are those which are easily identifiable, but do not justify being classified as conspicuous.

Stripes is the word used to indicate markings which are vertical, unless stated to be diagonal.

Tidal streams and currents are described by the direction towards which they flow.

Time is expressed in the four-figure notation beginning at midnight and is given in local time unless otherwise stated. Details of local time kept will be found in *Admiralty List of Radio Signals Volume 2*.

Winds are described by the direction from which they blow.

ABBREVIATIONS

The following abbreviations are used in the text:

AIS	Automatic Identification System		JRCC	Joint Rescue Co-ordination Centre
ALC	Articulated loading column			
ALP	Articulated loading platform		kHz	kilohertz
AMVER	Automated Mutual Assistance Vessel Rescue System		km	kilometre(s)
			kn	knot(s)
ASL	Archipelagic Sea Lane		kW	kilowatt(s)
°C	degrees Celsius		Lanby	Large automatic navigation buoy
CALM	Catenary anchor leg mooring		LASH	Lighter Aboard Ship
CBM	Conventional buoy mooring		LAT	Lowest Astronomical Tide
cm	centimetre(s)		LF	low frequency
CDC	Certain Dangerous Cargo		LHG	Liquefied Hazardous Gas
CVTS	Co-operative Vessel Traffic System		LMT	Local Mean Time
			LNG	Liquefied Natural Gas
DF	direction finding		LOA	Length overall
DG	degaussing		LPG	Liquefied Petroleum Gas
DGPS	Differential Global Positioning System		LW	Low Water
DMA	Dynamic Management Area			
DW	Deep Water		m	metre(s)
DSC	Digital Selective Calling		mb	millibar(s)
dwt	deadweight tonnage		MCTS	Marine Communications and Traffic Services Centres
DZ	danger zone			
			MF	medium frequency
E	east (easterly, eastward, eastern, easternmost)		MHz	megahertz
EEZ	exclusive economic zone		MHHW	Mean Higher High Water
ELSBM	Exposed location single buoy mooring		MHLW	Mean Higher Low Water
ENE	east-north-east		MHW	Mean High Water
EPIRB	Emergency Position Indicating Radio Beacon		MHWN	Mean High Water Neaps
ESE	east-south-east		MHWS	Mean High Water Springs
ETA	estimated time of arrival		MLHW	Mean Lower High Water
ETD	estimated time of departure		MLLW	Mean Lower Low Water
EU	European Union		MLW	Mean Low Water
			MLWN	Mean Low Water Neaps
feu	forty foot equivalent unit		MLWS	Mean Low Water Springs
fm	fathom(s)		mm	millimetre(s)
FPSO	Floating production storage and offloading vessel		MMSI	Maritime Mobile Service Identity
			MRCC	Maritime Rescue Co-ordination Centre
FPU	Floating production unit		MRSC	Maritime Rescue Sub-Centre
FSO	Floating storage and offloading vessel		MSI	Marine Safety Information
ft	foot (feet)		MSL	Mean Sea Level
			MSR	Mandatory Ship Reporting
g/cm³	gram per cubic centimetre		MV	Motor Vessel
GMDSS	Global Maritime Distress and Safety System		MW	megawatt(s)
GPS	Global Positioning System		MY	Motor Yacht
GRP	glass reinforced plastic			
gt	gross tonnage		N	north (northerly, northward, northern, northernmost)
			NATO	North Atlantic Treaty Organization
HAT	Highest Astronomical Tide		Navtex	Navigational Telex System
HF	high frequency		NE	north-east
hm	hectometre		NNE	north-north-east
HMS	Her (His) Majesty's Ship		NNW	north-north-west
hp	horse power		No	number
hPa	hectopascal		nt	nett tonnage
HSC	High Speed Craft		NW	north-west
HW	High Water			
			ODAS	Ocean Data Acquisition System
IALA	International Association of Lighthouse Authorities			
			PLEM	Pipe line end manifold
IHO	International Hydrographic Organization		POL	Petrol, Oil & Lubricants
IMO	International Maritime Organization		PSSA	Particularly Sensitive Sea Areas
ITCZ	Intertropical Convergence Zone		PWC	Personal watercraft

RCC	Rescue Co-ordination Centre		teu	twenty foot equivalent unit
RMS	Royal Mail Ship		TSS	Traffic Separation Scheme
RN	Royal Navy			
RoRo	Roll-on, Roll-off		UHF	ultra high frequency
RT	radio telephony		UKC	under keel clearance
			UKHO	United Kingdom Hydrographic Office
			ULCC	Ultra Large Crude Carrier
S	south (southerly, southward, southern, southernmost)		UN	United Nations
			UT	Universal Time
SALM	Single anchor leg mooring system		UTC	Co-ordinated Universal Time
SALS	Single anchored leg storage system			
SAR	Search and Rescue		VDR	Voyage Data Recorder
Satnav	Satellite navigation		VHF	very high frequency
SBM	Single buoy mooring		VLCC	Very Large Crude Carrier
SE	south-east		VMRS	Vessel Movement Reporting System
SMA	Seasonal Management Area		VTC	Vessel Traffic Centre
SPM	Single point mooring		VTMS	Vessel Traffic Management System
sq	square		VTS	Vessel Traffic Services
SRR	Search and Rescue Region			
SS	Steamship		W	west (westerly, westward, western, westernmost)
SSE	south-south-east		WGS	World Geodetic System
SSW	south-south-west		WMO	World Meteorological Organization
SW	south-west		WNW	west-north-west
SWATH	small waterplane area twin hull ship		WSW	west-south-west
			WT	radio (wireless) telegraphy

Chapter Index Diagram

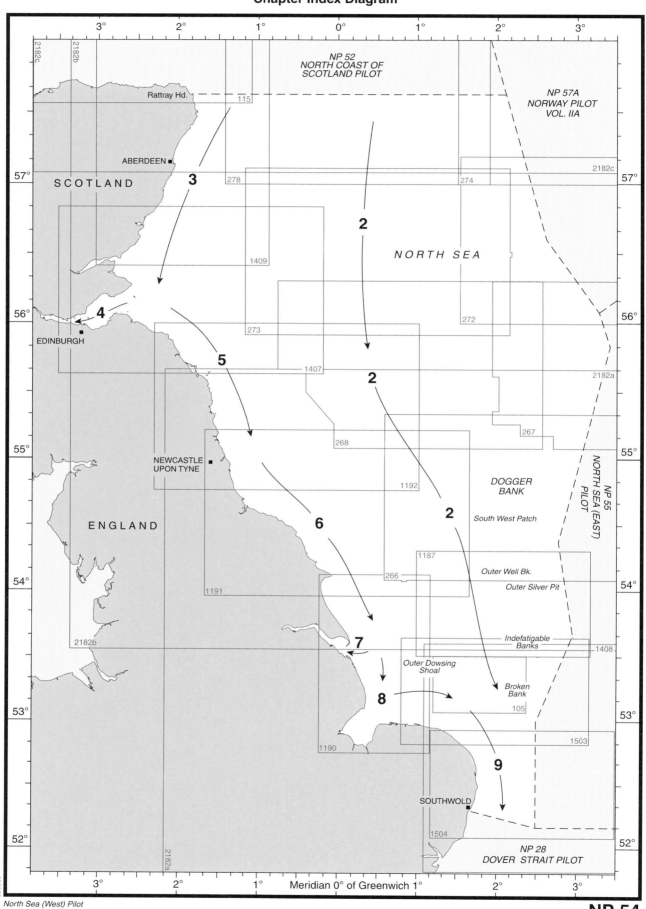

referenced to the Soviet Geocentric Co-ordinate System 1990 (SGS90) and positions must be adjusted, if necessary, to the datum of the chart being used.

3 Differential GPS (DGPS) compares the position of a fixed point, referred to as the reference station, with positions obtained from a GPS receiver at that point. The resulting differences are then broadcast as corrections to suitable receivers to overcome the inherent and imposed limitations of GPS. There are two stations within the coverage of this book, each having a range of 150 miles;

Girdle Ness Light (57°08'·3N 2°02'·9W),
Flamborough Head Light (54°07'·0N 0°05'·0W).

4 **Caution.** Total dependence on GNSS is unwise. Satellite navigation systems are under the control of the owning nation which may impose selective availability or downgrade the accuracy. Furthermore, the very low signal levels which reach receivers make GNSS systems vulnerable to inteference both intentional and unintentional. GNSS systems also suffer occasionally from undetected failures, for example a satellite clock error.

For full details of these systems see *Admiralty List of Radio Signals Volume 2.*

European Loran C System (Eurofix)
1.37

1 Loran-C provides position information from a source entirely independent of a GNSS. The two systems' positions can be compared and an alarm generated if they diverge beyond a set limit. Several equipment manufacturers supply combined GNSS/Loran-C receivers which produce position information from either system or both. Commonly, GNSS is used as the primary system with Loran-C providing an automatic back-up. Loran-C can provide alternative inputs to electronic charts, GMDSS radios and other onboard systems.

2 The Loran-C signal is transmitted at a much higher power and a lower frequency than GNSS thus making it less vulnerable to inteference.

For further details of the Eurofix chains see *Admiralty List of Radio Signals Volume 2.*

Radio aids to navigation
1.38

1 Full details of radio aids to navigation outlined below are given in *Admiralty List of Radio Signals Volume 2.* Individual stations and services which may be of assistance to the mariner are listed as necessary within the text of this volume.

2 **Radar beacons (racons)** transmit from numerous locations both fixed and floating, including offshore oil and gas field installations.

For further details see *Admiralty List of Radio Signals Volume 2.*

Automatic Identification System (AIS). For details see 1.47 and *Admiralty List of Radio Signals Volume 6 (1).* General information about AIS may be found in *The Mariner's Handbook.* AIS is also being fitted to offshore oil platforms, lighthouses and selected navigational buoys around the coast in order to enhance navigational safety.

3 **VHF direction finding service** for emergency use only is operated by UK Coastguard; see 1.70.

Marine Safety Information (MSI)
1.39

1 The area lies within the limits of NAV/METAREA I of the World-wide Navigation Warning Service; the Area Co-ordinator is the United Kingdom.

Within the NAV/METAREA, Coastal Warnings and Local Warnings may be transmitted. Coastal Warnings are promulgated mainly by the UK Hydrographic Office for navigational warnings and the Meteorological Office for weather forecasts and gale warnings. They cover a distance of 100-200 miles from the coast and are transmitted through a network of coast radio stations operated by the coastguard organisation (1.67). Local Warnings cover the area within the limits of jurisdiction of a Harbour or Port Authority VTS and are intended to supplement the Coastal Warnings by giving information not normally required by ocean-going shipping in transit.

2 NAVTEX, an international automated direct-printing service broadcasting on 518 kHz and 490 kHz for the promulgation of navigational warnings, meteorological warnings, and urgent information to ships, is available. Navtex messages for the waters described in this volume are broadcast from Cullercoats (55°04'N 1°28'W).

3 See *Admiralty List of Radio Signals Volume 3 (1)* and *The Mariner's Handbook* for further details.

Radio weather reports
1.40

1 Details of meteorological services for shipping, including broadcasts by BBC Radio 4 and radio-facsimile weather charts, are given in *Admiralty List of Radio Signals Volume 3 (1).*

The Meteorological Office transmits routine forecasts, gale warnings and strong coastal wind forecasts by internet, telephone and facsimile. See *www.metoffice.gov.uk.*

REGULATIONS-INTERNATIONAL

Submarine pipelines and cables
1.41

1 A number of submarine cables and pipelines cross the S part of the North Sea. They are shown on the charts and, in the case of the pipelines, which link the offshore oil and gas fields to the shore, marked with the appropriate legend (oil or gas).

2 Regulations to prevent damage to submarine cables and pipelines are contained in *The International Convention for the Protection of Submarine Cables 1884,* as extended by the *Convention on the High Seas, 1958.*

3 **Caution.** Mariners are advised not to anchor or trawl in the vicinity of pipelines. Gas from a damaged oil or gas pipeline could cause an explosion, loss of a vessel's buoyancy or other serious hazard. Pipelines are not always buried and may significantly reduce the charted depth. They may also span seabed undulations and cause fishing gear to become irrecoverably snagged, putting a vessel in severe danger.

4 See *The Mariner's Handbook* for further details.

Pollution of the sea

Marpol 73/78
1.42

1 *The Mariner's Handbook* gives a summary of *The International Convention for the Prevention of Pollution from Ships 1973,* as modified by the Protocol of 1978, and known as MARPOL 73/78.

Pollution reports. Under the Convention, a Master has a duty to report pollution incidents or damage and breakdowns affecting the safety of his vessel. For further details see *Admiralty List of Radio Signals Volume 1.*

Special areas
1.43

1   Under MARPOL 73/78 designated Special Areas, owing to their sensitive oceanographic and ecological conditions and to their maritime traffic, are provided with a higher level of protection and regulation than other areas of the sea. The North Sea region is regarded as a Special Area in respect of Annexes I (Oil) and V (Garbage from Ships) and, in respect of Annex VI (Air Pollution), it is a special SOx (sulphur oxide) Emission Control Area.

REGULATIONS – EUROPEAN UNION

Routeing and traffic

Directive 2002/59/EC
1.44

1   **General information.** This Directive establishes a common vessel traffic monitoring and information system throughout European Community (EC) waters. The principal provisions are described below. They apply in general to all commercial vessels over 300 gt but the rules concerning the notification of carriage of dangerous and polluting goods applies to all vessels regardless of size.

2   **Caution.** These extracts are for reference purposes only and are not to be regarded as a statement of the applicable law. The full text of the regulations is the sole authoritative statement of the applicable law and it is recommended that it is consulted. The regulations to which the following refers is *Directive 2002/59/EC* or the appropriate enabling legislation drafted by individual member states, which in the United Kingdom is *The Merchant Shipping (Traffic Monitoring and Reporting Requirements) Regulations 2004*, a copy of which can be obtained from The Stationery Office (www.tso.gov.uk).

1.45

1   **Ship reports.** All vessels bound for a port within the EC must report to the port authority at least 24 hours prior to arrival, or, if the voyage is less than 24 hours, no later than the time of departure from the previous port. The report shall include the following information:

    Name, call sign, IMO or MMSI number.
    Port of destination.
    ETA and ETD at port of destination.
    Total number of persons onboard.

2   Upon receipt of a ship's report, the port authority will notify the national coastguard authority by the quickest means possible. This information will then be pooled in the European-wide telematic network called SafeSeaNet.

    Any amendments to the initial ship report must be notified immediately.

    Mandatory ship reporting systems. All vessels shall report to the coastguard authority on entering an IMO adopted mandatory ship reporting system, the report being made in the recognised format (See *Admiralty List of Radio Signals Volume 6*). The coastguard authority is to be informed of any changes to the initial report.

1.46

1   **VTS.** All vessels are to participate in and comply with VTS systems operated by EC member states and also those systems operated by member states in conjunction with co-operating non-member states. This includes those systems operated by member states outside their territorial waters but which are operated in accordance with IMO guidelines.

    Routeing Schemes. All vessels must comply with IMO recommended TSS and Deep Water route regulations. (See IMO publication *Ships' Routeing Guide*).

1.47

1   **AIS and VDR.** All vessels are to be equipped with AIS and VDR. The systems shall be in operation at all times except where international rules provide for the protection of navigational information.

    All coastguard stations throughout the EC are required to be able to receive AIS information and to relay it to all other coastguard stations within the EC.

1.48

1   **Notification of dangerous and polluting goods.** All vessels leaving an EC port are to report dangerous and polluting goods as specified within the Directive to the harbour authority. Vessels arriving from outside EC waters must transmit a report to their first EC port or anchorage upon departure from their port of loading. If, at the time of departure, the port of destination in the EC is not known, the report must be forwarded immediately such information becomes known. Where practical, this report is to be made electronically and must include the information described in Annex 1(3) of the Directive.

2   When a harbour authority receives a dangerous or polluting cargo report, it shall retain the report for use in the event of an incident or accident at sea, forwarding it whenever requested by the national coastguard authority.

1.49

1   **Reporting of Incidents and Accidents.** Whenever a vessel is involved with one of the following, the coastguard authority of the EC coastal state is to be informed immediately;

    (a) any incident or accident affecting the safety of the ship;
    (b) any incident or accident which compromises shipping safety, such as a failure likely to affect a ship's manoeuvrability or seaworthiness;
    (c) any event liable to pollute the waters or shores of the coastal state;
    (d) The sighting of a slick of polluting material or drifting containers and packages.

    The owner of a vessel, who has been informed by the master that one of the above has occured, must inform the coastguard and render any assistance that may be required.

1.50

1   **Measures to be taken in the event of exceptionally bad weather or sea conditions.** If, on the advice of the national meteorological office, the coastguard authority deems a threat of pollution or a risk to human life exists due to impending severe weather, the coastguard authority will attempt to inform the master of every vessel about to enter or leave port as to the nature of the weather and the dangers it may cause.

2   Without prejudice to measures taken to give assistance to vessels in distress, the coastguard may take such measures as it considers appropriate to avoid a threat of pollution or a risk to human life. The measures may include:

    (a) a recommendation or a prohibition on entry or departure from a port;
    (b) a recommendation limiting, or, if necessary, prohibiting the bunkering of ships in territorial waters.

3   The master is to inform his owners of any measures or recommendations initiated by the coastguard. If, as a result of his professional judgement, the master decides not to act in accordance with measures taken by the coastguard, he shall inform the coastguard of his reasons for not doing so.

1.51

1   **Measures relating to incidents or accidents at sea.** The coastguard authority will take measures to ensure the safety of shipping and of persons and to protect the marine and coastal environment. Measures available to EC states include;

    (a) a restriction on the movement of a ship or an instruction to follow a specific course.

    (b) a notification to put an end to the threat to the environment or maritime safety;

    (c) sending an evaluation team aboard a ship to assess the degree of risk and to help the master remedy the situation;

    (d) instructing the master to put in at a place of refuge in the event of imminent peril, or, cause the ship to be piloted or towed.

2   The owner of the ship and the owner of the dangerous or polluting goods onboard must co-operate with the coastgurd authority when requested to do so.

1.52

1   **Places of refuge.** EC states are required to designate places of refuge where a vessel which has undergone an accident or is in distress can receive rapid and effective assistance to avoid environmental pollution.

Pollution of the Sea

Combating oil pollution

1.53

1   All countries which border the North Sea have agreed to co-operate in combating oil pollution by means of surveillance and in the pooling of resources in an emergency incident. Other European Community measures contributing to the subject include Port State Control Inspections (Directive 95/21/EC), Port Reception Facilities for Ship-Generated Waste and Cargo Residues (Directive 2000/59/EC), The Phasing Out of Single-Hull Tankers (Directive 417/2002/EC) and Sulphur Content of Marine Fuels (Directive 2005/33/EC). For further information see www.emsa.eu.int. and www.parismou.org.

Regulation No 417/2002/EC

1.54

1   This regulation establishes a timetable for the phasing out of all single-hull petroleum tankers of more than 5000 dwt in European waters. Ultimately only double-hull tankers or tankers of equivalent design will be permitted to visit European ports and offshore terminals.

The timetable is based upon a vessel's date of build, its design and the type of petroleum carried. The schedule for Category 1 tankers as defined by this regulation completed in 2007 and for Category 2 and 3 tankers will complete in 2015.

Measures to enhance maritime security

1.55

1   In compliance with Regulation 725/2004/EC, subject vessels are required to provide security information, as required by SOLAS XI-2 and the ISPS Code, to the appropriate national authority 24 hours prior to arrival. For further information see www.gisis.imo.org.

REGULATIONS - UNITED KINGDOM

Administration

1.56

1   The United Kingdom Maritime and Coastguard Agency is an executive agency of the Department for Transport. The agency is responsible for all aspects of maritime safety policy including the co-ordination of search and rescue at sea through Her Majesty's Coastguard (1.67). Other tasks include ship surveys and inspections and the issue of guidance and regulations.

2   The agency's address is:

    Maritime and Coastguard Agency,
    Spring Place, 105 Commercial Road,
    Southampton, Hampshire,
    SO15 1EG.

The website is www.mcga.gov.uk.

Quarantine

1.57

1   Vessels arriving at any of the ports covered by this pilot are subject to United Kingdom quarantine regulations which are enforced in accordance with *The International Health Regulations 1969.* Vessels entering territorial waters from abroad should hoist the appropriate International Code signal flag by day, or, a red light over a white light at night.

In British Territorial Waters, no person is permitted to leave a vessel coming from a foreign place, except in the case of an emergency, until pratique has been granted by the local authority.

2   A vessel bound for the United Kingdom is required to report to the Port Health Authority not later than 4 hours nor more than 12 hours prior to arrival if she has replied in the affirmative to any of the health questions posed in *The Maritime Declaration of Health* (IMO FAL). For further details see *Admiralty List of Radio Signals Volume 1 (1).*

For a list of ports which issue Ship Sanitation Certificates see 1.92.

Immigration

1.58

1   In 1995, the mainland states of the European Community ratified the Schengen Convention. The purpose of the convention was to allow unrestricted movement of EU citizens throughout Europe by eliminating internal border controls. The European Union now has one external border at its outer limits and this includes the ports and airports of the community. The United Kingdom and the Republic of Ireland, however, have not ratified the convention.

2   Prior to arrival in a United Kingdom port, a Crew and Passenger List (IMO FAL) should be prepared and forwaded to the ship's agent who will inform the appropriate authorities. After arrival alongside, no crew member will be allowed ashore until permission has been granted to do so.

The United Kingdom Border Agency is currently developing a programme which will introduce electronic border control to the United Kingdom by 2014. e-Borders will collect and analyse passenger and crew information provided by carriers (airlines, rail and shipping companies) before travel starts on all journeys to and from the United Kingdom. See www.ukba.homeoffice.gov.uk for further details.

Customs and Excise

1.59

1   The Cargo Manifest, Dangerous Goods Manifest, Crew Effects Declaration, and Stores Declaration should be prepared prior to arrival. Goods which are not to be cleared must be stored in the Bond Locker in order that the room can be officially sealed. Normally, cargo operations and the boarding or disembarkation of personnel will not be permitted until the vessel has been granted an inward clearance certificate by a Customs Officer. A vessel will not be allowed to proceed to sea until she has obtained an outward clearance certificate from Customs.

Protection of wrecks

General information

1.60

1   In waters around the United Kingdom, the sites of certain wrecks are protected by the *Protection of Wrecks Act (1973)* from unauthorised interference on account of their historic, archaeological or artistic importance. For further details and a list of protected wrecks see *The Mariner's Handbook* and Notice No 16 of the *Annual Summary of Admiralty Notices to Mariners.*

2   To prevent the disturbance of the dead, the terms of *Protection of Military Remains Act 1986* provides similar protection to certain other wrecks, including aircraft, which sank within the last 200 years.

Protected wrecks in the area covered by this volume are mentioned in the text.

Protection of wildlife

General information

1.61

1   Three separate councils are responsible for nature conservation; in England by English Nature, whose headquarters are at Northminster House, Peterborough PE1 1VA; in Scotland by Scottish Natural Heritage, 12 Hope Terrace, Edinburgh EH9 2AS, and in Wales by the Countryside Council for Wales, Ffordd Penrhos, Plas Penrhos, Bangor LL57 2LQ.

2   These conservation bodies give advice on nature conservation to government and to all those whose activities affect wildlife and wild places. They are also responsible for establishing, maintaining and managing a series of National Nature Reserves and Marine Reserves and identifying and notifying Sites of Special Scientific Interest. The work is based on detailed ecological research and survey.

3   Information concerning bye–laws, codes of conduct, descriptions and positions of nature reserves and sites of special scientific interest can be obtained from the councils.

4   **National Nature Reserves.** There are about 300 National Nature Reserves in the United Kingdom; only those which can be found on or near the coastlines and river estuaries contained in this volume and which may be of direct interest to the mariner are mentioned in the text. Reserves are shown on charts of the British Isles.

5   **Marine Nature Reserves** provide protection for marine flora and fauna and for geological and physiographical features in tidal waters; they also provide opportunities for study and research. Limits of marine nature reserves are shown on the chart.

6   **Local Nature Reserves.** Local authorities in England and Wales and district councils in Scotland are able to acquire and manage local nature reserves in consultation with the conservation councils.

    Conservation Trusts can also own and manage non–statutory local nature reserves. Where necessary, the appropriate Trust name is given within the text of this volume.

1.62

1   **Royal Society for the Protection of Birds (RSPB),** is an organisation whose primary interest lies in the preservation of the many species of wild birds seen in Britain. For the purposes of this volume, only important bird sanctuaries lying in and around the coastal areas which may be of direct interest to the mariner are mentioned.

    Visiting a sanctuary in many cases is not encouraged and often not permitted. In other cases, it is permitted but under arrangement and strict control.

    Further details can be obtained from: Head of Reserve Management, Royal Society for the Protection of Birds, The Lodge, Sandy, Bedfordshire SG19 2DL.

Regulations to prevent the spread of rabies

General information

1.63

1   Stringent regulations are in force to prevent the spread of Rabies into the United Kindom. The following regulations apply:

> *The Rabies (Importation of Dogs, Cats and Other Mammals) Order 1974.*
> *Pet Travel Scheme (Pilot Arrangements) (England) Order 1999.*

2   Any animal onboard a visiting vessel must be kept securely confined so that it cannot escape to shore or come into contact with another animal. If an animal escapes, the Master must immediately inform the police or an officer of HM Revenue and Customs or an Animal Health Officer of the State Veterinary Service.

DISTRESS AND RESCUE

General information

1.64

1   General arrangements for Search and Rescue (SAR) are given in *The International Aeronautical and Marine Search and Rescue (IAMSAR) Manual* published by IMO. Reference should be made also to Notice No 4 of *The Annual Summary of Admiralty Notices to Mariners.*

Global Maritime Distress and Safety System

1.65

1   The Global Maritime Distress and Safety System (GMDSS) enables SAR authorities on shore, in addition to shipping in the immediate vicinity of a vessel in distress, to be alerted rapidly to an incident so that assistance can be provided with the minimum of delay.

2   Mariners are reminded that active GMDSS receivers together with a continuous watch on the VHF radio distress frequency are most important factors in the arrangements for the rescue of people in distress at sea. Within the waters covered by this volume, MRCCs monitor VHF DSC (Channel 70). Certain stations also monitor MF DSC (2187·5 kHz). Distress Alerts by satellite are handled by MRCC Falmouth (50°09′N 5°03′W). For further details see *Admiralty List of Radio Signals Volume 5.*

3   In summer average sea states are more agreeable and waves generally only exceed 4 m on or about 4% of occasions in the N and 2% in the S.

Swell conditions
1.109

1   Diagrams 1.109.1 to 1.109.4 give swell roses for several areas for January, April, July and October. The roses show the percentage of observations recording swell waves for each sector and for several ranges of wave height.

2   The North Sea is particularly exposed to swell from the NW to NE and there is a high incidence of waves from this sector in spring and summer. The swell from SW to SE increases in frequency in autumn and winter. Over the open sea a heavy swell may arrive from any direction, particularly in winter, but waves between W and S are likely to be of shorter periods than from other directions especially in the S of the region.

SEA WATER CHARACTERISTICS

Density
1.110

1   Typical summer values are $1{\cdot}027$ g/cm^3 and winter values are $1{\cdot}025$ g/cm^3.

Sea surface salinity distribution
1.111

1   Summer surface salinity distribution varies from 34·50‰ around much of the coast to 34·75‰ towards the N of the region. During the winter lower salinity values of less than 34·00‰ are observed off Firth of Forth and the coast between latitudes 52°N and 53°N, reflecting high fresh water input from river run-off. Generally much of the coastal region has typical winter surface salinity values of 34·25‰. Winter and summer bottom salinities reflect the uniform nature of the water column.

Sea surface temperature
1.112

1   The diagrams in 1.112 show the mean sea surface temperature of the waters surrounding the British Isles for February, May, August and November.

2   In winter the sea surface temperature is governed by the influx of the warm water associated with the North Atlantic Current. The limit of this warm water is usually delineated by the 6°C isotherm. Minimum sea surface temperatures are normally recorded in February or early March when values average about 5°C to 6°C along the whole of the E coast. Temperatures are generally lower in the S than in the N, with the waters between 52°30′N and 54°00′N, being the coldest around the British coastline.

3   In spring and summer, the seas warm up much more rapidly in the S of the region than in the N. Generally the seas off the E coast of Britain are warmest in August with a mean sea surface temperature of around 16 to 17°C in the extreme S of the region and 13 to 14°C off the E coast of Scotland.

Variability
1.113

1   In the warmest summers, the coastal sea temperatures can reach 20°C in the S and 17°C in the N, whilst in the coldest of winters extreme temperatures of 1°C have been recorded in the S and 2°C to 3°C in the N.

CLIMATE AND WEATHER

General information
1.114

1   The following information should be read in conjunction with the relevant chapters of *The Mariner's Handbook*.

   Weather reports and forecasts which cover the area are regularly broadcast in a number of languages; see *Admiralty List of Radio Signals Volume 3 (1)*.

2   **Ice accumulation.** In certain weather conditions, ice accumulation on hulls and superstructures of ships can be a serious danger. This hazard occasionally occurs in the N part of the area covered by this book. See *The Mariner's Handbook* for details on the causes of ice accumulation and the recommended course of action.

General conditions
1.115

1   The climate is in general mild for the latitude with winds most usually from between S and NW. In winter, strong to gale force winds, cloudy to overcast skies and rain/snow are common, although precipitation amounts are not large. On occasions E winds can bring exceptionally cold weather to the region. Winter temperatures are broadly similar on the E coasts of both England and Scotland, but in the N the winter is longer, spring is later and cooler and summer and autumn a few degrees cooler than in the S.

2   In summer, gales become less frequent than in winter although winds are often fresh or strong. There is little seasonal variation in the rainfall and the summer months are often cloudy and cool. However there are occasional spells of hot dry weather when temperatures can exceed 30°C.

3   Fog occasionally affects the E coast, particularly in the N. Over the open sea fog is not especially frequent; in winter it is more likely in the S than in the N, but in the summer the N has the higher incidence.

Pressure

Mean pressure fields
1.116

1   The distribution of the mean atmospheric pressure over the area is shown in diagrams 1.116. In general, pressure increases from NW to SE across the area with the lowest pressure in the NW in autumn and winter and the highest in the SE in spring and summer.

2   It is emphasised that these mean pressure fields are the average of dissimilar and often rapidly changing day to day situations, indeed an important characteristic of the North Sea region is the mobility and irregularity of the pressure systems affecting it and the variable nature of the weather associated with them.

Variability
1.117

1   Extreme pressure values may vary between 1050 hPa (mb) and 950 hPa due to the movement of depressions and anticyclones. During disturbed weather large variations can occur with, on occasions, pressure changes of 40 hPa in a period of 24 hours, especially in winter.

Anticyclones

The Azores anticyclone
1.118

1   The weather of the region is much influenced by this anticyclone. It is usually centred at around 35°N but recedes to the S in winter. It is usually the source of the

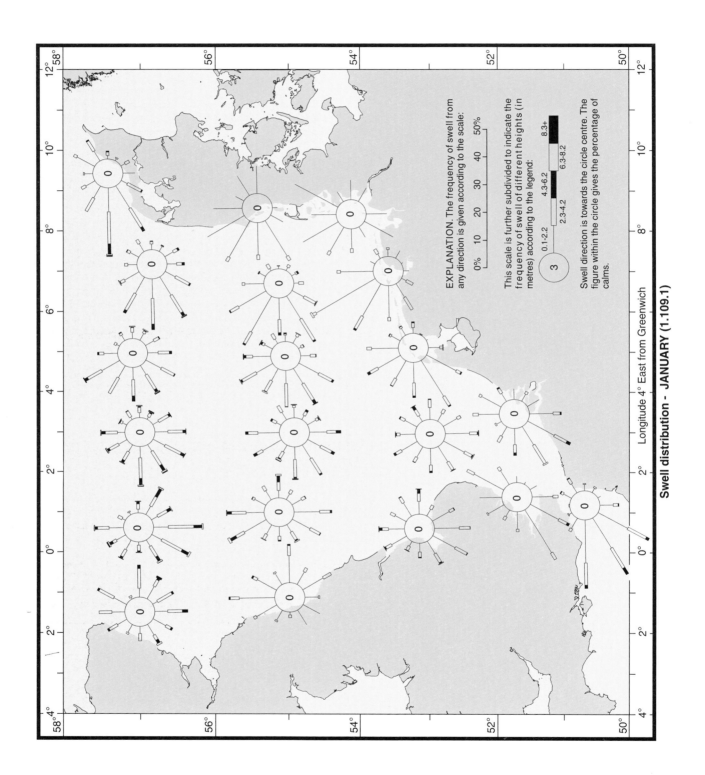

Swell distribution - JANUARY (1.109.1)

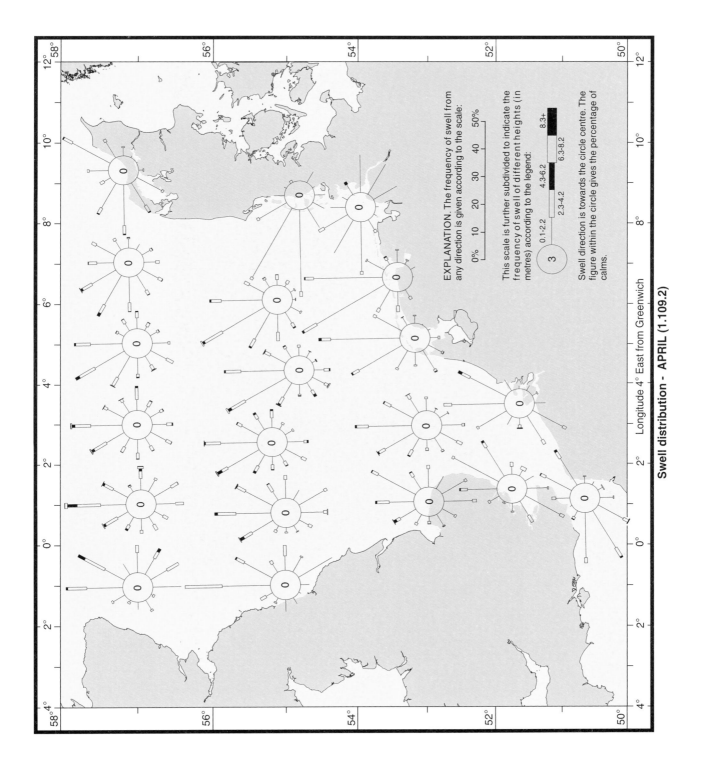

Swell distribution - APRIL (1.109.2)

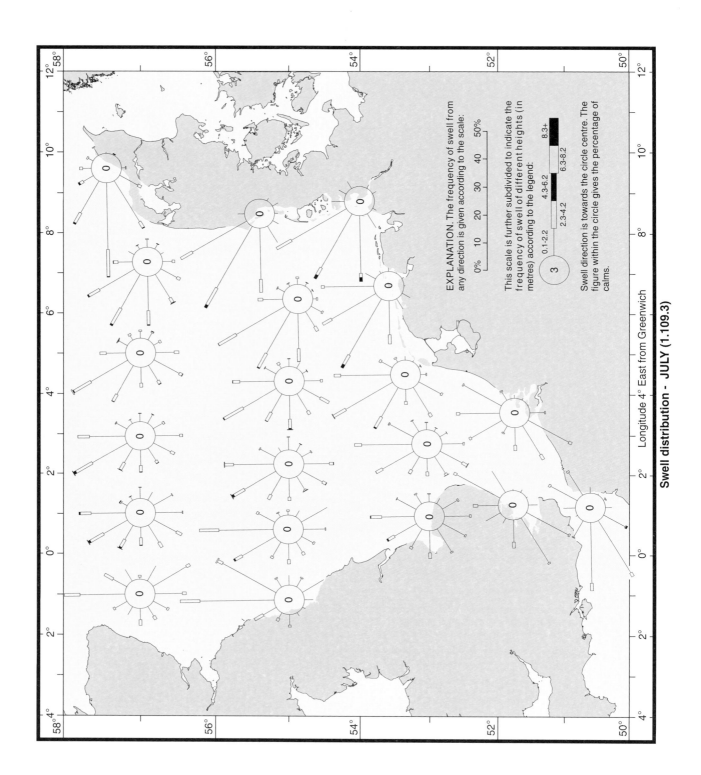

EXPLANATION. The frequency of swell from any direction is given according to the scale:

0%   10   20   30   40   50%

This scale is further subdivided to indicate the frequency of swell of different heights (in metres) according to the legend:

0.1-2.2   4.3-6.2   8.3+
2.3-4.2   6.3-8.2

Swell direction is towards the circle centre. The figure within the circle gives the percentage of calms.

Longitude 4° East from Greenwich

Swell distribution - JULY (1.109.3)

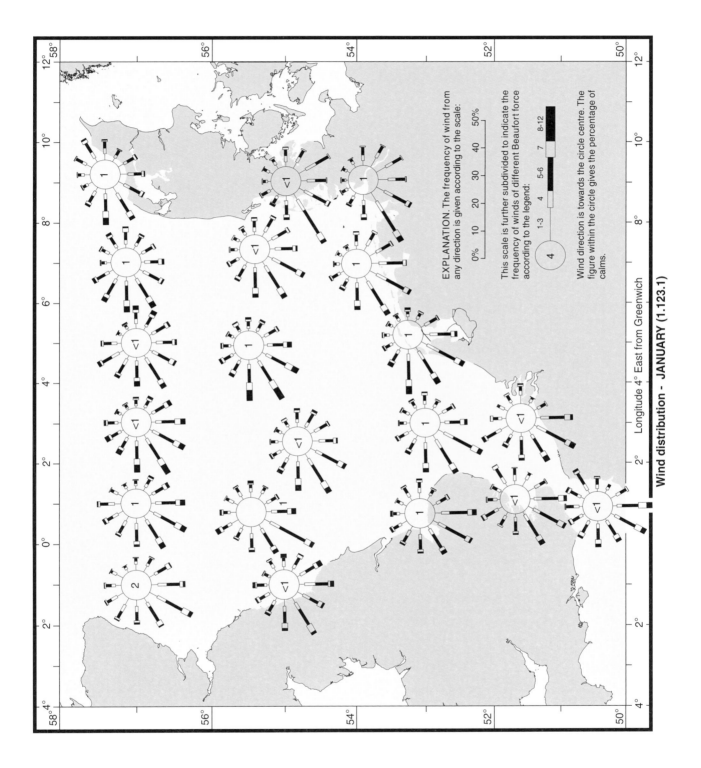

EXPLANATION. The frequency of wind from any direction is given according to the scale:

0% 10 20 30 40 50%

This scale is further subdivided to indicate the frequency of winds of different Beaufort force according to the legend:

1-3   4   5-6   7   8-12

Wind direction is towards the circle centre. The figure within the circle gives the percentage of calms.

Longitude 4° East from Greenwich

Wind distribution - JANUARY (1.123.1)

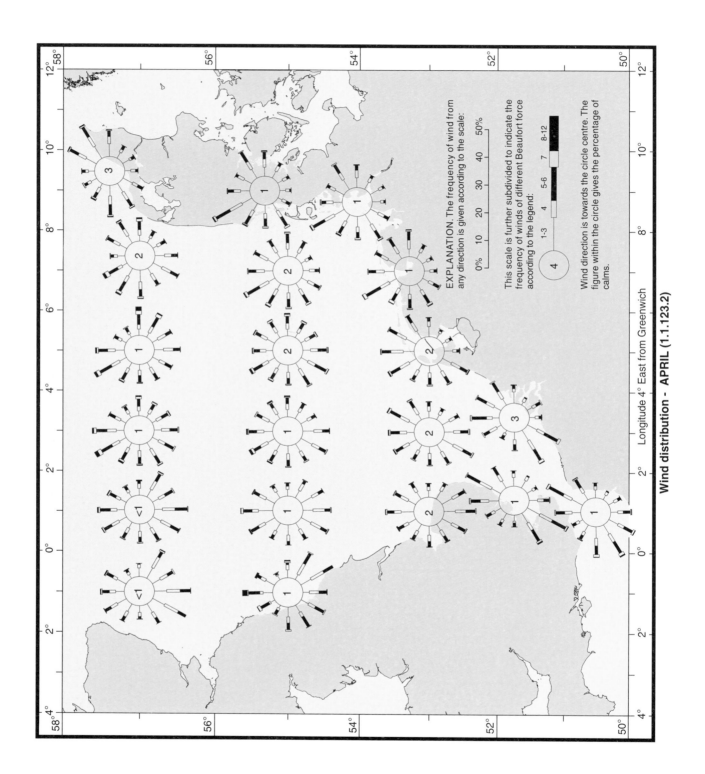

EXPLANATION. The frequency of wind from any direction is given according to the scale:

0% 10 20 30 40 50%

This scale is further subdivided to indicate the frequency of winds of different Beaufort force according to the legend:

1-3   4   5-6   7   8-12

Wind direction is towards the circle centre. The figure within the circle gives the percentage of calms.

Longitude 4° East from Greenwich

Wind distribution - APRIL (1.1.123.2)

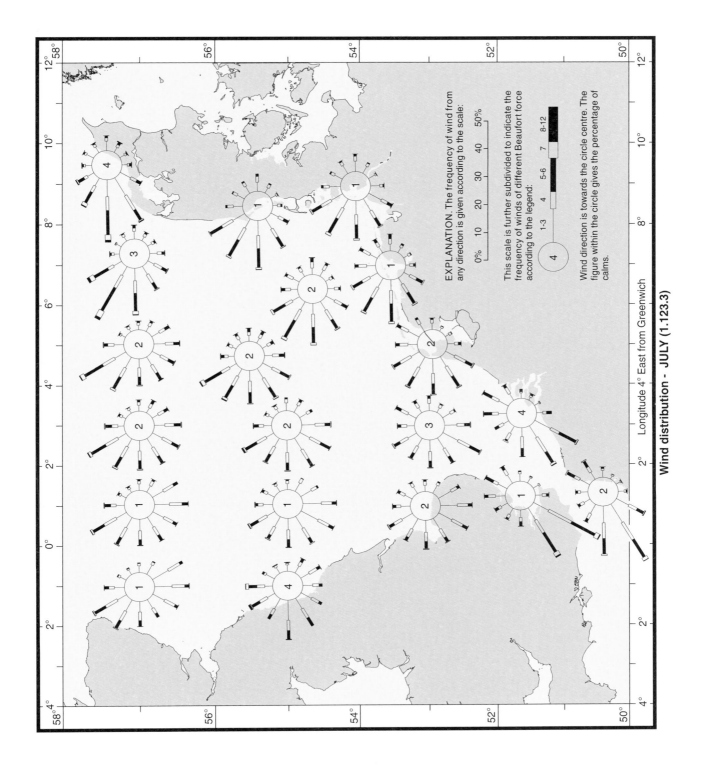

EXPLANATION. The frequency of wind from any direction is given according to the scale:

0%   10   20   30   40   50%

This scale is further subdivided to indicate the frequency of winds of different Beaufort force according to the legend:

1-3   4   5-6   7   8-12

Wind direction is towards the circle centre. The figure within the circle gives the percentage of calms.

Wind distribution - JULY (1.123.3)

Longitude 4° East from Greenwich

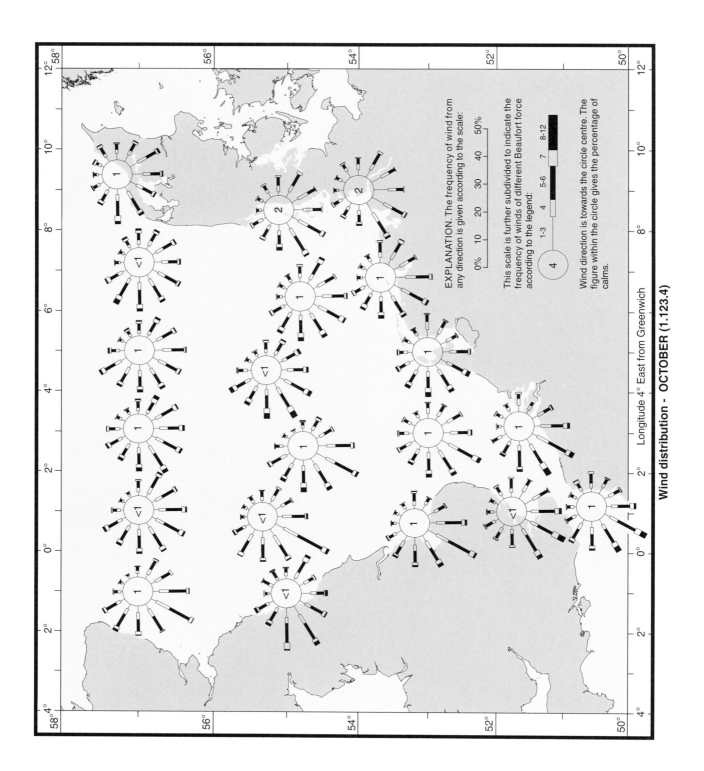

Wind distribution - OCTOBER (1.123.4)

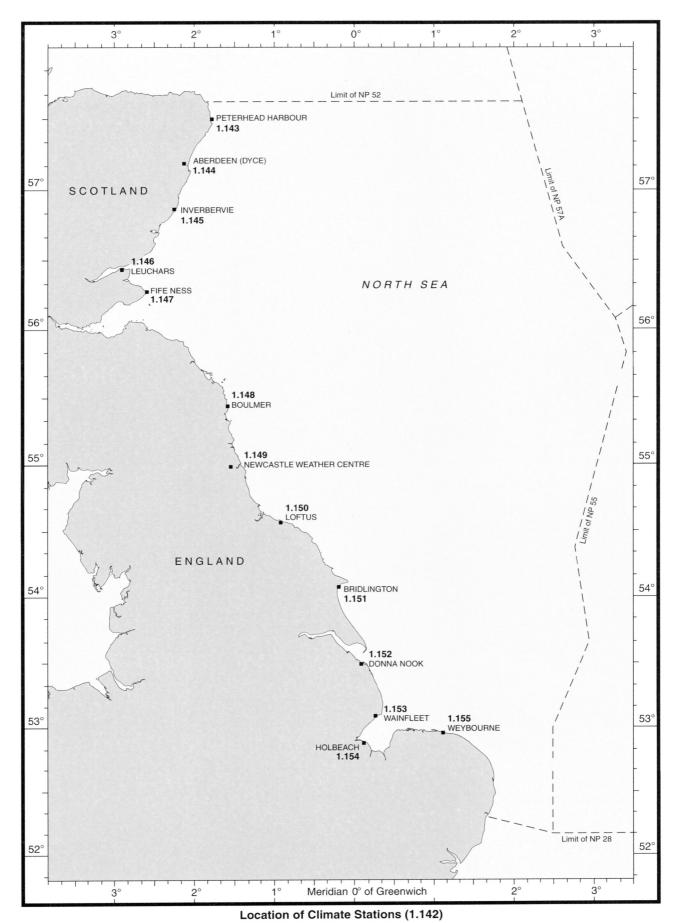

Location of Climate Stations (1.142)

WMO No 03092 PETERHEAD HARBOUR

57°30'N 01°46'W.   Height above MSL - 15 m Climate information for period 1996 - 2006

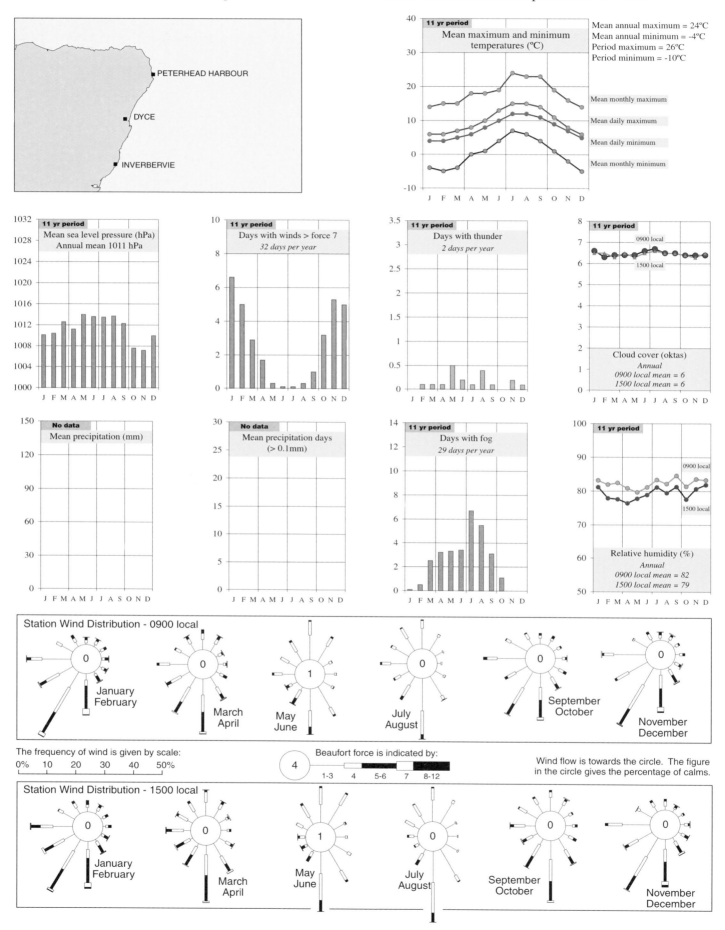

Mean annual maximum = 24°C
Mean annual minimum = -4°C
Period maximum = 26°C
Period minimum = -10°C

WMO No 03091 ABERDEEN (DYCE)

57°12'N 02°13'W.   Height above MSL - 69 m Climate information for period 1996 - 2006

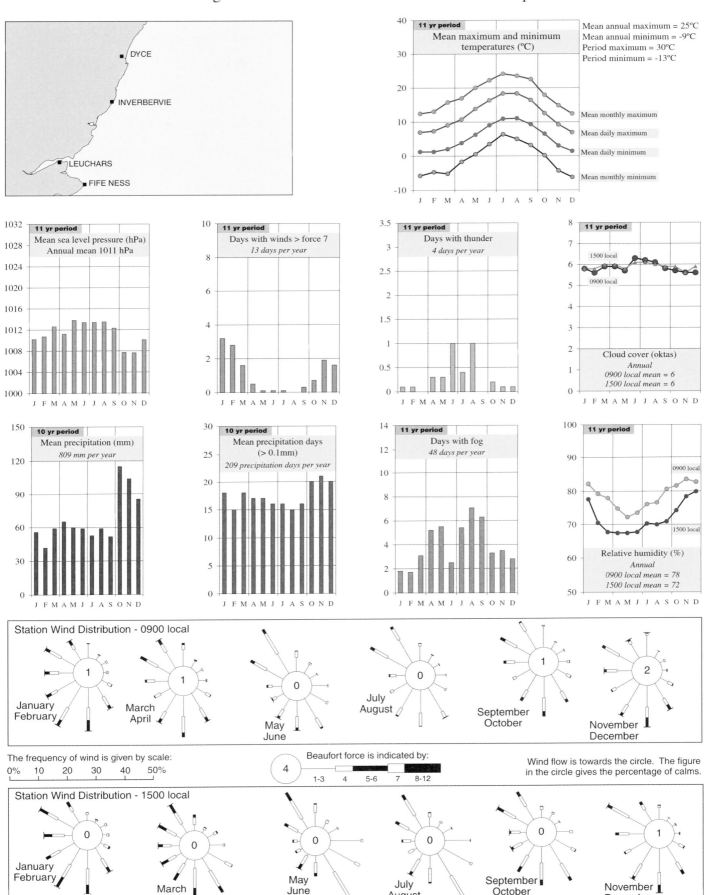

WMO No 03088 INVERBERVIE

56°51'N 02°16'W.   Height above MSL - 134 m Climate information for period 1996 - 2006

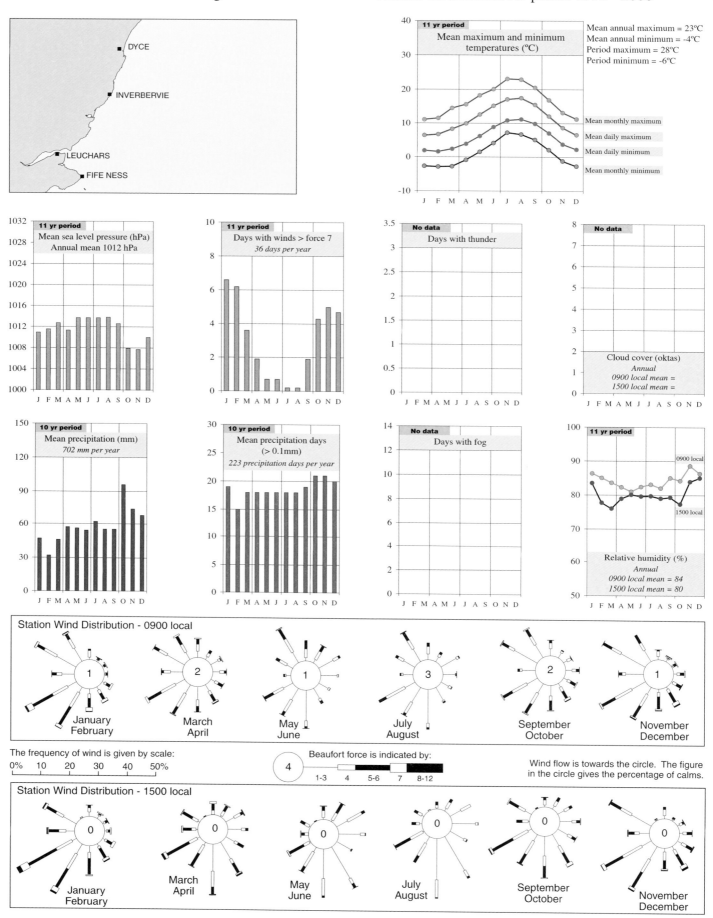

WMO No 03275 LOFTUS

54°34'N 00°52'W.   Height above MSL - 159 m Climate information for period 1996 - 2006

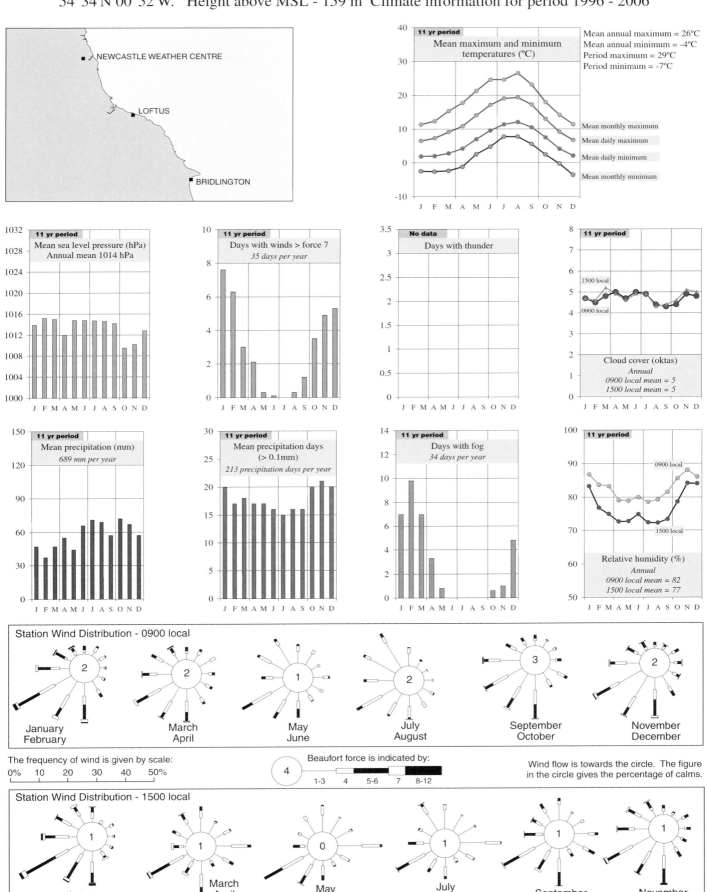

WMO No 03292 BRIDLINGTON

54°06'N 00°10'W.   Height above MSL - 19 m Climate Information for period 1996 - 2006

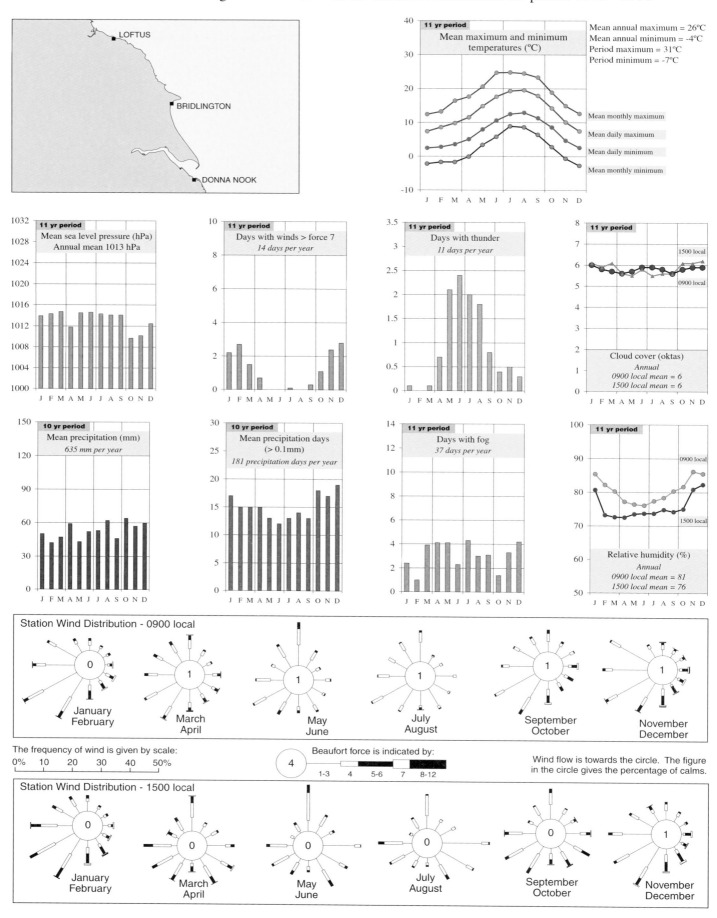

CHAPTER 2

THE WESTERN PART OF THE NORTH SEA

GENERAL INFORMATION

Charts 2182A, 2182B
Scope of the chapter
2.1

1 This chapter provides a general description of the off-lying features in the W part of the North Sea beyond a distance of about 20 miles from the coast. Several of the principal offshore routes are also described.

For an overview of maritime topography see 1.94.

Hazards
2.2

1 **Offshore oil and gas operations.** Numerous exploration and production rigs are located in the area. See 1.25 and 2.22. The rigs should be given as wide a berth as possible.

Exercise areas. Military aircraft, submarines and other naval vessels exercise in the area. See 1.20 and 2.3.

Fishing. Fishing vessels may be encountered throughout the waters of the North Sea. See 1.9.

2 **Wrecks** are numerous throughout the North Sea and some, particularly in the shallower parts, may be a danger to shipping. The positions of wrecks are best seen on the charts.

Unexploded munitions. Periodically unexploded munitions are recovered in fishing nets or located during offshore oil and gas operations. For instructions regarding munitions picked up at sea refer to *The Mariner's Handbook*.

Exercise areas
2.3

1 **Surface warships** exercise in the approaches to the Firth of Forth in an area centred on 56°10′N 2°00′W.

Submarines exercise in areas centred on 56°45′N 1°30′E, 54°05′N 2°32′E, the approaches to the Firth of Forth centred on 56°10′N 2°00′W and NE of Flamborough Head centred on 54°26′N 0°22′E.

2 **Aircraft.** Large areas of the W part of the North Sea are used for aerial exercises. Within the limits of this volume only one area, centred on a light buoy (special) in position 56°20′N 1°00′W, is used for surface weapon firing.

For further details see 1.20.

Dumping grounds
2.4

1 Underwater explosives may still remain in areas 40 miles E of Flamborough Head and 30 miles NE of Whitby, which were formerly used as dumping grounds.

2 Underwater explosives may also remain in former dumping grounds off East Anglia as follows:

Within an area bounded by 52°25′N, 53°12′N, 2°00′E, 3°15′E.

Within 3 miles either side of a line joining 52°05′N 2°32′E and 52°20′N 3°00′E.

In the vicinity of positions 52°46′·4N 1°41′·9E and 53°22′N 1°31′E.

Oceanographical data buoys
2.5

1 Data gathering and ODAS buoys may be encountered in the vicinity of the routes described in this chapter. For further information see 1.30.

Rescue
2.6

1 See 1.64.

Tidal streams
2.7

1 Details of tidal streams are given on the charts and in *Admiralty Tidal Stream Atlas: North Sea, Northwestern Part* and *Admiralty Tidal Stream Atlas: North Sea, Southern Part*. For details of the tidal regime see 1.96.

Tidal heights
2.8

1 See 1.105.

TOPOGRAPHY

Latitude of Rattray Head to Dogger Bank

Charts 267, 268, 272, 273, 278
General information
2.9

1 From the latitude of Rattray Head (57°37′N) to the Dogger Bank (54°45′N 2°15′E) the area is open with few marked features and depths are generally in excess of 50 m throughout. There are a number of North Sea oil fields along the N and E boundaries of this area, see 2.22.

Banks and deeps
2.10

1 Turbot Bank (57°27′N 0°50′W) lies in the NW corner of the area covered by this book. Aberdeen Bank is 22 miles S of Turbot Bank and Marr Bank a further 48 miles SSW. There are a number of wrecks and patches with less than 50 m over them, shown on the chart, to the NE and SE of Marr Bank.

2 There are several abrupt deeps on the E edge of The Long Forties (57°'N 0°E/W) of which the deepest is Devil's Hole having depths of more than 200 m in places.

Dogger Bank to Outer Silver Pit

Charts 266, 1191
General information
2.11

1 The W part of this area is a continuation of the generally featureless area described in 2.10. Dogger Bank (54°45′N 2°15′E) dominates the E half of the area. Several gas fields exist along its S edge.

Banks and deeps
2.12

1 The banks mentioned below all have depths of less than 30 m, with some, in particular Dogger Bank, having depths of less than 20 m. The individual depths are best seen on the chart.

2 Dogger Bank is roughly a circle, 25 miles in radius, centred on 54°45′N 2°15′E, with an arm extending 60 miles NE. The drab brown colour of the North Sea is due largely to stirred-up deposits of the bank held in suspension. It is a rich fishing area. South West Patch, having depths of less than 15 m, lies on the SW side of Dogger Bank. In bad weather the sea breaks heavily over it.

3 **Caution.** There are a number of dangerous wrecks on Dogger Bank and South West Patch. In addition, unexploded ordnance has been reported (1998) in 54°31′·2N 1°53′·6E.

3 Outer Well Bank, South-West Spit and The Hills are smaller shoals lying about 10 to 20 miles SW of Dogger Bank.

4 Outer Silver Pit (54°05′N 2°05′E) is a deep which separates the banks above from the large area of shoals which lie to the NE of the coast between the River Humber (53°30′N 0°10′E) and Great Yarmouth (52°36′N 1°44′E). The edges of the deep are often marked by tide ripples. The W end of Outer Silver Pit is known as Skate Hole and the E end as Botney Cut.

Outer Silver Pit to the latitude of Cromer

Charts 1187, 1503
General information
2.13

1 To S of Outer Silver Pit depths decrease gradually as the banks NE of the coast are approached. Sole Pit (53°40′N 1°33′E) with Well Hole, 11 miles E, and Coal Pit, 6 miles SE, are close N of the banks and intrude into them. The area between Sole Pit and Outer Dowsing Shoal (53°27′N 1°06′E) is typified by sandwave features (1.94). A disturbed sea surface sometimes indicates the shallower areas.

2 To S and SW of Outer Silver Pit, and interspersed between the banks which lie offshore, are numerous offshore gas fields, which form the greatest concentration of production platforms in the North Sea (2.22). Production platforms, wells and pipelines are shown on the charts.

Offshore banks
2.14

1 Indefatigable Banks (53°34′N 2°20′E), two narrow shoals, lie 52 miles offshore. They are the outermost of a series of narrow sandbanks running NW/SE in roughly parallel lines which lie to the SW of the Indefatigable Banks. Depths over the banks from Swarte Bank (53°24′N 2°12′E) SW are less than 10 m in places and over those farthest SW there are depths less than 5 m. The shallow areas may be indicated by smooth rippling when the tidal stream is strong; this rippling can be detected by radar. The sea breaks over the banks in rough weather. Depths between the banks may exceed 30 m but there are patches with depths of less than 15 m.

2 **Caution.** The banks are generally unmarked and care should be taken when approaching them. The banks should not be crossed, especially in rough weather, unless the position of the vessel is known accurately.

The channels described at 2.17, 2.18 and 2.19 are relatively narrow in places and the adjacent banks are liable to change.

ROUTES

Charts 2182A, 2182B
Deep-draught vessels
2.15

1 Deep-draught vessels on passage between Dover Strait and ports on the E coast of the United Kingdom are recommended to follow the DW Route via DR1 Light Buoy (53°06′·7N 2°40′·7E) (see *North Sea (East) Pilot*) and then to approach the coast through Outer Silver Pit (2.12).

This route avoids the offshore banks between Great Yarmouth and River Humber.

2 *Admiralty List of Radio Signals Volume 6 (1)* lists pilotage authorities bordering the English Channel, North Sea and NW Europe who provide licensed Deep Sea Pilots. Arrangements can be made to embark the pilot by helicopter.

German Bight to River Humber
2.16

1 Vessels proceed on a direct course W from the German Bight TSS (see *North Sea (East) Pilot*) to the River Humber. The track passes through Outer Silver Pit (2.12) and N of the offshore sandbanks (2.14).

In strong NW winds, vessels are advised to proceed SW of Leman Bank (53°07′N 1°56′E) and thence through Outer Dowsing Channel. See 2.17.

Outer Dowsing Channel and Leman Bank Route
2.17

1 The route, which is described at 9.7, passes through the channel between Leman Bank (53°07′N 1°56′E) and Smiths Knoll (52°53′N 2°12′E). It is used by vessels proceeding between ports on the E coast of the United Kingdom and the near continental ports of The Netherlands and Belgium. It is used also by vessels proceeding from ports on the E coast of the United Kingdom to the Thames Estuary and to Dover Strait. The latter vessels usually join the SW-going lane of the TSS to E of Falls Bank. See *Dover Strait Pilot*.

The Middle Ground Route
2.18

1 An alternative and well-used route passes between the routes described at 2.17 and 2.19. It leads SE over The Middle Ground (52°50′N 2°09′E) and passes between Haisborough Sand (52°55′N 1°42′E), Hammond Knoll (52°52′N 1°55′E) and Winterton Ridge (52°50′N 2°01′E) to SW and Smiths Knoll (52°53′N 2°12′E) to NW.

The Would and Haisborough Gat
2.19

1 The route, which is described at 9.15, is used by vessels proceeding between ports in the Wash or on the E coast of the United Kingdom and the near continental ports of The Netherlands and Belgium. It is used also by vessels proceeding S along the coast of the United Kingdom and by vessels proceeding to Dover Strait. The latter join the SW-going lane of the TSS to W of Falls Bank. See *Dover Strait Pilot*.

Northern United Kingdom to Near Continent
2.20

1 Vessels bound from Scotland or northern England to the near continental ports of The Netherlands or Belgium can proceed E of Indefatigable Banks (53°34′N 2°20′E) to join the shipping lanes of the S part of the North Sea (See *North Sea (East) Pilot* and *Dover Strait Pilot*). By so doing, the offshore sandbanks (2.14) and most of the oil and gas installations are circumvented.

Routes to North Sea Oil and Gas Fields
2.21

1 North Sea Oil and Gas Fields are served by a number of E coast ports. In the N, Peterhead (57°30′N 1°47′W) (3.14), Aberdeen (57°09′N 2°04′W) (3.56), Montrose (56°42′N 2°28′W) (3.115) and Dundee (56°28′N 2°57′W) (3.173) serve the oil fields which lie to their E and NE. In the S, Great Yarmouth (52°36′N 1°44′E) (9.60) and Lowestoft (52°28′N 1°45′E) (9.92) serve the concentration of gas

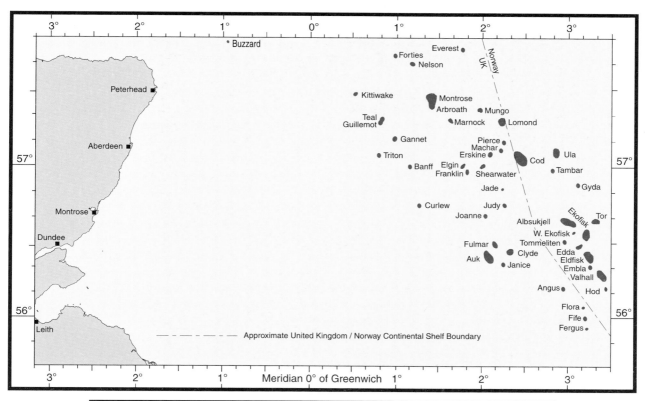

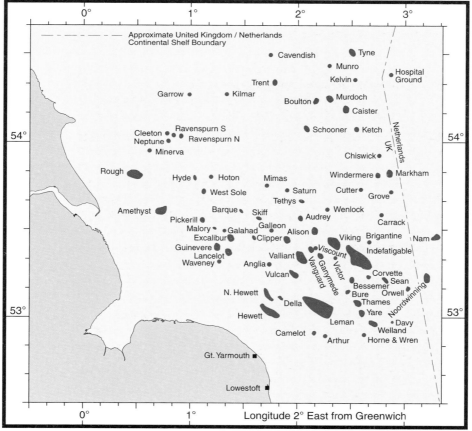

North Sea West - Major Oil and Gas Fields and Supply Bases (2.22)

fields in the S part of the North Sea. The approaches to these ports are therefore likely to be busy with supply-vessel traffic.

OIL AND GAS FIELDS

2.22

1   The major oil and gas fields which lie within the limits of this volume are in two main groups. Those which lie to the extreme NE are all oil fields with the exception of Lomond and Franklin Gas Fields. Those to the S are all gas fields. Most fields lie offshore but a few gas fields in the S are mentioned in the coastal route directions.

2   All the gas fields and some of the oil fields are connected to the shore by pipelines. Those oil fields which are not so connected rely on SPMs or FPSOs to offload their oil direct to tankers.

3   **Caution.** Production platforms and associated structures, including tanker moorings, storage tankers and platforms on pipelines, generally exhibit Mo (U) lights and aircraft obstruction lights and are fitted with audible fog signals. Unauthorised navigation is prohibited within 500 m of all such structures, including storage tankers, which can swing about their moorings. Tankers manoeuvring in the vicinity of platforms and offshore moorings should be given a wide berth. For further information see *The Mariner's Handbook.*

4   See diagram 2.22 for a general disposition of oil and gas fields in the waters of this book.

A list of all oil and gas production platforms in the North Sea is contained in *Admiralty List of Lights and Fog Signals Volume A.*

NOTES

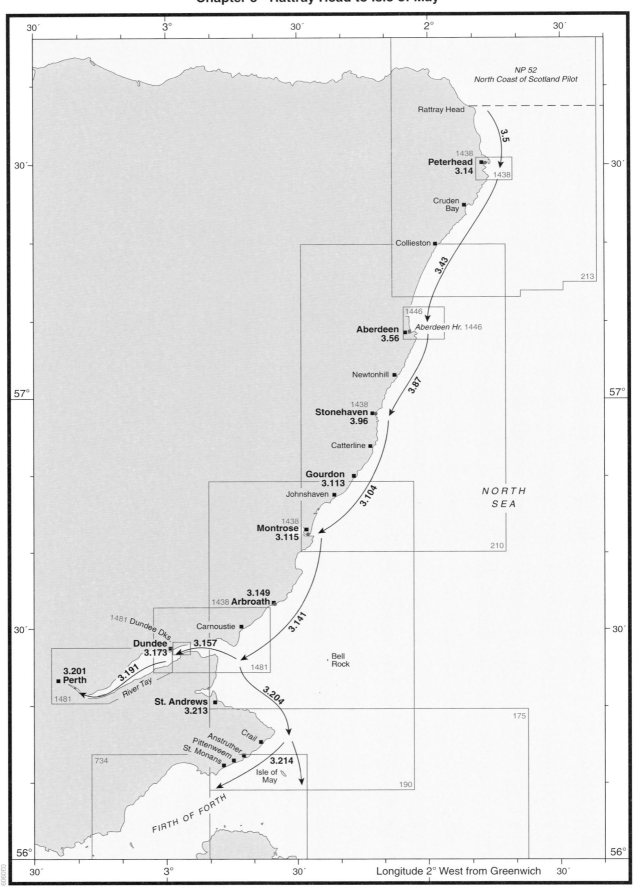

30′ 3° 30′ 2° 30′

NP 52
North Coast of Scotland Pilot

Rattray Head

3.5

1438
Peterhead
3.14
1438

Cruden
Bay

Collieston

213

1438

3.43

1446
Aberdeen
3.56
Aberdeen Hr. 1446

Newtonhill

3.87

1438
Stonehaven
3.96

Catterline

Gourdon
3.113

N O R T H
S E A

Johnshaven

3.104

1438
Montrose
3.115

210

3.149
1438 **Arbroath**

3.141

1481 Dundee Dks

Carnoustie

Bell
Rock

Dundee **3.157**
3.173

1481

3.201
■ **Perth**

3.191

River Tay

3.204

1481

St. Andrews
3.213

175

Crail
Anstruther
Pittenweem
St. Monans

3.214

734

Isle of
May

190

FIRTH OF FORTH

56°

30′ 3° 30′ Longitude 2° West from Greenwich 30′

57°

30′

56°

606000

54

CHAPTER 3

RATTRAY HEAD TO ISLE OF MAY

GENERAL INFORMATION

Charts 1409, 1407
Scope of the chapter
3.1

1   In this chapter the coastal passage from Rattray Head (57°37′N 1°49′W) to Isle of May about 90 miles SSW is described, together with the ports of Peterhead (3.14), Aberdeen (3.56), Stonehaven (3.96), Montrose (3.115), Arbroath (3.149), Dundee (3.173) and Perth (3.201). For a description of features lying farther offshore than 20 miles see Chapter 2.

Topography
3.2

1   From Rattray Head (57°37′N 1°49′W) the coast runs in a generally SSW direction for 85 miles to Fife Ness; Isle of May (3.215) lies 5 miles SSE of Fife Ness, towards the centre of the approach to Firth of Forth.

2   The coast is mainly composed of rocky cliffs, fringed by reefs, which dry 1 to 2 cables offshore but occasionally dry 5 cables to seaward. There are several sandy stretches; from Rattray Head to Peterhead, the 12 mile stretch lying NNE of Aberdeen, the 4 miles NNE of Montrose, Lunan Bay just S of Montrose and the mouth of River Tay.

3   The approach to River Tay lies between Whiting Ness (56°34′N 2°33′W) and Fife Ness 17 miles S. Bell Rock lies 9½ miles SE of Whiting Ness.

Outlying banks and deeps
3.3

1   Attention is drawn to the following:
   Buchan Deep charted within a 100 m depth contour lies 12 to 20 miles E of Buchan Ness (57°28′N 1°46′W) and extends 18 miles NNE/SSW.
   A deep, charted within a 100 m depth contour, lies 12 miles ESE of Girdle Ness (57°08′N 2°03′W).

2   **Scalp Bank** a flat patch with a least depth of 31 m lies 17 miles E of Red Head (56°37′N 2°29′W). Similar patches lie 5 miles S of Scalp Bank and midway between the bank and Red Head.
   Wee Bankie with a least depth of 31 m, lies 16 miles E of the Isle of May (56°11′N 2°33′W).

Tidal streams
3.4

1   Tidal streams are given on the charts and in *Admiralty Tidal Stream Atlas: North Sea, Northwestern Part.*
   The offshore stream runs generally N and S from Rattray Head to Bell Rock. The E-going stream out of the S part of Moray Firth sets in the direction of the coast, that is gradually SE and S round Rattray Head before joining the S-going offshore stream. The N-going offshore stream divides N of Rattray Head, part of it sets NW and W into Moray Firth and part of it continues N.

2   The change from the S-going to the N-going stream is through W and from the N-going to the S-going stream through the E.

South of Bell Rock, clear of the land and in the outer part of Firth of Forth the tidal streams are weak, spring rate 1 kn, but run in various directions throughout the tidal cycle as shown in *Admiralty Tidal Stream Atlas: North Sea, Northwestern Part.*

RATTRAY HEAD TO BUCHAN NESS

General information

Chart 213
Route
3.5

1   From Rattray Head (57°37′N 1°49′W) the route leads S for a distance of 9 miles to a position E of Buchan Ness, crossing the approaches to Peterhead 2 miles N of Buchan Ness.

Topography
3.6

1   The coast between Rattray Head and Buchan Ness consists of fairly low-lying sandhills as far as South Head (2 miles N of Buchan Ness), the E extremity of the promontory on which Peterhead stands. There are two bays, Peterhead Bay and Sandford Bay, between South Head and Buchan Ness.

Rescue
3.7

1   A Coastal Rescue Team is maintained at Peterhead. See 1.67.
   An all-weather lifeboat is stationed at Peterhead. See 1.72.

Tidal streams
3.8

1   Tidal streams for the area are shown on the charts and in *Admiralty Tidal Stream Atlas: North Sea, Northwestern Part.*
   The spring rate in either direction is 1¾ kn.

Directions
(Directions for passage N are given in North Coast of Scotland Pilot)

Principal marks
3.9

1   **Landmarks:**
   Mormond Hill (57°36′N 2°02′W) with buildings and Television mast on its summit.
   Radio Mast (red lights) (57°37′·1N 1°53′·3W).
   Radio Mast (red lights) (57°36′·7N 1°53′·6W).
   Radio Mast (red lights) (57°36′·4N 1°52′·9W).
   Power station chimney (lit) at Peterhead (57°29′N 1°47′W).
   Buchan Ness Lighthouse (white tower, red bands, 35 m in height) (57°28′N 1°46′W).

2 **Major Lights:**

Rattray Head Light (white tower, lower part granite, upper part brick, 34 m in height) (57°37′N 1°49′W) stands on a rock called The Ron.

Buchan Ness Light (above).

Rattray Head Light (3.9)
(Original dated 2008)

(Photograph – Drew Given)

Buchan Ness Light from S (3.9)
(Original dated 2009)

(Photograph – Drew Given)

Other aids to navigation
3.10

1 **Racons:**

Rattray Head Light (57°37′ 1°49′W).

Buchan Ness Light (57°28′N 1°46′W).

For details see *Admiralty List of Radio Signals Volume 2.*

Rattray Head to Buchan Ness
3.11

1 From a position off Rattray Head (57°37′N 1°49′W), a sandhill partly covered by bent grass and higher than the surrounding sandy ridges, the coastal passage leads 9 miles S to a position E of Buchan Ness, passing (with positions from Rattray Head):

2 E of Rattray Hard (2 miles ENE), an uneven rocky patch on which dangerous seas are raised during onshore gales, thence:

E of Rattray Bay (1½ miles S), which lies between Rattray Hard and Scotstown Head. Submarine pipelines run to offshore oilfields from the gas terminal at Saint Fergus. Thence:

3 E of Scotstown Head (3¼ miles S) off which Scotstown Hard extends 5 cables to seaward, thence:

E of Kirkton Head (4 miles S) with dangerous rocks extending 5 cables to seaward, thence:

E of The Girdle Wears (5½ miles SSE) a patch of rocks close NE of Buchanhaven, thence:

E of North Head (6½ miles S) (chart 1438) with North Head Rock 1½ cables NE, thence:

4 E of South Head (6¾ miles S) (chart 1438) and the dangers extending ½ cable E, covered by the red sector of N Breakwater light at Peterhead, thence:

E of The Skerry (8 miles S) an isolated rock in Sandford Bay, thence:

E of Buchan Ness (8½ miles S) a rocky, rugged peninsula bordered by rocky ledges and connected to the mainland by a narrow isthmus. The lighthouse (3.9) stands in the centre of the peninsula.

Clearing Bearings
3.12

1 Buchan Ness Light (57°28′N 1°46′W) (3.9) bearing more than 184° and open to the E of the lights of the town of Peterhead passes E of the dangers off Rattray Head, Scotstown Head and Kirkton Head.

The alignment (203°) of The Skerry (3.11) with Buchan Ness Lighthouse (5½ cables SSW), passes 4 cables E of South Head.

(Directions continue for Peterhead at 3.34 and for coastal route S at 3.49)

Buchanhaven
3.13

1 Buchanhaven (57°31′N 1°48′W) is a small fishing village with a boat harbour among the rocks. It lies on the S side of the mouth of the River Ugie.

A jetty which extends 127 m N from the shore affords a landing for boats at all states of the tide.

PETERHEAD

General information

Chart 1438 plans of Approaches to Peterhead and Peterhead Harbour

Position
3.14

1 Peterhead (57°29′·81N 1°46′·42W) on the NE coast of Scotland is 23 miles NNE of Aberdeen.

Function
3.15

1 Peterhead is a major supply base for the offshore oil and gas industry and the most important fishing port in the

United Kingdom for white and pelagic species. Additionally, the port handles tankers, general cargo ships and cruise liners.

The town of Peterhead has a population of about 21 000.

Topography
3.16

1   Peterhead Bay is a deep indentation in the coast between Keith Inch, a promontory to the N, and Salthouse Head to the S. The bay is open to the SE but protected by breakwaters. The breakwaters afford a good measure of protection from E winds, particularly in the S of the Bay, although seas frequently break over both breakwaters and there may be a heavy groundswell in the Bay; see 3.25.

2   The harbour for fishing vessels at the N end of the bay is protected to the E by Keith Inch.

Port limits
3.17

1   The port limits lie 1½ miles E of the coast between Keith Inch and Buchan Ness but exclude Sandford Bay and The Skerry. See chart for details.

Approach and entry
3.18

1   Peterhead Bay is approached from SE and entered between a pair of breakwaters.

Traffic
3.19

1   In 2008, Peterhead was used by 2501 vessels including fishing boats.

Port Authority
3.20

1   Peterhead Port Authority, Harbour Office, West Pier, Peterhead, AB42 1DW.
Website: www.peterheadport.co.uk

Limiting conditions

Controlling depth
3.21

1   The approach to Peterhead Bay is in depths greater than 20 m. The least depth in the E part of the bay inside the breakwaters is 11·2 m.

Deepest and longest berth
3.22

1   Tanker Jetty (3.37).

Tidal levels
3.23

1   See *Admiralty Tide Tables Volume 1*. Mean spring range about 3·3 m; mean neap range about 1·5 m.

Maximum size of vessel handled
3.24

1   The Oil jetty (3.37) can accept vessels up to 250 m LOA and draught 10·5 m.

Local weather and sea state
3.25

1   During E gales, the backwash caused by the breakwaters causes a turbulent sea which is most extreme in their close vicinity.

2   Small vessels attempting to enter Peterhead Bay in these conditions are advised to join the leading line (3.35) at a position no closer than 5 cables SE of the harbour entrance, and to remain on the leading line until inside the harbour.

Similarly, if small vessels are leaving harbour in these conditions, the alignment, astern, of the leading lights should be maintained until the vessel is 5 cables SE of the entrance.

Arrival information

Vessel traffic service
3.26

1   A VTS with radar surveillance is maintained for the advice of shipping. For details see *Admiralty List of Radio Signals Volume 6 (1)*.

Notice of ETA required
3.27

1   See 1.45. Vessels should contact the VTS 1 hour prior to arrival and should also make contact when 2 miles from the breakwater.

Pilotage and tugs
3.28

1   **Pilotage** is compulsory for:
Vessels exceeding 3500 gt.
Laden oil tankers.
Vessels carrying hazardous cargoes or dangerous goods in bulk or quantities of 100 tonnes or more.
Vessels carrying more than 1 tonne of IMO Class 1 explosives.

2   All vessels, which in the opinion of the Harbour Master or his appointed deputies, are defective, damaged or handicapped to such an extent that a pilot is required.

3   All vessels when, in the opinion of the Harbour Master or his appointed deputies, a pilot is required because there is an obstruction in Peterhead Bay Harbour.

4   The pilot boards within 2 miles SE of the breakwater entrance, except in bad weather when he boards inside the breakwaters.

Tugs. One small tug for vessels up to 120 m LOA. Larger tugs, although not permanently stationed in Peterhead, are normally available at 24 hours notice.

Traffic regulations
3.29

1   The following regulations apply:
Vessels shall not obstruct the harbour entrance.
Within the harbour there is a speed limit of 5 kn.
Vessels shall keep 50 m clear of other vessels working dangerous or polluting cargoes.

2   The harbour may be closed to either incoming or outgoing traffic at any time at the discretion of the Harbour Master.

3.30

Navigation Channel. A navigation channel, which is the width of the harbour entrance on an axis of 314°, is deemed to exist within the harbour limits. Within this channel the following regulations apply:

1   Vessels shall not anchor or remain without permission.
Small vessels shall not obstruct large vessels.
Vessels shall keep to starboard. Large vessels requiring the use of the whole channel, shall only enter the channel when it is clear of other vessels.
Vessels following one another shall keep at least 70 m apart.
There shall be no overtaking.

Peterhead Harbour from SE (3.31)
(Original dated 2000)

(Photograph - Air Images)

Harbour

General layout
3.31

1   The entrance to Peterhead Bay faces SE and is 208 m wide between the breakwaters. Within the entrance there is a tanker jetty in the lee of South Breakwater.

North Base, situated at the N end of the harbour, consists of an open pile jetty and berths on the inside of North Breakwater. It is used by the offshore oil industry for construction and enginering projects.

2   South Base, situated on the S side of the harbour, is used primarily as a supply base for the offshore oil industry. Princess Royal Jetty extends 175 m NE from the NW extremity of South Base; a sectored light marks the end of this jetty. The jetty is used both by supply vessels and by general cargo ships.

3   Peterhead Bay Marina, enclosed by two breakwaters each with a light exhibited from its head, lies W of Princess Royal Jetty. A seasonal light buoy (starboard hand) is moored 40 m NNW of the E breakwater head.

4   The inner harbour at the N end of the Bay consists of four interconnected tidal basins and is used primarily by fishing vessels. The outer basin, enclosed by Merchants Quay, West Quay and Albert Quay, is entered directly from Peterhead Bay. Lights are exhibited from the end of West Quay and Albert Quay. South Harbour is entered from the outer basin, and leads to North Harbour and Alexandra Basin, and thence to Port Henry Harbour which is entered from the W side of North Harbour.

Development
3.32

1   In the North Harbour, a 150 m long deepwater berth with a depth of 10 m is being developed along Smith Embankment, centred on 57°30'·11N 1°46'·73W, to accommodate large pelagic trawlers. At the same time, Albert Quay breakwater will be extended by rock armour in a W direction by about 80 m. Additionally, the fairway to the existing fishing harbour and the new berth will be dredged to 9·0 m.

Natural conditions
3.33

1   **Tidal streams.** The tidal stream across the breakwater entrance and up to 3 cables offshore, depending on tidal range, is usually as follows:

> Flood tide (S setting) starts approximately 30 mins to 1 hour before LW Peterhead.
>
> Ebb tide (N setting) starts approximately 1 to 2 hours before HW Peterhead.

2   Tidal streams vary between 1 kn and 3 kn but stronger currents can be experienced occasionally due to weather effects. Inside the breakwaters, however, there is no appreciable tidal stream.

It is recommended that tidal information is confirmed with the VTS or pilot prior to arrival.

3   **Climate information.** See 1.142 and 1.143.

Directions for entering harbour
(Continued from 3.12)

Principal marks
3.34

1   **Landmarks:**

North Breakwater Light (white metal tripod, 10 m in height) (57°29′·8N 1°46′·3W).

South Breakwater Light (white metal tower, black base, 17 m in height) (1 cable WSW of N breakwater light).

Buchan Ness Lighthouse (57°28′N 1°46′W) (3.9).

2   Town Hall Spire (57°30′·3N 1°46′·7W) (illuminated clock face).

Kirktown Spire (57°30′·3N 1°47′·0W), 1¾ cables W of Town Hall Spire.

Reform Tower (square) (57°29′·5N 1°47′·9W) standing on Meet Hill.

Power station chimney (lit) (57°28′·7N 1°47′·4W).

Major light:

Buchan Ness Light (above).

Approaches to Peterhead Bay
3.35

1   **Kirktown Leading Lights:**

Front light (fluorescent orange triangle point up on orange lattice mast) (57°30′·2N 1°47′·2W).

Rear light (fluorescent orange triangle point down on orange lattice mast) (91 m NW of front light).

The alignment (314°) of the above leading lights leads through the entrance to Peterhead Bay, passing (with positions from the front light):

2   NE of Buchan Ness (2 miles SSE) (3.11), thence:

NE of The Skerry (1½ miles SSE) (3.11), thence:

NE of Sandford Bay (1¼ miles S), which is fringed by drying rocky ledges and has a light buoy (special) in its centre marking the seaward end of two outfall pipes, thence:

To Peterhead Bay entrance (5 cables SE), lying between the breakwater heads on which stand lights (3.34).

Approach to Outer Basin
3.36

1   From a position within the breakwater heads the track continues NW on the alignment (314°) until the light on Albert Quay (3.31) is abeam to starboard. Thence course is altered to E in order to enter the basin between the heads of Albert Quay and Merchants Quay finger jetty.

Basins and berths

Vessels are advised not to anchor in the area centred 1 mile E of Keith Inch (57°30′·15N 1°46′·20W) due to the risk of a fouled anchor from discarded wires on the seabed.

Peterhead Harbour Master

(SDD 2011000 162692)

[38/11]

eterhead Bay offers an anchorage in depths The best holding ground is under the lee eakwater consisting of fine sand over blue ith occasional boulders.

er vessels anchored in Peterhead Bay have drag anchor. While at anchor vessels must d lookout and a continuous VHF radio are to be held ready for immediate use.

Berths (Positions given from South ıt (3.34)):

(2½ cables SW), with a depths between and 11·0 m alongside, for vessels up to in length, draught 10·5 m and about lwt. The berth is also used by cruise ships.

3   ASCO North Base Jetty (2½ cables NNE): 100 m long with depths reducing from 13·4 at the outer end to less than 5 m at the inner end.

ASCO South Base (4 cables SW): length of quay 480 m, depths of 6·2 m to 7·3 m alongside.

Princess Royal Jetty: 170 long with depths of 7 m to less than 5 m alongside.

4   North and South Breakwaters: 640 m of quayside with depths between 13·1 and 7·9 m. The North Breakwater incorporates a purpose-built mooring system for oil and gas installations.

Inner Harbour
3.38

1   Albert Quay: length of quay 340 m, depth alongside between about 8·0 m and 10·1 m; can accept vessels up to 160 m LOA and draught 8·5 m.

Merchants Quay finger jetty: 60 m of quay each side, depth 9·0 m.

Merchants Quay: length of quay 130 m, depth 6·2 m; fish market adjacent.

2   South Harbour: 350 m of quayside, depth 3·1 m; can accept vessels up to 92 m LOA and draught 6·1 m at HW Springs.

North Harbour: Two jetties and 400 m of quayside, depths between about 2 m and 3 m.

Port Henry Harbour: One jetty and 740 m of quayside, depths between about 1 m and 3 m.

Port services

Repairs
3.39

1   Dry dock; length overall 58 m; floor length 53 m; breadth 10·3 m; sill depth 0·5 m below chart datum; block depth 0·3 m at entrance reducing to nil at dock head.

There is a slipway capable of taking four vessels up to 27·5 m in length and 300 tonnes.

2000 tonne shiplift serving one covered berth and one outside berth.

Divers available.

Other facilities
3.40

1   Ship Sanitation Certificates issued (1.92); oily waste disposal by road tanker; hospitals. Four Yokohama fenders are available.

Supplies
3.41

1   Marine diesel at all quays; other fuels by road tanker; water at all quays; provisions.

Communications
3.42

1   There is a heliport 2½ miles W of Peterhead and helicopter landing sites at Keith Inch and Boddam (2 miles S of the town).

BUCHAN NESS TO ABERDEEN

General information

Charts 213, 210

Route
3.43

1   From a position E of Buchan Ness (57°28′N 1°46′W) the route leads SSW for a distance of 22 miles to Fairway Light Buoy 1 mile NE of the entrance to Aberdeen Harbour.

Topography
3.44

1   The coast from Buchan Ness to Bay of Cruden (5 miles SSW) is composed of red granite cliffs, up to 73 m in height. Bay of Cruden is sandy and backed by sandhills. At the S extremity of the Bay is a reef, The Skares (57°23′N 1°51′W) from which rocky cliffs continue 5 miles SSW to Hackley Head. The coast is then sandy, backed by grass-covered sandhills and curves gently SSW 12 miles to Aberdeen (57°09′N 2°04′W) and Girdle Ness which is 1 mile E of Aberdeen.

Hazards
3.45

1   **Firing Danger Areas** exist as follows:

Drums Links Firing Range 1¾ miles S of Newburgh (3.55), with radius 1·6 miles centred 57°17′·4N 2°00′·6W. Firing activity takes place seawards.

Black Dog Rifle Range (57°13′N 2°03′W) marked by DZ buoys (special) moored 1½ miles ENE and 1 mile E of Blackdog Rock. Red flags and occasionally red lights are displayed from flagstaffs on the shore when firing is taking place.

2   **Salmon Fisheries.** Numerous bag nets of considerable size and strength are placed off the coast between Newburgh (57°19′N 2°00′W) and Aberdeen. They are obstructions to small craft navigating inshore.

Dumping ground
3.46

1   A disused explosives dumping ground lies 3 miles E of the Aberdeen harbour entrance.

Rescue
3.47

1   There is an MRCC at Aberdeen and Coastal Rescue Teams are located at Aberdeen, Bay of Cruden (57°25′N 1°51′W) and Collieston (57°21′N 1°56′W) See 1.67.

2   An all-weather lifeboat and an inshore lifeboat are stationed at Aberdeen. See 1.72.

Tidal streams
3.48

1   See *Admiralty Tidal Stream Atlas: North Sea, Northwestern Part* and information on charts. The maximum rate in either direction is 3 kn in the N of the area but reducing farther S.

Directions
(Continued from 3.12)

Principal marks
3.49

1   **Landmarks:**

Buchan Ness Lighthouse (57°28′N 1°46′W) (3.9).

Radar aerial, charted as a structure, (57°28′N 1°49′W).

Oil tanks, (57°23′N 1°53′W).

2   Silo, 2 cables SW of the Hill of Strabathie, (57°13′N 2°04′W).

Radio mast, on the summit of Brimmond Hill, (57°10′N 2°14′W).

Radio mast (57°10′N 2°09′W).

Major lights:

Buchan Ness Light (above).

Girdle Ness Light (3.75) (57°08′·3N 2°02′·9W).

Other aids to navigation
3.50

1   **Racons:**

Buchan Ness Light (57°28′N 1°46′W).

Aberdeen Fairway Light Buoy (57°09′·3N 2°01′·9W).

For details see *Admiralty List of Radio Signals Volume 2.*

Buchan Ness to Aberdeen
3.51

1   From a position off the rocky peninsula of Buchan Ness (57°28′N 1°46′W) the coastal passage leads 22 miles SSW running parallel to the coast, to the Fairway Light Buoy off the entrance to Aberdeen Harbour, passing (positions given from Buchan Ness):

ESE of Ward Point (4 miles SSW), the N entrance point of Bay of Cruden. Castle ruins lie close N and Slains Lodge, a large rectangular building stands 7½ cables N of the point, thence:

2   ESE of The Skares (5½ miles SSW), several patches of rock which extend 3½ cables from the S entrance point to Bay of Cruden. They are marked by a light buoy (port hand). Thence:

ESE of Blindman Rock (8 miles SW) which lies close off Old Slains Castle, a dark prominent tower standing on the headland. There is a boat landing close S of the castle.

3   The route continues SSW of Hackley Head (57°20′N 1°57′W), which marks the change along the coast from cliffs to grass covered sandhills, passing (with positions from Newburgh Bar (57°18′N 1°59′W)):

ESE of Drums Links Firing Range (3.45) (centred 1·1 miles SSW), thence:

ESE of Black Dog Rifle Range (3.45) (5½ miles SSW). Submarine cables run E through the area. The landing positions, close N of Blackdog Rock are marked by beacons. Thence:

4   ESE of River Don Entrance Light (white tower) (8½ miles SSW). The entrance to the river is the only interruption in the sandy coast between Blackdog Rock and Aberdeen, thence:

To the vicinity of Fairway Light Buoy (safe water) (9 miles SSW) off the entrance to Aberdeen and 1 mile NNE of Girdle Ness.

3.52

1   **Useful marks:**

Stirling Hill (57°27′·5N 1°47′·5W), granite quarries are close by.

River Don Bridge (4 arches) (57°10′·5N 2°05′·4W).

(Directions continue for Aberdeen at 3.75 and coastal passage S at 3.92)

Minor harbours
Port Erroll
3.53

1   **General information.** Port Erroll (57°24′·67N 1°50′·68W) is a small boat harbour at N end of Bay of Cruden. It can be entered by vessels drawing 3 m at HW Springs.

Useful mark:

Church spire (1½ miles W).

Collieston
3.54

1   **General information.** Collieston (57°20′·84N 1°56′·08W) is a fishing village with a small harbour formed by a pier.

Useful mark:

Church (57°21′N 1°56′W) at Kirktown of Slains.

W end:
Fish Market Quay with a dredged depth of 6·0 m.

Victoria Dock
3.80
Waterloo Quay West and East, 380 m long, alongside
depths 9·3 m and 6·0 m respectively.
Regent Quay, 250 m long, 9·3 m alongside depth.
Upper Dock, 6·0 m alongside depth.
Blaikie's Quay, 635 m long, 6·0 m alongside depth,
includes a RoRo berth at the W end.
Matthews Quay, 160 m long, 9·0 m alongside depth,
includes a RoRo berth.

Tidal Harbour
3.81
Telford Dock: Four quays with alongside depth of
9·0 m and an offshore pocket dredged to 11·0 m.
The dock is used primarily for the final assembly
and loading of equipment for the offshore oil and
gas industry.
A drydock and ship repair facility.
Pocra Quay, 166 m long, 6·0 m alongside depth, an
offshore supply base.

River Dee
3.82
A total of 928 m of quayside with depths alongside
ranging from 4·1 m to 6·5 m, the longest berth being
Mearns Quay with a length of 320 m. The area is used by
supply vessels serving the offshore oil and gas industry.

Port services

Repairs
3.83
Repairs of all kinds can be carried out and divers are
available. There is a dry dock, length 112·8 m, breadth
21·33 m, depth 6·5 m.

Other facilities
3.84
Ship Sanitation Certificates issued (1.92); oily waste
reception facilities; several hospitals. Mobile heavy lift
cranes up to 1000 tonnes can be hired.

Supplies
3.85
Bunkers, fresh water and provisions available.

Communications
3.86
There are daily passenger ferry services to the Orkney
and Shetland Islands and weekly general cargo and RoRo
services to Scandinavia, Holland and Belgium.
Dyce airport (57°12′N 2°13′W) is 5 miles from
Aberdeen.

ABERDEEN TO STONEHAVEN

General information

Chart 210
Route
3.87
From a position E of Girdle Ness (57°08′N 2°03′W) the
coastal route leads SSW for 12 miles to a position E of
Stonehaven.

Topography
3.88
Nigg Bay (3.103) lies between Girdle Ness and Greg
Ness, 6 cables S. Thence the coast from Greg Ness to
Garron Point, at the N entrance to Stonehaven Bay, runs
10 miles SSW. It is composed of nearly perpendicular cliffs
of mica slate over granite, topped by grassy slopes, with
bare hills of moderate elevation in the background. The
coast is mainly steep-to with the 30 m depth contour lying
parallel to the coast approximately one mile offshore. In
places the cliffs are fringed by reefs and isolated rocks up
to three cables to seaward. Stonehaven is at the head of
Stonehaven Bay, which lies between Garron Point and
Downie Point, 1½ miles SSW.

Rescue
3.89
For details of Coastguard at Aberdeen see 3.47. There is
a Coastal Rescue Teams at Stonehaven.

Hazards
3.90
Oil rigs are frequently anchored about 5 miles SE of
Greg Ness and in Nigg Bay.
Bag nets of considerable size and strength are placed off
every point during the fishing season, and are obstructions
to small craft navigating inshore.

Tidal streams
3.91
Tidal streams which run parallel to the coast in either
direction, are shown on the charts and in *Admiralty Tidal
Stream Atlas: North Sea, Northwestern Part*. The spring
rate close inshore in either direction is 2½ kn.
A race forms off Girdle Ness during the S-going stream.

Directions
(continued from 3.52)

Principal Marks
3.92
Radio masts (57°07′N 2°06′W).
Radio mast (57°05′N 2°09′W).
Memorial tower on Hill of Auchlee (57°04′N
2°11′W).
Radio mast on summit of Cairn-mon-earn (57°01′·1
2°21′·5W).
TV mast, red obstruction lights (57°00′·0N 2°23′·4W).
Major light:
Girdle Ness Light (57°08′·3N 2°02′·9W) (3.75).

Other aids to navigation
3.93
Racons:
Aberdeen Fairway Light Buoy (57°09′·3N 2°01′·9W).
Girdle Ness Light (57°08′·3N 2°02′·9W).
For details see *Admiralty List of Radio Signals Volume 2.*

Girdle Ness to Downie Point
3.94
From a position E of the rocky promontory of Girdle
Ness (57°08′N 2°03′W), the coastal passage leads SSW to
a position off Downie Point, 2 cables SE of Stonehaven
Harbour. The track runs parallel to the coast and passes
(with positions from Findon Ness (57°04′·1N 2°05′·6W)):
ESE of Girdlestone (4¾ miles NNE), a rocky patch
1½ cables E of Girdle Ness,which covers and
uncovers, thence;
ESE of two rocky patches (4½ miles NNE) which
dry, thence;

3   ESE of Greg Ness (4 miles NNE), the S entry point of Nigg Bay, thence;

ESE of Hasman Rocks (3 miles NNE), which dry and lie 1 cable offshore, thence;

ESE of Mutton Rock (2 miles NNE), which dries and lies 1½ cables offshore of the fishing village of Cove Bay. The village is at an elevation of 61 m with a small harbour below in the rocks. Thence;

4   ESE of Findon Ness, a steep-to headland. Findon village stands on sloping ground rising to elevations of between 60 and 90 m, close W of the headland, thence;

ESE of Portlethen (1 mile SSW) a fishing village with a landing place for boats, fronted by a drying reef. Seal Craig, lying 3 cables offshore, is the E extremity of the reef. Thence;

5   ESE of Newtonhill (3 miles SSW), a village with a boat landing over a gravel beach, thence;

ESE of Grim Brigs (3¾ miles SSW), a small headland close E of the village of Muchalls, thence;

6   ESE of Garron Point (6 miles SSW), a high rocky promontory. It shelves 2½ cables from the summit and is steep-to terminating in Garron Rock. Skatie Shore a rocky ledge extends 1 cable to the N of the point. Boat landing can be made S of the point. Thence;

7   ESE of Stonehaven Bay (7 miles SSW), lying between Garron Point and Downie Point (11½ miles SSW). The bay has a sandy bottom but there are rocky ledges extending as far as 2 cables offshore.

8   **Caution.** Depths are irregular in places and soundings give little guidance. There is no reason to stand close inshore as the coast is straight and the strength of the tidal stream does not diminish close inshore.

Useful marks
3.95

Glenury Viaduct (56°58′N 2°13′W) (3.100).
War Memorial (56°57′·3N 2°12′·2W) (3.100).
(Directions continue for Stonehaven at 3.100 and for coastal passage S at 3.108)

Stonehaven

Chart 1438 plan of Stonehaven Harbour
General information
3.96

1   **Position.** Stonehaven (56°58′N 2°12′W) stands at the mouth of River Carron at the head of Stonehaven Bay.

Function. Formerly a fishing port, it is now mainly a holiday resort and is used only by recreational craft and a few small inshore fishing boats.

The population is about 9600.

2   **Approach and entry.** Stonehaven is approached from the E through the S part of Stonehaven Bay (3.94).

Port Authority. Harbour Office, Old Pier, Stonehaven, AB39 2LU.

Limiting conditions
3.97

1   **Depths.** There are depths between 0·6 and 1·8 m in the outer harbour. The inner harbour dries 3·4 m sand and mud.

Tidal levels: see *Admiralty Tide Tables Volume 1*. Mean spring range about 3·9 m; mean neap range about 1·9 m.

Maximum size of vessel handled. Length 34 m, draught 3 m.

2   **Local weather and sea state.** During NE and E gales vessels cannot lie alongside in the outer harbour. A boom is placed across the entrance to Inner Basin in NE and E gales.

In E gales the sea breaks beyond the S entrance point to Stonehaven Bay, 1½ cables E of the harbour, and even bursts over the breakwaters.

Arrival information
3.98

1   **Anchorage** may be obtained in Stonehaven Bay as indicated on the chart, in depths of 11 m, good holding ground, 7¾ cables E of Bay Hotel (3.100), with the ruins of Dunnottar Castle (3.100) seen over Bowdun Head, bearing 194°.

2   Small craft may anchor closer into the shore but should keep Garron Rock (3.94) (Chart 210) open to the E of the land to the NE.

Pilotage is not compulsory.

Harbour
3.99

1   **General layout.** There is an outer harbour, protected on its N side by a breakwater and to the S by Downie Point. Middle Basin lies W of the outer harbour and is protected by breakwaters on its E and S sides and by the land to the N and W. Inner Basin, also protected by breakwaters, is entered from Middle Basin.

2   **Boom signal.** When the entrance to Inner Basin is closed, a green light is exhibited from the concrete post 7 m in height, standing in the NE corner of the Inner Basin Breakwater.

Tidal stream is weak in Stonehaven Bay with a spring rate of 1 kn.

Directions for entering harbour
(continued from 3.95)
3.100

1   **Principal marks:**

Glenury Viaduct (56°58′N 2°13′W), to the NW of Stonehaven.
Bay Hotel (three gables) (56°58′·0N 2°12′·7W).
War Memorial (monument) (56°57′·3N 2°12′·2W), standing on Black Hill.
Dunnottar Castle (56°56′·7N 2°11′·8W), in ruins.

2   **Approach to outer harbour.** From a position about 1 mile ENE of Downie Point (3.94) the route leads WSW within the white sector (246°–268°) of the Outer Breakwater Light (post, 2 m in height), passing (with positions from the Outer Breakwater Light):

3   NNW of a light buoy (special) (5 cables E), thence:

SSE of a 4 m shoal (3 cables ENE), thence:

About ½ cable NNW of Downie Point (1½ cables E), rocky ledges run WSW of the point, and:

SSE of Bellman's Head (1 cable NE), a ledge and rocky shoals that run to the SW of it, thence:

To a position ½ cable ENE of the Outer Breakwater Light where the track rounds to the S of the Outer Breakwater head into the outer harbour.

4   **Approach to Middle Basin.** The alignment (273°) of the leading lights at the W side of the Middle Basin leads through its entrance, from the S side of which a light (post, 7 m in height) is exhibited:

Front light (mast, 5 m in height) (56°57′·6N 2°12′·2W).

Rear light (lantern on building, 7 m in height) (10 m W of front light).

Signal Tower

West Breakwater   *Harbour Pier*

Arbroath Harbour from SE (3.149)
(Original dated 2000)

(Photograph - Air Images)

2   **Tidal levels:** see *Admiralty Tide Tables Volume 1*. Mean spring range about 4·5 m; mean neap range about 2·2 m.
   Maximum size of vessel handled: length 67 m, beam 11 m, draught 4 m.

3   **Local weather and sea state.** During strong onshore winds there can be a heavy groundswell in the entrance and entry is unsafe. Additionally, tidal streams can set strongly across the harbour entrance at springs.

Arrival information
3.151
1   **Port radio.** The Harbour Master can be contacted on VHF Channels 16 and 11 during working hours.
   Pilotage is not available.
   Traffic regulations.
      All vessels entering or being within the harbour shall be in all respects under the control of the Harbour Master, whose directions shall be implicitly obeyed in all matters within his jurisdiction.
2   No vessel shall anchor or lie within 76 m of the pierhead and no vessel shall at any time obstruct the fairway.
      No vessel when entering, approaching or leaving the harbour, shall overtake or attempt to pass abreast or ahead of any other vessel so approaching, entering, or leaving.

Harbour
3.152
1   **General layout.** The harbour is open to the SE but protected by Harbour Pier to the NE and by West Breakwater, which is detached, to the S. The harbour contains a tidal basin and an inner basin leading off the tidal basin. The outer tidal basin, with an entrance 15 m wide, dries, the bottom being muddy. The inner basin is enclosed by a pair of half-tide gates and has a depth of 2·5 m. The entrance to the inner basin is 12·2 m wide.

2   **Traffic signal.** At night, when it is unsafe to enter harbour, the light on Harbour Pier (3.153) is changed to fixed red.

Directions for entering harbour
3.153
1   **Principal marks:**
      Clump of trees on Dickmount Law (56°35′N 2°34′W) (Chart 190) (3.145).
      Abbey ruins with a circular window (56°33′·8N 2°34′·9W).
      Saint Mary's Church (spire) (56°33′·7N 2°34′·6W).
      Presbyterian Church (spire) (56°33′·6N 2°34′·9W).
2   Signal Tower (56°33′·3N 2°35′·2W) (disused), a white castellated structure with a flagstaff.
      Reservoir Tower (56°33′·4N 2°35′·7W), standing on Keptie Hill and resembling a castle from seaward.

Signal tower

West Breakwater   *Leading Lights*   *Harbour Pier*

Arbroath Harbour entrance from SE (3.153)
(Original dated 2000)

The extremities of the Harbour Pier and the West Breakwater, which flank the harbour entrance, (56°33'·2N 2°35'·0W) are painted white and are prominent.

3.154

1   **Caution.** An unmarked dangerous wreck lies 1½ miles ESE of the harbour entrance in position 56°33'·0N 2°32'·5W.

Leading Lights:

Front Light (white column, 4 m in height) (56°33'·3N 2°35'·2W).

Rear Light (white column, 9 m in height) (50 m WNW of the front light).

From a position about 1 mile ESE of the harbour entrance the alignment (299¼°) of these lights leads through the dredged channel to the Harbour entrance, passing (with positions from the front light);

2   NNE of the seaward end of an outfall (6½ cables S), extending 5½ cables S from the shore and marked by a light buoy (special), thence:

NNE of Cheek Bush and Chapel Rock (3½ cables SE and 4 cables SSE respectively), thence:

SSW of Knuckle Rock (3½ cables ESE), thence:

3   NNE of two rocks (2½ cables SE) which dry 0·2 m and 0·5 m respectively, thence:

NNE of a light beacon (special) (2¼ cables SE) marking the seaward end of an outfall, thence:

4   To the harbour entrance (1 cable SE) which lies between the heads of Harbour Pier (light: white tower, 9 m in height) and West Breakwater (light: white metal post, 2 m in height). Inshore of West Breakwater, clear of the fairway, the bottom is rocky and dries. Thence:

To the entrance to the tidal basin (½ cable ESE).

5   **Alternative leading marks.**

Saint Thomas Church (56°33'·4N 2°35'·4W) (twin towers) bearing 298° between the harbour entrance lights, leads through the harbour entrance.

Reservoir Tower, Keptie Hill (3.153) bearing 299° and seen between the twin towers of Saint Thomas Church leads through the harbour entrance.

Port services

3.155

1   **Repairs.** Timber, steel and mechanical repairs can be undertaken. There is a patent slip capable of handling vessels up to 30·5 m LOA and 250 tonnes.

Other facility: hospital with helicopter landing pad.

2   **Supplies:** marine diesel and water at the quays; fresh provisions.

3   **Rescue.** There is an all-weather lifeboat and an inshore lifeboat. See 1.72.

Anchorage

Chart 190
Lunan Bay

3.156

1   Lunan Bay (56°39'N 2°28'W) which lies between Boddin Point and Red Head, is sandy and free from dangers, apart from the rocky ledges off the Point and Head. There is a good anchorage in the bay, indicated on the chart, 1 mile E of the ruins of Red Castle (3.148) in depths of 14 m, sand over clay.

2   Small craft can anchor in Ethie Haven which lies in the SW corner of Lunan Bay.

RIVER TAY ENTRANCE TO TAY ROAD BRIDGE

General information

Chart 1481
Description

3.157

1   River Tay flows into the sea between Buddon Ness (56°28'N 2°44'W) and Tentsmuir Point (56°27'N 2°49'W). Dundee Harbour (56°27'·82N 2°56'·37W) is 7 miles W of Buddon Ness. Tay Road Bridge lies at the W end of Dundee Harbour and connects Dundee with the S bank of the Tay in the vicinity of Newport-on-Tay.

2   Tayport Harbour (3.172), a small tidal basin, lies on the S bank of River Tay, 5 miles W of Buddon Ness.

3   There is a bar 3 miles E of Buddon Ness. The buoyed channel across the bar and through the entrance lies between extensive drying sandbanks, Gaa Sand to the N and Abertay Sands to the S. Both banks are liable to change especially during bad weather from the E. Abertay Sands has been extending E for many years and its extension, the Elbow, together with the river bar, have been moving SE. However depths over the bar have remained fairly constant.

4   Within the entrance, the channel is narrow with a minimum width of about 1½ cables and is encumbered with sandbanks as far as Broughty Ferry, 4½ miles W of Buddon Ness. The channel broadens out in the final approach to Dundee.

5   A National Nature Reserve (1.61) covers Abertay Sands and the sands off Tentsmuir Point.

Depths

3.158

1   The controlling depth to Dundee is at Lady Shoal (3.170) where there is a least depth of 4·8 m in mid-channel. Depths in the buoyed channel across The Bar are about 5 m providing the centreline is maintained.

Deep-draught vessels should arrive at Fairway Light Buoy at least 3 hours before HW in order to berth on the same tide.

2   **Caution.** Depths in the channel are liable to change and the VTS should be consulted for the latest information.

Tidal levels

3.159

1   See *Admiralty Tide Tables Volume 1*.

The Bar: mean spring range about 4·5 m; mean neap range about 2·3 m.

Dundee: mean spring range about 4·8 m; mean neap range about 2·3 m.

Pilotage and tugs

3.160

1   **Pilotage** is compulsory in the Dundee Port Authority Area which extends from close W of the Fairway Light Buoy upriver to Balmerino, 2 miles W of Tay Bridge. For pilotage between Balmerino and Perth see 3.194.

2   Pilots board passenger vessels, vessels carrying dangerous goods or which are empty but not gas-free, vessels over 90 m LOA and any other vessels that specifically request, at the outer pilot station which is in the vicinity of the Fairway Light Buoy (56°28'·3N 2°36'·6W). The inner pilot station, which is SW of Buddon Ness, is used as the boarding point for small vessels. Tankers less than 90 m LOA in ballast but not gas-free may board the pilot at the inner station providing all pre-arrival checks are in order. For further details see *Admiralty List of Radio Signals Volume 6 (1)*.

Buddon Ness   Tentsmuir Point

River Tay Estuary from NE (3.157)

(Original dated 2000)

(Photograph - Air Images)

3   The pilot boats are launches of 15 m in length with a dark hull, white superstructure and marked "Dundee Pilot" on both sides. A pilot boat is only on station when a vessel is expected.

Tugs. Two tugs are available at Dundee; additional tugs may be obtained by prior arrangement.

Vessel traffic service
3.161
1   VTS and radar surveillance for monitoring shipping in River Tay as far up river as Balmerino is maintained by Forth and Tay Navigation Service at Grangemouth. The call sign is DUNDEE HARBOUR RADIO.

2   Between Balmerino and Perth there is no VTS. The local authority is Perth and Kinross Council and communications should be addressed to Perth Harbour. See *Admiralty List of Radio Signals Volume 6 (1)* for details.

Notice of ETA required
3.162
1   Vessels over 300 gt and all vessels carrying dangerous cargoes should give 24 hours notice of their ETA to Dundee Harbour Radio. An update should be signalled 6 hours and 2 hours in advance.

See *Admiralty List of Radio Signals Volume 6 (1)* for further details.

Outer anchorage
3.163
1   Anchorage in a depth of about 20 m is available in the vicinity of the Fairway Light Buoy (56°28'·3N 2°36'·6W). There is also an anchorage 6 cables WSW of Buddon Ness, close to the inner pilot boarding position (3.160). Depth in this latter anchorage is about 6 m.

Dundee Port Authority may occasionally anchor vessels in the vicinity of West Deep Light Buoy (56°27'·1N 2°56'·2W), particularly vessels bound for Perth and awaiting HW. Vessels bound for Perth may also anchor to W of Tay Bridge, see 3.196.

2   **Prohibited anchorage.** Vessels are prohibited from anchoring in the vicinity of submarine cables crossing the river close W of Tayport High Lighthouse and the submarine gas pipeline (1.41) which runs NNE across the river from Tentsmuir Point. The landing places of the pipeline are marked by light beacons.

Anchoring is also prohibited off Dundee Harbour as indicated on the chart.

Exercise area
3.164
1   A military exercise area exists at Buddon Ness. Ranges fire WSW and S across Monifieth Bay and E across Carnoustie Bay. The firing ranges operate a clear range procedure; exercises and firing only take place when the area is considered to be clear of shipping. See *The Mariner's Handbook*.

Rescue
3.165
1   An all-weather and an inshore lifeboat are maintained at Broughty Ferry (3.157). See 1.72.

Natural conditions
3.166
1   **Tidal streams** in the vicinity of the entrance to River Tay are shown on the chart. In the buoyed channel between the Inner Light Buoys and Tentsmuir Point, a NW set occurs on the flood tide which is especially noticeable in the vicinity of North Lady Light Buoy before Abertay Sands (3.170) are covered.

2   Tidal streams run strongly in the channel S of Horse Shoe (56°27'·4N 2°50'·0W) (3.170), where the in-going stream sets towards Tayport and the out-going stream towards Green Scalp (3.170). There is usually some turbulence between Horse Shoe and Broughty Castle (3.167), especially during the E going stream with W winds.

3   Off Dundee docks, the in-going stream sets across the entrance to Camperdown Dock (3.186) at less strength than in the centre of the river. The stream is weak or slack from 30 minutes to 40 minutes before HW which is the best time for entry into the enclosed dock system.

Both the duration and rate of the out-going stream may be increased and the in-going stream correspondingly reduced during and after heavy rain or when snow is melting.

4   **Climate information.** See 1.142 and 1.146.

Directions
(continued from 3.148)

Principal marks
3.167

1   **Landmarks:**
Old High Lighthouse on Buddon Ness (white tower) (56°28′·1N 2°45′·0W), now disused.

Old High and Old Low Lighthouses on
Buddon Ness (3.167)
(Original dated 2008)

(Photograph - Drew Given)

Broughty Castle (56°27′·8N 2°52′·2W), a conspicuous square building.

Broughty Castle from SE (3.167)
(Original dated 2008)

(Photograph - Drew Given)

2   Two wind turbines (56°29′·1N 2°53′·9W and 56°29′·0N 2°53′·7W) (uncharted) on hill to N of Broughty Ferry (3.157).
Television mast (56°26′·7N 2°55′·5W), close SE of Tay Road Bridge.
Monument (56°26′·8N 2°56′·0W), close SE of Tay Road Bridge.
War Memorial on summit of Dundee Law (56°28′·2N 2°59′·4W).
Television mast 140 m N of War Memorial (above).
Building (56°28′·0N 2°55′·7W).

War Memorial on Dundee Law from SE (3.167)
(Original dated 2008)

(Photograph - Drew Given)

3   Buildings (4 blocks of flats) (56°28′·1N 2°58′·2W).
Saint Paul's Church Spire (56°27′·7N 2°58′·1W) in SE part of Dundee.
Building, 180 m S of Church Spire (above).
Building (56°27′·5N 2°58′·8W). Another building lies close W and a third close SE.

4   **Major light:**
Tayport High Light (white tower, 23 m in height) (56°27′·2N 2°53′·9W).

Tayport High Light from NE (3.167)
(Original dated 2008)

(Photograph - Drew Given)

Other aid to navigation
3.168

1   **Racon:**
Abertay Light Buoy (56°27′·4N 2°40′·3W).
For details see *Admiralty List of Radio Signals Volume 2.*

Fairway Light Buoy to Buddon Ness
3.169

1   From the vicinity of Fairway Light Buoy (safe water) (56°28′·3N 2°36′·6W) the route leads WSW thence W to a position in the channel S of Buddon Ness, passing (with positions from Buddon Ness):

Over The Bar (3 miles E), passing between Middle Light Buoys (lateral), which are 4¼ cables apart, thence:

2 NNW of Elbow (2 miles SE), a spit extending 3 miles ENE from Abertay Sands, with depths of less than 5 m, thence:

Between the Abertay Light Buoys (E cardinal and port hand) (2 miles ESE), 4 cables apart.

3 Thence the line of bearing 269° within the narrow white sector (268°–270°) of Tayport High Light leads in the channel, passing (with positions from Buddon Ness):

Between Inner Light Buoys (lateral) (1 mile SE), thence:

S of Gaa Sand and Gaa Spit, which extend 2 miles E of Buddon Ness. Gaa Sand dries up to 1½ miles E of Buddon Ness, thence:

S of Buddon Ness, consisting of grass covered sand dunes up to 9 m high on its E side.

4 **Cautions.** When entering River Tay during onshore gales from the NE or SE, the tidal set must be watched carefully in order to keep in the buoyed channel. It might be dangerous to cross The Bar in these conditions, particularly during the out-going stream; depths might alter and light buoys drag out of position. The best time to cross The Bar is from 2 hours before HW to HW.

Passage across Abertay and Gaa Sands can be highly dangerous and should not be attempted.

Buddon Ness to Tayport High Lighthouse
3.170

1 From a position in the channel S of Buddon Ness the route leads W, remaining in the narrow white sector (268°–270°) of Tayport High Light as far as Horse Shoe Light Buoy. Thence course is adjusted WNW until Tayport High Lighthouse is abeam. The track passes (with positions from Tayport High Lighthouse):

2 N of Abertay Sands (4½ miles E), a drying bank on the S side of the channel which extends 3½ miles E of Tentsmuir Point, thence:

N of Lady Shoal (4 miles E), an extension N of Abertay Sands, which almost forms an inner bar, thence:

3 Between North Lady and South Lady Light Buoys (lateral) (4 miles E). North Lady Light Buoy (starboard hand) marks the S limit of Lady Bank which fills the greater part of the bay lying between Buddon Ness and Broughty Castle. South Lady Light Buoy (port hand) lies just inside the narrow white sector of Tayport High Light. Thence:

4 N of Pool Light Buoy (3 miles E) (port hand), thence:
N of Tentsmuir Point (2½ miles ESE), which is low and sandy and fronted by Green Scalp, a bank of sand and gravel which dries, thence:

5 S of Horse Shoe (2 miles E), a patch of foul ground to the W of Lady Bank, marked on its S side by Horse Shoe Light Buoy (S cardinal). A light buoy (special) marking the seaward end of Dighty outfall lies 2½ cables ENE of Horse Shoe Light Buoy. The channel is only 1 cable wide at this point and shoal patches, with depths of less than 3 m lie close S of the white sector of Tayport High Light. Thence:

6 NNE of Lucky Scalp (2 miles E) an islet, and Larick Scalp, a drying bank, to its W. The drying bank of sand and gravel lies W of Green Scalp and fills

the bay between Tentsmuir Point and Tayport (3.172). Scalp Light Buoy (port hand) is moored close N of Larick Scalp. Thence:

7 SSW of Broughty Castle (1 mile NE) (3.167). Lights (grey column 3 m in height) are exhibited from close S of the castle. The S extremity of Broughty Castle in transit with Old High Lighthouse bears 084½° and provides a useful compass check for vessels leaving Dundee. And:

8 NNE of Tayport (6 cables E). The ruins of Larick Beacon lie 3 cables ENE of the harbour entrance; an outfall extends from Tayport to a position ¾ cable WNW of Larick Beacon.

Tayport High Lighthouse to Tay Road Bridge
3.171

1 From a position in the channel NNE of Tayport High Lighthouse, the route leads W for 1 mile then SW for a further mile to the navigation spans under the Tay Road Bridge (56°27′N 2°57′W), passing (with positions from navigation spans):

2 N of Newcome Shoal (1½ miles ENE), marked on its NE extremity by Newcome Light Buoy (port hand). From this point vessels can proceed to Dundee Docks, 1½ miles to the W. Thence:

N of Tayport High Lighthouse (1½ miles E), thence:

SE of Middle Bank (2½ cables N), which lies in the centre of the river on both sides of the road bridge, and is marked at its NE extremity by Middle Bank Light Buoy (E cardinal), thence:

3 NW of West Deep Light Buoy (port hand) (2 cables NE), thence:

To the navigation spans under Tay Road Bridge.
(Directions continue at 3.197)

Tayport Harbour

General information
3.172

1 Tayport Harbour (56°27′N 2°53′W) is a small tidal basin. The entrance is 25 m wide and marked on either pierhead by beacons (white and red bands). There are depths of 1·2 m to 1·5 m at the entrance and within are 488 m of quays and pontoon berths for small craft. Vessels that use the harbour take the mud at LW.

The harbour is privately owned.

DUNDEE

General information

Chart 1481 and plan of Dundee Docks
Position
3.173

1 The City of Dundee (56°28′N 2°57′W), spreads out along the N bank of River Tay over a distance of several miles. Two bridges cross River Tay at Dundee; Tay Road Bridge, which runs from the centre of the City and Tay Bridge, a railway bridge, 1½ miles to the W.

Function
3.174

1 The port handles general cargo, including forest products and agricultural commodities, and imports crude oil. The repair and servicing of offshore oil and gas installations is undertaken also.

The population of the city is about 155 000.

Dundee Harbour from E (3.173)
(Original dated 2000)

(Photograph - Air Images)

Port limits
3.175
1   The E limit of Dundee Port Authority is 8 cables W of the Fairway Light Buoy (3.169); the W limit lies at Balmerino, 2 miles W of Tay Bridge. The limits are shown on Chart 1481.

Traffic
3.176
1   In 2008 Dundee was visited by 330 vessels and handled 932 000 tonnes of cargo.

Port Authority
3.177
1   Forth Ports PLC, Port of Dundee, Stannergate Road, Dundee DD1 .3LU.
       Website: www.forthports.co.uk

Limiting conditions

Controlling depths
3.178
1   See 3.158.

Deepest and longest berth
3.179
1   Deepest berth: Caledon West Wharf. Longest berth: King George V Wharf. See 3.185.

Tidal levels
3.180
1   See 3.159.

Maximum size of vessel handled
3.181
1   Vessels with a maximum length of 260 m, beam 45 m and draught up to 8·8 m can be accommodated at Caledon West Wharf (3.185).

Arrival information

Traffic regulations
3.182
1   Subject to the requirements of maintaining steerage way, vessels shall not exceed 8 kn to the W of 2°53′W. Within the docks and tidal basin the speed limit is 3 kn.

2   Vessels crossing, turning or manoeuvring in a fairway shall only do so when it is clear and not impede other vessels navigating in the fairway.
       Power-driven vessels navigating against the stream shall slow or stop to allow vessels navigating with the stream to pass clear.

Harbour

General layout
3.183
1   Dundee Docks consist of a number of riverside berths which extend downstream from the NW end of Tay Road Bridge. There are two non-tidal docks, Camperdown Dock, entered directly from River Tay and Victoria Dock entered via Camperdown Dock. Restrictions on dock gate opening apply (3.186).

Directions for entering harbour
3.184
1   Directions are given at 3.167 to 3.171.

Basins and berths

Riverside berths
3.185
1   King George V Wharf, 445 m long, 8·5 m depth alongside.
       Caledon West Wharf, 76 m long, is dredged W in front of King George V Wharf and E in front of Princess Alexandra Wharf to provide a berth 300 m long and 55 m wide, with 9·5 m depth alongside and is used principally for oil tankers.

Dundee Law   *Broughty Castle*

Approaches to Dundee Harbour from ESE (3.183)
(Original dated 2008)

(Photograph - Drew Given)

2   Princess Alexandra Wharf, 256 m long, 8·0 m depth alongside the E 180 m.

Eastern Wharf, 213 m long, 8·0 m alongside, with a RoRo berth at the E end with a depth of 7·0 m in front of the linkspan.

3   Prince Charles Wharf, depth 9·0 m, total length 318 m, of which 115 m at the E end utilised for offshore oil industry vessels berthing alongside. The remainder to the W, including an 8·0 m depth box to the S, is for the fitting out of offshore oil rigs.

Queen Elizabeth and Caledon East wharves are disused. Obstructions in the form of old piles exist adjacent to the W part of the Queen Elizabeth Wharf.

There is a tidal basin at the E end of the riverside berths, which is reserved for use by the port authority.

Docks
3.186

1   Camperdown and Victoria docks are no longer in commercial use. They are available only to leisure craft and for limited lay-up. The dock gates may be opened on request from 1 to 2 hours before and until HW. However, no vessel should approach the locks at Camperdown Dock without first receiving permission from Dundee Harbour Radio. The approaching vessel should stand off and not approach the lock entrance until permission to proceed has been received.

Camperdown Dock has 560 m of quays and is entered through dock gates facing S, immediately W of King George V Wharf. The entrance is 15 m wide and the nominal bottom of the dock is LAT; there are depths inside the dock of 4·0 m.

2   Victoria Dock has 680 m of quays and is entered from the W side of Camperdown Dock. Depths within the dock are similar to Camperdown Dock.

Port services

Repairs
3.187

1   Ship and engine repairs can be carried out.

Other facilities
3.188

1   Ship Sanitation Certificates issued (1.92); reception of oily waste; hospitals. There is a helicopter landing site at Ninewells Hospital, 2 miles WNW of Tay Road Bridge.

Supplies
3.189

1   Fuel and diesel oils; water; provisions of all kinds.

Communications
3.190

1   Dundee Airport (56°27′N 3°01′W) is situated close W of Tay Bridge.

TAY ROAD BRIDGE TO PERTH

General information

Chart 1481
Description
3.191

1   From Tay Road Bridge to Perth is a distance of 19 miles. Above the railway bridge, River Tay broadens out to a width of 3 miles but gradually narrows thereafter until just W of Mugdrum Island, 10 miles SW of Tay Bridge,

where it is only 2 cables wide and continues to narrow farther upstream. For the 10 miles to Mugdrum Island the N side of the river is heavily encumbered with dryingbanks up to 2 miles wide. The S side of the river is relatively free of banks but there are a number of banks in mid-river.

Dundee Harbour and Tay Bridges from ENE (3.191)
(Original dated 2000)

(Photograph - Air Images)

Depths
3.192

1   Depths in River Tay are uncertain but recent mapping and dredging has been carried out to improve access to Perth. Vessels are advised to leave Dundee 2 hours before HW Dundee in order to arrive at HW Perth.

There is a tide gauge at Newburgh (56°21′·4N 3°13′·7W) and at Ribny Beacon (56°22′·5N 3°20′·3W).

Flow
3.193

1   Under normal conditions, the following flows are experienced:

	Half-flood	*Half-ebb*
Springs	3 kn	4 to 5 kn
Neaps	1½ kn	3 kn

2   After heavy rains or melting snows, a spate is experienced which can considerably increase the height of the river and the strength of the current.

Pilotage and tug
3.194

1   **Pilotage.** Navigation on the River Tay between Dundee and Perth is difficult and can be hazardous. Pilotage is not compulsory but masters are strongly advised to make use of the services of a local pilot who can be arranged by Perth Harbour and who will board off Balmerino at the W limit of Dundee Port Authority. For further details see *Admiralty List of Radio Signals Volume 6 (1)*.

Tug. A small tug is available at Perth.

Local knowledge
3.195

1   The passage between Tay Bridge and Perth should not be attempted without local knowledge.

Anchorage
3.196

1   An anchorage area, as indicated on the chart, is located 5 cables SW of No 3 Light Buoy (port hand) (56°25′·2N 3°02′·0W).

Directions
(continued from 3.171)

Tay Road Bridge
3.197

1   Tay Road Bridge spans the river from Newport-on-Tay (56°27′N 2°56′W) NW to Dundee. There are two navigation spans, the N span between piers 31 and 32, and the S span between 32 and 33. The width of the spans is 76 m. Lights are exhibited on the piers and in the centre of each span, together with daymarks (cone, point down, black and white diagonal stripes). Inbound vessels proceeding from E to W must use the N span and outbound vessels the S span. Use of the two spans either side of the navigation spans is not permitted.

2   **Vertical clearance** under the centre of the spans is 21 m.

Tay Road Bridge to Tay Bridge
3.198

1   From a position close W of the road bridge the route leads WSW for 1¾ miles to the navigation spans of the railway bridge, passing:

2   SSE of Middle Bank (56°27′N 2°58′W) (3.171), and: NNW of Newport-on-Tay (56°26′N 2°56′W). A submarine cable area runs between Newport-on-Tay and Dundee as shown on the chart. Vessels are cautioned against anchoring in the area. The NE limit of the area is marked by beacons on either bank. Thence:
To the navigation spans of the railway bridge.

Tay Bridge
3.199

1   Tay Bridge (56°26′N 2°59′W), a railway bridge, spans the river at the W end of Dundee and has thirteen high spans. The navigable channel is under the fifth high span from S. Lights and daymarks on both sides of the bridge indicate the navigation channel; see Diagram 3.199. The channel between the fourth and fifth piers from the N is obstructed by the remains of an old bridge, and must not be used for navigation.
Vertical clearance under the bridge is 21 m.

Tay Bridge to Perth
3.200

1   The river between the railway bridge and Perth is encumbered by mud and sand banks which dry; the channel is marked by light buoys and light beacons (lateral).

2   **Submarine cables and pipelines.** Two submarine power cables cross the river at Cairnie Pier (56°21′·5N 3°18′·1W). Their landings are marked by light beacons (special). A gas pipeline crosses the river in the close vicinity of Inchyra Light (56°22′·2N 3°19′·6W) and two oil pipelines cross the

river 8 cables farther upriver in the vicinity of Elcho Castle. Their landings are marked by light beacons (lateral).

3   **Vertical clearances.** Between the railway bridge and Perth there are power cables (56°22′N 3°19′W) spanning the river with a minimum safe overhead clearance of 23 m. Friarton Road Bridge, (56°23′N 3°25′W), which is marked by lights, has a vertical clearance of 24 m.

Perth

General information
3.201

1   The Royal Burgh of Perth (56°23′·79N 3°26′·05W) is on the W bank of River Tay, 17 miles above Tay Bridge at Dundee. The population of Perth is about 43 000.
Perth Tidal Harbour (56°22′·87N 3°25′·72W), 5 cables S of Perth, is also on the W bank of the river. The small commercial port has 417 m of quay providing four berths. It handles wheat, animal feeds, packaged timber, chemical salt and road salt In 2008, the port was visited by 96 vessels totalling 136 964 gt. Trade is mostly with Continental Europe and the Baltic Sea.

2   **Port Authority.** Perth & Kinross Council, Economic Development, 5 High Street, Perth PH1 5JS. Communications should be addressed to the Harbour Master, Perth Harbour Office, Friarton Road, Perth PH2 8BB.

Perth Tidal Harbour from S (3.201)
(Original dated 2000)

(Photograph - Air Images)

Limiting conditions
3.202

1   **Tidal levels.** See *Admiralty Tide Tables Volume 1*. Mean spring range about 3·1 m; mean neap range about 1·6 m.
Maximum size of vessel handled. The port can accept vessels up to 90 m LOA. Subject to the discretion of the Harbour Master, normal transit draught in the upper river is set at the height of tide on the day of transit up to a maximum draught in fresh water of 4·2 m.
Vessels lie aground at LW on a bottom of soft mud.

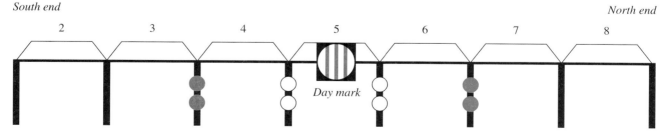

Tay railway bridge inbound view (3.199)

Port services
3.203
1   **Repairs.** Small repairs can be carried out locally; major repairs at Dundee.

Other facilities. Oily waste reception facilities using road tankers available by arrangement with vessel's agents. There is a hospital.

2   **Supplies:** marine diesel by road tanker; water at quays; provisions.

RIVER TAY TO FIFE NESS

General information

Chart 190
Route
3.204
1   From the vicinity of the Fairway Light Buoy (56°28′·3N 2°36′·6W) off the entrance to River Tay, the coastal route leads SSE for a distance of 12 miles to a position E of Fife Ness.

Topography
3.205
1   Saint Andrews Bay lies between Tentsmuir Point the S entrance point of River Tay and Fife Ness. Tentsmuir Point is at the W end of Abertay Sands (3.170) and from here the coast runs S for 6 miles to the town of Saint Andrews. This part of the coast is fronted by Tentsmuir Sands and backed by sandhills. There is a nature reserve (1.61) on Tentsmuir Sands. The mouth of River Eden is 2 miles N of Saint Andrews. The coast forming the S part of the bay between Saint Andrews and Fife Ness, 8 miles ESE, is generally rocky, with cliffs in places rising to 30 m.

Rescue
3.206
1   Forth MRCC is based at Fife Ness (56°17′N 2°35′W) and there is a Coastal Rescue Team at Saint Andrews. See 1.67.

Natural conditions
3.207
1   **Tidal streams** are shown on the chart and in *Admiralty Tidal Stream Atlas: North Sea, Northwestern Part.*

Climate information. For Leuchars see 1.142 and 1.146: for Fife Ness see 1.142 and 1.147.

Directions
(continued from 3.148)

Principal marks
3.208
1   **Landmarks:**
    Old High Lighthouse (56°28′N 2°45′W) (3.167).
    Regulus Tower at Saint Andrews (56°20′N 2°47′W).
    Silo, position approximate, 1¼ miles SSW of Kinkell Ness (56°20′N 2°45′W).
2   **Major lights:**
    Bell Rock Light (56°26′N 2°23′W) (3.145).
    Fife Ness Light (white building, 5 m in height) (56°17′N 2°35′W).
    Isle of May Light (56°11′N 2°33′W) (3.220).

Other aid to navigation
3.209
1   **Racon:**
    Bell Rock Light (56°26′N 2°23′W).
    For details see *Admiralty List of Radio Signals Volume 2.*

River Tay to Fife Ness
3.210
1   From the vicinity of Fairway Light Buoy (56°28′·3N 2°36′·6W) off the entrance to River Tay, the route leads SSE to Fife Ness, passing (with positions from Fife Ness):

2   ENE of Saint Andrews Bay (7 miles WNW), with the town of Saint Andrews (3.213) at its head. The W coast of the bay is fronted by shoal water with depths of less than 5 m. Thence:

3   ENE of North Carr Rocks (1 mile NNE), which dry. The rocks have a prominent beacon (red column on a stone base, globe topmark, all supported by six metal stays) and lie at the NE extremity of foul ground extending 1 mile NE of Fife Ness. North Carr Light Buoy (E cardinal) is moored 1 mile NE of North Carr Rocks, which are also covered by the red sector (197°–217°) of Fife Ness Light. Thence:

4   ENE of Fife Ness, a dark cliff, 10 m high, above a rocky foreshore.

Useful marks
3.211
1   University spire (56°20′·5N 2°47′·7W).
    Cathedral ruins (56°20′·4N 2°47′·2W) (3.213).
    Kingsbarn village church spire (56°18′N 2°40′W).
    Balcomie Tower (56°17′N 2°36′W), square tower and outbuildings, standing close W of Fife Ness.
    Coastguard radio tower on Fife Ness (56°17′N 2°35′W).
    (Directions continue for coastal passage at 3.220)

Minor harbours

Guardbridge
3.212
1   **General information.** Guardbridge (56°21′N 2°53′W) (Chart 1407) is situated about 3 miles above the bar of River Eden, where the river is spanned by a road bridge.

Local knowledge is required for the river passage.

2   **Directions for entering harbour.** The River Eden bar dries 1·7 m (2003). Within the bar there are depths of 3 m reducing to 2 m at Guardbridge. The bar itself is constantly changing and the channel to Guardbridge, via the River Eden, is narrow and bounded by wide sand flats.

Berths. There is a quay near the bridge and the tall chimney of a paper mill stands close N of the quay.

Saint Andrews
3.213
1   **General information.** Saint Andrews (56°20′N 2°48′W), population about 14 000, stands on a flat table–land 18 m high, 6 miles S of Tentsmuir Point. It has a small harbour, which dries, used by fishing boats and pleasure craft. The harbour lies at the mouth of Kiness Burn. Long Pier, 213 m long, protects the harbour and is built on The Skellies, a rocky ledge running ESE for 3 cables. Other ledges lie close S of and parallel to The Skellies.

2   The harbour lies S of Long Pier and there is a short pier extending NE from the opposite shore close S of Long Pier. It is divided into an outer and inner harbour by an entrance 8 m wide, spanned by a movable pedestrian bridge. Both the harbours are tidal. At MHWS depths of

*Regulus
Tower*

Saint Andrews Harbour from E (3.213)
(Original dated 2003)

(Photograph - Crown Copyright)

4 m to 5 m have been reported in the approach channel and 4 m in parts of the outer harbour. These depths are liable to change.

3 **Principal marks:**
Regulus Tower (56°20'·4N 2°47'·2W) conspicuous, in the E side of the town.
University Spire (56°20'·5N 2°47'·7W).

4 Cathedral ruins (56°20'·4N 2°47'·2W), close N of Regulus Tower.
Drumcarrow Craig 56°18'·6N 2°52'·5W(215 m high) (3½ miles SW of Regulus Tower) a rugged topped hill, surmounted by a mast (Chart 1407).

5 **Directions for entering harbour.** From a position NNE of Long Pier, the approach leads close to the SE extremity of the pierhead, about 16 m off, and thence close S of Long Pier and parallel to it, and keeping N of the ledges on the S side of the channel. A light (metal post) is exhibited from the head of Long Pier.
Caution. The passage between Long Pier and the ledges is narrow. In E gales there is a considerable swell in the outer harbour.

6 **Boat Landing.** There are steps, available at half tide, within Long Pier.
Facilities: limited supplies of water; slipway for small boats only; cottage hospital.

FIFE NESS TO ELIE NESS AND ISLE OF MAY

General information

Charts 175, 734
Routes
3.214

1 Two routes are described, the first being a route which enters Firth of Forth from NW and the second being the N part of the route across the approaches to Firth of Forth.
The fishing ports of Crail (3.224), Anstruther (3.225), Pittenweem (3.226) and St Monans (3.227) are also described.

Topography
3.215

1 From Fife Ness (56°17'N 2°35'W) the coast runs in a SW direction for 9½ miles to Elie Ness. The coast consists of low cliffs and grassy banks above a rocky foreshore, and is mostly foul up to 2 cables offshore.

2 Isle of May is 5 miles S of Fife Ness. It is composed of dark grey greenstone, with an elevated grassy surface. The W side is formed by cliffs, up to 62 m high, which slope irregularly E to a rocky coast indented by deep fissures. The NW end of the island is lower and terminates in rocks offshore. The island has a bird observatory and is a National Nature Reserve (1.61).

Isle of May from S (3.215)
(Original dated 2000)

(Photograph - Air Images)

Exercise area
3.216

1 Submarines and other naval vessels exercise in the approaches to and within the Firth of Forth. See 1.20.

Dumping ground
3.217

1 There is a disused dumping ground for ammunition and boom defence gear 2½ miles E of Isle of May (3.215). A second disused dumping ground lies close SW of it. Both are shown on the chart.

Rescue
3.218

1 An all-weather lifeboat is stationed at Anstruther (56°13'N 2°42'W). See 1.72.

Natural conditions
3.219

1 **Tidal streams** for the area are shown on the chart and in *Admiralty Tidal Stream Atlas: North Sea, Northwestern Part.* The spring rate in either direction is 1 to 1½ kn off salient points.
Climate information. See 1.142 and 1.147.

Directions
(continued from 3.211)

Principal marks
3.220

1 **Landmarks:**
West Lomond (56°15'N 3°18'W), a sugar loaf mountain (Chart 1407).
East Lomond (56°14'N 3°13'W), a sugar loaf mountain (Chart 1407).
Largo Law (56°14'N 2°56'W), a notched summit and stone cairn (Chart 1407).
Kellie Law (56°15'N 2°47'W), a ridge to E of Largo Law (Chart 1407).

2 **Major lights:**
Fife Ness Light (56°17'N 2°35'W) (3.208).
Elie Ness Light (white tower 11 m in height) (56°11'N 2°49'W), on SW point of Elie Ness.

Isle of May and Light from WSW (3.220)
(Original dated 2009)

(Photograph - Gareth Kirk, MV Logos II)

Isle of May Light (square tower on stone dwelling 24 m in height) (56°11′N 2°33′W).

Fife Ness to Elie Ness
3.221

1 From a position E of Fife Ness (56°17′N 2°35′W), the coastal passage leads 12 miles SW to a position S of Elie Ness, passing (with positions from Fife Ness):

SE of an outfall extending 4 cables SE from Kilminning Craig (6 cables SW) (3.222) and marked by a light buoy (special), thence:

2 Depending on draught, clear of Hurst (1½ miles SSE), a 10·2 m rocky patch, thence:

SE of Crail (2 miles SW) (3.224), a village lying in Roome Bight, 7 cables wide between Roome Ness and West Ness. The coast between Kilminning Craig and Roome Ness is foul up to 4 cables offshore. Thence:

3 SE of Caiplie Rock (3½ miles SW) with a depth of 3·7 m, which lies off Caiplie village. The Coves, several caverns in the face of the coastal banks, lie 8 cables N of Caiplie Rock. Thence:

SE of Anstruther Easter (5 miles SW) and its harbour (3.225). Anstruther Easter is the central part of a long straggling town with Cellardyke at the E end

[handwritten overlay:]
r Paragraph 3.221 5 line 3 Insert:

Caution. Extensive static creel pot fishing is *ertaken* to the N and W of Isle of May between *Ness* and Pittenweem. Mariners navigating in this *should* avoid fouling the pots, which are marked *unlit* orange floats.

h Ports Ltd
D 2011000 196226)   [45/11]

3.222

1 **Useful marks:**

Kilminning Craig (56°16′N 2°36′W), a prominent high black rock.

Pittenweem Church (clock tower and short spire) (56°13′N 2°44′W).

2 St Monans sector light (breakwater head) (56°12′·2N 2°45′·9W).

St Monans Church (spire) (56°12′N 2°46′W), at W end of the village.

Newark Castle (ruins) (56°12′N 2°47′W), 5 cables SW of St Monans Church.

(Directions continue for Firth of Forth at 4.16)

Fife Ness to the Isle of May
3.223

1 From a position E of Fife Ness the route leads S in open sea to pass clear of Isle of May (3.215).

(Directions continue for coastal passage S at 5.11).

Minor harbours and anchorage
Crail Harbour
3.224

1 **General information.** Crail Harbour (56°15′N 2°38′W) stands at the SW end of the village and is formed by a main pier to the S and a small jetty on the W side. The inner approach to the harbour is obstructed by rocky ledges, but vessels drawing up to 3 m may enter at HW.

Crail Harbour from S (3.224)
(Original dated 2000)

(Photograph - Air Images)

2 **Harbour Authority.** Fife Council, County Buildings, St. Catherine Street, Cupar, KY15 4TA.

Directions for entering harbour. From SE of the harbour the alignment (295°) of the leading lights leads to the harbour entrance which is 7 m wide:

Front light (white stone beacon, 6 m in height) on cliff (56°15′·5N 2°37′·8W).

Rear light (similar beacon, 5 m in height) (30 m WNW of front beacon).

3 **Caution.** NE gales cause a heavy swell in the harbour, and it is not possible to enter in strong NE or SE winds.

Useful mark:

Crail Church (square tower surmounted by spire) (56°15′·8N 2°37′·6W).

Facilities: limited small craft berths and facilities available; there is a slipway; hospital at Saint Andrews.

Anstruther from SSW (3.225)
(Original dated 2000)

(Photograph - Air Images)

Chart 734
Anstruther Harbour
3.225

1   **General information.** Anstruther Harbour (56°13′N 2°42′W), a fishing and recreational harbour, is close SW of Anstruther Easter (3.221). There are 1170 m of quays in the harbour. It is formed by E and W piers (both lighted at their heads) with an entrance which faces SW. The outer and inner harbours dry, the former on sand and rock, the latter on soft mud.

2   **Harbour Authority.** Fife Council, Fife House, North Street, Glenrothes, Fife KY7 5LT. The harbour authority is represented by a Harbour Master who may be contacted by telephone or VHF radio; see *Admiralty List of Radio Signals Volume 6 (1)* for details.

3   **Directions for entering harbour.** From S of the harbour the alignment (019°) of leading lights leads to the harbour entrance:

> Front light (white mast 6 m in height) (56°13′·1N 2°41′·8W).
> Rear light (white mast 8 m in height) (38 m NNE of front light).

Caution. Entry should not be attempted in strong winds from the E and S.

4   **Repairs.** Minor repairs can be carried out. There is a slipway and a beaching area.

Supplies: marine diesel by road tanker; water; provisions.

Hospital at Saint Andrews.

Pittenweem Harbour
3.226

1   **General information.** Pittenweem Harbour (56°13′N 2°44′W) is a busy fishing port which can be used by vessels up to 27·5 m in length. It is formed by three piers, with an entrance 23 m wide facing SW. The small inner basin has an entrance 8 m wide. Both the entrance channel and inner basin are dredged to a depth of 1·8 m at MLWS.

The inner basin is liable to be congested and the Harbour Master must be consulted before berthing.

Church

Light-beacon

Pittenweem from S (3.226)
(Original dated 2000)

(Photograph - Air Images)

2   **Harbour Authority.** Fife Council, .County Buildings, St. Catherine Street, Cupar, KY15 4TA The harbour authority is represented by a Harbour Master who may be contacted by telephone or VHF radio; see *Admiralty List of Radio Signals Volume 6 (1)* for details.

3   **Directions for entering harbour.** The W side of the approach channel is marked by a light beacon and the E side by a sector light on the head of the breakwater. From

Outer anchorages

4.51

1 Vessels bound for Leith normally use Aberlady Bay Anchorage (4.22) or Inchkeith Small Vessel Anchorage (4.84).

2 There are three designated anchor berths, L1, L2 and L3, in Leith Road and a small vessel anchorage to N of Granton. However, these anchorages lie within the area of compulsory pilotage (4.4).

A dredging area on Middle Bank (56°01′N 3°11′W) (4.82) adjoins the N limit of the Leith Road anchorage.

Pilotage and tugs

4.52

1 **Pilotage.** See 4.4.

Tugs are available.

Harbour

General layout

4.53

1 The harbour is enclosed by East and West Breakwaters and is entered via a lock which lies 1½ cables within the breakwater entrance. The harbour entrance is marked by East Breakwater Light (red lantern on concrete base, 4 m in height). The lock is 259 m long and 33·5 m wide.

2 The harbour is divided into Western Harbour, which is the largest and deepest area in the harbour, and a complex of older and smaller docks in the E part. The deepest part of Western Harbour is marked by buoys and has a dredged depth of 10·3 m.

3 A substantial area of the W part of Western Harbour has been reclaimed for land based development (2009).

Traffic signals

4.54

1 Lights (Diagram 4.54) controlling entry and departure from the entrance lock are exhibited from both ends of the lock.

Signal	Meaning
●	Harbour is closed.
●	Vessel may enter lock.
● ●	Indicates side of lock to which vessel will be secured.

Traffic signals (4.54)

Tidal streams

4.55

1 The tidal streams set strongly across the approach channel at rates up to 1½ kn in a 080°/260° direction. Great care is required to maintain the correct approach. An eddy forms off Leith breakwater heads during in-going stream.

Directions for entering harbour
(continued from 4.19)

Principal marks

4.56

1 **Landmarks:**

Salisbury Crags (55°56′·8N 3°10′·5W).
Arthur's Seat (55°57′N 3°10′W) (4.42).
Nelson's Monument (55°57′·3N 3°11′·0W).
Edinburgh Castle (55°56′·9N 3°12′·0W).
Saint Mary's Cathedral, three spires, (55°56′·8N 3°13′·0W).
Two buildings (55°58′·6N 3°10′·7W), tower blocks.

2 **Major light:**

Inchkeith Light (56°02′N 3°08′W) (4.16).

Leith Channel

4.57

1 Leith Channel commences close S of Fairway Light Buoy (56°03′·5N 3°00′·1W) and runs 4¼ miles SW through South Channel and Narrow Deep to a position SE of Inchkeith Lighthouse, passing (with positions from Inchkeith Lighthouse):

NW of North Craig (2½ miles ESE), a rocky shoal, marked on its NW side by Narrow Deep Light Buoy (port hand), thence:

2 NW of Craig Waugh (2¾ miles SE), a shoal which dries and which is marked by a light buoy (isolated danger), thence:

SE of Herwit (1 mile SE), a rocky ledge which dries, with Little Herwit close NNW. A conspicuous stranded wreck lies on Herwit. Thence:

SE of Inchkeith (4.93).

Inchkeith to Leith

4.58

1 From a position in the channel SE of Inchkeith Lighthouse, the route leads 1½ miles WSW, thence 2 miles W, through South Channel and Leith Road to the approach to the dredged channel which leads SSE to the harbour entrance, passing (with positions from East Breakwater Light (55°59′·5N 3°11′·0E)):

2 SSE of Briggs (2½ miles NE), a rocky ledge which dries; foul ground extends 1 cable farther SE, thence:

N of a buoy (N cardinal) (1¾ miles E), marking the seaward end of an outfall which extends 1½ miles N from the coast, thence:

Inchkeith Island and Light from SSW (4.57)
(Original dated 2009)

(Photograph - Gareth Kirk, MV Logos II)

Limiting Marks

Leith Entrance Lock from NW (4.58)
(Original dated 2004)

(Photograph - MV Doulos)

3   Clear of the anchorages in Leith Road (4.51), thence:
N of Leith Approach Light Buoy (port hand) (6 cables NW).

4   Thence course is adjusted SSE into the dredged approach channel which is 122 m wide with a centreline bearing of 147°. The E side of the approach channel is marked by Leith Approach Light Buoy and a light beacon, 5 cables SE. The W side of the approach channel is marked by a directional light beacon and beacons in transit (4.59). Between the light beacon on the E side of the approach channel and the lock are a line of dolphins and a projecting approach wall about 280 m in length running parallel to East Breakwater.

Both sides of the lock have a line of lamp posts which can be used as visual references in the approach to the lock.

4.59

1   **Limiting light.**
Directional light beacon (144°-145°) (steel pole, 4 m in height (55°59'·3N 3°10'·9W).

2   **Limiting marks.**
Front mark: Red triangle apex up (55°59'·3N 3°10'·9W).
Rear mark: Red triangle apex down (720 m SE).
By day the alignment (146°) of the above marks, and by night the narrow (144°-145°) light sector of the above light, indicates the W limit of the dredged approach channel.

Basins and berths

Western Harbour

4.60

1   Cruise Liner Terminal: 570 m of quayside available, including one berth 375 m in length; depth 10·3 m.
Imperial Basin: 200 m long, 9·5 m alongside.

Outer Harbour

4.61

1   Nos 8, 10 and 12 berths: 305 m long, 9·5 m alongside.
No 6 berth: 149 m long, 8 m alongside.

Docks

4.62

1   Imperial Dock: 1396 m of quayage, depth 9·5 m, can accommodate vessels up to 30 m beam.
Albert Dock, 844 m of quayage, depth 8 m, entrance width 18·2 m, includes a RoRo berth.
Edinburgh Dock, 1120 m of quayage, depth 8 m, entrance width 18·2 m.

Port services

Repairs

4.63

1   Limited repairs can be carried out. There are two dry docks.
Largest dock: length 167·6 m overall, floor breadth 21·3 m, depths (below chart datum) sill 1·9 m and blocks 1·8 m.

Other facilities

4.64

1   Hospitals; helicopter landing site at Royal Infirmary Edinburgh; reception of oily waste; Ship Sanitation Certificates issued (1.92).

Supplies

4.65

1   Marine diesel oil from road tanker or small coastal tanker; fresh water at working berths; stores and provisions.

Granton

Charts 735, 736

General information

4.66

1   **Position.** Granton Harbour (55°59'·30N 3°13'·31W) lies 1½ miles W of Leith (4.40).
Function. Granton, formerly a small commercial port, is now used by leisure craft and also by pilot boats and work boats.
Approach and entry. Granton is approached through South Channel (4.57) and Leith Road (4.58) and entered from the N.
Port Authority: see 4.45.

Limiting conditions

4.67

1   **Controlling depths.** The depth in the harbour entrance is 3·4 m and the depth alongside the head of Middle Pier is 2·6 m. Depths are liable to change and the Harbour Master at Leith should be consulted prior to arrival.
Tidal levels: see *Admiralty Tide Tables Volume 1.* Mean spring range about 4·8 m; mean neap range about 2·4 m.

Arrival information

4.68

1   **Vessel traffic service.** See 4.50.
Anchorage. There is an anchorage for small vessels 1 mile N of the harbour entrance. Anchoring is prohibited within 2½ cables of the harbour entrance.
Pilotage. See 4.4. The Forth Pilots base is at the head of Middle Pier.

Harbour
4.69

1   **General layout.** The harbour is formed by Eastern and Western Breakwaters and divided into two by Middle Pier, which runs N/S with its head a cable inside the entrance. The harbour entrance faces N and is 104 m wide. Much of the harbour dries and is being reclaimed for land development.

    Middle Pier is a timber pile jetty about 140 m in length.

2   **Tidal streams.** The tidal streams set strongly across the entrance to the harbour.

Directions for entering harbour
4.70

1   **Principal marks:**

    See 4.56 for marks in the approach channel.
    Gasholder (55°58′·8N 3°14′·7W).

2   **Approach.** Commercial and naval vessels of more than 50 gt bound for Granton from E should approach through Leith Channel (4.57), passing to the N of Leith Approach Light Buoy (port hand) and thence S of the small vessel anchorage (4.68) to a position N of the harbour entrance.

3   **Useful marks:**

    East Breakwater light (white square brick building, 5 m in height) (55°59′·3N 3°13′·3W).

Newhaven Harbour

Chart 735
General information
4.71

1   Newhaven Harbour (55°59′N 3°12′W) lies on the W side of the root of West Breakwater, Leith (4.40). The harbour dries 1 to 3 m and it is used by fishing vessels and recreational craft.

2   A disused lighthouse, 15 m in height, is located on the N side of the entrance.

    The harbour has no direct connection with Leith, but is administered by Forth Ports PLC (Leith and Granton).

FAIRWAY LIGHT BUOY TO INCHCOLM

General information

Charts 735, 736
Route
4.72

1   From the vicinity of Fairway Light Buoy, the route leads 5 miles W following Forth Deep Water Channel to a position N of Inchkeith (56°02′N 3°08′W), thence the route leads 6 miles WSW remaining in the channel to a position SW of Inchcolm, passing the port of Burntisland and the marine terminal at Braefoot, which lie N of the fairway.

Topography
4.73

1   Between Inchkeith (56°02′N 3°08′W) and Inchcolm, the Firth of Forth narrows from a width of about 5 miles to 2 miles. Outside urban areas, the N and S shores are largely covered by woodland. The N coast is somewhat irregular with a number of sandy bays separated by rocky headlands. The island of Inchcolm lies about 5 cables off the N bank and is separated from it by Mortimer's Deep, a narrow, deep water channel. The islands of Oxcars, Cow and Calves, Inchmickery and Cramond are located on the extensive banks of mud and sand which lie between Forth Deep Water Channel and the S shore.

Depths
4.74

1   Between Fairway Light Buoy and Inchcolm depths in Forth Deep Water Channel are greater than 19 m.

Traffic regulations
4.75

1   See Appendix I.

    Vessels with a draught in excess of 10 m may display the signals prescribed for a vessel constrained by her draught in Rule 28 of *The International Regulations for Preventing Collisions at Sea (1972)* and should follow the recommended channel for deep-draught vessels between the Fairway Light Buoy and Grangemouth.

2   Vessels which are not confined to a fairway shall not obstruct other vessels which can only navigate within such fairway and shall give such vessels a clear course and as wide a berth as safe navigation requires.

    In complying with the above, outbound vessels with a draught of less than 10 m may often pass S of Forth Deep Water Channel between No 2 Light Buoy (56°02′·9N 3°03′·7W) and No 10 Light Buoy (56°02′·1N 3°13′·3W) but keeping a safe distance N of Inchkeith.

Protected wrecks
4.76

1   Restricted areas are established 1 mile SSE and SSW of Burntisland (56°03′N 3°14′W) to protect two historic wrecks. See 1.60.

Degaussing range
4.77

1   A DG range, the limits of which are shown on the chart, is centred 5 cables SW of Burntisland Harbour entrance (56°03′N 3°14′W). Within the range anchoring and fishing are prohibited and vessels should keep clear of vessels using the range.

    A restriction on the operation of the range occurs whenever tankers bound for Braefoot Terminal are manoeuvring in Mortimer's Deep.

Cow and Calves   Oxcars Light   Forth Bridges   Inchcolm   Braefoot Terminal

Forth Deep Water Channel from ESE (4.72)
(Original dated 2006)

(Photograph - HMSML Gleaner)

Rescue
4.78
1   There is a Coastal Rescue Team and an inshore lifeboat at Kinghorn (56°04′N 3°10′W). See 1.67 and 1.72.

Tidal streams
4.79
1   In the seaward approaches to Inchkeith the tidal stream is more or less rotary. It changes direction rapidly around slack water and sets SW or NE when full with a rate at springs of about ¾ kn to 1 kn.

    Between Inchkeith and Inchcolm the tidal stream runs in the direction of the deep water channel with a maximum rate of about 1 kn to 1½ kn at springs.

2   Tidal conditions in the Firth of Forth are greatly affected by the meteorological conditions in the North Sea and by melting snow and rain inland.

    For further information see tidal stream data on the chart.

Directions
(continued from 4.19)

Principal marks
4.80
1   **Landmarks:**
        Radio mast (56°04′N 3°14′W).
        Church tower (56°04′N 3°13′W).
        Church tower (56°03′N 3°14′W).
        Radar tower (56°03′N 3°14′W).
        Shed (56°03′N 3°14′W).

2   Square tower of Saint Colm's Abbey (56°02′N 3°18′W).
        Arthur's Seat (55°57′N 3°10′W) (4.42).
        Nelson's Monument (55°57′N 3°11′W).
        White Houses (55°59′N 3°18W).
    Major light:
        Inchkeith Light (56°02′N 3°08′W) (4.16).

Other aid to navigation
4.81
1   **Racon:**
        No 7 Light Buoy (56°03′N 3°11′W).

Fairway Light Buoy to Inchcolm
4.82
1   From a position N of Fairway Light Buoy (56°03′·5N 3°00′·1W) the route leads 5 miles W, thence 6 miles WSW, following Forth Deep Water Channel, which is marked by light buoys and runs through North Channel, to a position 5 cables SW of Inchcolm. The route through Forth Deep Water Channel passes (with positions from Inchkeith Light (56°02′·0N 3°08′·2W)):

2   N of Inchkeith (4.93), thence:
    N of Rost Bank (1 mile NNW), which lies close S of the fairway. During spring tides or strong winds there are tide rips over the bank. Thence:
    SSE of Kinghorn Ness (2 miles NNW), fringed by a rocky bank, thence:
3   SSE of Blae Rock (2 miles NW), marked on its SE side by No 7 Light Buoy (starboard hand). In E gales the sea breaks heavily on the rock, thence:

NNW of Gunnet Ledge (1½ miles WSW), marked on its E and W sides by light buoys (cardinal). The ledge stands on Middle Bank, an extensive bank of mud, gravel and shells that separates North Channel from South Channel (4.57).

4   The route continues WSW in the deep water channel, passing (with positions from Oxcars Light (56°01′·4N 3°16′·8W)):
    SSE of Lammerlaws Point (3 miles NE) close E of Burntisland (4.86) and the W point of a bay which extends to Kinghorn Ness, 1½ miles ENE. The bay is fronted by a sand flat and has Black Rocks (4.83) near its entrance. Heuchboy, a rocky ledge, marked by a beacon, lies close SSE of the point. Thence:
5   SSE of No 9 Light Buoy (starboard hand) (2¼ miles ENE) moored near the entrance to a channel leading to Braefoot Marine Terminal (4.100), thence:
6   NNW of Oxcars, a rocky islet on which stands a light (4.83). The islet lies at the W end of Oxcars Bank.Thence:
7   To a position SW of Inchcolm (7 cables NW), a rocky island. A light (4.83) stands on its SE corner. The island is hilly at either end and the ruins of Saint Colm's abbey (4.80) lie in the centre. The island lies at the SW corner of a bank, 1½ miles long, running ENE/WSW, which separates the main channel to the SE from Mortimer's Deep (4.102) to the NW. Meadulse Rocks, a group of drying rocks, lie on the bank to the N of Inchcolm; a ruined beacon stands near their W end and the islet Car Craig lies at their E end, 4 cables NE of Inchcolm. There are depths of less than 5 m up to 1 mile to the NE of Inchcolm.

Useful marks
4.83
1   Black Rocks (56°03′·4N 3°12′·6W), W of Kinghorn Ness.
    Flagstaff (white, about 10 m in height) (56°02′N 3°18′W), close E of Saint Colm's Abbey.
    White building (56°03′N 3°17′W).
2   Oxcars Light (white tower, red band, 22 m in height) (56°01′N 3°17′W).

Oxcars Light from ENE (4.83)
(Original dated 2006)

(Photograph - HMSML Gleaner)

Inchcolm Light (grey metal framework tower, 10 m in height) (56°02′N 3°18′W).

Inchcolm Light from SE (4.83)
(Original dated 2006)

(Photograph - HMSML Gleaner)

Flagstaff (55°59′N 3°18′W) at head of the breakwater.
*(Directions continue for Forth Bridges
and River Forth at 4.135.
Directions for Braefoot Marine Terminal
are given at 4.119)*

Anchorages

Inchkeith
4.84

1   **Inchkeith Small Vessel Anchorage** is 5 cables E of the island. The anchorage is controlled by the VTS; inbound vessels should request an anchorage berth before passing Fairway Light Buoy and outbound before passing Inchkeith. Generally the anchorage is for vessels up to 100 m LOA and 5 m draught but subject to the port authority's approval.

Burntisland Road
4.85

1   There are three designated anchorage berths in Burntisland Road which is situated between the port of Burntisland (4.86) (56°03′N 3°14′W) and the Forth Deep Water Channel. The anchorages, numbered B1, B2 and B3, are allocated by the VTS.

Burntisland

Chart 733
General information
4.86

1   **Position.** Burntisland (56°03·22′N 3°14′·20W) stands 8 cables S of The Binn of Burntisland (chart 735), a steep-sided and prominent hill.

Function. Burntisland, population about 5700, is a small commercial port handling general cargoes.

2   **Approach and entry.** There is unimpeded access from Forth Deep Water Channel, which passes 1 mile S of the port.

Traffic. In 2008, the port was used by 37 vessels.

Port Authority. The harbour is administered by Forth Ports PLC (4.2).

Limiting conditions
4.87

1   **Controlling depths.** The depth at the harbour entrance is 2·2 m.

East Dock has a depth of 8·5 m over the sill at HW springs; West Dock has a depth of 6·3 m over the sill at HW springs. For the latest information on the depths inside both docks, the Harbour Master should be consulted.

Tidal levels: see *Admiralty Tide Tables Volume 1.* Mean spring range about 4·7 m; mean neap range about 2·3 m.

2   **Maximum size of vessel handled.** The East Dock can accommodate vessels up to 122 m in length, beam 16·8 m, draught 6·7 m.

Arrival information
4.88

1   **Vessel traffic service.** See 4.7.

Anchorage. There is a recommended anchorage in Burntisland Road, 2 cables SSW of the harbour entrance in a depth of 10·4 m on a mud bottom. Additionally, there are three numbered anchor berths (4.85).

2   **Pilotage** is compulsory. See 4.4.

Tugs are available from Leith.

Traffic regulations. Vessels must reduce speed and keep well clear of vessels anchored in Burntisland Road if such vessels have barges alongside.

Harbour
4.89

1   **General layout.** The port consists of two wet docks leading off a tidal Outer Harbour, which is formed by two breakwaters. The harbour entrance is 76 m wide. East Dock, entrance 18·29 m wide, is approached from the E side of Outer Harbour through a pair of dock gates, which are opened from 2 hours before HW to HW by arrangement. West Dock is approached from the NW corner of Outer Harbour and entered through a half-tide gate. A shelter for small craft enclosed by a lay-by jetty lies just inside the harbour entrance on the E side.

2   **Degaussing range.** The harbour entrance lies within the restricted limits of a DG range (4.77).

Directions for entering harbour
4.90

1   **Principal marks:**
Radio mast (56°04′N 3°14′W) (Chart 735).
Erskine church (tower surmounted by small spire) (56°03′·8N 3°13′·5W).
Church Tower (56°03′·5N 3°13′·9W).
Radar tower (56°03′·3N 3°14′·1W).
Shed (56°03′·5N 3°14′·4W).
Radio mast (56°03′·7N 3°15′·2W).

2   **Approach.** From a position in Forth Deep Water Channel between No 7 and No 9 Light Buoys (starboard hand), the route leads 1½ miles NW to the harbour entrance passing clear of any vessels anchored in Burntisland Road (4.85). The harbour entrance lies between breakwaters on which stand lights; E pierhead (pole, 5 m in height), W pierhead (white tower, 6 m in height).

Berths
4.91

1   The NW quay of East Dock is the principal cargo berth.

The quay on the W side of West Dock is used as the base for a fabrication yard. The berth can accommodate vessels up to 150 m in length and beam 23 m.

Port services
4.92

1 **Repairs** of a limited nature can be carried out.

Other facilities: Ship Sanitation Certificates issued (1.92); reception of oily waste; hospital at Kirkcaldy (4.32).

Supplies: fuel of all types by road; water at the quays; provisions and stores.

Minor harbours and landings

Chart 735
Inchkeith
4.93

1 **Inchkeith** (56°02′N 3°08′W) has a central ridge up to 55 m in height, terminating in a point at its S end. Elsewhere it descends regularly to the coast, which is fringed with rocks. It is generally forbidden to land on the island. West Harbour, on the W side of the island is formed by piers and has depths of 1 to 2 m. The harbour is protected from all but the S.

2 **Inchkeith Small Vessel Anchorage.** See 4.84.

Pettycur
4.94

1 Pettycur Harbour (56°04′N 3°11′W) lies 3 cables WSW of Kinghorn Ness. The harbour, which dries 1·5 m, is formed by a curved pier.

Chart 733
Carron Harbour
4.95

1 Carron Harbour (56°03′·6N 3°15′·4W) has a boat yard and a pier. The harbour dries.

Aberdour
4.96

1 Aberdour (56°03′N 3°18′W) has a small harbour at the mouth of Dour Burn which dries. The harbour is formed by a pier extending ESE from the W side of the burn, with a depth of 2·7 m at HW springs on its inner side. Within the pier the bottom is soft mud and vessels are well protected from every direction. There are moorings and an anchorage for small craft at the entrance to the bay.

Inchcolm
4.97

1 Inchcolm (56°02′N 3°18′W) (4.82) has a boat landing on its N side, 1 cable to the E of the ruined abbey (4.82).

Chart 736
Inchmickery
4.98

1 Inchmickery (56°01′N 3°16′W) (4.73) has a boat pier on its W side.

Cramond
4.99

1 Cramond (55°58′·7N 3°18′·1W) lies at the mouth of River Almond. The harbour is approached via a winding channel leading in a SW direction from a position close W of Cramond Island, which is located on sand flats 6 cables offshore and connected to it by a causeway. The channel, marked by perches on the starboard hand side, is subject to considerable change. Craft with a draught of 1·2 m can enter the river about 2 hours either side of HW but care should be taken to avoid grounding on a stone sill across the river mouth.

BRAEFOOT MARINE TERMINAL

General information

Chart 733, 736
Position
4.100

1 Braefoot Marine Terminal (56°02′·14N 3°18′·63W) is situated on the NW side of Mortimer's Deep, 3 cables ENE of Braefoot Point.

Function
4.101

1 Braefoot is a gas tanker terminal serving the Mossmorran petro-chemical complex. Shell Jetty exports propane, butane and natural gasoline and Exxon Jetty exports ethylene.

Approach and entry
4.102

1 The Braefoot Marine Terminal is approached from Forth Deep Water Channel via Mortimer's Deep, the channel between Inchcolm and the N side of the firth. The terminal may be approached from either end of the deep.

Traffic
4.103

1 In 2008 the terminal was used by 314 vessels. About 3 million tonnes of cargo is exported annually.

Terminal operators
4.104

1 Shell UK Exploration and Production, PO Box 16, Mossmorran, Cowdenbeath, Fife.

Exxon Mobil Chemicals Ltd., Exxon Mobil House, Ermyn Way, Leatherhead, Surrey, KT22 8UX.

Limiting conditions

Controlling depths
4.105

1 Controlling depth in the E approach is 10 m on the leading line (4.120). In the SW approach the controlling depth is 14·2 m, 3 cables SW of Haystack (56°01′·7N 3°19′·3W).

Deepest and longest Berth
4.106

1 Shell Jetty (4.116).

Tidal levels
4.107

1 See Leith (4.48).

Density of water
4.108

1 The dock water density is 1·025 g/cm^3.

Maximum size of vessel handled
4.109

1 Shell Jetty can accommodate tankers up to 60 000 cubic metres capacity, 220 m LOA and draught 13·0 m. The Exxon Jetty is used by tankers up to 20 000 dwt, 165 m LOA and draught 9·5 m.

Arrival information

Port operations
4.110

1 Local VHF frequencies are manned 2 hours before a vessel's arrival. See *Admiralty List of Radio Signals Volume 6 (1)*.

Braefoot Terminal

Inchcolm   *Abbey*

Mortimer's Deep from SE (4.102)

(Original dated 2000)

(Photograph - Air Images)

Notice of ETA required
4.111

1   See 4.7. Notice of ETA should be sent to the terminal 72 hours in advance and amended for any change greater than 12 hours. ETA should be confirmed 24 hours in advance and amended for any change greater than 4 hours.

Outer anchorages
4.112

1   See 4.8.

Pilotage and tugs
4.113

1   **Pilotage.** See 4.4.
    Tugs are available.

Traffic regulations
4.114

1   The following rules apply to the movement of tankers using Braefoot Marine Terminal. See also Appendix I:

    No vessel shall enter Mortimer's Deep without the express permission of the Forth and Tay Navigation Service, unless the vessel is destined for Braefoot Marine Terminal. This Byelaw shall not apply to pleasure boats less than 12 m in length provided they shall reduce speed as low as possible and do not approach within 100 m of vessels berthed at the terminal.

2   Every tanker destined for the terminal shall regulate its approach so as not to arrive before the agreed berthing time.

    Berthing and unberthing at the terminal will not be permitted when visibility is less than 5 cables.

    Tankers approach the jetties via either the E or W channels of Mortimer's Deep and berth stemming the tide.

3   Tankers departing the terminal may be directed via the E or W channel. Tankers may be required to swing with aid of tugs on departure.

    No vessel shall enter Mortimer's Deep, or the channels leading to it, when the terminal is occupied or when a tanker is manoeuvring in the area, except that a second tanker may enter once the first tanker is securely berthed.

4   Radio transmissions and the operation of radar are prohibited in the vicinity of the terminal, except that a vessel's normal equipment may be tested provided that a source of ignition is not present and that the Chief Harbour Master's permission has been obtained.

Foul ground
4.115

1   There are two areas of foul ground in Mortimer's Deep, one of which encompasses the approaches to the terminal. See chart for details.

Terminal

General layout
4.116

1   There are two jetties, Shell Jetty to the W, which is 85 m long with a swept depth alongside of 15 m (1984) and Exxon Jetty to the E, with a swept depth alongside of 13 m (2002). The seaward ends of both jetties are flanked by berthing and mooring dolphins, which are marked by lights and joined by catwalks.

Traffic signal
4.117

1   A yellow flashing light exhibited from the main jetty 2 hours prior to and during a tanker movement, warns other mariners that a movement is imminent or in progress.

Tidal streams
4.118

1   Tidal streams can attain rates of up to 2½ kn through Mortimer's Deep.

Braefoot Terminal from SE (4.116)
(Original dated 2003)

(Photograph - Forth Ports PLC)

Directions

Principal marks
4.119

1   **Landmarks:**
Square tower of Saint Colm's Abbey (56°02′N 3°18′W).
White building on Hawkcraig Point (56°03′N 3°17′W).

Approach from the east
4.120

1   **Hawkcraig Point leading lights:**
Front light (white tower, red band, 4 m in height) (56°03′·0N 3°17′·1W).
Rear light (white tower, red band, 8 m in height) (96 m WNW of front light).

2   From a position in Forth Deep Water Channel SSE of No 9 Light Buoy (56°02′·4N 3°13′·4W) (4.82), the alignment (292°) of these lights leads WNW for about 1½ miles through a recommended channel, which is 200 m wide and marked by a pair of light buoys (lateral) near its inner end. The track passes (with positions from front leading light):

3   SSW of Burntisland Docks (1½ miles E) and the anchor berths in Burntisland Road (4.85), thence:
Across the S extremity of the degaussing range (1 mile ESE) (4.77), thence:

4   To the E end of Mortimer's Deep (6 cables ESE).
4.121

1   **Braefoot Bay Terminal leading lights:**
Front light (triangle point up, white post on dolphin, 2 m in height) (56°02′·2N 3°18′·7W).

White Building

Hawkcraig Point Leading Lights (4.120)
(Original dated 2006)

(Photograph - HMSML Gleaner)

Rear light (triangle point down, white post on jetty, 2 m in height) (88 m from front light).

2   From a position on the leading line at the E end of Mortimer's Deep, the alignment (247¼°) of these lights leads WSW for 1½ miles to the marine terminal. The channel, which is 1 cable wide at its narrowest part and marked by light buoys (lateral), passes (with positions from the front light):
SSE of Hawkcraig Point (1¼ miles NE), a bold cliffy headland, thence:

3   NNW of Car Craig (8 cables E), an islet standing at the E end of Meadulse Rocks, a rocky reef extending about 7 cables farther W, thence:

SSE of Craigdimas (6 cables NE), a rocky ledge which dries and which is marked by a ruined beacon, thence:

SSE of Vault Point (3 cables NE).

Approach from the south-west
4.122

1   **Inchcolm lights in line:**

Common rear light (white tower, 2 m in height) (56°01′·8N 3°18′·2W).

S front light (white tower, 2 m in height) (84 m WSW of rear light).

N front light (white tower, 2 m in height) (80 m WSW of rear light).

2   The S front light in line with the rear light (066°) and the N front light in line with the rear light (076¾°) mark the limits of the channel leading into Mortimer's Deep from WSW.

3   From a position about 2½ cables NNW of No 17 Light Buoy (starboard hand) (56°01′·2N 3°19′·8W), the track leads ENE within the channel for 5 cables to a position 1 cable SE of Haystack, passing (with positions from rear leading light):

SSE of Dalgety Bay (1 mile WNW), which dries and lies between Braefoot Point and Downing Point, 1 mile WSW, thence:

4   SSE of Haystack (6 cables W), a bare rock, 5 m high, with No 9 Light Buoy (starboard hand) moored close SE of it, and:

NNW of No 14 Light Buoy (W cardinal) (5 cables WSW) marking the extremity of a coastal bank extending WSW from Inchcolm.

5   Thence course is adjusted NNE to the terminal, 5 cables distant.

6   **Caution.** A shoal patch with a depth of 3·2 m extends 1 cable SSW of Haystack and is inside the 076¾° clearing line.

A shoal patch with a depth of 10·5 m lies a ½ cable W of No 14 Light Buoy and is just outside the 066° clearing line.

4.123

1   **Beacons in line:**

Front beacon (red pole on dolphin surmounted by a triangle point up) (56°02′·1N 3°18′·9W).

Rear beacon (post surmounted by a triangle point down) (220 m NNE of front beacon).

The alignment (017½°) of the beacons marks the approach to the terminal from SSW. A beacon (red pole surmounted by a triangle point up) (56°02′·1N 3°18′·8W) in line (014½°) with the rear beacon marks the E limit of this approach.

Leading line: The transit (231°) of Haystack (4.122) with the centre of the S span of Forth Railway Bridge leads through the centre of Mortimer's Deep.

Marine terminal services

Facilities
4.124

1   Ship Sanitation Certificates issued (1.92); hospital at Kirkcaldy.

Supplies
4.125

1   Fresh water; provisions; marine diesel at Shell Jetty only.

INCHCOLM TO FORTH BRIDGES

General information
Chart 736
Route
4.126

1   From a position SW of Inchcolm the route leads 3 miles WSW to a position close W of the bridges.

Topography
4.127

1   Between Inchcolm and the two bridges both shores are wooded. The N shore consists of sandy bays separated by rocky headlands and the S shore trends NW to Hound Point. Forth Road Bridge is 5 cables W of Forth Railway Bridge. Both bridges cross River Forth where the river narrows to 1 mile between Queensferry on the S bank and the peninsula to the N on which North Queensferry stands. The port of Rosyth (4.151) lies 1½ miles NW of Forth Road Bridge on the N bank of the river.

Depths
4.128

1   Within Forth Deep Water Channel, which terminates in the vicinity of Hound Point Marine Terminal, there is a least depth (2006) of 18·4 m in 56°00′·6N 3°21′·4W. Continuing WSW on the recommended route depths are generally in excess of 20 m except for a shoal patch with a depth of 12·3 m in 56°00′·5N 3°22′·5W.

Radar interference
4.129

1   It has been reported that due to the Forth bridges, vessels leaving Rosyth Main Channel (56°01′N 3°26′W) and small craft leaving Port Edgar (56°00′N 3°25′W) are unlikely to be detected on radar by vessels approaching from E. However, vessels with an aerial height of between 12 m and 24 m, when between the bridges, should have no difficulty with radar interference.

Traffic regulations
4.130

1   **Hound Point anchorage** (4.144). Passing vessels are to keep at least 200 m away from vessels at anchor in this anchorage.

2   **Hound Point Marine Terminal** (4.138). Vessels must reduce speed if necessary and must not approach within 100 m when passing vessels berthed at the terminal. A maximum speed limit of 10 knots over the ground is imposed when passing within 5 cables of a vessel berthed alongside the terminal.

Anchoring is prohibited between the terminal and the shore at Whitehouse Point, where pipelines are laid.

3   **Passage beneath the Forth Bridges.** Vessels may not pass or run parallel to another vessel under Forth Railway Bridge whether in conditions of good visibility or not. In the event of vessels approaching the bridge from opposite directions, the outward bound vessel shall have priority of passage under the bridge and the inbound vessel shall keep clear.

4   In conditions where visibility is less than 5 cables, an inward bound vessel shall not, under any circumstances, pass No 19 Light Buoy (56°00′·7N 3°22′·5W) unless clearance to do so has been obtained from the Forth and Tay Navigation Service.

Vessels must not approach within 100 m of the main piers of the Forth Road Bridge.

5   **Port of Rosyth Ferry Operations.** When departing from Rosyth, the ro-pax ferry to Zeebrugge will normally have right-of-way when entering the main channel unless otherwise directed by the VTS. See Appendix I (Byelaw No 28).

On both inbound and outbound passages under Forth Railway Bridge, the ferry has priority unless otherwise directed by the VTS.

Vertical clearances - Forth Bridges
4.131

1   **Rail Bridge.** The central part of the two navigation spans is level for 146 m and has a minimum safe vertical clearance of 42 m above HAT below the painting and maintenance platforms.

2   **Road Bridge.** With painting and maintenance platforms fitted, there is a minimum safe vertical clearance above HAT of 40 m between the green and red lights, rising to 41 m under the central white light.

Rescue
4.132

1   There are Coastal Rescue Teams at Rosyth and Queensferry; see 1.67.

An inshore lifeboat is permanently stationed at Queensferry; for details of lifeboats see 1.72.

Local magnetic anomaly
4.133

1   A compass deflection of up to 11° has been observed by vessels passing under the rail bridge. Vessels steering on a magnetic compass are therefore advised to steady on a distant object before passing under the bridge.

Tidal streams
4.134

1   The strength of the tidal stream attains 2¾ kn at springs through the channels under the bridges. There may be turbulence in North Channel off North Queensferry (56°01′N 3°24′W).

During the W-going tidal stream eddies around Beamer Rock (56°00′·3N 3°24′·7W) extend up to 2 cables WNW.

2   During the E-going tidal stream eddies exist between Beamer Rock and Long Craig (3 cables ENE) and at springs can extend E as far as Inch Garvie (9 cables ESE). In addition the E-going stream sets strongly onto Inch Garvie.

Directions
(continued from 4.83)

Inchcolm to Hound Point
4.135

1   From a position SW of Inchcolm (56°02′N 3°18′W) the route leads WSW in Forth Deep Water Channel, passing (with positions from Inchcolm):

NNW of Drum Flat (1 mile S), an extensive bank of sand and mud which stretches 4½ miles ENE from Hound Point. To S of Drum Flat, Drum Sands occupies the bight between Hound Point and Granton (4.66). Thence:

2   SSE of Haystack (4.122) (5 cables W), thence:

SSE of Dalgety Bay (4.122) (1 mile WNW), thence;

SSE of Inverkeithing Bay (2½ miles WSW) which lies between Battery Point and Downing Point, 1¾ miles NE. The bay is shallow with depths of less than 5 m at its entrance. Inverkeithing Harbour (4.147) is situated in an inlet at the W end of the bay.

Thence the track leads to a position NW of Hound Point (2 miles SW) and the Marine Terminal (4.138).

Forth Bridges
4.136

1   From a position NW of Hound Point the track leads 7 cables WSW to the Forth Railway Bridge, thence 5 cables W through the two bridges, passing:

2   NNW of Inch Garvie, a rocky island on which stands the centre span of the rail bridge. A light (black round beacon, white lantern, 10 m in height) is exhibited from the NW end of the island. Thence:

3   Under Forth Railway Bridge, which has two navigation spans, each 521 m wide, N and S of Inch Garvie. Lights are exhibited on each side of the bridge, at the centre of the navigation spans and near the ends of the cantilevers, so defining the N and S channels under the bridge. The bridge is floodlit. The normal tracks, both W-bound and E-bound, pass under the N navigation span. However, vessels may also pass under the S navigation span if required and with the permission of the VTS. Thence:

4   Under Forth Road Bridge, which is a suspension bridge of three spans. The two towers supporting the centre span of the bridge lie either side of the navigable channel and are just over 1000 m apart. Lights are exhibited on both sides of the bridge at the centre, midway between the centre and the supports, and at the supports themselves.

Useful marks
4.137

1   Radio masts (56°01′·7N 3°24′·9W).
(Directions continue for Rosyth at 4.165 and for River Forth at 4.179)

Hound Point Marine Terminal
General information
4.138

1   **Position and function.** Hound Point Marine Terminal (56°00′·42N 3°21′·61W) is an offshore terminal located 3 cables NW of Hound Point. It lies at the W extremity of Forth Deep Water Channel. The terminal exports crude oil from the North Sea.

Approach and entry. The terminal is approached directly from Forth Deep Water Channel. From the Fairway Buoy the distance to the terminal is 12½ miles.

2   **Traffic.** In 2008 the terminal was used by 277 vessels. About 24 million tonnes of crude oil is exported annually.

Terminal operator. The terminal is owned and operated by BP Exploration Operating Company Ltd., BP Dalmeny, PO Box 30, Bo'ness Road, Grangemouth, FK3 9XQ.

Limiting conditions
4.139

1   **Controlling depths.** At the outer end of Forth Deep Water Channel there is a charted depth of 19·4 m in the vicinity of No 1 Light Buoy (chart 735). Departing deep-draught tankers should leave the berth no later than 2 hours before HW Leith.

Hound Point Marine Terminal and Forth Bridges from ENE (4.136)
(Original dated 2003)

(Photograph - Forth Ports PLC)

The least depth on No 1 and No 2 berth is 24·5 m and 22·0 m respectively.

It should be noted that there is an 18·4 m patch (56°00'·6N 3°21'·4W) 1 cable off the E end of the terminal.

Tidal levels. See Rosyth (4.158).

Density of water is 1·020 to 1·025 g/cm^3.

2   **Maximum size of vessel handled.** The terminal can accommodate tankers up to 335 m LOA and about 300 000 dwt. Maximum sailing draughts are calculated on an individual vessel basis.

Local weather and tidal streams. The tidal stream attains a rate of 2½ kn at springs but the flow can exceed 3½ kn at times.

Arrival information
4.140

1   **VTS.** See 4.7.

Notice of ETA required. The terminal requires 72, 48 and 24 hours notice.

Outer anchorage. See 4.8.

Pilotage. See 4.4.

Tugs are available; all are equipped for fire-fighting and anti-pollution operations. They are normally moored at buoys 1¼ cables SW of the terminal.

2   **Regulations.** For traffic regulations see Appendix I. Berthing will not be attempted if:

The wind exceeds 20 kn on/off the berth.

The wind exceeds 30 kn in any direction.

The visibility is less than 1 mile.

Terminal
4.141

1   **General layout.** The terminal consists of two berths, each with a concrete island structure flanked by berthing and mooring dolphins linked by catwalks; a central island structure connects the two berths. The line of the terminal runs ENE/WSW along the S edge of the Forth Deep Water Channel. The berths and the outer mooring dolphins are marked by lights and the W island structure displays an aero obstruction light.

2   Berth 1 at the W end of the terminal is designed to accept vessels up to 335 m LOA and between 50 000 and about 300 000 dwt. Berth 2 at the E end is designed to accept vessels up to 300 m LOA and between 50 000 and 150 000 dwt.

Load rates are between 7000 and 15 000 tonnes per hour and vessels must be able to deballast simultaneously.

Directions
4.142

1   See 4.135. Vessels with a sailing draught of more than 16·5 m are required to berth starboard side to.

Port services
4.143

1   **Repairs.** Minor repairs and maintenance permitted: no hot or cold work.

Supplies. No fresh water, fuel or provisions on the berth but provisions can be supplied in the anchorage.

Other facilities. Reception of garbage; Ship Sanitation Certificates issued (1.92); hospital.

Communications. Launch service to Hawes Pier at Queensferry (4.149). Airport at Edinburgh.

2   **Terminal regulations.** There are stringent regulations concerning the state of moorings. The terminal is entitled to suspend operations and/or summon tugs in the absence of an alert and efficient deck watch or if it appears that a vessel's movement will endanger the flow arms. A minimum of six mooring lines is required at each end; the springs are to be wire with or without synthetic fibre tails.

3   Tankers must be equipped with segregated ballast tanks, an inert gas system and a vapour emission control system. Sampling devices should be used in conjunction with approved vapour locks.

Anchorage and mooring

Hound Point Anchorage
4.144

1   An uncharted anchorage, 5 cables downstream of Forth Railway Bridge in position 56°00'·3N 3°22'·5W and occupying a swinging circle of 1000 m diameter, is used by cruise ships. Throughout a vessel's stay at this berth a pilot will be embarked and, depending upon the vessel's length and other circumstances, a tug will remain attached aft in order to swing the vessel clear of the main channel. Depth in the anchorage is 24 m; the bottom mud.

No 1 Mooring Buoy
4.145

1   No 1 Mooring Buoy (56°01'·1N 3°21'·2W) lies close N of Forth Deep Water Channel and is used occasionally by warships and other government vessels.

Minor harbours

Saint David's Harbour
4.146

1   **General information.** Saint David's Harbour (56°02'N 3°22'W) is on the NE side of Inverkeithing Bay. The harbour is in a poor state of preservation and the inner basin dries 3·1 m.

Directions for entering harbour. The harbour is 3 cables N of Saint David's Light Beacon (4.147) but there are no other navigational marks. The entrance, 62 m wide faces W and is formed by two piers.

Inverkeithing Harbour
4.147

1   **General information.** Inverkeithing Harbour (56°01'·45N 3°23'·57W), a natural inlet at the W end of Inverkeithing Bay, is used for the export of scrap and stone and the import of sawn timber. In 2008 the port was used by 69 vessels.

2   **Port Authority.** The berth on the N side, at East Ness Pier, is operated by Forth Bridge Stevedoring Ltd., East Ness Pier, Preston Crescent, Inverkeithing, KY11 1DS. The berths on the S side are operated by Port Services (Inverkeithing) Ltd, The Bay, Inverkeithing, Fife KY1 2HR.

3   **Maximum size of vessel handled.** LOA about 110 m: maximum draught is equal to the predicted height of tide at Leith.

Controlling depth. 0·5 m in the harbour approach.

Pilotage. See 4.4.

Directions for entering harbour. From a position in Forth Deep Water Channel S of Doig Rock (56°01'·4N 3°21'·5W), the track leads 1 mile WNW to the harbour entrance, passing (with positions from the harbour entrance):

4   SSW of Saint David's Light Beacon (green square on pile) (6 cables E), thence:

S of a light buoy (starboard hand) (2 cables E) marking the SW extremity of the drying bank which lies N of the channel, thence:

N of a light buoy (port hand) (1 cable E), thence:

5   S of Prestonhill Wharf (1¼ cables ENE), a T-shaped jetty (disused), lying close E of East Ness which forms the N side of the entrance to the harbour, thence:

To the harbour entrance which is 120 m wide and lies between two piers extending from the shore at East Ness and West Ness. A light beacon (port hand) marks the N extremity of the drying bank extending from the shore at West Ness.

Useful mark. White obelisk (56°01'·7N 3°22'·7W).

6   **Berths.** Vessels up to about 90 m in length load stone and scrap at the Deep Water Berth and No 1 Berth. The berth at the S end of East Ness Pier is primarily for the import of sawn timber and can handle vessels up to 110 m LOA.

North Queensferry
4.148

1   **General information.** North Queensferry harbour (56°01'N 3°24'W), which dries, lies between the N

landings of the two bridges. Town Pier is at the E end of the town, with Railway Pier 1½ cables to the W.

Berths. Small craft moorings lie between the two piers.

Queensferry
4.149

1 **General information.** Hawes Pier (55°59′·6N 3°23′·2W) lies close W of the rail bridge and there are a number of small craft moorings to the E of the rail bridge.

There is a small harbour at Queensferry, 3 cables W of the pier, which is densely occupied with small craft moorings.

Port Edgar
4.150

1 **General information.** Port Edgar (56°00′N 3°25′W) is situated close W of Forth Road Bridge, and accommodates a yacht marina administered by City of Edinburgh Council. Limited commercial berths are available by prior arrangement.

Port Edgar from NW (4.150)
(Original dated 2000)

(Photograph – Air Images)

2 **Harbour.** The harbour is formed by two breakwaters with an entrance open N and 222 m wide. East and West Piers lie within the breakwaters and extend from the shore. The marina lies between these two piers and is protected from the N by a floating breakwater.

3 **Directions for entering harbour.** The line of bearing (244°) of West Breakwater Light (white blockhouse, 4 m in height) (55°59′·8N 3°24′·8W) leads to the harbour entrance.

Caution. Vessels up to 18 m in length can use the harbour at all states of the tide. On both the in-going and the out-going tides, a weak eddy opposing the main stream is set up just outside the line of the breakwater heads and vessels should guard against a sheer when entering.

4 **Berths.** The commercial berths are at a finger pier in the SW part of the harbour.

ROSYTH

General information

Chart 736, 728

Position and function
4.151

1 Rosyth (56°01′·20N 3°26′·44W) is situated on the N side of River Forth, 1½ miles WNW of Forth Road Bridge. Formerly a naval base, Rosyth is now a commercial port handling general cargo and cruise ships. Additionally, there is a RoRo passenger and freight service to Zeebrugge.

Approach and entry
4.152

1 Rosyth is approached from a position close W of Forth Road Bridge and entered via a main channel which is one mile in length and marked by light buoys and a directional light.

Traffic
4.153

1 In 2008 the port was used by 237 vessels.

Port Authority
4.154

1 Forth Ports plc, Exmouth Building, Port of Rosyth, Fife KY11 2XP.

The enclosed dock, Main Basin, is operated by Babcock BES, Rosyth Business Park, Rosyth KY11 2YD.

Website: www.forthports.co.uk

Limiting conditions

Controlling depths
4.155

1 Main Channel leading to Rosyth is maintained by dredging to a depth of ~~8·8 m~~ but due to silting depths less than the maintained depth are likely to exist. The Harbour Master should be consulted for the latest information. *[handwritten annotation: 8·3m ✗ UKSC]*

Vertical clearance
4.156

1 See 4.131.

Deepest and longest berths
4.157

1 Deepest berth: Main Basin (4.167); longest berth: North Wall (4.167).

Tidal levels
4.158

See *Admiralty Tide Tables Volume 1.* Mean spring range about 5·0 m; mean neap range about 2·5 m.

Maximum size of vessel handled
4.159

1 For vessels using the tidal harbour there is no restriction on length and beam but maximum permitted draught is 7·8 m.

For vessels entering Main Basin through the Direct Entrance the maximum dimensions are 195 m LOA and 32·0 m beam; for the Entrance Lock, the maximum dimensions are 185 m LOA and 22·8 m beam.

Arrival information

Vessel traffic service
4.160

1 See 4.7.

Outer anchorages
4.161

1 See 4.8.

Pilots and tugs
4.162

1 **Pilotage** is compulsory. See 4.4.
Tugs are available.

Harbour

General layout
4.163

1 The harbour runs roughly ESE/WNW along the N bank of River Forth. At the E end is North Wall, a long straight

Rosyth from SE (4.163)
(Original dated 2000)

(Photograph - Air Images)

quay, in the middle are two relatively small basins and at the W end is Main Basin, a large square-shaped wet dock. The commercial Port of Rosyth operates North Wall and the two tidal basins. Main Basin is operated by a separate organisation and it contains three drydocks and a synchrolift, the latter giving access to an enclosed repair facility.

2 Main Basin has two entrances, a direct entrance and a lock to S of it. A central island stands between the two entrances. Works are in progress (2009) to widen the Direct Entrance.

The direct entrance has a maintained depth of 6·6 m and its gate can be opened on a rising tide between the time that the tide reaches a height of 4·25 m and 30 minutes before HW. A tide gauge stands at the E end of the central island.

Tidal stream
4.164

1 In Main Channel the in-going stream begins at about –0530 HW Rosyth and the out-going stream at –0045 HW Rosyth. Both run for about 4 hours, with maximum spring rates of 1½ kn. The in-going stream runs out through the boat channel (56°01'·0N 3°26'·6W) at the W end of Main Channel to rejoin the main stream in the river. Conversely, a branch of the out-going stream sets through the boat channel to join the out-going stream in Main Channel.

2 In the vicinity of North Wall and the immediate approaches to Main Basin, eddies, with rates not exceeding ½ kn, occur on both the in-going and out-going streams. A strong SW set has been reported on the N side of Middle Jetty (56°01'·3N 3°26'·7W), one hour before HW.

Directions for entering harbour
(continued from 4.137)

Landmarks
4.165

1 Flagstaff (56°00'·8N 3°24'·5W).
Radio masts (56°01'·7N 3°24'·9W).
Rosyth Castle (56°01'·4N 3°25'·9W), a ruin.
Beamer Rock Light Tower (white tower, red top) (56°00'·3N 3°24'·7W).

Chimney (185)

Beamer Rock Light from E (4.165)
(Original dated 2006)

(Photograph - HMSML Gleaner)

Main Channel
4.166

1 From a position close W of Forth Road Bridge within the white sector (321°-326°) of Alpha Directional Light Beacon (red square daymark on white post with red bands) (56°01'·2N 3°25'·6W), the track leads NW through the channel, which is marked by light buoys (lateral), passing (with positions from Light Beacon A):

2 NE of Beamer Rock (1 mile SSE) (4.180), thence:
SW of onshore Beacon C (red rectangular daymark with white triangle apex down on white beacon, red bands) (1 mile SE), thence:
SW of offshore Beacon D (black triangular daymark apex up on black and white post) (6 cables SE), thence:
NE of No 2 Light Buoy (E cardinal) (5 cables SSE) marking the E end of Whale Back (4.180), thence:
NE of No 4 Light Buoy (port hand) (4 cables SSE).

3 Thence course is adjusted WNW to the harbour entrance, a distance of about 5 cables. The fairway is 1 cable wide and passes S of the coastal bank and N of Whale Back.

Useful mark
4.181

1 Culross church tower (56°03′·5N 3°37′·5W).
*(Directions continue for the entrance lock
at 4.205, and for Stirling at 4.219)*

Anchorages

Rosyth
4.182

1 Anchorages R1 to R4, lie in the fairway SW of Rosyth (56°01′·5N 3°27′·0W).

Tancred Bank
4.183

1 There are four anchor berths numbered T1 to T4 each with a swinging radius of 1 cable in mid-river WNW of Tancred Bank (56°01′·5N 3°33′·0W).

Minor harbours

Bruce Haven
4.184

1 Bruce Haven (56°02′N 3°29′W), 8 cables W of Rosyth, is formed by a curved pier extending SSW from Capernaum Point. Rocks marked by a beacon at their SW extremity, lie on the E side of the entrance. The haven dries.

Limekilns
4.185

1 Limekilns (56°02′N 3°29′W) has a boat harbour protected to the W by Limekilns Pier. The harbour dries.

Charlestown
4.186

1 Charlestown Harbour (56°02′N 3°30′W) is formed by piers and now only used as a sailing centre. It is protected from all winds and has depths of 4 m, soft mud, at HW springs.

Charlestown Harbour from SSW (4.186)
(Original dated 2000)

(Photograph - Air Images)

Bo'ness Harbour
4.187

1 Bo'ness Harbour (56°01′N 3°36′W) is used by recreational craft and there are long term plans for further development. The outer harbour dries; the inner half-tide dock is heavily silted and remains closed (2009).

The harbour entrance is marked by lights. A beacon (N cardinal) close N of West Pier marks an obstruction which covers at HW.

Blackness Harbour
4.188

1 Blackness Harbour (56°00′·3N 3°31′·3W), which dries, consists of a stone pier surrounded by moorings. The pier can be approached 2 hours either side of HW.

GRANGEMOUTH

General information

Chart 741, 737

Position
4.189

1 Grangemouth (56°02′·18N 3°40′·89W) is situated on the S bank of River Carron, where the latter enters River Forth.

Function
4.190

1 Grangemouth, having a population of about 17 800, is the second largest port in Scotland and handles all types of vessels including container vessels, tankers and LPG carriers.

Topography
4.191

1 The greater part of Grangemouth Docks lies on a promontory which juts NE from the S bank of River Forth. River Carron runs parallel to and immediately adjacent to the W side of the promontory. It is contained to its W by an embankment, marked by stone beacons.

2 Grangemouth lock is located at the head of the promontory and much of the surface is occupied by oil storage tanks. The promontory is flanked on either side by alluvial mud flats. Part of the bay to the E of the promontory has been reclaimed.

Approach and entry
4.192

1 Grangemouth Docks are approached from the E via a short marked channel which gives access to a lock.

Traffic
4.193

1 In 2008, Grangemouth was used by 2242 vessels. About 157 000 containers are handled annually.

Port Authority
4.194

1 The harbour is administered by Forth Ports PLC, Grangemouth Port Office, Central Dock Road, Grangemouth, FK3 8UE.
Website: www.forthports.co.uk

Limiting conditions

Controlling depth
4.195

1 The entrance channel is dredged to 6·5 m but is subject to occasional silting. The entrance lock has a depth of 5·9 m. The Harbour Master should be consulted for the latest information on depths.

Deepest and longest berths
4.196

1 Tanker berths, Eastern Channel (4.207); other vessels, Grange Dock (4.207).

Tidal levels
4.197

1 See *Admiralty Tide Tables Volume 1*. Mean spring range about 5·2 m; mean neap range about 2·6 m.

Density of water
4.198

1   Average density of dock water is 1·020 g/cm³.

Maximum size of vessel handled
4.199

1   Grangemouth Docks can accept vessels up to 32 000 dwt, length 187 m, beam 27 m and draught 10·7 m (tankers) and 7·4 m (other vessels).

Arrival information

Port operations
4.200

1   Grangemouth Locks should be contacted for berthing information and for the depth over the sill at the lock.

Vessel traffic service
4.201

1   See 4.7.

Pilotage and tugs
4.202

1   **Pilotage.** See 4.4.

Tugs are available. Inbound vessels requiring tugs are met S of Hen and Chickens (4.180).

Traffic regulations
4.203

1   See Appendix I.

Harbour

General layout
4.204

1   There are four interconnected basins which lie in a NE/SW direction over a distance of 1½ miles. The lock lies SE of an old entrance now disused and sealed–off; its approach is flanked by West and East Jetties. The lock leads into Eastern Channel, which leads to Grange Dock via East Cut. Western Channel runs W from Grange Dock and thence into Carron Dock via West Cut. Two small docks, Old Dock and Junction Dock, lie to the W of Carron Dock but are no longer in use.

Directions for entering harbour
(continued from 4.181)

Principal mark
4.205

1   **Landmark:**

Group of oil tanks (56°02'·2N 3°41'·5W), 2 cables W of entrance lock.

Lock approach
4.206

1   From a position at the W end of the approach channel the track leads 3 cables SW between West and East Jetties and thence to the lock entrance. The lock is 238 m long, 31 m wide (29·1 m between fenders) and lies on an axis 062°/242°. Lights (fixed red and fixed green) at the NE and SW corners of the lock indicate the alignment of the entrance and the position of the lock gates.

Basins and berths
4.207

1   Eastern Channel: six tanker jetties, largest 210 m long, 11·6 m depth alongside; one LPG berth depth 8·5 m.

Grange Dock: 2175 m of quayside, depth 7·7 m, includes container terminal, forest products terminal and RoRo berth.

Carron Dock: 355 m of quayside, depth 6·4 m.

Grangemouth Harbour from NE (4.204)
(Original dated 2003)

(Photograph – Forth Ports PLC)

Port services

Repairs
4.208
1   **Repairs** of all kinds can be carried out.

One dry dock; length 105·4 m; floor length 104 m; breadth 16·1 m; depth over the blocks 6·1 m at MHWS but never less than 5·6 m.

Other facilities
4.209
1   Reception of oily waste; Ship Sanitation Certificates issued (1.92); hospital at Falkirk.

Supplies
4.210
1   Fuel oils of all types at oil jetties in Eastern Channel, elsewhere by road tanker; fresh water; stores and provisions.

Forth and Clyde Canal

General information
4.211
1   Passage to the Scottish W coast is possible using the Forth and Clyde Canal. Entry is obtained via a marked channel in River Carron (4.191) and a sea lock at 56°01'·2N 3°45'·4W. At MLW there is a vertical clearance of about 3 m below the Kerse Road Bridge on River Carron. Within the canal the following limits apply: 1·83 m depth; 3 m vertical clearance; 6 m width; 20·88 m LOA.

Passage to Edinburgh is possible via the Forth and Clyde Canal and the Union Canal. It is limited at the Falkirk Wheel by a depth of 1·37 m and a vertical clearance of 2·74 m.

GRANGEMOUTH TO STIRLING

General information

Chart 741
Route
4.212
1   From a position (56°02'N 3°41'W) off the lock at Grangemouth, the route follows River Forth for a distance of 17 miles to Stirling, passing the towns of Kincardine and Alloa.

Depths
4.213
1   W of the maintained channel leading to Grangemouth, the river shoals considerably. At MHW vessels of about 3 m draught can proceed as far as Alloa (56°06'N 3°48'W) and vessels of about 1·5 m draught can reach Stirling.

Pilotage and local knowledge
4.214
1   Pilotage (4.4) is compulsory as far as Kincardine Bridge but no pilots are available above the bridge. For safety reasons there is an embargo on commercial movements above the bridge and the channel is not buoyed. The channel, which dries in places, is continually changing and the chart should not be relied upon completely. Local knowledge is necessary for small craft to proceed above Kincardine Bridge.

Vessel traffic service
4.215
1   See 4.7.

Traffic regulations
4.216
1   **Regulations for Kincardine Bridge.** See Appendix I.

Vertical clearances
4.217
1   Kincardine Bridge (56°04'N 3°44'W) has a safe vertical clearance of 8·3 m. Clackmannanshire Bridge (56°04'·4N 3°44'·2W) has a safe vertical clearance of 8·5 m. There are two more bridges in the vicinity of Stirling with vertical clearances of less than 3·5 m.

2   A number of power cables cross the river but all have a vertical clearance well in excess of the bridge clearances.

Tidal streams
4.218
1   Tidal streams run as follows:

Time from HW Leith	*Remarks*
Kincardine	
−0400 to −0330	In-going stream commences
+0300 to +0100	Out-going stream commences. Spring rate 2¾ kn.
Alloa	
−0400	In-going stream commences
+0100	Out-going stream commences. Spring rate 3 kn.

2   At Kincardine the channel contracts, causing the tide to accelerate up to 4 kn. Above and below Kincardine there is a local phenomenon, the "Leaky Tide", when the in-going/out-going stream is interrupted soon after it begins by a short period of out-going/in-going stream.

Between Alloa and Stirling the river bed rises by about 3 m reducing a 5 m tidal range at Alloa to 3 m at Stirling. This also has an effect on the time of HW at Stirling which is ½ hour later than Alloa.

Directions
(continued from 4.181)

Grangemouth to Kincardine Bridge
4.219
1   From a position NE of the lock at Grangemouth, the route leads 2½ miles NW to Kincardine Bridge, passing (with positions from Kincardine Bridge):

2   SW of Longannet Power Station (1¾ miles ESE) standing on Longannet Point which is low-lying. A T-jetty with a depth alongside of 5·7 m extends offshore from the power station and a light is exhibited from the E arm of the jetty. The jetty also serves as a cooling water intake. And:

3   NE of the mouth of River Carron (2 miles SE) (4.191) marked by a light buoy (port hand) and a light beacon (starboard hand), the latter at the extremity of a training wall. A beacon (special) marking the seaward end of an outfall lies 2 cables NW of the entrance. Thence:

NE of a bank (1 mile SSE) running NW/SE for a distance of 1½ miles. The bank fronts a bight which extends to Kincardine Bridge. Between this bank and the bank off Longannet the channel is 2 cables wide. Thence:

4   SW of Inch Brake (4 cables SE), a shoal marked by a buoy (starboard hand), thence:

To Kincardine Bridge. The bridge is 4½ cables long and was formerly a swing bridge. It has two navigation spans each 46 m wide divided by a 143 m long timber jetty.

No directions can be given above Kincardine Bridge and Clackmannanshire Bridge due to the continually changing nature of the channel.

Useful marks
4.220

1   Chimney (56°02'·9N 3°41'·0W) at Longannet Power Station.

Longannet Power Station chimney from E (4.220)
(Original dated 2000)

(Photograph - Air Images)

Clock tower (56°04'·1N 3°43'·1W).
Buildings (56°04'·3N 3°42'·8W).
Church Tower (56°04'·3N 3°43'·0W).
Town pier (56°03'·9N 3°43'·4W).

2   Clackmannan Tower (56°06'·5N 3°45'·6W) in ruins.
Spire (56°06'·8N 3°47'·8W).
Chimney (56°06'·7N 3°47'·9W).
Tower (56°06'·7N 3°48'·2W).

Minor harbours

Kincardine
4.221

1   Kincardine (56°04'N 3°43'W) lies 2 miles NNW of Grangemouth on the N bank of the River Forth. There are no shipping facilities but boats can land at Town Pier.

Alloa
4.222

1   Alloa (56°06'N 3°48'W), population about 19 000, lies 3½ miles NW of Kincardine. Shallow-draught vessels may lie alongside a pier on the N bank.

Stirling
4.223

1   Stirling (56°07'N 3°56'W) is 54 miles from the entrance to Firth of Forth and may be considered the head of navigation in the River Forth.

NOTES

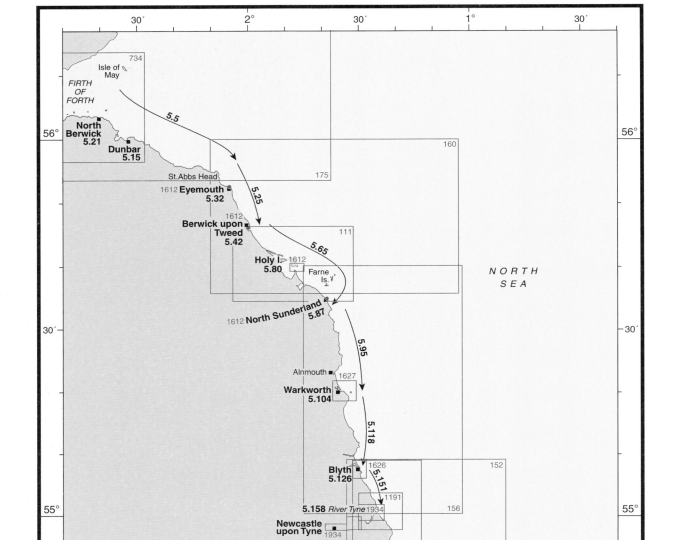

30′   2°   30′   1°   30′

734

Isle of
May

*FIRTH
OF
FORTH*

**North
Berwick
5.21**

**Dunbar
5.15**

56°

160

175

St.Abbs Head

1612 **Eyemouth
5.32**

5.5

5.25

1612
**Berwick upon
Tweed
5.42**

111

5.65

**Holy I.
5.80**

1612

Farne Is.

*NORTH
SEA*

1612 **North Sunderland
5.87**

30′

5.95

Alnmouth

1627

**Warkworth
5.104**

5.118

**Blyth
5.126**

1626

152

5.151

156

55°

1191

5.158 *River Tyne* 1934

**Newcastle
upon Tyne** 1934

1935

30′   Longitude 2° West from Greenwich   1°   30′

56°

30′

55°

606060

ISLE OF MAY TO RIVER TYNE

GENERAL INFORMATION

Charts 1407, 1192
Scope of the chapter
5.1

1   In this chapter the coastal passage from Isle of May (56°11′N 2°33′W) (3.215) to River Tyne, 85 miles SSE, is described together with the ports of Eyemouth (5.32), Berwick-upon-Tweed (5.42), Warkworth (5.104), Blyth (5.126) and the Port of Tyne (5.158).

Topography
5.2

1   Isle of May lies 10 miles NE of Fidra (56°04′N 2°47′W) (4.18). From Fidra the coast continues 24 miles ESE to Saint Abb's Head, thence 60 miles SSE to the mouth of River Tyne. The coast is a mixture of rocky cliffs fringed with reefs and sandy bays and includes Holy Island (55°41′N 1°48′W) and the Farne Islands, 6 miles ESE.

2   This particular stretch of coast is dangerous. Within the 30 m depth contour, which elsewhere is less than 2 miles offshore but here lies up to 5 miles off the mainland, there are many shoals and rocks and extensive sands to the W and N of Holy Island.

Outlying banks and deeps
5.3

1   Spittal Hirst, a bank charted within the 30 m depth contour, lies 4½ miles E of Berwick-upon-Tweed (55°46′N 2°00′W).

    Newton Skere, a rocky bank charted outside the 30 m depth contour, lies 4½ miles E of Beadnell Point (55°33′N 1°37′W).

2   Craster Skeres, a rocky patch close to the 50 m depth contour, lies 5 miles E of Castle Point (55°30′N 1°35′W).

    Farn Deeps, spread over an area 15 miles by 12 miles, lie E of Castle Point (55°30′N 1°35′W) about 20 miles off the coast.

Tidal streams
5.4

1   The offshore streams are not strong with spring rates being about 1 kn. They are regular and run in the direction of the coast. The tidal streams are given on the charts and in *Admiralty Tidal Stream Atlas: North Sea, Northwestern Part.*

ISLE OF MAY TO SAINT ABB'S HEAD

General information

Charts 734, 175
Route
5.5

1   From a position midway between Isle of May (56°11′N 2°33′W) (3.215) and Fidra (10 miles SW) (4.18) the route leads ESE for a distance of 22 miles to a position NE of Saint Abb's Head.

    Traffic recommendation. A recommendation has been adopted by IMO that laden tankers should avoid the area between Bass Rock and the coast.

Topography
5.6

1   Fidra lies 5 cables off the coast, which runs 5½ miles E to Great Car (5.13). As far as North Berwick (5.21), 2½ miles E of Fidra, the coast is low and sandy, with occasional clumps of trees and fringed by rocky ledges up to 4 cables offshore which are interrupted by sandy beaches. To the E of North Berwick, the coast is composed of cliffs and steep slopes with somewhat narrower rocky ledges offshore. Apart from Fidra there are the islets of Lamb, Craigleith and Bass Rock (5.13) lying offshore. Bass Rock is the most northerly and 1¼ miles off the coast. At Great Carr the trend of the coast turns to ESE as far as Saint Abb's Head (5.13), a distance of 19 miles. Initially the coast is rocky thence sandy to Dunbar (5.15), 4½ miles ESE of Great Carr. The coast to the ESE of Dunbar is backed by high ground with a flat foreground on which the railway is occasionally visible. About 5 miles short of Saint Abb's Head the coast becomes bold and rugged, backed by elevated land which is nearly bare of trees, and slopes steeply forming cliffs in places.

Exercise area
5.7

1   Naval vessels and submarines exercise in the approaches to and within the Firth of Forth (1.20).

Measured distance
5.8

1   A measured distance is charted close W of Saint Abb's Head (55°55′N 2°08′W).

        Limit Marks. Two pairs of beacons, surmounted by triangles with the front triangles point down.
        Distance. 1849 m.
        Running track. 111°/291°.

2   Beyond 2 miles offshore the W beacons are difficult to see against the background of dark fir trees.

    It is reported that the beacons are no longer maintained.

Rescue
5.9

1   There are Coastal Rescue Teams at North Berwick and Dunbar; see 1.67.

    An all-weather lifeboat is stationed at Dunbar; inshore lifeboats are stationed at Dunbar and North Berwick. See 1.72.

Tidal streams
5.10

1   The offshore streams are weak, with rates not exceeding 1 kn, and change regularly. Near the land the tidal stream follows the line of the coast. In the entrance to Firth of Forth spring rates are 1½ kn but SE of Barns Ness (55°59′N 2°27′W) rates reduce to 1 kn. The tidal stream runs strongly round Saint Abb's Head and there is turbulence especially with opposing winds. Details of the tidal streams are given on the chart and in *Admiralty Tidal Stream Atlas: North Sea, Northwestern Part.*

2   **Caution.** During onshore gales the sea breaks heavily over the submerged rocks and ledges fronting the coast between Great Car and Saint Abb's Head. As the SE-going stream sets strongly towards Saint Abb's Head, it should be given a wide berth.

Directions
(continued from 3.223)

Principal marks
5.11

1   **Landmarks:**
Bass Rock (56°05′N 2°38′W) (5.13).
North Berwick Law (56°03′N 2°43′W), a conical hill covered in grass.

North Berwick Law from N (5.11)
(Original dated 2003)

(Photograph - Crown Copyright)

Traprain Law (55°58′N 2°40′W), a remarkable isolated hill not to be confused with North Berwick Law.
House (56°00′·2N 2°32′·3W) of brown brick, slate roof and tall chimneys.
Church Tower at Dunbar (56°00′N 2°31′W).

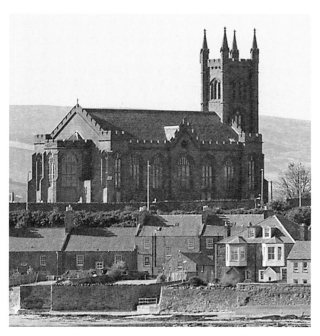

Church with Tower at Dunbar (5.11)
(Original dated 2003)

(Photograph - Crown Copyright)

2   Mast (55°56′N 2°27′W).
Torness Power Station (55°58′N 2°25′W) (5.13).
Major lights:
Isle of May Light (56°11′N 2°33′W) (3.220).
Fidra Light (56°04′N 2°47′W) (4.16).
Saint Abb's Head Light (white tower and buildings, 9 m in height) (55°55′N 2°08′W).

Other aid to navigation
5.12

1   **Racon:**
Saint Abb's Head Light (55°55′N 2°08′W).
For details see *Admiralty List of Radio Signals Volume 2.*

Isle of May to Saint Abb's Head
5.13

1   From a position midway between Isle of May (56°11′N 2°33′W) and Fidra (10 miles SW) the coastal route leads ESE to a position NE of Saint Abb's Head, passing (with positions from Barns Ness Lighthouse (disused) (55°59′·2N 2°26′·8W)):
NNE of Craigleith (56°04′N 2°43′W), a rocky islet 6 cables N of North Berwick. A similar but smaller islet, Lamb, lies 1 mile WSW of Craigleith. Thence:

2   NNE of Bass Rock (8½ miles WNW), a conspicuous pyramidal rock which is precipitous on all sides, particularly the NE and NW. Its cliffs are a brilliant white from the droppings of seabirds. Bass Rock Light (white tower and dwellings, 20 m in height) stands on its S side. An area in which experimental buoys, both lit and unlit, are regularly moored is centred 2½ miles NE of Bass Rock, as shown on the charts. The buoys are of no navigational significance. Thence:

Bass Rock from S (5.13)
(Original dated 2008)

(Photograph - Nigel Hoy)

3   NNE of Satan Bush (6½ miles NW), a rocky patch. Great Car, a ledge of rocks which nearly covers at HW, lies 1 mile W of Satan Bush. South Carr Beacon (black round stone tower, surmounted by a cross) stands at the N extremity of Great Carr. Thence:

4   NNE of Lady Ground (4½ miles WNW), a steep-to patch. Whitberry Point, a low dark point, with a small conical hill near its centre, lies 9 cables W of Lady Ground and at the SE end of Peffer Sands. Thence:

5   NNE of Dunbar (5.15) (2½ miles WNW). Belhaven Bay, which fronts Tyne Sands, lies between Dunbar and Whitberry Point. A pillar buoy (special) marks the outlet of a sewage outfall 1 mile ESE of Whitberry Point. Thence:

6   NNE of Sicar (2 miles NW), an isolated rock on which the sea breaks heavily during onshore gales, thence:
NNE of Barns Ness, a low point fringed by rocky ledges. Barns Ness Lighthouse (disused) (white round tower, 37 m in height) stands on the point.

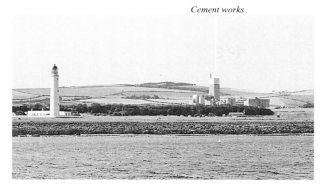

Cement works

Barns Ness Lighthouse (disused) from N (5.13)
(Original dated 2003)

(Photograph - Crown Copyright)

Saint Abb's Head from ENE (5.13)
(Original dated 2001)

(Photograph - Crown Copyright)

7   Ruddystone, a rocky shoal, lies 5 cables N of the point. Thence:

NNE of Torness Point (2 miles ESE), from which rocky ledges extend 2½ cables offshore. Torness Power Station lies 2½ cables SW of the point. Skateraw Harbour, now unusable, is 6 cables W of the point. Thence:

Two chimneys (55°59′N 2°28′W).
(Directions continue at 5.29)

Dunbar

General information
5.15

1   **Position.** Dunbar (56°00′·43N 2°31′·16W) mostly built of dark coloured stone, stands at the E end of Tyne Sands (5.13).

Function. The harbour, called Victoria Harbour, is only used for landing fish and by recreational craft. The population is about 6400.

Port Authority. Victoria Harbour is administered by Dunbar Harbour Trust, Castlegate, Dunbar, East Lothian, EH42 1HX.

Power Station at Torness Point from NE (5.13)
(Original dated 2003)

(Photograph - Crown Copyright)

8   NNE of Cove Harbour (5.22) (4½ miles ESE) with Pease Bay 7 cables SE. The Bay lies at the mouth of a deep, well-wooded ravine, spanned by a stone viaduct with four unequal arches. Thence:

NNE of Fast Castle Head (8 miles ESE). The ruins of Fast Castle stand on the head and a wind turbine is located on Telegraph Hill, 5 cables SSW. Thence:

9   NNE of Saint Abb's Head (56°55′N 2°08′W), a bold promontory of dark rock which rises almost vertically. The face of the rock is broken by deep fissures. Parts of the cliff have become detached but the head is steep-to. Between the head and Cross Law, 2 miles W, is a valley which causes the head to appear as an island from the NW or SE. Saint Abb's Head Light (5.11) stands on the head, which is a National Nature Reserve (1.61).

Useful marks
5.14

1   Tantallon Castle (56°03′·3N 2°39′·0W), a ruin on the edge of a cliff.

Doon Hill (55°58′N 2°30′W) with a well defined NW escarpment.

Dunbar Harbour from NW (5.15)
(Original dated 2000)

(Photograph - Air Images)

Limiting conditions
5.16

1   **Controlling depth** is 5·6 m in the approach channel at HW springs and 4·6 m at HW neaps. Within the harbour Middle Quay has a depth alongside of 5·3 m at HW springs.

Tidal levels: see *Admiralty Tide Tables Volume 1*. Mean spring range about 4·4 m; mean neap range about 2·1 m.

2   **Maximum size of vessel handled.** Length 30 m, draught 4 m at HW springs. Vessels lie aground on a sandy bottom at LW.

Local weather and sea state. When the wind is strong from between WNW through N to E, the harbour is difficult to enter and the berths may be untenable due to a heavy swell in the harbour. In these conditions vessels move into Old Harbour (5.18).

Castlefoot Rock   *Harbour Entrance*   *Leading Lights*   *Scart Rock*

Approach to Dunbar Harbour from NNE (5.19)
(Original dated 2003)

(Photograph - Crown Copyright)

Arrival information
5.17
1   **Pilotage** is not available.

Outer anchorage, shown on the chart, may be obtained in Dunbar Roads in depths of 13 m, 4 cables NW of the harbour entrance.

Harbour
5.18
1   **General layout.** Victoria Harbour lies at the NW end of Dunbar and has 183 m of quays. It is protected from the N by a breakwater and the entrance, cut through solid rock, lies on the W side of the harbour and faces NW. Old Harbour is close E of Victoria Harbour and is entered through a 12 m wide passage in East Quay which is spanned by a lifting bridge.

Directions for entering harbour
5.19
1   **Leading lights:**
> Front leading light (column, orange triangle point up, 4m in height) (56°00'·3N 2°31'·2W).
> Rear leading light (column, orange triangle point down, 4 m in height).

2   From a position NNE of the harbour entrance, the alignment (198°) of these lights leads SSW to a positon NW of the entrance, passing (with positions from the front light):

3   ESE of Scart Rock (2¾ cables N), an above water rock, thence:
> WNW of Castlefoot Rock (2¾ cables NNE), an above water rock, thence:
> To a position close NW of the harbour entrance whence a direct approach may be made.

4   **Alternative approach from NW.** The line of bearing 132° of the harbour entrance, with the light on Middle Quay (column, 5 m in height) seen through it, leads to the harbour entrance, passing (with positions from the harbour entrance):

NE of Wallace's Head (2½ cables WNW), a rock which dries 1 m and is marked by a metal perch, thence:

5   SW of Half Ebb Rock (1¾ cables NW), which dries 2·1 m and is marked by a metal perch, thence:
To the harbour entrance.

If weather permits (5.16), it is best to enter harbour within 1 hour of HW.

Caution. There are several isolated rocks, known as The Yetts (56°00'·5N 2'30'·7W), lying E–W in the approach to Dunbar.

Port services
5.20
1   **Repairs.** Minor repairs can be carried out.

Other facilities. The nearest hospital for accidents and emergencies is at the Royal Infirmary, Edinburgh.

Supplies: marine diesel by road tanker; water at Middle Quay; provisions.

Minor harbours, anchorages and boat landings

North Berwick
5.21
1   **General information.** North Berwick (56°04'N 2°43'W) stands partly within a black rocky point and partly at the foot of North Berwick Law (5.11). The harbour is mainly used by recreational craft, but a few fishing boats remain. The harbour is owned and operated by the East Lothian Council (5.15).

2   **Limiting conditions.** The harbour dries at LW, but has depths of 5 m at HW springs. NE gales raise heavy seas and a scend in the harbour and in these conditions the harbour might be closed by booms so that vessels can lie safely. The harbour should not be used without local knowledge.

3   **The harbour** is formed by piers. The entrance is 8 m wide and faces SW. The quays are 30 m and 91 m in length.

North Berwick Harbour from WSW (5.21)
(Original dated 2000)

(Photograph - Air Images)

Principal marks:
North Berwick Law (56°03′N 2°43′W) (5.11).
Church (spire) (56°03′·6N 2°43′·1W).
Church (56°03′·5N 2°43′·2W).

4　**Directions for entering harbour.** In approaching from N, vessels should note off-lying rocks which encircle the NW part of West Bay (56°03′·6N 2°43′·3W). A light (post, 3 m in height) is exhibited on North Pier Head. This light is extinguished when vessels cannot enter the harbour. A second light (bracket on building) is exhibited 1 cable S of North Pier Head.

Supplies: marine diesel by road tanker.

Cove Harbour
5.22
1　**General information.** Cove Harbour (55°56′N 2°21′W), which is privately owned, is a small fishing harbour formed by piers. The village of Cove is on top of the cliff close W of the harbour.

2　**Limiting conditions.** The entrance is 22 m wide and has a depth in it of 3·7 m at HW springs. Within the harbour there are depths of 3 m at HW springs. The bottom of the harbour is mainly sandy, but there are occasional rocky patches. Onshore gales throw a heavy sea into the harbour.

3　**Caution.** There are below water rocks 3 cables E of the entrance.

Landmark. Dunglass Mansion (55°56′·3N 2°22′·5W) stands in a wood 8 cables W of Cove.

Anchorages
5.23
1　In addition to the anchorage off Dunbar (5.17) there are anchorages for small craft, shown on the chart, as follows:
Three cables E of Fidra Light (4.16) in W winds.

2　Off the W end of Craigleith (5.13), sand and clay. E of the anchorage position the bottom is foul and uneven.

In Scoughall Road, 7 cables NNW of Whitberry Point (56°01′N 2°35′W), in depths of 9 to 11 m, clay, during offshore winds.

Boat landings
5.24
1　Available at:
Bass Rock (5.13). Moderate or good weather only, SW side below ruins of castle.
Redheugh (55°55′·5N 2°16′·8W), at a position shown on the chart.

Pettico Wick (55°55′N 2°09′W), at a position shown on the chart.

SAINT ABB'S HEAD TO BERWICK-UPON-TWEED
General information
Chart 160
Route
5.25
1　From a position NE of Saint Abb's Head (55°55′N 2°08′W) the coastal route leads 12 miles SSE to a position E of Berwick-upon-Tweed, which stands at the mouth of River Tweed.

Topography
5.26
1　From Saint Abb's Head as far as Hare Point, 3 miles SE, the coast is rugged and bleak and backed by high land which rises boldly and has few identifiable features. Eyemouth (5.32), close S of Hare Point, stands on low ground. To the SSE, as far as Burnmouth (5.39), 2¼ miles from Eyemouth, the coast ascends again reaching an elevation of 101 m. Between Burnmouth and Berwick-upon-Tweed, a further 5 miles SSE, the coast consists of a steep bank and low cliffs, about 18 m high, which decrease in height towards Berwick-upon-Tweed. Rocks fringe the coast up to 3½ cables offshore. The coast is backed by Lamberton Hill, 1½ miles SSW of Burnmouth and Halidon Hill, 3½ miles S of Burnmouth, and the railway which skirts the bases of the two hills is usually in sight from seaward. Otherwise the background is generally bare and featureless. The Scotland-England border lies midway between Burnmouth and Berwick.

Rescue
5.27
1　There are Coastal Rescue Teams at St Abb's, Eyemouth and Berwick. See 1.67.

All-weather lifeboats are stationed at Eyemouth and at Berwick; inshore lifeboats are stationed at Berwick and St Abb's. See 1.72.

Tidal stream
5.28
1　Tidal stream information is given on the chart and in *Admiralty Tidal Stream Atlas: North Sea, Northwestern Part.*

Directions
(continued from 5.14)

Principal marks
5.29
1　**Landmarks:**
Mast (radio/TV) (55°50′N 2°05′W).
Berwick Town Hall (spire) (55°46′·2N 2°00′·2W).
Berwick Lighthouse (white round stone tower, red cupola and base, 13 m in height) (55°45′·9N 1°59′·1W).
Chimney (55°45′·6N 1°59′·6W).

2　**Major lights:**
Saint Abb's Head Light (55°55′N 2°08′W) (5.11).
Longstone Light (55°39′N 1°37′W) (5.71).

Other aid to navigation
5.30
1　**Racon:**
Saint Abb's Head Light (55°55′N 2°08′W).
For details see *Admiralty List of Radio Signals Volume 2.*

Saint Abb's Head to Berwick-upon-Tweed
5.31

1 From a position NE of Saint Abb's Head (55°55′N 2°08′W) the coastal route leads 12 miles SSE to a position E of Berwick Lighthouse, passing (with positions from Berwick Lighthouse):

ENE of Fold Buss (8 miles NNW), a rock with a depth of 13·3 m, which lies to the N of Eyemouth, thence:

2 ENE of Gunsgreen Point (7½ miles NNW) which is fringed by rocky ledges and which lies 3 cables ESE of Hare Point The two points enclose the small bay that has Eyemouth (5.32) at its head. Thence:

ENE of Ross Carrs (5½ miles NNW), two rocks which dry and and which lie 4 cables NNE of Burnmouth Harbour, thence:

3 ENE of South Carr (5 miles NNW), a rock which lies to the ESE of Burnmouth Harbour, thence:

ENE of Seal Carr (1¼ miles NNW), a rocky ledge extending 3 cables NNE of Sharper's Head, thence:

ENE of Berwick Lighthouse (55°45′·9N 1°59′·1W) (5.29).

(Directions for coastal passage continue at 5.71 and for Berwick-upon Tweed at 5.56)

Eyemouth

Chart 1612 plan of Eyemouth Harbour
General information
5.32

1 **Position.** Eyemouth (55°52′·49N 2°05′·09W) stands on low ground on the W side of Eye Water, 3 miles SSE of Saint Abb's Head. The harbour is on the E side of the town in the SE corner of the bay which fronts the town and lies between Hare Point and Gunsgreen Point.

2 **Function.** Eyemouth Harbour is the base for a fishing fleet and fish are processed locally. The harbour also accommodates visiting recreational craft. The population is about 3 400.

3 **Approach and entry.** The harbour is approached from the N across the bay and thence by an entrance channel, 17 m wide and 300 m long. The channel is protected by East and West Breakwaters.

4 **Port Authority.** Eyemouth Harbour Trust, Gunsgreen Basin, Eyemouth, TD14 3TX.

Limiting conditions
5.33

1 **Controlling depths.** The harbour entrance channel has a dredged depth of 2·0 m (2005) and Gunsgreen Basin has a

| *Hurkars* | *Luff Hard Rock* | *Hare Point* | *Hairy Ness* |

Approaches to Eyemouth from N (5.32)
(Original dated 2000)

(Photograph - Air Images)

maintained depth of 2·0 m. The inner harbour is maintained to a depth of 0·9 m at LW springs and 2·0 m at LW neaps.

Tidal levels see *Admiralty Tide Tables Volume 1*. Mean spring range about 4·3 m; mean neap range about 2·1 m.

2   **Maximum size of vessel handled**. Vessels up to 4·6 m draught can enter the harbour at HW springs.

Local weather and sea state. While there is some protection given from the N and E by a group of rocks, the Hurkars (5.36), Eyemouth should not be attempted in strong winds from these directions as the bay is a mass of broken water.

Arrival information
5.34

1   **Outer anchorage.** An anchorage shown on the chart, is available in depths of 5 m in the bay to the SW of the Hurkars.

Pilotage is not compulsory. The pilot boards from an open fishing boat. Vessels requiring a pilot should contact the Harbour Office during working hours or otherwise the Forth Coastguard.

Harbour
5.35

1   **General layout.** The outer harbour consists of Gunsgreen Basin, a tidal basin for large fishing vessels, which lies on the E side of the harbour at Gunsgreen Point. The basin, 185 m long and 60 m wide, has 230 m of quayside berthing.

Eyemouth Harbour from N (5.35)

(Original dated 2000)

(Photograph - Air Images)

2   The inner harbour is a long, thin tidal basin lying NNE/SSW. The main berthing is on the W side at Saltgreens Quay, 244 m in length, with Gunsgreen Quay and Middle Quay on the E side.

The inner harbour is protected against freshets by Middle Quay.

3   **Traffic signals.** A red light is exhibited from the E end of the promenade when it is considered unsafe to enter either the bay or the harbour.

Directions for entering harbour
5.36

1   **Leading lights:**

> Front light (orange column, 4 m in height) (55°52′·5N 2°05′·3W).
>
> Rear light (orange column, 6 m in height) (55 m S of front light).

2   **Northern approach.** From a position N of Hare Point (55°52′·7N 2°05′·5W) the alignment (174°) of these lights standing on West Breakwater leads to the harbour entrance, passing (with positions from front light):

> W of a light buoy (N cardinal) (3¼ cables N), marking the N extremity of the Hurkars, a group of dark rugged rocks which dry, extending 2 cables S of the light buoy; and:
>
> E of a dangerous wreck (3 cables NNW), thence:

3
> E of Luff Hard Rock (2½ cables N), an above water rock which lies off Hare Point, thence:
>
> W of Hinkar (2½ cables NNE), an above water rock lying in the centre of the Hurkars, thence:
>
> Close W of Inner Buss (2 cables N), a small underwater rock, thence:
>
> To the harbour entrance channel, which is 15m wide and lies between West and East Breakwaters. Within the breakwaters, the channel is marked by light beacons (port and starboard hand). Smeaton Quay Head Light Beacon (port hand) marks the entrance to Gunsgreen Basin.

4   **Eastern approach.** From a position ENE of Gunsgreen Point (55°52′·5N 2°05′·0W), the route leads WSW close inshore NNW of Nestends and Dulse Craig and thence joins the N approach on the alignment (174°) of the leading lights (above), passing (with positions from front leading light):

> NNW of Gunsgreen Point (1½ cables ENE) (5.31), thence:

5
> SSE of the Hurkars (2½ cables NNE) (above), thence:
>
> NNW and W of Hettle Scar (1 cable NE), a drying reef off the NW edge of the rocky ledges fronting Gunsgreen Point, thence:
>
> To the harbour entrance channel (above) on the alignment (174°) of the leading lights.

Port services
5.37

1   **Repairs.** There is a slip at the boatyard in Eye Water and a cradle for vessels up to 21 m in length and draught 2 m. Engine repairs can be carried out.

Other facilities: day-hospital at Berwick-upon-Tweed; ice plant.

Supplies: marine diesel at Gunsgreen Basin and by road tanker at other berths; fresh water at Gunsgreen Basin, Saltgreens Quay and Middle Quay; provisions.

Minor harbours and anchorage

Chart 160
Saint Abb's Boat Harbour
5.38

1   **General information.** Saint Abb's Boat Harbour (55°54′N 2°08′W) is 1¼ miles S of Saint Abb's Head. The entrance, 6 m wide, faces N and lies between piers, which together with a central jetty form an outer and inner harbour. There are depths in places of 2 m in the outer harbour. The inner harbour dries.

2   **Directions for entering harbour.** From a position close E of Maw Carr (150 m NNW of the entrance), a reddish rock with vertical sides, the alignment (165°) of the following leading lights leads to harbour entrance:

> Front light (white post, red bands, 2 m in height, on head of inside jetty) (55°53′·9N 2°07′·7W).
>
> Rear light (mast with red rectangle, white stripe, 10 m in height, SW corner of old harbour).

A number of rocky ledges lie to the NE and E of the harbour.

Burnmouth Harbour
5.39

1 **General information.** Burnmouth (55°50′N 2°04′W) is a fishing village at the mouth of a deep ravine. The small harbour, which dries, is formed by a pier at the inner end of an opening in the rocks, and is well-protected.

2 **Directions for entering harbour.** The alignment (241°) of the leading lights on the shore close by old coastguard houses and church leads to a position NNE of the harbour, which opens up the entrance, whence the track leads SSW to the harbour:
>   Front leading light (white post, 2 m in height) (55°50′·6N 2°04′·1W).
>   Rear leading light (white post, 2 m in height) (45 m from front light).

The white posts are difficult to distinguish by day.

Burnmouth Harbour from NE (5.39)
(Original dated 2001)

(Photograph - Crown Copyright)

Coldingham Bay
5.40

1 Anchorage at a position shown on the chart might be obtained in Coldingham Bay (55°53′N 2°07′W) 4 cables S of Saint Abb's Boat Harbour (5.38). The bay is generally foul and the anchorage rarely used except in the summer during offshore winds.

Marshall Meadows Bay
5.41

1 Boat landing can be made in Marshall Meadows Bay (55°48′N 2°02′W).

BERWICK-UPON-TWEED

General information

Chart 1612 plan of Berwick Harbour
Position
5.42

1 Berwick-upon-Tweed (55°45′·84N 1°59′·07W) stands on the N side of the mouth of River Tweed. Tweedmouth and Spittal lie on the S side of the entrance.

Function
5.43

1 The harbour is a small commercial and fishing port. The population is about 25 950.

Topography
5.44

1 The harbour is formed by the sea reach of River Tweed. The river has a large catchment and runs generally E for 96 miles. It rises at an elevation of 457 m, falling rapidly at first but at less than 0·6 m a mile for its last 8 miles. The harbour lies between a breakwater on the N side and a drying sandy spit extending from Spittal Point on the S side. The spit serves as a natural breakwater.

2 To the N of the breakwater the coast is fringed by ledges and the ground is foul for a distance of 4 cables offshore. Between the E extremity of the sandy spit, Sandstell Point, and the head of the breakwater there is a bar composed of sand and rocky boulders.

Port Authority
5.45

1 Berwick Harbour Commission, Harbour Master's Office, Tweed Dock, Tweedmouth, Berwick-upon-Tweed. TD15 2AB.

Limiting conditions

Controlling depths
5.46

1 The depth at the bar is 1·1 m. The depth in the approach channel to the dock is 0·9 m. Depths are liable to change and the Harbour Master should be consulted for the latest information.

Deepest and longest berth
5.47

1 West Quay in Tweed Dock.

Tidal levels
5.48

1 See *Admiralty Tide Tables Volume 1*. Mean spring range about 4·1 m; mean neap range about 2·5 m.

Maximum size of vessel handled
5.49

1 Vessels exceeding 87 m LOA must be fitted with a bowthrust unit. A vessel of 116 m LOA equipped with bow thrust and twin screws has used the port. The Harbour Master should be consulted prior to entry.

Vessels up to 4·6 m draught at MHWS and 3·7 m draught at MHWN can be accepted into Tweed Dock. Vessels lie aground on a bottom of level mud at LW.

Arrival information

Notice of ETA required
5.50

1 Notice of ETA together with pre-arrival information should be sent to the ship's agent or the Harbour Office 24 hours prior to arrival.

Outer anchorage
5.51

1 An anchorage in depths of 13 to 15 m can be found 7 cables ESE of the Breakwater Lighthouse on the alignment (294°) of the Breakwater Lighthouse with Berwick Town Hall spire (5.56). The anchorage is indicated on the chart.

Pilotage
5.52

1 Pilotage is compulsory. If vessels are expected, the pilot boat monitors VHF from 3 hours before HW to HW, which

is the only time pilotage is normally carried out. Weather permitting, the pilot boards 5 cables outside the breakwater. See *Admiralty List of Radio Signals Volume 6 (1)*.

Local knowledge
5.53

1 The sandbank off Spittal Point (5.44) is liable to much alteration. Considerable shoaling may take place in the entrance to the harbour especially after W gales. Due to these frequent changes local knowledge is advisable.

Harbour

General layout
5.54

1 The mouth of River Tweed is U-shaped with the entrance facing E. Tweed Dock (5.61) is situated at the W end of the mouth just below Berwick Bridge.

Tidal streams
5.55

1 Tidal streams to the E of the harbour entrance are given on chart 160. Within the river the in-going stream commences +0515 HW Tyne and the out-going stream at −0100 HW Tyne. Spring rates in both directions are fairly strong. During freshets the durations and rates of the out-going streams are increased and the in-going streams correspondingly reduced. The surface of River Tweed may be strewn with floating debris brought down by freshets.

2 An indraught into Berwick Bay has been reported after strong E winds.

Caution. It is considered dangerous to enter or leave harbour on the out-going stream during freshets.

Directions for entering harbour
(Continued from 5.31)

Principal marks
5.56

1 **Landmarks**
2 Town Hall (spire) (55°46′·2N 2°00′·2W).
Berwick Lighthouse (55°45′·9N 1°59′·1W) (5.29).
Saint Mary's Church (spire) (55°46′·4N 2°00′·5W).
Presbyterian Church (spire) (55°46′·3N 2°00′·1W).
Chimney (55°45′·6N 1°59′·6W).

Outer approaches
5.57

1 From a position about 2 miles to seaward of Berwick-upon-Tweed (chart 160), the track leads to the harbour entrance on the line of bearing 281° of Berwick Lighthouse.

Caution. Vessels approaching from N are advised to keep to seaward of the 20 m depth contour. Vessels approaching from the S see 5.73.

Berwick Lighthouse to Crabwater Rock
5.58

1 From the harbour entrance, the channel which is about 100 m wide, leads WNW for a distance of 2½ cables, passing (with positions from Berwick Light):
   SSW of Berwick Light and the breakwater itself which lies along the N side of the channel, and:
2 NNE of the drying spit which has Sandstell Point (1 cable SSW) as its E extremity. The bar (5.46) lies between Sandstell Point and the E end of the breakwater. Thence:
   NNE of a light buoy (port hand) (2½ cables W) marking the NW extremity of the drying sands off Spittal Point, and:

Berwick -upon-Tweed from ESE (5.54)
(Original dated 2000)

(Photograph - Air Images)

Berwick Harbour Entrance from ESE (5.57)

(Original dated 2001)

(Photograph - Crown Copyright)

3   SSW of the root of the breakwater (2½ cables WNW) which is marked by a light (starboard hand). Crabwater Rock, awash, lies ¼ cable WSW of the root.

Crabwater Rock to Spittal
5.59

1   **Leading Lights:**
    Front light (orange triangle point down, orange mast, black bands, 4 m in height) (55°45'·6N 1°59'·8W).
    Rear light (similar structure, 12 m in height) (55m SSW of front light).

Spittal leading marks (207°) from NE (5.59)

(Original dated 2001)

(Photograph - Crown Copyright)

From a position in mid channel, SW of the root of the breakwater, the alignment (207°) of these lights leads SSW in the channel, passing (with positions from front light):

2   ESE of Calot Shad (1½ cables N), a bank of sand and stones which dries, and which extends from the S side of Berwick nearly across the entire harbour. It is marked on its E side by a light beacon and light buoys (starboard hand). And:
    WNW of the sandspit (2½ cables ENE) extending between Spittal Point and Sandstell Point, thence:
    WNW of Spittal Point (1½ cables ENE).

Spittal to Tweed Dock
5.60

1   From a position in mid channel WNW of Spittal Point the track leads W and NW for a distance of 3½ cables to Tweed Dock, passing (with positions from Tweed Dock entrance):
    S of a buoy (starboard hand) (2½ cables SE) marking the SW corner of Calot Shad (5.59), and:
    N of Carr Rock Jetty (2½ cables SE), the end of which is marked by a light (port hand), thence:

2   To the entrance of Tweed Dock, which is entered between a docking pier on the S side from which a light (port hand) is exhibited and the beacon (black and yellow with diamond-shaped topmark) that marks a drying bank on the N side of the entrance. A groyne extending SE from the E dock wall has its outer extremity close NW of the beacon. The entrance to the dock is 17·5 m wide. The dock is tidal. A light buoy (special, conical) is moored on the W side of Calot Shad and marks the swinging area limit E of Tweed Dock entrance. This buoy might be moved as necessary.
    Between the dock entrance and Berwick Bridge there is an off-lying detached stone and gravel wall which uncovers at half-tide. It is used by salmon fishermen.

Berths

Alongside berths
5.61

1   Tweed Dock has 329 m of quays available for commercial shipping, providing three berths. West Quay is 124 m in length and has an alongside depth of 1·2 to 1·5 m.
    Stoneberth (55°45'·7N 2°00'·0W) at Spittal is no longer used commercially.

Port services

Repairs
5.62

1   Minor repairs to the hull; major engine repairs; small boat grid.

Other facilities

5.63

1   Boat landing at Salmon Jetty (55°46′·1N 2°00′·3W); Hospital with helicopter landing site close E of the coastguard station; SSCECs and extensions issued (1.92).

Supplies

5.64

1   Marine diesel by road tanker; water at the quays; provisions.

BERWICK-UPON-TWEED TO NORTH SUNDERLAND, INCLUDING FARNE ISLANDS

General information

Chart 111
Route
5.65

1   From a position E of Berwick-upon-Tweed (55°46′N 2°00′W), the coastal route leads 13 miles ESE to a position NE of Longstone, the E point of Farne Islands, and thence 2 miles S to a position 3½ miles NE of North Sunderland Harbour. An alternative inshore route to W of Farne Islands is described also.

Topography

5.66

1   The coast between Berwick-upon-Tweed and Snook (5.101), the point 4 cables SE of the entrance to North Sunderland Harbour, is the most dangerous in NE England, N of River Humber. Numerous dangers front this part of the coast, with Farne Islands and associated shoals extending 4½ miles NE of Snook. These dangers, with the exception of Spittal Hirst (55°46′N 1°51′W), lie within the 20 m depth contour.

2   Berwick Bay lies between Spittal Point (55°46′N 1°59′W) and Snipe Point, 8 miles to the SE, the N extremity of Holy Island. Initially the coast of the bay is sandy but it is then fronted by a narrow rocky ledge extending as far as Cheswick, 3½ miles SE of Spittal Point. The central part of this ledge is backed by cliffs about 30 m high. SE of Cheswick there are low sand dunes fronted by sand flats which broaden out from the coast and eventually meet Holy Island at Snipe Point, 5 miles ESE of Cheswick, forming Cheswick Sands, Goswick Sands and Sand Ridge. To the W and S of Holy Island lie further extensive tracts of flats, Holy Island Sands and Fenham Flats. The sands are intersected at LW by rivulets which connect to the sea and are passable on foot in many places at LW. Holy Island is based on limestone rock and is a moderately elevated plain, sloping SW with scarcely a tree or shrub upon it. A causeway crosses a tract of sand 7 cables wide and connects the shore at Beal Point with The Snook, a long narrow ridge of sandhills extending W from the main part of Holy Island.

3   South of Holy Island the coast runs 7 miles SE to Snook near North Sunderland Harbour. It is generally sandy, fringed by rocks in places and in the S backed by low undulating country. Budle Bay lies between Ross Links, a sandy ridge, at the N end of this stretch of coast and Budle Point, 4 miles NW of Snook. Warnham Flats, which dry, occupy the greater part of Budle Bay.

4   Farne Islands, a chain of rocky islets, reefs and shoals are divided by Farne Sound and Staple Sound (5.79). Inner Farne (5.77) (55°37′N 1°39′W), the innermost island, lies 2¼ miles E of Blackrocks Point and is separated from the mainland by Inner Sound (5.77). Due to the considerable tidal range, about 4·5 m, the islands present very different aspects at HW and LW. The islands are owned by the National Trust and are a nature reserve (1.61) and a bird sanctuary (1.62).

Hazards

5.67

1   The area E of Longstone (55°39′N 1°36′W) is a focal point for shipping. Whirl Rocks extend to its NE and Crumstone, which is not lit, lies 1 mile SSE. Whirl Rocks are steep-to and there are depths of 45 to 55 m within one mile of them. In poor visibility, or at night, vessels should not attempt to pass E of Longstone in depths of less than 65 m which occur about 3 miles E of the islet. Due allowance should be made for the tidal stream.

Sandwaves

5.68

1   An area of sandwaves exists up to a distance of about 15 miles offshore from N to E of the Farne Islands. See *The Mariner's Handbook.*

Rescue

5.69

1   There are Coastal Rescue Teams at Holy Island village and at North Sunderland Harbour; see 1.67.

   An all-weather lifeboat and an inshore lifeboat are stationed at North Sunderland Harbour. See 1.72.

Farne Island Lighthouse   *E Wideopen*
Farne Islands from SW (5.66)
(Original dated 2000)

(Photograph - Air Images)

Natural conditions
5.70

1   **Tidal streams.** Offshore streams are regular and rarely exceed 1 kn at springs. They are given on the chart and in *Admiralty Tidal Stream Atlas: North Sea, Northwestern Part.*

2   The streams are strong near Farne Islands and at a position 1 mile NE of Longstone (5.72) spring rates are 3½ to 4 kn, decreasing seaward. There is turbulence over Knivestone and Whirl Rocks which lie to the NE of Longstone. Within Inner Sound (5.77) the spring rate in each direction is 2½ kn.

3   **Current.** A weak current runs S off the coast. Strong and continued NW and N winds increase its rate and the current may be strong enough to affect navigation. Conversely SE and S winds reduce its rate and if prolonged may reverse its direction.

Directions
(continued from 5.31)

Principal marks
5.71

1   **Landmarks:**
    Tower (55°42′N 1°54′W) at Goswick Links.
    Holy Island Castle (55°40′N 1°47′W), surmounted by a flagstaff and standing on a rocky hill.
    Emmanuel Head Beacon (51°41′·2N 1°46′·8W), a white pyramid standing on a cliff 3 m in height.
    Bamburgh Castle (55°36′·6N 1°42′·6W), standing on a high rock that rises abruptly from a flat beach. Its principal tower is square with a turret.
    Bamburgh Church Tower (55°36′·5N 1°43′·1W).
    Longstone Lighthouse (red tower, white band, 26 m in height) (55°38′·6N 1°36′·7W).

Longstone Lighthouse from NE (5.71)
(Original dated 2001)

(Photograph - Crown Copyright)

2   Tower (55°38′N 1°37′W) on Staple Island.
    Tower (2½ cables NNW of Staple Island Tower) on Brownsman islet.
    Inner Farne Lighthouse (white round tower, 13 m in height) (55°37′N 1°39′W).
    Tower (1 cable N of Inner Farne Lighthouse).

3   **Major Lights:**
    Saint Abb's Head Light (55°55′N 2°08′W) (5.11).
    Blackrocks Point Light (white building, 9 m in height) (55°37′N 1°43′W).
    Longstone Light (as above).

Coastal Route
5.72

1   From a position E of Berwick-upon-Tweed, the coastal route leads 13 miles ESE to a position NE of Longstone, thence 2 miles S to a position 3½ miles NE of North Sunderland Harbour, passing (with positions from Emmanuel Head Beacon (15 m in height) (55°41′N 1°47′W)):

2   SSW of Spittal Hirst (55°45′·7N 1°51′·2W) (5.3), thence:
    NNE of Outer Tours (3½ miles NNW), thence:
    NNE of Tours and Park Dyke (2 miles NW), two rocky shoals lying within 3 cables of each other, thence:

3   NNE of Emmanuel Head which is surmounted by a beacon (5.71), thence:

Emmanuel Head Beacon from E (5.72)
(Original dated 2000)

(Photograph - Air Images)

4   NNE of Goldstone (2 miles ESE), a rock which dries, marked by a light buoy (starboard hand) on its W side. Stiel Reef extends 1¼ cables ESE of Goldstone, and Saint Nicholas Rock, on which the sea breaks heavily, lies 3 cables NW. Thence:

5   NNE of Whirl Rocks (55°39′N 1°36′W), on which the sea breaks heavily, lying 6 cables NE of Longstone. The island, on which stands a lighthouse (5.71), is the outermost of the Farne Islands. At LW Longstone appears as one island, but at HW it is divided into several parts.

6   The route continues S, passing (with positions from Longstone Lighthouse (55°39′N 1°36′W) (5.71)):
    E of Whirl Rocks, thence:
    E of Crumstone (1 mile SSE), a flat black rock. Callers, a reef, extends 2½ cables WNW of Crumstone and is part of the bank surrounding the latter. Thence:

7   To a position NE of North Sunderland Harbour (5.87). (4 miles SSW).

8   Farne Islands and the dangers surrounding them are covered by a red sector of Blackrocks Point Light (238°–275°) (5.71) and by the red sector of Inner Farne Light (119°–280°) (5.71).

Clearing bearing
5.73

1   The alignment (162°) of the beacon on Emmanuel Head (5.72) with Newtown Hill summit 4½ miles SSE of the beacon passes E of Spittal Hirst and the dangers which lie SE of Spittal Hirst in Berwick Bay (5.66).

Useful mark
5.74
1   The Cheviot (55°29′N 2°09′W), at an elevation of 813 m and marked by a large cairn (Chart 1192).

(Directions for North Sunderland continue at 5.91 and for coastal passage S at 5.100)

Inshore route via Inner Sound
5.75
1   From a position ENE of Emmanuel Head Beacon (51°41′·2N 1°46′·8W) (5.71), the alignment (162¼°) of Megstone (black rock, 5 m high) (55°38′N 1°40′W) with North Sunderland Lighthouse (white tower, 8 m in height) (2¾ miles SSE of Megstone) leads about 3 miles SSE to a position ENE of Tree o'the House and E of the dangers which lie to the E of Holy Island, passing (with positions from Megstone):

2   ENE of Saint Nicholas Rock (3½ miles NNW) (5.72), thence:

ENE of Goldstone (3 miles NNW) (5.72), thence:

ENE of Guzzard (2½ miles NNW), a shoal, thence:

To a position ENE of Tree o'the House (2 miles NNW).

The dangers above are covered by a red sector of Blackrocks Point Light (175°–191°).
5.76
1   From a position ENE of Tree o'the House the line of bearing 206° of Blackrocks Point Lighthouse (5.71) leads 1½ miles SSW until Holy Island Castle (5.71) bears 312°, or at night Inner Farne Light (5.71) shows white bearing 119°, passing:

2   WNW of Oxscar, also known as South Goldstone (4½ cables NE), a rock which dries, thence:

WNW of Megstone (5.75), thence:

To a position WNW of Swedman (4 cables W), a drying reef which is marked by a light buoy (starboard hand) moored 4½ cables to the W.
5.77
1   The line of bearing 312° (astern) of Holy Island Castle leads 3½ miles SE through Inner Sound, passing:

NE of Blackrocks Point Lighthouse (2 miles WSW) (5.71), thence:

SW of Swedman (4 cables W) (5.76), thence:

NE of Islestone (1¼ miles SSW) a rocky reef which dries and which is covered by a green sector (289°–300°) of Blackrocks Point Light, thence:

2   SW of Inner Farne (Farne Island) (1 mile SE). The island is the most SW of the group and is also the highest; much of its surface is covered by grass. A bold cliff of columnar basalt, 15 m high, stands on its SW side and slopes gradually to the NE. Inner Farne Lighthouse (5.71) stands on the SW extremity of the island. Thence:

3   NE of Shoreston Outcars (2¼ miles SSE), a ledge of rocks which dries and is marked by a light buoy (port hand) moored 3 cables to the NE of the ledge, thence:

To a position NE of North Sunderland Harbour (3 miles SSE).

(Directions for North Sunderland Harbour continue at 5.91 and for coastal passage S at 5.100)

Side channels

Goldstone Channel
5.78
1   As an alternative to the inshore route (5.75 to 5.77) Goldstone Channel may be used. From a position NNE of Emmanuel Head Beacon (55°41′·1N 1°46′·8W) (5.71), the line of bearing 171° of Blackrocks Point Lighthouse (55°37′N 1°43′W) (5.71) or by night in a white sector (165°–175°) of the light, leads about 4½ miles S through Goldstone Channel and passes (with positions from Blackrocks Point Lighthouse):

2   E of Emmanuel Head Beacon (4½ miles NNW) (5.71), thence:

E of Outer Wingate (3¾ miles NNW) with Wingate, a group of rocks close SW. The sea breaks over Outer Wingate, thence:

W of Saint Nicholas Rock (3½ miles N) (5.72), thence:

3   E of Plough Seat Reef (3½ miles NNW), which dries, marked on its E side by a Plough Seat Light Buoy (port hand). Plough Rock, a drying rock 2 cables W of the reef, is marked on its W side by a light buoy (W cardinal). Thence:

4   W of Goldstone Light Buoy (starboard hand) marking a rock which dries (3¼ miles N), thence:

W of Guzzard (2¾ miles N) (5.75), thence:

5   W of Tree o'the House (2¼ miles N) (5.75).

The track continues S until Holy Island Castle bears 312°, or, at night the white sector of Inner Farne Light is opened on a bearing of 119°, whence the track through the Inner Sound (5.75) is joined.

Caution. Goldstone Channel should only be used when the marks and lights can be seen clearly, as the soundings are irregular and the tidal streams are strong.

Staple Sound
5.79
1   **Caution.** The passage through Staple Sound, which separates the outer group of Farne Islands from the inner group, is seldom used. The tidal stream is strong, with spring rates up to 4 kn, and there are no leading marks so that accurate fixing is essential. The track lies on the NE side of Staple Sound and not in the apparent mid–channel between Staple Island (55°38′N 1°37′W) and the islets NE of Inner Farne.

2   From the vicinity of 55°38′·9N 1°40·0′W, the route leads about 3 miles SE through Staple Sound, passing (with positions from the tower on Staple Island (5.71)):

NE of Oxscar (1½ miles W) (5.76), thence:

NE of Glororum Shad (1 mile WNW). N of this shoal depths are irregular. Thence:

SW of North Wamses and South Wamses (5 cables NNW), two rocky islets, thence:

3   NE of Islestone Shad (7 cables E), a rocky patch over which the sea breaks in bad weather, thence:

SW of Gun Rocks (2 cables WNW) which dry 3·6m. They lie at the extremity of the reef running NW from the S point of Staple Island. Thence:

4   NE of Knoxes Reef (7 cables SW), which dries and extends 6 cables ENE of Inner Farne. An islet and rock lie on its SW side. Thence:

SW of Staple Island, with a conspicuous tower (5.71). The S side of the island is a bold cliff with Pinnacles, detached steep-to rocks resembling broken pillars, lying close E. The island is swarmed by birds. Thence:

5   NE of The Bush (8 cables SSW), a rocky ledge which dries and lies E of the islets of East Wideopen and West Wideopen, thence:

SW of Fang (8 cables ESE), a spit extending S from Crumstone (5.72) and clear of Staple Sound.

Holy Island Harbour

Chart 1612 plan of Holy Island Harbour

General information

5.80

1   **Position.** Holy Island Harbour (55°40′N 1°48′W) is on the S side of Holy Island.

Function. The harbour is small although it appears large at HW. It is secure and sheltered and has proved useful as a port of refuge. During E winds, when it is impracticable to enter Berwick Harbour (5.42), it might be possible to use Holy Island Harbour.

The population of Holy Island is about 150.

2   **Approach and entry.** The harbour is approached from the SE of Holy Island and entered by a narrow channel between Castle Point on the island and Guile Point, the N extremity of Old Law, a low-lying headland that has become detached at its S end. Both Castle Point and Guile Point are fringed by extensive reefs of rock and stone which dry.

Port Authority. The Harbour Master, Falkland House, Holy Island.

Limiting conditions

5.81

1   **Controlling depths.** The least depth in the harbour approach is 1·6 m on the Nob (55°39′·6N 1°46′·6W), a patch of stony ground.

Tidal levels. Mean spring range about 4·2 m; mean neap range about 2·2 m. See *Admiralty Tide Tables Volume 1.*

Arrival information

5.82

1   **Outer anchorage** is available in depths of 8 m, 4½ cables E of Castle Point (55°40′·1N 1°46′·7W) or in Skate Road (Chart 111), 1¼ miles SSE of Castle Point. Both anchorages are exposed.

Hole Mouth (55°40′N 1°47′W), a small opening between Castle Point and Ridge End (5.84) has a depth of 2·5 m in it and has been used as a haven by small craft driven too close inshore to pass round Ridge End.

2   **Pilotage** is not available.

Harbour

5.83

1   **General layout.** There are no alongside berths apart from a jetty 60 m long at Steel End (55°40′·1N 1°47′·7W), which is used to land fish. There is a slipway equipped with an electric winch 2 cables W of the jetty.

Within the harbour an anchorage may be found in depths of between 5 m and 7 m, bottom sand.

2   **Tidal streams** run strongly into and out of Holy Island Harbour as follows:

Time from HW Tyne	Remarks
+0510	W-going stream begins
−0045	E-going stream begins

3   The sands between the W extremity of Holy Island at Snook Point, and the nearest point of the mainland, Beal Point (5.66), are only covered for about 3 hours at springs, between −0215 and +0045 HW Tyne, and scarcely at all at neaps. Throughout this period there is a SE-going stream off the coast but in the harbour initially there is a W-going

Steel End

Castle   *Castle Point*

Holy Island from ESE (5.80)

(Original dated 2000)

(Photograph - Air Images)

stream and then an E-going stream. When the sands are covered the W-going stream from the harbour runs across the sands, turns E along the N coast of the island and then joins the SE-going stream off the coast. When there is an E-going stream in the harbour, the SE-going coastal stream runs across the sands and joins the E-going harbour stream.

Directions for entering harbour
5.84

1   **Landmarks:**
      Holy Island Castle (55°40′N 1°47′W) surmounted by a flagstaff and standing on a rocky hill.
      Ruined chapel (55°40′·1N 1°48′·4W) standing on the summit of Saint Cuthbert's Islet.
      Tower at Heugh Hill (55°40′·1N 1°48′·1W).

2   **Approach.** From a position ESE of Castle Point (55°40′·1N 1°46′·7W), the transit (260°) of Old Law East Light Beacon (stone obelisk, 21 m in height) (55°39′·5N 1°47′·6W) with Old Law West Beacon (stone obelisk, 25 m in height) (120 m W), or, at night, the narrow white sector (258½°–261°½) of East Light Beacon (Guile Point Light Beacon), leads to the harbour entrance, passing (with positions from the light):

Old Law Beacons from E (5.84)
(Original dated 2000)

(Photograph - Air Images)

3   S of Plough Seat Reef (1½ miles NE) (5.78), thence:
      S of Ridge Light Buoy (E cardinal) (9 cables ENE), marking Ridge End, the E extremity of a reef that borders the E side of Holy Island Harbour, thence:
      S of Triton Shoal (6 cables ENE), composed of large stones covered in kelp. It is marked on its SW corner by Triton Light Buoy (starboard hand) moored close W of Nob (5.81), thence:

4   N of Parton Stiel (5 cables ESE), a stony patch. The Bar lies between Triton Shoal and Parton Stiel. The bottom is chiefly of stones covered with kelp and patches of sand in between.

5.85

1   **Inner leading marks:**
      Heugh Light Beacon (black triangle apex up, on framework tower, 8 m in height) (55°40′·1N 1°48′·0W) standing on Heugh Hill, a dark cliff 14 m high.
      Saint Mary's Church belfry (200 m NW of Heugh Beacon).

2   From a position close S of Triton Light Buoy (starboard hand), the alignment (309°) of these marks, or at night the white sector of Heugh Light Beacon (308°–311°) leads through Burrow Hole, the inner channel, and into the

harbour (5.82). The track passes (with positions from Heugh Beacon):
      NE of Black Law (4½ cables SSE), an islet covered in grass. Two dangerous underwater rocks lie 1¼ cables NE of the islet. And:

3   SW of Stone Ridge (5 cables ESE), composed of large stones running W from Ridge End (5.84), thence:
      NE of Seal Spit (4 cables SE), the N extremity of the bank surrounding Black Law, thence:

4   SW of Wheel Shoal (3 cables ESE), the W extremity of Stone Ridge.
      Thence course is adjusted W to the inner anchorage as shown on the chart.

   Caution. The channel through Burrow Hole is less than 1 cable wide and it is necessary to adjust from the outer to the inner marks rapidly.

Supplies
5.86

1   Limited supplies of fresh water and provisions.

North Sunderland (Seahouses) Harbour

Chart 1612 plan of North Sunderland Harbour
General information
5.87

1   **Position.** North Sunderland Harbour (55°35′N 1°39′W) lies on the mainland S of the Farne Islands. Seahouses village stands on the SW side of the harbour and the town of North Sunderland is 5 cables inland.
   Function. The harbour is used only for fishing vessels and recreational craft which can lie aground.
   Port Authority. North Sunderland Harbour Commissioners, Harbour Office, Harbour Road, Seahouses, Northumberland, NE68 7RN.

Limiting conditions
5.88

1   **Controlling depths.** The Outer Harbour is dredged to 0·7 m above chart datum.
   The Inner Harbour has depths of 4·0 m at HW springs and 2·8 m at HW neaps.
   Tidal levels: see *Admiralty Tide Tables Volume 1*. Mean spring range about 4·1 m; mean neap range about 2·1 m.
   Maximum size of vessel handled is length 30·5 m and 2·75 m draught at HW springs. Vessels smaller in length may enter with a maximum draught of 3·7 m at HW springs.

Arrival information
5.89

1   **Pilotage** is not compulsory.

Harbour
5.90

1   **General layout.** The small artificial harbour is protected by a low-lying rocky headland to the SE, a detached breakwater to the NE and from the NW by Outer or North West Pier. Middle Pier divides Outer Harbour from Inner Harbour. The latter lies at the inner end of the breakwater and has an entrance 18 m wide facing E.
   The Inner Harbour is used primarily by fishing craft and by small commercial craft which carry passengers. The Outer Harbour is only suitable in fair weather but in bad weather accommodation may be available in Inner Harbour.

2   Private moorings for small craft are laid in Fluke Hole off Seahouses Point (53°34′·9N 1°38′·8W). Fluke Hole is

North Sunderland Harbour from NE (5.90)
(Original dated 2000)

(Photograph - Air Images)

accessed from Outer Harbour by a short channel which is marked by stakes.

3   **Traffic signal** A fixed red light exhibited above the normal fixed green light at North Sunderland Light indicates that it is dangerous to enter harbour.

Night	*Position*
	The main Lighthouse.

Traffic signals (5.90)

Directions for entering harbour
(Continued from and 5.74 and 5.77)
5.91

1   **Landmark:**
      North Sunderland Lighthouse (55°35′·0N 1°38′·9W) (white tower, 8 m in height).
    Approach. From a position NE of the harbour, the route leads SW to a position NNW of the entrance whence course is adjusted SSE to pass between the breakwaters. The track passes:
      NW of Carr End (55°35′·1N 1°38′·7W), a steep-to rocky ledge that dries and which extends 1½ cables seaward of the detached breakwater. Southend Rock, 1 cable SE of Carr End, is the E extremity of this ledge. The end of an outfall pipe extends about ½ cable E of Southend Rock. Thence:

2   To the harbour entrance, which is 61 m wide, facing N. The entrance lies between the heads of Outer Pier, on which stands North Sunderland Lighthouse and the detached breakwater, with a light (metal tripod) at its NW extremity.

Port services
5.92

1   **Repairs** to fishing craft can be undertaken. There is a slipway and a boat hoist of 20 tonnes.
    Supplies: marine diesel (light); lubricating oil; limited fresh water; provisions.

Anchorages and boat landings
Chart 111
Anchorages
5.93

1   In fair weather there is an anchorage in 16 m, 3 cables SE of Inner Farne (55°37′N 1°39′W) as indicated on the chart.
    There is an anchorage in favourable conditions for small craft in The Kettle (55°37′N 1°39′W), a natural basin on The N side of Inner Farne. The anchorage is in a depth of 4·3 m, clean sand, good holding and is indicated on the chart. Vessels approaching this anchorage should do so on the alignment of Emmanuel Head Beacon (5.72) with the E extremity of Megstone (5.75).

2   Anchorage for small craft may also be found about 4 cables NE of Inner Farne Island in a depth of about 5 m as indicated on the chart.

Landings
5.94

1   There are landings at:
      Granary Point (55°40′N 1°52′W) where, with local knowledge, small craft can take the ground safely.
      Warren Mill (55°36′N 1°46′W) at the head of Warren Burn in the SW corner of Budle Bay (5.66). Warnham Bar, with a depth of 4 m at HW springs, shifts occasionally and should not be attempted without local knowledge.
      Inner Farne (55°37′N 1°39′W) (5.77) in the small bay at the N end of the island.

NORTH SUNDERLAND TO COQUET ISLAND

General information

Chart 156
Route
5.95

1   From a position 3½ miles NE of North Sunderland Harbour (55°35′N 1°39′W) the route leads 18 miles S to a position E of Coquet Island.

Topography
5.96

1   The coast is formed by a number of headlands with off-lying ledges and rocks extending up to 1 mile offshore. Between the headlands there are several sandy bays. The land backing the coast is generally grassy and rises to a moderate elevation with the rounded mass of The Cheviot (5.74), the highest point in the distance. Coquet Island, which is a bird sanctuary owned by the Royal Society for the Protection of Birds (1.62), lies 1 mile ESE of Warkworth Harbour (5.104).

Depths
5.97

1   The 30 m depth contour runs parallel to the coast about 2½ miles offshore, but closes the land in the vicinity of Coquet Island. The island is 7 cables offshore and separated from the mainland by Coquet Channel. There are no dangers outside the 30 m depth contour but there are two off-lying rocky banks, Newton Skere and Craster Skeres (5.3), which are 6½ miles SE and 10½ miles SSE respectively of Longstone (55°39′N 1°36′W) (5.72). The sea breaks heavily over these patches in bad weather.

Rescue
5.98

1 There are Coastal Rescue Teams at Craster (55°28′N 1°35′W), Boulmer (55°25′N 1°35′W) and Amble (55°20′N 1°34′W); see 1.67.

An all-weather lifeboat is stationed at Amble; inshore lifeboats are stationed at Amble and Craster. See 1.72.

Natural conditions
5.99

1 **The tidal streams** run in the direction of the coast and are of no great strength, except off salient points where there may be eddies. Tidal streams are given on the chart and in *Admiralty Tidal Stream Atlas: North Sea, Northwestern Part.*

Climate information for Boulmer: see 1.142 and 1.148.

Directions
(continued from 5.74 and 5.77)

Principal marks:
5.100

1 **Landmarks:**

Hepburn Hill (55°31′N 1°52′W) (chart 1192).
Radio Tower (55°31′·2N 1°36′·8W).
Dunstanburgh Castle (55°29′·4N 1°35′·7W), a ruin.
Heiferlaw (55°27′N 1°45′W) (chart 1192).
Radar aerials (55°25′N 1°46′W) (chart 1192).
Radio mast (55°23′N 1°47′W), a framework tower (chart 1192).

2 Alnmouth Church (spire) (55°23′·3N 1°36′·8W).
Warkworth Castle (55°21′N 1°37′W), a conspicuous tower.
Coquet Lighthouse (white square tower, turreted parapet, lower half grey, 22 m in height) (55°20′N 1°32′W).

3 **Major lights:**

Longstone Light (55°38′·6N 1°36′·7W) (5.71).
Coquet Light (above).

North Sunderland to Coquet Island
5.101

1 From a position NE of North Sunderland Harbour (55°35′N 1°39′W), the coastal route leads S to a position E of Coquet Island, passing :

E of Snook (North Sunderland Point) (55°34′·7N 1°38′·4W). Snook is a headland about 9 m in height. Its foreshore comprises extensive rocky and parallel ledges dipping S. The Falls, a spit, extends 4 cables ESE of Snook and Grimstone, an isolated rock that dries, lies 2 cables E of Snook. The foregoing dangers are marked by N Sunderland Light Buoy (port hand) moored at the SE entrance to Inner Sound (5.77). Thence:

2 E of Beadnell Point (55°33′·1N 1°37′·2W), which is low and wedged shaped with strata that dips to the south. Red Brae, a dark low projecting cliff is 4 cables NW of the point. Thence:

3 E of Barnyard and Faggot (55°32′·0N 1°36′·3W), two rocks marked by Newton Rock Light Buoy (port hand) moored 9½ cables NE of Snook Point. Beadnell Bay with sandy shores and off-lying foul grounds lies between Snook Point and Beadnell Point. Thence:

E of Ice Carr (55°31′·4N 1°36′·4W) lying 2 cables NE of Newton Point, a rounded point surmounted by a conspicuous radio tower, thence:

4 E of Castle Point (55°29′·6N 1°35′·5W), which has shelving black perpendicular pillars on its E and S sides. The ruins of Dunstanburgh Castle stand prominently on the N side of the point. Embleton Bay lies between Castle Point and a group of rocks 1¼ miles NNW of the point. The rocks run 5 cables to seaward with Fills, an extensive rocky patch, at their extremity. Thence:

5 E of Longhoughton Steel (55°25′·9N 1°34′·6W), where the coast is low and sandy, Thence:

E of Seaton Point (55°24′·4N 1°34′·9W), which is low, round and sandy. Between this point and Longhoughton Steel to the N, the coast is fronted by a series of rocky ledges extending up to 6 cables offshore. Boulmer Stile, a rocky ledge, with Seaton Shad, a shoal extending 7 cables to its S, form the SE point of these ledges and are covered by a red sector (163° - 180°) of Coquet Island Light (5.100). Thence:

6 E of Alnmouth Bay (55°22′·3N 1°34′·0W). The bay lies between Seaton Point to the N and Coquet Island, 4½ miles SSE of the point. Aln Harbour (5.116) lies at its N end and Warkworth Harbour (5.104) at the S end. The coast of the bay is mainly of sandhills, broken by a cliff at its midpoint at the foot of which is a rocky ledge, Birling Carrs. Thence:

7 To a position E of Coquet Island (55°20′N 1°32′W) with a light on its SE side (5.100). Two detached shoals, Steel Bush with 1·2 m and North East Bush with 2·8 m, lie 2½ cables NNE of the island.

Useful marks
5.102

1 Tank (55°35′N 1°40′W).
Beadnell Church (spire) (55°33′N 1°38′W) showing above woods W of Beadnell Point.
White house (55°20′·2N 1°34′·3W).
Spire (55°20′N 1°34′W).
(Directions continue for coastal passage at 5.122)

Side Channel
Chart 1627 plan of Warkworth Harbour
Coquet Channel
5.103

1 Coquet Island (55°20′N 1°32′W) is separated from the mainland by Coquet Channel. The channel, which lies between Law Briggs, drying rocks on the mainland and foul ground on the SW side of the island, is two cables wide and has a least depth of 0·8 m. There are no navigation marks and local knowledge is required for passage through the channel.

Warkworth
Chart 1627, plan of Warkworth Harbour
General information
5.104

1 **Position.** Warkworth Harbour or Amble (55°20′N 1°34′W) is situated at the mouth of River Coquet, at the S end of Alnmouth Bay. The river is 27 miles long and after heavy rain is liable to flood but at other times its volume is inconsiderable. Amble lies on the S bank of the entrance to River Coquet and all the business of the port is conducted there. Warkworth village is 1½ miles NW of the port.

2 **Function.** Warkworth Harbour is a small port used mainly by the fishing industry. There is also a marina.

The population of Amble is about 5 600.

Warkworth

Coquet Island and Channel from SE (5.103)
(Original dated 2000)

(Photograph - Air Images)

Warkworth Harbour from E (5.104)
(Original dated 2000)

(Photograph - Air Images)

3   **Approach and entry.** The harbour is approached from the NNE across Alnmouth Bay and entered through breakwaters which form the entrance.

Port Authority. Warkworth Harbour Commissioners, Quayside, Amble, Northumberland, NE65 0AP.

Limiting conditions
5.105

1   **Controlling depths.** There is a least charted depth over the bar at the harbour entrance of 0·6 m. Depths are liable to change due to silting and the Harbour Master should be consulted for the latest information.

Tidal levels: see *Admiralty Tide Tables Volume 1*. Mean spring range for Amble about 4·2 m; mean neap range about 2·2 m.

2   **Maximum size of vessel handled.** Vessels up to about 40 m in length and 4·0 m draught can enter the harbour at HW.

Local weather and sea state. NE gales cause the worst seas with broken water extending from the harbour

entrance to Coquet Island. The harbour should not be approached in these conditions.

When a swell is running a dangerous short sea builds up over Pan Bush (5.108), 4 cables ENE of the entrance. In these conditions small craft should not attempt to cross the shoal even at HW.

Arrival Information
5.106

1   **Port radio:** VHF R/T watch maintained during office hours Monday to Friday.

Notice of ETA required: 24 hours notice is required for commercial vessels. Notice is not required for fishing vessels or recreational craft.

Outer anchorage with South Pier light bearing 200° in 9 m, sand and mud, is available for vessels awaiting the tide to enter Warkworth Harbour. An anchorage position is indicated on the chart.

Harbour
5.107

1   **General layout.** The harbour is formed at the lower reach of River Coquet by two outer breakwaters and within the breakwaters North and South Jetties, the latter extending W into Broomhill Quay. Fish Dock lies between Broomhill Quay and Radcliffe Quay.

Tidal streams: see 5.117. The S–going stream sets across the entrance.

Directions for entering harbour
5.108

2   **Landmarks:**

    Warkworth Castle (55°21′N 1°37′W) (5.100).
    Coquet Lighthouse (55°20′N 1°32′W) (5.100).
    White house (55°20′·2N 1°34′·3W).
    Spire (55°20′N 1°34′W).
    Water Tower (55°19′·6N,1°37′·6W) (Chart 156), which is mushroom shaped.

3 **Outer approach.** From a position in Alnmouth Bay to the NNE of the harbour entrance the line of bearing 190° of the spire (55°20′N 1°34′W) leads to a position ENE of the entrance, passing (with positions from the spire):

Through the anchorage (1 mile NNE) (5.106), thence:
W of Pan Bush (6½ cables NNE), a rocky shoal which lies at the N end of a rocky spit, thence:
W of a wreck (4½ cables NNE) with a least depth of 1·8 m.

4 **Harbour entrance.** From a position ENE of the harbour entrance and clear W of the wreck, the alignment (248°) of North Jetty with the water tower (see above) leads through the entrance, passing (with positions from the entrance):

5 NNW of Pan Rocks (1 cable SE) extending 1½ cables NE of Pan Point, which is cliffy and lies E of South Pier. The rocks are marked close to their NE extremity by a beacon which has toppled and is covered at half tide. The rocks are crossed by an outfall marked at its seaward end by a light buoy which is moored about 2 cables E of the beacon. Thence:

6 To the harbour entrance, which is 68 m wide and lies between the heads of North and South Piers, on which stand light beacons, (North:green pole. South: white round tower, red bands, white base, 8 m in height).

Berths
5.109

1 There is berthing available alongside Broomhill Quay and Radcliffe Quay, although the former is normally used by fishing vessels. These jetties have depths alongside of more than 1 m and a total length of about 250 m.

Port services
5.110

1 **Repairs.** Minor repairs can be carried out. There is a boat building yard with a small basin containing a 50 tonne boat hoist.

Supplies: marine diesel; water at the berths on Broomhill Quay; provisions.

Rescue. See 5.98.

Minor harbours and anchorages

Chart 156
Beadnell Harbour
5.111

1 Beadnell Harbour (55°33′N 1°38′W), which lies on the SW side of Beadnell Point is a small drying harbour formed by two piers with an entrance between the piers 8 m wide. Local knowledge is required. There are depths of 2 m in the harbour at HW springs, bottom silt over rock except in the elbow of South Pier where sand accumulates. Beadnell Point affords good protection and there is little sea in the harbour other than in SE gales.

Newton Haven
5.112

1 Newton Haven (55°31′N 1°37′W) is an opening in the rocks abreast the village of Low Newton-by-the-Sea. The haven with depths of 3·5 m is formed by Fills (5.101) and Emblestone, a drying rocky ledge, on its E and S sides. It is exposed to heavy seas during strong winds between N and ENE and should only be used with local knowledge.

Craster Harbour
5.113

1 **General information.** Craster Harbour (55°28′N 1°35′W) is formed by two piers, the N pier is 76 m long and the S pier 91 m long and marked by the base of a tower. The harbour which dries has depths of 4 m at HW springs.

2 **Directions for entering harbour.** Little Carr and Great Carr are two drying ledges lying N and S of the harbour respectively. Little Carr is marked by a concrete beacon and the recommended track lies to the W of the beacon when entering harbour. Local knowledge is required.

Boulmer Haven
5.114

1 **General information.** Boulmer Haven (55°25′N 1°35′W) is a small drying harbour among the rocks within the N part of Marmouth Scars, a rocky ledge off Seaton Point (5.101). The entrance, named The Marmouth, is 37 m wide and dries.

2 **Directions for entering harbour.** The alignment of the leading beacons close S of Boulmer village leads through The Marmouth to the Haven:

Front beacon (red and white, white triangular topmark, 10 m in height) (55°24′·9N 1°34′·9W).
Rear beacon (red and white, topmark two red triangles points together, 11 m in height) (55 m W of front beacon).

Local knowledge is required.

Fluke Hole
5.115

1 **General information.** Fluke Hole (55°24′N 1°35′W) is a small bay between the S end of Marmouth Scars, off Seaton Point (5.101) and Marden Rocks which dry. Local knowledge is required.

Anchorage is available in depths of 5 m, 5 cables SSE of Seaton Point. This anchorage is used by coasters on a temporary basis during N winds.

Aln Harbour
5.116

1 **General information.** Aln Harbour (55°23′N 1°37′W) is formed by the lower reach of River Aln. It is little used except for a few fishing boats and recreational craft which lie aground at LW. Alnmouth village, with a conspicuous church spire, is on the N side of the harbour and Church Hill, 13 m high, on the S side.

Alnmouth

Aln Harbour from ENE (5.116)
(Original dated 2000)

(Photograph - Air Images)

Depths at HW springs are 3·5 m both at the bar and in the harbour.

2 **Harbour.** Some protection is afforded to the harbour during N winds by the foul ground off Seaton Point

(5.101), but in E gales there is a heavy sea. There is a considerable scend in the harbour but this is lessened if the sea breaks outside the bar. However the entrance is not considered as dangerous as those of some of the neighbouring harbours.

3   **Directions.** The channel is easiest after freshets, which occur in the winter, but the width of the channel and the position of the bar is constantly changing and local knowledge is required.

Anchorage, as indicated on the chart, is available for vessels waiting the tide in a depth of 3·4 m, 8 cables ESE of Alnmouth Church on the alignment (198°) of Birling Carrs (5.101) with Warkworth Castle.

Coquet Road

Chart 1627 plan of Warkworth Harbour
5.117

1   **General information.** Coquet Road (55°20′N 1°33′W) lies between Coquet Flat, which extends 6 cables N of Coquet island and the spit with Pan Bush at its N extremity. Both Pan Bush and Coquet Flat are covered by red sectors of Coquet Light (5.100), which is on the SE side of the island. Coquet Road is sheltered from the SE, through S to NW, but is otherwise exposed and should only be used in an emergency. In particular a dangerous sea builds up over Pan Bush and the shoals to its N.

2   **Tidal streams.** In Coquet Road and Coquet Channel the S-going stream commences at −0515 HW Tyne and the N-going stream at +0045 HW Tyne. The stream is not strong in the Coquet Road but the S-going stream runs strongly across North Steel, a drying rocky ledge extending 2½ cables N of Coquet Island. In Coquet Channel the streams run strongly SE-NW when the rocks off Hauxley Point are dry but more N-S when the rocks are covered.

3   **Directions.** From a position N of Coquet Road the alignment (181°) of Hauxley Point (55°19′N 1°33′W) with the point 6 cables S of it leads between Pan Bush (5.108) and Coquet Flat into Coquet Road.

COQUET ISLAND TO BLYTH

General information

Chart 156
Route
5.118

1   From a position E of Coquet Island (55°20′N 1°32′W) the route leads 14½ miles S to a position SE of Blyth.

Topography
5.119

1   Hauxley Point, which is on the mainland 1 mile SW of Coquet Island, and its vicinity are fronted by drying rocky ledges extending up to 6 cables offshore. Bondicarr Bush, the extremity of the ledges and rocks, is 5 miles N of Snab Point. Druridge Bay, which lies between the two, has a low, sandy coast backed by moderately high land. From Snab Point to Newbiggin Point (5.123), 3 miles SSE, the coast is low and sandy and fronted by rocky ledges in most places. Between Newbiggin Point and Link End (5.123) near the entrance to Blyth Harbour, lies Cambois Bay. The bay is rocky as far as River Wansbeck, at its mid-point, thence sandy for its S half. Two outfalls, the S of which is unmarked, extend into the bay as shown on the chart.

Rescue
5.120

1   There are Coastal Rescue Teams at Newbiggin and Blyth; see 1.67.

An all-weather lifeboat is stationed at Blyth; inshore lifeboats are stationed at Blyth and Newbiggin. See 1.72.

Tidal stream
5.121

1   Tidal streams run in the direction of the coast and are of no great strength except off salient points where there may be eddies. They are shown on the chart and in *Admiralty Tidal Stream Atlas: North Sea, Northwestern Part.*

Directions
(continued from 5.102)

Principal marks
5.122

1   **Landmarks:**
    Coquet Lighthouse (55°20′N 1°32′W) (5.100).
    Chimney (red obstruction lights) (55°12′N 1°31′W) at an aluminium smelting plant.
    Tower (55°11′·4N 1°30′·3W).

2   Two wind turbines with white towers (lighted: 57 m in height) on yellow bases standing on North Spit (55°08′·2N 1°29′·4W).
    East Pier Lighthouse (white tower, 14 m in height) (55°07′N 1°29′W) at Blyth.
    Nine wind turbines (55°07′N 1°29′W) on Blyth East Pier.

3   **Major lights:**
    Coquet Light (above).
    East Pier Light (above).

Coquet Island to Blyth
5.123

1   From a position E of Coquet Island the coastal route leads S to a position SE of Blyth, passing (with positions from Beacon Point (55°12′N 1°30′W)):
    E of Hauxley Head (7½ miles NNW), the E extremity of the drying ledges off Hauxley Point (5.119). Open cast mines are visible S of Hauxley Point. Thence:

2   E of Bondicarr Bush (7 miles N) (5.119), thence:
    E of Northern Hill (6 miles N), a rocky patch off the N end of Druridge Bay, thence:
    E of Cresswell Skeres (3 miles N), two offshore rocky patches, thence:
    E of Snab Point (2 miles NNW) (5.119), thence:

3   E of Newbiggin Ness (7 cables SE), a shoal 4 cables E of Newbiggin Point. Between the point, which is 12 m high, and Beacon Point to the N, the coast is fringed by drying reefs and rocks up to 4 cables offshore. A light buoy (special) marks the seaward end of a sewer outfall 1 mile S of Newbiggin Ness, and a diffuser with a least depth of 12·2 m lies 2 miles S of Newbiggin Ness, at the seaward end of an outfall extending 1½ miles from the shore. Thence:

4   To a position SE of East Pier Lighthouse (4¾ miles S) at the head of East Pier and 8 cables SSE of Link End (55°07′·7N 1°29′·9W) (Chart 1626). Link End is the SE extremity of a low and sandy peninsular having rocky ledges extending up to 3 cables to seaward. These dangers are further extended by North Spit and South Spit, two shoals,

respectively 5 cables NE and 5 cables E of Link End. Two wind turbines (5.122) stand on North Spit.

Useful marks
5.124

1 Shirlaw Pike (55°20′N 1°51′W) (Chart 1192).
Cresswell Hall (cupola) (55°14′N 1°33′W).
Newbiggin Church (spire) (55°11′N 1°30′W).
Sculpture (uncharted) on Newbiggin breakwater (55°10′·9N 1°30′·6W).
(Directions continue for coastal passage S at 5.155 and for Blyth at 5.141)

Anchorages and landing
5.125

1 **Anchorage** may be obtained in Druridge Bay (55°16′N 1°33′W) (5.119) in depths of 9 m to 11 m about 2½ miles N of Snab Point (5.119).

Anchorage may be obtained in Newbiggin Bay, which lies between Newbiggin Point (55°11′N 1°30′W) (5.123) and Spital Point (8 cables SW), in depths between 5 m and 9 m. The anchorage is sheltered from NW winds.

Chart 1627 plan of Warkworth Harbour

2 **Landing** may be made by small boats in Hauxley Haven (55°19′N 1°32′W), a small opening in the rocks close S of Hauxley Point (5.119).

BLYTH
General information
Chart 1626
Position
5.126

1 Blyth Harbour (55°06′·98N 1°29′·29W) lies at the mouth of the River Blyth.

Function
5.127

1 Blyth is a commercial port handling alumina, aluminium, forest products, grain, animal feeds, fertilisers, aggregates, coal and general cargoes including containers and RoRo. The port contains a fishing harbour and a marina.
The population is about 35 000.

Port limits
5.128

1 The port limits extend up to 1¼ miles from the entrance, covering the port and the immediate approaches, and are shown on the chart.

Traffic
5.129

1 In 2008, the port was visited by 346 vessels totalling 1·0 million dwt.

Port Authority
5.130

1 Blyth Harbour Commission, South Harbour, Blyth Harbour, Northumberland, NE24 3PB.

Blyth Harbour from SE (5.126)
(Original dated 2000)

(Photograph – Air Images)

Limiting conditions

Controlling depths
5.131

1 The approach channel from the Fairway Light Buoy to the heads of the breakwaters, which is about 1 cable wide, is dredged to 8·5 m. Within the harbour, there is a least depth (2009) of 7·6 m in the fairway as far as Alcan Bulk Terminal (5.145) and 6·7 m as far as Battleship Wharf (5.145).

Deepest and longest berths
5.132

1 Alcan Bulk Terminal and Battleship Wharf (both 5.145).

Tidal levels
5.133

1 See *Admiralty Tide Tables Volume 1.* Mean spring range about 4·2 m; mean neap range about 2·2 m.

Tidal heights are increased by strong N winds and decreased by strong S winds.

Maximum size of vessel handled
5.134

1 Vessels up to 175 m in length and draught of 9·0 m can use the Alcan Bulk Terminal berth. Vessels up to 185 m in length and draught 9·0 m can use Battleship Wharf.

2 With the approval of the Harbour Master, larger ships may be accommodated.

Arrival information

Port radio
5.135

1 For details of Blyth Port Control see *Admiralty List of Radio Signals Volume 6 (1).*

Notice of ETA required
5.136

1 Twenty four hours' notice of entry is required. VHF contact should be established with the port 2 hours and 1 hour prior to arrival.

Outer anchorage
5.137

1 Anchorage can be obtained in a position about 1 mile E of East Pierhead in depths of 17 m (Chart 1935).

✳ WK 12/10

Pilotage and tugs
5.138

1 **Pilotage** iscompulsory for vessels over 50 m in length, and for vessels towing other vessels or objects when the combined length of tow exceeds 50 m. For further details see *Admiralty List of Radio Signals Volume 6(1).*

~~sub standard or hampered in any way;~~
~~commanded by a Master who is visiting the port for the first time;~~
~~without a fully corrected copy of chart BA1626 or equivalent.~~

2 The pilot normally boards within 2 miles of the harbour entrance but in bad weather the pilot boards in the vicinity of the pierheads.

Tugs can be ordered on request from the Tyne. A small harbour pushing tug of 600 hp is available. There is a boat service for running lines.

Harbour

General layout
5.139

1 The harbour, which is artificial and formed from the course of River Blyth, is about 2 miles long running NNW/SSE. It is protected from the E by Link End which culminates in East Pier extending a farther 8 cables to the SSE.

2 Most of the berths lie along the river. South Harbour is close W of the harbour entrance and there is a tidal basin at the N end of the harbour. Lights are exhibited from the extremities of most jetties, piers and berths.

Natural conditions
5.140

1 **Tidal streams** in the dredged areas in the approaches to Blyth might set across the line of the leading lights.

In the harbour the streams are of no great strength and run as follows:

Time from HW		Remarks
−0600	Blyth	In-going stream commences
+0015	Blyth	Out-going stream commences

2 Details of the streams to seaward are shown on Chart 1935 and in *Admiralty Tidal Stream Atlas: North Sea, Northwestern Part.*

Directions for entering harbour
(Continued from 5.124)

Principal marks
5.141

1 **Landmarks:**
East Pier Lighthouse (55°07'·0N 1°29'·2W) (5.122).
Tower (55°06'·3N 1°30'·0W) at a cemetery.
Two wind turbines on North Spit (55°08'·2N 1°28'·4W) (5.123).
Nine wind turbines positioned along East Pier (5.122).

2 **Major Light:**
East Pier Light (above).

Approach
5.142

1 **Outer Leading Lights:**
Front light (orange diamond on framework tower) (55°07'·4N 1°29'·8W).
Rear light (orange diamond on framework tower) (180 m NW of front light).

2 From a position about 2 miles SE of the harbour entrance the alignment (324°) of Blyth Outer Leading Lights leads through the approach channel and harbour entrance to a position 3 cables inside the entrance, passing ~~(with positions from the entrance):~~

✳ WK 24/11

~~SW of Blyth Light Buoy (starboard hand) (5½ cables SE).~~

3 Through the harbour entrance, which is 1 cable wide facing SSE and lies between East Pierhead on which stands the lighthouse (5.122) and West Pierhead on which stands a light (white tower, 4 m in height).

5.143

1 **Link End Inner Leading Lights:**
Front light (white 6-sided tower, 4 m in height) (55°07'·7N 1°29'·9W).
Rear light (white triangle on mast, 7 m in height) (87 m NNW of front light).
The alignment (338°) of Link End Inner Leading Lights leads through the south part of the harbour.

Basins and berths

South Harbour
5.144

1 There are two general cargo berths: North Quay has an alongside depth of 8·5 m and can accept vessels up to 200 m LOA; West Quay is 170 m long with an alongside depth of 7·3 m and has a RoRo pontoon at its S end.

River berths east side
5.145

1 Alcan Bulk Terminal has a berth 152 m long and a depth alongside of 9 m.

Battleship Wharf, lies 5½ cables NW of Alcan Terminal. The quay provides four berths and has a total length of 435 m. No 1 Berth is 120 m long with an alongside depth of 5·5 m and is used by coasters. The three remaining berths have alongside depths ranging from 8·5 m to 9·0 m.

River berths west side
5.146

1 There are six berths of which Dun Cow Quay is the longest and deepest, being 220 m in length with an alongside depth of 8·5 m. A RoRo berth at the NW end of Wimborne Quay is reported (2008) to be in poor condition. Bates Wharf, a bulk loading terminal, is constructed of timber and has a depth alongside of 7·6 m.

Turning Basin
5.147

1 The Turning Basin, the NW limits of which are marked by four beacons, lies to the W of Battleship Wharf. The Turning Basin is dredged to a depth of 6·7 m.

Port services

Repairs
5.148

1 Deck and engine repairs can be carried out.

Other facilities
5.149

1 Refuse disposal; Ship Sanitation Certificates issued (1.92); hospitals.

Supplies
5.150

1 Water at all loading and discharging berths; fuel by road tanker.

BLYTH TO TYNEMOUTH

General information

Chart 1935
Route
5.151

1 From a position SE of the entrance to Blyth Harbour (55°07′N 1°29′W) the route leads 5 miles SE to a position ENE of Tynemouth.

Topography
5.152

1 Initially the coast is low and sandy as far as Seaton Sluice, 2 miles SSE. Thence there is a rocky cliff, fringed by ledges extending up to 3 cables offshore, which extends to Saint Mary's Island (5.156) 1¼ miles farther SE. The island is connected by a causeway to Curry's Point, 1 cable SW. From Curry's Point to Brown's Point, 2 miles SSE, the coast has a sandy foreshore backed by a bank. Brown's Point itself is low and fringed by rocky ledges. The final stretch of 1½ miles to Tynemouth is fronted by rocks and ledges.

Rescue
5.153

1 There is a Coastal Rescue Team at Blyth and Volunteer Life Brigades at Tynemouth and South Shields; see 1.67.

An all-weather lifeboat and an inshore lifeboat are stationed at Tynemouth; an inshore lifeboat is stationed at Cullercoats. See 1.72.

Tidal streams
5.154

1 Tidal streams are given on the chart and in *Admiralty Tidal Stream Atlas: North Sea, Northwestern Part*.

Directions
(continued from 5.124)

Principal marks
5.155

1 **Landmarks:**
East Pier Lighthouse (55°07′N 1°29′W) (5.122).
Saint Mary's Island Lighthouse (disused) (white tower, 37 m in height) (55°04′N 1°27′W).

Saint Mary's Island Lighthouse from NE (5.155)
(Original dated 1995)

(Photograph - Simmons-Aerofilm Ltd.)

White building (55°03′·4N 1°27′·4W).
White dome (55°02′·9N 1°26′·9W).
Saint George's Church (spire) (55°01′·8N 1°25′·9W).
Congregational Church (spire) (55°01′·0N 1°25′·5W).

2 **Major lights:**
East Pier Light (above).
North Pier Light (Tynemouth) (grey round masonry tower, white lantern, 23 m in height) (55°00′·9N 1°24′·2W).

Blyth to Tynemouth
5.156

1 From a position SE of Blyth Harbour (55°07′N 1°29′W) the coastal route leads SE to a position ENE of Tynemouth, passing (with positions from Tynemouth entrance):
Clear, depending on draught, of a wreck with a depth of 10·2 m (5½ miles NNW), thence:
2 NE of Saint Mary's Island (4 miles NNW) on which stands a disused lighthouse (5.155). The island lies towards the seaward extremity of rocky ledges and off-lying rocks which encumber the coast in that vicinity. Thence:

Clear of a light buoy (special) (3¼ miles NNW) marking an explosives dumping area. Vessels should avoid anchoring in its close vicinity. Thence:

3   NE of Bellhues Rocks (1 mile N) which lie 8 cables ESE of Brown's Point (5.152) and within the green sector (161°–179°) of Tynemouth South Pier Light (5.178). Whitley Bay lies between Brown's Point and Saint Mary's Island. Thence:

To a position ENE of Tynemouth.

(Directions continue for coastal passage S at 6.13 and for Port of Tyne at 5.177)

Minor harbour

Cullercoats
5.157

1   A boat harbour (55°02′N 1°26′W) lies between Brown's Point (5.152) and George Point, 2½ cables S of Brown's Point. The harbour is approached through a gap in the ledges.

2   **Leading lights.** The alignment (256°) of Cullercoats Leading Lights leads into the boat harbour:

Front light (post, 3 m in height) (55°02′·0N 1°25′·9W).

Rear light (column, 4 m in height) (38 m WSW of front light).

Local knowledge is required.

PORT OF TYNE

General information

Charts 1935, 1934
Position
5.158

1   Port of Tyne (55°00′·78N 1°24′·13W) lies along both banks of River Tyne which enters the sea at Tynemouth (55°01′N 1°25′W). From the entrance at Tynemouth, the river is navigable to Newcastle Swing Bridge (5.181) 10 miles up river. The river banks are heavily industrialised and lined with numerous berths.

2   Tynemouth lies on the N bank of the river, as do North Shields, Wallsend, the city of Newcastle upon Tyne, Scotswood and Lemington. The towns of South Shields, Jarrow, Hebburn, Gateshead and Blaydon lie on the S bank.

Function
5.159

1   Port of Tyne is a busy port, with a diverse trade ranging from automobiles, grain, coal, timber, oil and chemicals to scrap metal and sea-dredged aggregates. Vehicle and passenger ferries use the port, and there are container handling facilities. The port is a base for the offshore oil and gas industry.

2   Ship conversion and repair are also significant activities. Modules for North Sea oilfields have been constructed within the port.

North Shields is an important fishing port.

The population of Tyneside is about 795 000 and that of Newcastle upon Tyne is about 256 000.

Port limits
5.160

1   The seaward limit of the port authority is bounded by an arc, radius 1 mile, drawn from the entrance between the breakwaters. The Port of Tyne Authority exercises certain powers outside its seaward limit (5.173).

Traffic
5.161

1   In 2008, the port was visited by 2100 vessels and handled about 5 million tonnes of cargo.

Port Authority
5.162

1   The Port of Tyne Authority, Maritime House, Tyne Dock, South Shields NE34 9PT. The Harbour Master's Office is at Neville House, Bell Street, North Shields NE30 1LJ.

Tynemouth from NE (5.158)
(Original dated 2000)

(Photograph - Air Images)

Limiting conditions

Controlling depths
5.163

1 Maintained depths are as follows:

Tyne Piers (Entrance Reach) to Jarrow Quay Corner (1°28′·2W)	9·1 m
Jarrow Quay Corner to Jarrow Staith W end (1°30′·7W)	6·0 m
Jarrow Staith W end to Tyne Bridge (1°36′·3W)	5·2 m

West of the Swing Bridge depths are not maintained.

2 Silting is liable to occur and the VTS (5.169) should be consulted for the latest information on depths.

Vertical clearances
5.164

1 A power cable, safe overhead clearance 64 m, crosses the River Tyne at Jarrow (1°28′·4W).

Seven bridges span the River Tyne at Newcastle. The minimum vertical clearance of these bridges is 23 m. See 5.181 for details of bridges.

Deepest and longest berth
5.165

1 Riverside Quay (S bank, 1°27′W) (5.185).

Tidal levels
5.166

1 North Shields (55°00′W, 1°26′W): mean spring range about 4·3 m; mean neap range about 2·1 m.

Newcastle upon Tyne (54°58′N 1°36′W): mean spring range about 4·5 m; mean neap range about 2·2 m.

See *Admiralty Tide Tables Volume 1*.

Maximum size of vessel handled
5.167

1 There are no length or beam restrictions at the harbour entrance. Riverside Quay (5.185) has an alongside depth of 12·1 m and the adjacent swinging circle a diameter of 360 m. In 2008 the berth accommodated a vessel of 225 m LOA and draught 12·17 m.

Local weather and sea state
5.168

1 The heaviest seas in the entrance are caused during NE gales when the out-going stream is running strongly. In such conditions it is preferable to enter while the in-going stream is still running, noting that at this time it also sets across the entrance. At other times there should be no difficulty in entering the port.

2 In N gales vessels should keep close under the lee of North Pier and in S gales, especially when the out-going stream is running, close under the lee of South Pier.

Arrival information

Vessel traffic service
5.169

1 An Information Service, Tyne VTS, is in operation for the control of shipping; for details see *Admiralty List of Radio Signals Volume 6 (1)*. Positions of the reporting points are shown on the chart.

Tyne VTS is situated in North Shields (55°00′·4N 1°26′·4W).

Notice of ETA required
5.170

1 All vessels over 50 gt should send their ETA, together with a request for a pilot, to Tyne VTS 24 hours in advance, or, on sailing from the previous port if within 24 hours steaming. ETA should be confirmed by VHF approximately 2 hours in advance. See *Admiralty List of Radio Signals Volume 6 (1)*.

Outer anchorage
5.171

1 An outer anchorage, whose limits are shown on the chart, lies 1½ miles NE of North Pier head. Depth in the middle of the anchorage is about 27 m.

Pilotage and tugs
5.172

1 Pilotage is compulsory for all vessels of 50 m LOA or more with the following exceptions:

Vessels being moved within the harbour outside the main navigable channel.

Vessels transiting the seaward approaches (5.173) bound for another port.

Vessels anchoring in the outer anchorage.

Vessels exempt by law.

2 Normally the pilot boards within 3 miles of the pier heads. In bad weather the pilot vessel waits inside the harbour entrance and will lead a vessel into the harbour where the pilot will board. The pilot vessel has a black hull, orange wheelhouse and "PILOTS" painted on both sides.

Tugs are available at 3 hours notice.

Traffic regulations
5.173

1 **Seaward Approaches** is defined as the sector with a radius of 3 miles which lies between the light on North Pier bearing 242° and the light on South Pier bearing 288°. Except in an emergency or with prior permission of the Harbour Master, no vessel should anchor or stop in the seaward approaches in such a manner as to cause an obstruction to other vessels approaching or leaving the port.

2 **Manoeuvering regulations.** *The International Regulations for Preventing Collisions at Sea (1972)* apply, subject to certain bye-laws of which the most important are:

Vessels shall only enter, cross, or turn in the fairway when the fairway is clear and in such a manner as shall not impede or endanger any other vessel.

3 If it is unsafe for two vessels to pass one another when proceeding in opposite directions, the vessel which is proceeding against the tide shall give way to the other vessel.

A vessel intending to turn about in the river shall sound four short and rapid blasts followed by one short blast if turning to starboard, or, two short blasts if turning to port. This signal is to be repeated from time to time during the turning manoeuvre.

4 No vessel shall proceed at a speed greater than 6kn over the ground in the port W of Herd Groyne Light (55°00′·5N 1°25′·4W).

5 **Vessels under 20 m LOA** should report to Tyne VTS when approaching the harbour entrance and on leaving their berth in the river.

6 **Wrecks** are marked in accordance with the IALA Maritime Buoyage System (Region A).

7   **Quayside obstructions** likely to damage vessels when berthing or lying alongside will be marked by a yellow flag placed adjacent to the obstruction and illuminated by night

Harbour

General layout
5.174

1   The majority of berths are riverside. Tyne Dock is the only enclosed dock.

For details see 5.183 to 5.186.

Traffic signals
5.175

1   International Port Traffic Signals Nos 2 and 3 are used to control traffic into and out of Tyne Dock (5.184). The signals are displayed at both ends of the lock.

Natural conditions
5.176

1   **Tidal streams.** The tidal stream sets SSE across the harbour entrance about 4 hours before HW Tyne, with spring rates in excess of 1 kn. The tidal stream reverses to a NNW direction 2 hours after HW Tyne. See Chart 1935.

Within the harbour the tidal streams run in the direction of the channel but set towards the outer bank at the bends in the river. In The Narrows (55°00′·5N 1°26′·0W) the flood tide has a rate of 3 kn at springs and the ebb tide a rate of 2½ kn.

2   The streams set as follows:

Position	In-going begins from HW Tyne	Out-going begins from HW Tyne
River entrance	−0530	+0040
Whitehill Point	−0540	+0020
Newcastle Quay	−0540	+0010

3   Due to the elevations of its sources in Cumberland and the borders of Scotland, River Tyne is subject to sudden and heavy freshets, when an immense body of water is discharged. In these conditions both the duration and rate of the out-going stream are increased and the in-going stream correspondingly reduced.

Wind. Much of the length of the river is in a fairly deep valley which tends to funnel the wind up and down river. However, there are places where this effect ceases and unexpected cross-winds can be experienced.

4   **Climate information:** see 1.142 and 1.149.

Directions for entering harbour
(continued from 5.156)

Principal marks
5.177

1   **Landmarks** (Approaches):
   White building (55°03′·4N 1°27′·4W).
   White dome (55°02′·9N 1°26′·8W).
   Lighthouses (disused) (55°00′N 1°26′W) at North Shields.
   Saint George's Church (spire) (55°01′·8N 1°25′·9W).
   Congregational Church (spire) (55°01′·0N 1°25′·5W).
   North Pier Lighthouse (grey round masonry tower, white lantern, 23 m in height) (55°00′·9N 1°24′·2W).
   Water Tower (54°58′N 1°24′W) at Cleadon Waterworks.
   Lighthouse (disused) (54°58′·2N 1°21′·9W).

Lighthouses (Disused) from SE (5.177)
(Original dated 2006)

(Photograph - Crown opyright)

2   **Major lights:**
   North Pier Light (above).
   Herd Groyne Directional Light (red pile structure, red and white lantern) (55°00′·5N 1°25′·4W).

Herd Groyne Light from NE (5.177)
(Original dated 2006)

(Photograph - Crown Copyright)

3   **Landmarks** (River passage):
   Tynemouth Head and castle buildings (55°01′N 1°25′W).
   Collingwood's Monument (55°00′·9N 1°25′·2W).
   South Shields Town Hall (cupola) (54°59′·7N 1°25′·8W).
   North Shields Gasworks (55°00′·2N 1°27′·3W).
   Pylon (54°59′·1N 1°28′·4W) on Jarrow Quay.

Approaches
5.178

1   From a position about 2 miles ENE of the harbour entrance the white sector (246½°–251½°) of Herd Groyne Directional Light (5.177), shown throughout 24 hours, leads to the harbour entrance which is 366 m wide and lies between North Pier Light (5.177) and South Pier Light (grey round stone tower, red and white lantern, 12 m in height).

Herd Groyne Light   *Lighthouses (Disused)*

Entrance to River Tyne from ENE (5.178)

(Original dated 2007)

(Photograph - Crown Copyright)

Several wrecks lie in the approach to the harbour and within the entrance itself. However, the depth over them is greater than the maintained depth in Entrance Reach (5.163).

Harbour Entrance to The Narrows
5.179

1   From a position in the centre of the harbour entrance, when the white sector of Herd Groyne Directional Light should be disregarded, the route leads WSW through Entrance Reach and is marked by light buoys (lateral). The route passes (with positions from North Pier Light):

2   NNW of Herd Groyne (8 cables WSW), marked by a light (5.177) at its E extremity, thence:

To a position SSE of Fish Quay (1 mile WSW), which is 1 cable W of No 1 Groyne. No 1 Groyne is marked by a light (green metal beacon, 4 m in height). The Narrows lie between Fish Quay and The Lawe on the S bank of the river.

The Narrows to Newcastle upon Tyne
5.180

1   From The Narrows to Newcastle upon Tyne the river consists of a series of reaches with maintained depths. There are few navigational marks although lights are exhibited from most piers, jetties and berths.

2   In sequence the reaches are:

Shields Harbour Reach, (1½ miles in length). The entrances to Royal Quays Marina and Tyne Dock (5.184) lie within this reach. A ferry plies between North and South Shields as shown on the chart.

3   Long Reach, (2½ miles in length). A swinging area of about 360 m in diameter is situated at the E end of the reach. An overhead power cable (5.164) spans the river 3 cables W of the swinging area.

Bill Reach, (1½ miles in length). A light beacon (starboard hand) standing about 1 cable offshore marks the inside of the bend at the S end of the

4   Saint Anthony's Reach (5 cables in length). The bend at the W end is marked by a light beacon (green structure, 10 m in height) close SW of St Anthony's Point. On the S bank there is a light beacon (red column) 1 cable S of the point.

5   Felling Reach (7 cables in length). Saint Peter's Light Beacon (green pile structure with platform) stands on the N bank, 5 cables NW of Saint Anthony's Point.

~~Felling Reach~~
~~Light Beacon (red pile structure with platform, 7 m in height) stands on the S bank, 3½ cables WNW~~

~~of Saint Anthony's Point and Saint Peter's Light~~
~~Beacon (green pile structure with platform) stands~~
~~on the N bank, 5 cables NW of the point.~~

6   Saint Peter's Reach, (8 cables in length). Newcastle Quayside (5.186) and The Newcastle Bridges (5.181) commence at the NW end of the reach.

Newcastle bridges
5.181

1   Requests to open the Millenium and Swing Bridges should be made to Tyne VTS 24 hours in advance. The Swing Bridge can only be opened in daylight hours.

2   The seven Newcastle bridges spanning the River Tyne are:

Millennium Bridge (54°58′N 1°36′W) a single arch footbridge with a clear channel width of 30 m. When closed there is a vertical clearance of 3·7 m ...and when open a vertical clearance of 24 m. At all times the following lights are shown from the bridge:
An occulting white light is shown from the centre line.
A flashing green light is exhibited from the N side.
A flashing red light is exhibited from the S side.
A flashing white light is exhibited from the support span when the bridge is open to indicate the centre of the bridge and the best point of passage.

Tyne Bridge, 2½ cables above Millennium Bridge. A single span road bridge with a width of 114 m and a vertical clearance of 24 m.

3   **Newcastle Swing Bridge**, ¾ cable above Tyne Bridge, has four spans of which the centre two swing on a central pier to provide a channel 31 m wide on the N side and 29 m wide on the S side. When closed there is a vertical clearance of 3·8 m.

4   **Newcastle High Level Bridge**, ¼ cable above the swing bridge. The swing bridge central pier projects under the bridge dividing the channel, giving a N channel 27 m wide and a S channel 30 m wide. The vertical clearance is 23 m.

Queen Elizabeth II Bridge, 2¼ cables above the High Level Bridge. The vertical clearance is 24 m.

5   **King Edward Bridge**, 1 cable above the Queen Elizabeth II Bridge. The vertical clearance is 24 m.

Redheugh Bridge 1 cable above King Edward Bridge. The vertical clearance is 28 m.

River Tyne above Newcastle
5.182

1   Mariners wishing to navigate above Redheugh Bridge should consult the VTS to check that sufficient water is available.

Shields Harbour Reach from NNE (5.183)
(Original dated 2000)

(Photograph - Air Images)

The river is crossed by several bridges and power cables between Newcastle and Lemington. Scotswood Rail Bridge is the lowest, with a vertical clearance of 5·4 m.

Basins and berths

Shields Harbour Reach
5.183

1   Fish Quay and Western Quay at the N end of the reach are used by fishing vessels.

Northumbrian Quay, used primarily by cruise ships, has a length of 335 m and depth 9·0 m. It is the largest berth in the reach and lies on the river wall forming Royal Quays Marina. To SW of Northumbrian Quay lie No 3 and No 4 RoRo berths at the International Passenger Terminal and Whitehill Point Jetty, which is used for the import of cars.

Tyne Dock
5.184

1   Tyne Dock (54°59'·1N 1°26'·9W) is a non-tidal basin which is entered via half-tide gates through an entrance which is 21·3 m wide. There is a depth in the outer basin of 3·6 m and within the dock between 7·7 m and 6·7 m. There are two quays in the dock with a total length 440 m.

2   Vessels up to LOA 122 m, beam 19 m and draught 7·6 m can use the dock at HW springs.

Long Reach
5.185

1   Riverside Quay at the E end of Long Reach is the largest berth in Port of Tyne with a length of 540 m and a depth alongside of 12·1 m. The berth handles containerised and general cargoes. Tyne Bulk Terminal, depth alongside 12·1 m, is close W of Riverside Quay and Tyne Car Terminal, consisting of three jetties having depths alongside between 7·0 and 10·0 m, is close W again. On the N bank

of the river there are three tanker berths, one of which may be used as a tanker cleaning berth. To the W of these berths is a sludge jetty and W again Howdon Jetty is used for the discharge of aggregates. Northumberland Dock, largely reclaimed except for a small tidal basin, lies between the tanker berths and the sludge jetty.

Newcastle
5.186

1   Newcastle Quayside (54°58'N 1°36'W) lies on the N bank and extends upriver from Saint Peter's Reach to Tyne Bridge. Tyne VTS should be consulted for latest depths.

Port services

Repairs
5.187

1   Repairs of all kinds can be carried out. There is one dry dock 259 m in length and 44 m wide and several slipways.

Other facilities
5.188

1   Ship Sanitation Certificates issued (1.92); hospitals at North and South Shields, Wallsend and Newcastle.

Facilities for reception of oily waste and for the disposal of garbage vary depending upon the berth. The VTS should be contacted before arrival.

Supplies
5.189

1   All types of fuel oil; fresh water at most berths or by water boat.

Communications
5.190

1   There are daily ferry services to IJmuiden. There is an airport at Newcastle serving UK and European cities.

Port Authority
6.19

1   Port of Sunderland, Capstan House, Greenwells Quay, South Dock, Barrack Street, Sunderland, SR1 2BU. Website: www.portofsunderland.org.uk

Limiting conditions

Controlling depths
6.20

1   The entrance channel within the outer harbour has a maintained depth of 7·8 m and a depth of 7·6 m is maintained in the outer part of the inner harbour for a distance of 5 cables. Thence there is a maintained depth of 5·7 m as far as Wearmouth Bridge (6.21).

2   **Caution.** Depths are maintained by dredging every two years and significant shoaling can occur towards the end of the intervening period. Because of silting and possible obstructions depths should be checked with the Harbour Master and reliance not placed solely on published data. Local charts showing depths and temporary obstructions can be obtained from the port authority.

Vertical clearance
6.21

1   The river is spanned by Wearmouth Bridge, 1 mile from the entrance, and close W by Sunderland Railway Bridge. The latter is the lower bridge, with a vertical clearance of 24 m; gauges either side of the bridge indicate the actual clearance and the height of tide. Queen Alexandra Bridge, 1¼ miles above the rail bridge, has a greater vertical clearance.

Deepest and longest berth
6.22

1   Corporation Quay (6.39).

Tidal levels
6.23

1   See *Admiralty Tide Tables Volume 1*. Mean spring range about 4·4 m; mean neap range about 2·2 m.

    Winds between WNW and NNE increase the height of sea level, and winds between SSW and SSE have the opposite effect.

Maximum size of vessel handled
6.24

1   Riverside berths 183 m LOA and 8·2 m draught; South Docks 141·8 m LOA and 8 m draught at MHWS (7·16 m at MHWN).

Local weather and sea state
6.25

1   Gales from the ENE and ESE send a heavy sea into the outer harbour. Souter Point (6.14) affords some protection to the entrance to the harbour during gales from the N.

Arrival information

Port operations
6.26

1   A port radio station is maintained. See *Admiralty List of Radio Signals Volume 6 (1)*.

2   **Traffic signal.** When there is a danger in the harbour, three red flashing lights disposed vertically are exhibited from a framework tower on Old North Pier (54°55'·1N 1°21'·6W). This signal indicates vessels must not enter or leave harbour.

Notice of ETA required
6.27

1   See 1.45. Twelve hours notice of ETA is required with amendments at least 2 hours in advance.

Outer anchorage
6.28

1   There is an anchorage 1 mile E of Roker Pier Lighthouse (6.13), good holding ground, in depths of 12 m to 14 m. Care must be taken to avoid wrecks in the vicinity.

Pilotage and tugs
6.29

1   **Pilotage** is compulsory within the South Docks complex, upriver of the W end of Corporation Quay and for vessels carrying dangerous substances, under tow or with any mechanical or navigational defect.

2   The pilot usually boards within a 1½ mile radius of Roker Pier Lighthouse from a vessel, similar to a fishing vessel, painted black with red boot topping and the word "Pilots" forward on the wheelhouse. There is also a black pilot launch.

    In poor visibility a vessel requiring a pilot should sound morse code letter G.

    Tugs are available but are supplied either from Newcastle or Teesport.

Traffic regulations
6.30

1   Tanker distinguishing signals are required to be shown when nearing or in the harbour. By day the signal is a red flag and by night a red light at the masthead or where it can best be seen, in addition to other lights required by law.

Harbour

General layout
6.31

1   The port consists of an outer and inner harbour. The outer harbour is formed by two piers, Roker Pier to the N and New South Pier to the S. Roker Pier curves 4½ cables ESE and New South Pier curves 4 cables NNE from the coast. Rocky ledges extend up to 3½ cables offshore N and S of the two piers.

2   The inner harbour is entered between Old North Pier and Old South Pier which lie close to the entrance. There are a number of riverside berths and South Docks consisting of two enclosed docks, Hudson Dock and Hendon Dock, running S from the S bank of the river.

Traffic signals
6.32
1 South Docks traffic signals (Diagram 6.32) are displayed from the framework tower on Old North Pier and from a tower at No 3 Gateway at the N end of Hudson Dock when the docks are open for traffic. These lights are fixed lights, in contrast to the danger signal described at 6.26.

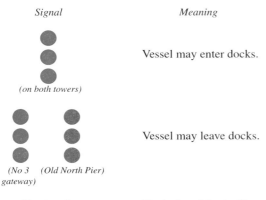

Signal	Meaning
(on both towers)	Vessel may enter docks.
(No 3 gateway) (Old North Pier)	Vessel may leave docks.
No signal	Dock closed for traffic.

Traffic signals (6.32)

Swing bridge
6.33
1 When the swing bridge is across the entrance to Hudson Dock, and the dock gates are open, two red lights disposed vertically are exhibited at the entrance to the dock. No signal is exhibited when the lock gates are shut.

A vessel may indicate that she wishes to enter or leave the dock by sounding a succession of "K"s in morse code.

Natural conditions
6.34
1 **Tidal streams** to seaward of the harbour entrance are given on the chart. In River Wear, which is subject to freshets, the streams in the vicinity of Sunderland run as follows:

Time from HW Tyne	Remarks
–0605	In-going stream commences
–0005	Out-going stream commences

2 **Flow.** After prolonged N winds a strong southerly flow with a rate of about 3 kn may be experienced in the approach to the harbour entrance.

Directions for entering harbour
(continued from 6.14)

Principal marks
6.35
1 **Landmarks:**
 Roker Pier Lighthouse (54°55′·3N 1°21′·1W) (6.13).
 Lighthouse (disused, white tower) (54°55′·9N 1°22′·0W).
 Blocks of Flats (54°55′·0N 1°22′·2W) (6.13).
 Blocks of Flats (54°54′·2N 1°22′·3W) (6.13).
 Chimney (54°53′·2N 1°21′·8W) at Sunderland Paper Mill.

2 **Major light:**
 Roker Pier Light (above).

Approach and entry
6.36
1 From a position ENE of the harbour entrance the line of bearing 251° of Old North Pierhead (54°55′·1N 1°21′·6W), on which stands a light (mast), leads through the outer harbour entrance whence the track alters WSW for the inner harbour entrance, passing (with positions from Old North Pier Light):
 SSE of the wreckage (7 cables ENE), least depth 7·2 m, thence:

2 To the outer harbour entrance (3 cables ENE), 200 m in width, lying between Roker Pierhead, on which stands Roker Pier Lighthouse (6.13), and an obstruction marked by a buoy (port hand) 40 m N of New South Pierhead. A light (white metal tower, 10 m in height) stands close to the pierhead. Thence:

3 To the inner harbour entrance which is 100 m wide lying between Old North Pier and Old South Pier, from which a light (red can on red metal framework tower) is exhibited.

Once clear of the entrance a direct approach can be made to the riverside berths and Half Tide Basin which leads to the enclosed docks.

Enclosed docks
6.37
1 The enclosed docks are entered at their N end through Half Tide Basin, which has a tidal swinging basin to its N. Half Tide Basin is entered through No 1 Gate which is 21·3 m wide with a depth over the sill of 9·6 m at MHWS.

2 Hudson Dock is entered from Half Tide Basin through No 3 Gate, which is 19·2 m wide between fenders and has a depth of 9·0 m over the sill at MHWS. The gates are normally open from 2 hours before to 30 minutes after HW, but vessels may lock in at any time provided notice is given by the previous HW and subject to the vessel's draught.

3 Hendon Dock is entered through a waterway at the S end of Hudson Dock which is 27 m wide and 62 m long with a depth of 9·4 m at MHWS.

Depths in the docks are not uniform and may be less than the depth over the entrance sill. See 6.20.

Useful mark
6.38
1 Saint Andrew's Church (tower) (54°55′·6N 1°22′·2W).

Basins and berths

Riverside berths
6.39
1 Corporation Quay, 323 m long, depth alongside 8·8 m. Greenwells Quay, with RoRo berth at S end, overall length 250 m, depth alongside 6·3 m.
Fish Quay, length 90 m, maintained depth at SW end 5·7 m.

2 Palmer's Hill Quay, Manor Quay and Strand Quay, all on the N side of the harbour, overall length 570 m, charted depths between 0·1 m and 4·0 m.

Wylam Wharf and Scotia Quay on the S side of the harbour, overall length 180 m, charted depths between 1·0 m and 1·4 m.

South Docks
6.40
1 Hudson Dock, 1490 m of quays, depths 6 m to 9 m. RoRo berth at N end of East Quay.

Hendon Dock, 700 m of quays, depth 9 m when newly dredged.

North Dock
6.41
1   North Dock is occupied by Sunderland Marina.

Port services

Repairs
6.42
1   All kinds of repairs can be undertaken.

There is a dry dock in Half Tide basin; length 115·3 m; breadth 16·6 m.

Other facilities
6.43
1   Hospital with helicopter landing site; Ship Sanitation Certificates issued (1.92); facilities for the reception of oily waste; diving services.

Supplies
6.44
1   Fuel oils by road tanker; fresh water; provisions.

SUNDERLAND TO TEES BAY

General information

Charts 152, 2567
Route
6.45
1   From a position ENE of Sunderland (54°55′N 1°22′W) the route leads 15 miles SSE to a position ESE of The Heugh, the E extremity of Hartlepool peninsula, which is the N entrance point to Tees Bay.

Topography
6.46
1   Initially the coast S of Sunderland is heavily industrialised, but this gives way to a grassy bank fringed by rocky ledges and shoals up to 4 cables offshore, as far as Seaham 5 miles SSE of Sunderland. From Seaham to The Heugh, 10 miles SSE, the coast is backed by cliffs between 20 and 30 m high. The coast itself is fronted by rocky ledges as far as Moorstack and Dogger Rocks which lie 3½ miles SSE of Seaham, thence it is composed of gravel and sand with the occasional rocky ledge as far as The Heugh which is low and rocky. The whole length of the coast from Sunderland to The Heugh is intersected by ravines known locally as denes. Castle Eden Denes, in the vicinity of Moorstack Rocks, is a nature reserve (1.61).

Submarine cable
6.47
1   An isolated submarine cable (experimental length 5 cables) lies 2¼ miles NE of Black Halls Point (54°44′·6N 1°16′·0W).

Rescue
6.48
1   There are Coastal Rescue Teams at Seaham and Hartlepool. See 1.67.

An all-weather lifeboat and an inshore lifeboat are stationed at Hartlepool. See 1.72.

Tidal streams
6.49
1   Tidal streams off the coast are weak. For details see charts and *Admiralty Tidal Stream Atlas: North Sea, Northwestern Part.*

Directions
(continued from 6.14)

Principal marks
6.50
1   **Landmarks:**

For marks in Sunderland see 6.35.
Chimney at Ryhope (54°51′·9N 1°22′·4W).
Ryhope Pumping Station (charted as water tower) (54°51′·8N 1°22′·7W) with a pronounced collar at the top.
Steetly Magnesite Works Chimney (54°42′·5N 1°12′·8W).

2   **Major Lights:**

Tynemouth North Pierhead Light (55°00′·9N 1°24′·2W) (5.155).
Roker Pier Light (54°55′·3N 1°21′·1W) (6.13).
The Heugh Light (white metal tower, 13 m in height) (54°41′·8N 1°10′·6W).

Other aid to navigation
6.51
1   **Racon:**

Tees Fairway Light Buoy (54°41′N 1°06′W).
For details see *Admiralty List of Radio Signals Volume 2.*

Sunderland to The Heugh
6.52
1   From a position ENE of Sunderland the route leads 15 miles SSE to a position ESE of The Heugh, passing (with positions from the entrance to Seaham Harbour (54°50′N 1°19′W)):

ENE of Hendon Rock (4 miles N); two wrecks lie 4 cables NE and the seaward end of an outfall lies 1 cable SSE. White Stones, a group of rocky shoals, lie 6 cables S of Hendon Rock. Thence:

2   ENE of Salterfen Rocks (2¾ miles NNW), extending 3 cables offshore, with Pincushion Rock 9 cables S, thence:

ENE of Seaham Harbour (6.53). A shoal with a depth of 8·6 m known as Louis Rocky Patch lies 6 cables E of the entrance. Thence:

ENE of a light buoy (port hand) (1½ miles SE), marking the seaward end of an outfall, thence:

3   ENE of Beacon Point (2¼ miles S) with Beacon Hill close W, thence:

ENE of Black Halls Point (6 miles SSE) fronted by Black Halls Rocks, thence:

4   To a position ESE of The Heugh (10 miles SSE) the E extremity of Hartlepool Peninsula on which stands a lighthouse (6.50). Two jetties, the larger of which is marked by a light beacon, lie 1½ miles NW of The Heugh and there are several outfalls marked by beacons along this length of coast. Tees Fairway Light Buoy (safe water) in the centre of Tees Bay, is 2½ miles ESE of The Heugh.

(Directions continue for Hartlepool at 6.80, for Tees Bay and the River Tees at 6.111 and for passage S at 6.129)

Seaham Harbour from SE (6.53)
(Original dated 2000)

(Photograph - Air Images)

Seaham

Chart 1627 plan of Seaham Harbour
General information
6.53

1   **Position.** Seaham Harbour (54°50′·23N 1°19′·27W) lies 5 miles S of Sunderland.

Function. Seaham, population about 22 000, is a commercial port handling steel coil, forest products, cement and dry bulk cargo.

2   **Topography.** The town lies in a break in the limestone cliffs, which are about 15 to 18 m high, and run to the N and S of the port. There are rocky ledges and detached rocks extending up to 3 cables offshore on either side of the breakwaters protecting the harbour.

Traffic. In 2008 the port was used by 180 vessels totalling 574 898 dwt.

3   **Port Authority.** The Seaham Harbour Dock Company, Cargo Durham Distribution Centre, Seaham, County Durham, SR7 7NZ.

Website: www.seahamharbour.com

Limiting conditions
6.54

1   **Controlling depth.** There is a least depth of 1·4 m in the channel leading to South Dock (6.58). A rocky patch, charted depth of 1·9 m, lies 1 cable ESE of the harbour entrance. Depths are liable to change after gales.

Deepest and longest berth is in South Dock (6.58).

2   **Tidal levels.** Mean spring range about 4·5 m; mean neap range about 2·1 m. See *Admiralty Tide Tables Volume 1*.

Maximum size of vessel handled. Length 120 m, beam about 18 m, draught between 5·5 and 6·7 m dependent upon height of tide. Larger vessels may be accommodated by prior agreement.

3   **Local weather and sea state.** ESE gales cause the heaviest seas in the approach; in these conditions Port Control should be contacted before attempting entry.

Arrival information
6.55

1   **Port radio.** A port radio service is maintained from 2½ hours before HW to 1½ hours after HW and during office hours. For further information see *Admiralty List of Radio Signals Volume 6 (1)*.

Notice of ETA required. 24 hours notice of ETA is required with updates as necessary. See 1.45.

2   **Outer anchorage** may be obtained to the ENE of North Pier from 3 cables to 1 mile off in depths between 8 and 16 m, sand, fairly clear of rocks. There is no protection except in offshore winds. It should be noted that the bottom is foul to the S of a line of bearing 070° from the head of North Pier.

Pilotage is not compulsory but is recommended for strangers. The pilot cutters are on station over the HW period when a vessel is expected.

Tug. A tug is available on request by VHF.

3   **Local knowledge.** Depths in the approach to the harbour are extremely irregular within the 5 m depth contour and strangers are advised not to approach the harbour at night.

Traffic regulation. The speed limit in the harbour is 5 kn.

Harbour
6.56

1   **General layout.** The harbour consists of an outer tidal harbour and an inner enclosed dock, South Dock. The entrance lies between two piers which curve ESE and NE 3½ cables from the shore and act as breakwaters to protect the outer harbour. Within the outer harbour there are wave screens protecting the entrance to South Dock.

On the NW side of the harbour there is a small tidal basin leading to North Dock, which is tidal, dries and is used only by fishing boats.

2   **Traffic signals** are displayed from the roof of the Port Control building at the N side of the entrance to South Dock:

    Fixed red light; vessels may enter dock.

    Fixed green light; vessels may leave dock.

Other than vessels entering and leaving under the guidance of the Port Control, no vessel movements may take place within South Dock, the harbour channel or its approaches when the traffic signals are displayed. Vessels should also contact Port Control on VHF.

Directions for entering harbour
6.57

1   From a position 1 mile ESE of the harbour entrance the route leads WNW to the entrance, passing (with positions from the harbour entrance, (54°50′·2N 1°19′·3W)):

SSW of Louis Rocky Patch (6 cables E), thence:
NNE of North Scar, a rock, (2 cables SE) the E point of Liddle Scars, thence:

2 Close SSW of a rock (6.54) (1 cable E) the S point of North East Bush, a rocky patch, thence:

To the harbour entrance between the piers, which faces ESE and is 85 m wide. The pier heads both exhibit lights. Thence:

3 To the dock entrance passing through the wave screen which exhibits three red lights in a triangle (red metal column, 4 m in height) on its S side. The docks gates are 19·8 m wide and operated from 2½ hours before HW to 1½ hours after HW. They cannot be operated during SE gales due to scend. There is a depth over the sill of 3·0 m at LAT.

4 **Useful marks.**
North Pier Head Light (white metal column, black bands, 10 m in height) (54°50'·3N 1°19'·3W).
South Pier Head Light (red metal column, 7 m in height).

Berths
6.58
1 South Dock has 900 m of quays available giving eight berths. A depth of at least 6·1 m is maintained in the dock.

Port services
6.59
1 **Repairs** of a limited nature can be undertaken.
Other facilities. Reception of oily waste; hospital at Sunderland (6.43); SSCECs and extensions issued (1.92).
Supplies. Fuel oil by road tanker; fresh water at the quays; provisions.

HARTLEPOOL

General information
Chart 2566 plans of Hartlepool Bay and Tees Bay
Position
6.60
1 Hartlepool Harbour (54°41'·59N 1°11'·18W) lies on the N side of Hartlepool Bay, 3 miles NNW of the entrance to the River Tees.

Function
6.61
1 Hartlepool, population 87 000, is a medium-size commercial port handling a wide range of cargoes including forestry products, steel products, refrigerated produce and automobiles. There are facilities for general cargo ships, RoRo and dry bulk vessels.

Platforms and pipelines for North Sea oil fields are constructed at Hartlepool.

Topography
6.62
1 The Heugh (6.52), which is the E extremity of Hartlepool Peninsula, lies to the E of the port. Its cliffs suffer from erosion and are protected by a sea wall. The seaward side of the peninsula as a whole is fronted by rocky ledges extending up to 2 cables offshore.

Port limits
6.63
1 See 6.92.

Approach and entry
6.64
1 Hartlepool Bay, which lies at the N end of the larger Tees Bay, is approached from E and its harbour is entered via a short dredged channel marked by a directional light and light buoys (lateral).

Hartlepool Harbour from SE (6.60)
(Original dated 2000)

(Photograph - Air Images)

Traffic
6.65

1   See 6.94.

Port Authority
6.66

1   PD Teesport Limited, Queens Square, Middlesbrough TS2 1AH.

Website: www.pdports.co.uk

Limiting conditions

Controlling depths
6.67

1   There is a nominal depth in the dredged approach channel of 5·7 m. The channel is subject to silting and the Harbour Master should be consulted for the latest information.

Deepest and longest berth
6.68

1   Irvines Quay (6.83).

Tidal levels
6.69

1   Mean spring range about 4·6 m; mean neap range about 2·4 m. See *Admiralty Tide Tables Volume 1.*

Maximum size of vessel handled
6.70

1   Vessels up to length 190 m, beam 33 m and draught 8·4 m can be handled. The Harbour Master should be consulted in all cases.

Arrival information

Vessel traffic service
6.71

1   Tees Port Control, a Port Operations and Information Service with full radar surveillance, is maintained for the control of shipping in Tees Bay, the approaches to Hartlepool and seawards for 12 miles. See *Admiralty List of Radio Signals Volume 6 (1).*

Notice of ETA required
6.72

1   Vessels over 300 gt should notify the VTS of their ETA at least 24 hours in advance and all vessels over 20 m in length should contact the VTS at least 6 hours prior to ETA.

Outer anchorage
6.73

1   See 6.103.

Pilotage and tugs
6.74

1   **Pilotage** is compulsory inwards of No 1 Light Buoy (54°41′·3N 1°10′·7W).

Compulsory pilotage applies to:
Vessels over 95 m LOA,
Vessels of more than 4000 gt,
Vessels of more than 4000 dwt,
Vessels of more than 20 m LOA carrying dangerous or polluting goods in bulk,
Vessels requiring a tug.

2   The pilot boards either 2 miles NNE or 1 mile E of Tees Fairway Light Buoy (54°40′·9N 1°06′·5W), as shown on Chart 2567.

Tugs are available.

Local knowledge
6.75

1   Entry into Hartlepool should not be attempted without local knowledge.

Traffic regulations
6.76

1   The Master of a vessel which is approaching or departing from Hartlepool or crossing Tees Bay shall not cause it to cross the approach to the River Tees at any point between Tees Fairway Light Buoy (54°40′·9N 1°06′·5W) and the South Gare Breakwater Light (54°38′·8N 1°08′·2W) in such manner as to embarrass or hamper the safe navigation of a vessel requiring to use Tees Approach Channel (6.113).

2   Vessels over 20 m in length entering Hartlepool must contact the VTS and confirm that:
The vessel is seaworthy in every respect.
All secondary power or mechanical systems are in operation and are immediately available in the event of failure of any primary system, and all main propulsion units, including thrusters, have been tested in both directions.
The steering is under direct manual control and not by any device or equipment designed to function in place of the steersman.
Anchors are cleared away ready for use.

Harbour

General layout
6.77

1   **Hartlepool Harbour** is entered through a dredged approach channel leading NW to Victoria Harbour, a tidal basin. North Basin, a non-tidal dock lies in the W corner of Victoria Harbour.

2   **Hartlepool Marina** is located in a separate harbour about 4 cables SW of the commercial port. The marina is approached through an outer harbour protected by outer and inner breakwaters (lighted) and is enclosed in a non-tidal basin with a lock. The approach channel dries 0·6 m; the lock can accommodate craft up to 48·7 m in length.

Traffic signals
6.78

1   International Port Traffic Signals Nos 2 and 5 are displayed from the head of Middleton Breakwater (54°41′·6N 1°11′·3W). See *The Mariner's Handbook.*

Tidal streams
6.79

1   For tidal streams see the tidal information on the chart. Both the in-going and out-going streams set across the approach and there are eddies in the outer harbour between the breakwaters and Victoria Harbour.

Directions for entering harbour
(continued from 6.52)

Principal marks
6.80

1   **Landmark:**
Chimney (54°42′·5N 1°12′·8W) (Chart 2567).
Church tower (54°41′·7N 1°10′·9W).
Major lights:
The Heugh Light (54°41′·8N 1°10′·6W) (6.50).
South Gare Breakwater Light (54°38′·8N 1°08′·2W) (6.111).

Approach

6.81

1 From a position 1½ miles ESE of The Heugh (54°42′N 1°11′W), the track leads about 1½ miles W to a position about 8 cables SE of the harbour entrance passing (with positions from the harbour entrance (54°41′·6N 1°11′·2W)):

2 N of Longscar Light Buoy (E cardinal) marking the NE extremity of Long Scar, a rocky ledge with outcrops extending up to 1 mile offshore. Longscar Light Buoy and two isolated rock pinnacles close SW of it are covered by the white sector (317°–325°) of Old Pier Light (6.82). And:

S of Heugh Breakwater (4 cables E) projecting 2 cables SSE from the Heugh. The Stones, detached rocks, lie close NE of the breakwater head.

Inner approaches

6.82

1 From a position about 8 cables SE of the harbour entrance, the line of bearing (325°) of a directional light (metal tower) (54°42′·0N 1°11′·7W) leads 1 mile NW through Hartlepool Approach Channel to Victoria Harbour. The channel which is marked by light buoys (lateral) passes:

2 Through the harbour entrance, which is 80 m wide and lies between Old Pier on the E side on which stands a light (white wooden framework tower, red bands, 12 m in height) and Middleton Breakwater on the W side from where traffic signals (6.78) are displayed.

3 The dredged channel continues through the outer harbour into Victoria Harbour from where direct approach can be made to North Basin (6.84).

Basins and berths

Victoria Harbour

6.83

1 Deep Water Berth, 290 m long, depth alongside 9·5 m, with a moveable pontoon and a link span bridge providing a RoRo berth at the NE corner of the berth; Victoria Quay, 140 m long, depth alongside 9·5 m; Irvines Quay, 380 m long, depth alongside 9·5 m; Fish Quay.

Basin

6.84

1 North Basin is entered through a pair of half-tide gates which can be opened around HW. The opening is 21·3 m wide. The basin has 494 m of quays and a depth of 2·5 m below datum. There are three RoRo berths. North Basin can accept vessels up to 170 m LOA and 20 m beam.

Port services

Repairs

6.85

1 Repairs of a limited nature can be carried out.

Other facilities

6.86

1 Ship Sanitation Certificates issued (1.92); four hospitals.

Supplies

6.87

1 Fuel oil; water at the quays; provisions.

TEES BAY AND RIVER TEES

General information

Charts 2567, 2566 plans of Tees Bay and River Tees

Position

6.88

1 Tees Bay is 6 miles across and lies between The Heugh (54°41′·79N 1°10′·52W) and Salt Scar (54°37′·68N 1°03′·00W) off Redcar. Hartlepool Bay and the port of Hartlepool lie in the NW corner of the bay; the mouth of River Tees (54°38′·87N 1°08′·58W), which gives access to Teesport, is located in the middle of the bay.

Function

6.89

1 Teesport lies at the centre of several major petro–chemical complexes within the Tees Valley region. In addition to petroleum products, the port also handles LNG, iron ore and other dry bulk cargoes, containers, RoRo and general cargoes.

The population of the area is about 370 000.

Topography

6.90

1 The coast either side of the mouth of River Tees is generally sandy and backed by low sandhills. Long Scar (54°40′·5N 1°10′·9W) and Little Scar, 5 cables SSW, are rocky ledges in the N of Tees Bay; West Scar (54°37′·5N 1°04′·0W) which runs E into Salt Scar are similar features at the SE extremity of the bay. The entrance to River Tees is formed between two breakwaters, North and South Gare. Shoals lying either side of the dredged approach channel extend up to 1 mile offshore.

2 There are numerous storage tanks and chimneys on either bank of River Tees. At night the glare from the flares and blast furnaces is visible a long way to seaward.

Historic wreck

6.91

1 A restricted area established to protect a historic wreck is centred on 54°39′·51N 1°10′·82W and has a radius of 100 m. See 1.60.

Port limits

6.92

1 Tees Bay and Hartlepool Bay lie within the jurisdiction of The Tees and Hartlepool Bay Authority. The seaward limits of the authority are shown on the chart. The inner limit lies 1 cable downstream of Tees Barrage (54°33′·9N 1°17′·2W).

Approach and entry

6.93

1 Tees Bay is approached from E and River Tees is entered from the vicinity of Tees Fairway Light Buoy (54°40′·9N 1°06′·5W) via Tees Approach Channel which is marked by a pair of leading lights and light buoys (lateral).

Traffic

6.94

1 The ports of Teesport and Hartlepool between them handle in the region of 50 million tonnes of cargo per year, including petroleum products, liquid and dry bulk, containers, general cargo and RoRo services. In 2008, 5075 vessels used the ports.

* WK
25/10
North Gare L   South Gare Breakwater   North Gare Breakwater   *South Gare Breakwater*

Entrance to River Tees from NE (6.93)
(Original dated 2000)

(Photograph - Air Images)

(Photograph - Air Images)

Port Authority
6.95
1 PD Teesport Limited, Queen's Square, Middlesbrough. TS2 1AH. The Harbour Master's office is at Tees Dock (6.119).

   Website: www.pdports.co.uk

Limiting conditions

Controlling depths
6.96
1 Tees Approach Channel has a dredged depth of 15·4 m reducing to 14·1 m within the breakwater entrance. Upriver of the major terminals at the river mouth the dredged depth reduces progressively until Billingham, 7 miles from the entrance, where it is 4·5 m. Above Billingham the channel is not dredged.

2 All areas are subject to siltation and depths less than the dredged depth may be encountered. For the latest information mariners are advised to consult the Harbour Master.

Vertical clearances
6.97
1 The power cable between Teesport (54°36'·0N 1°10'·2W) and North Tees Terminal has a safe overhead clearance of 61·3 m. There is a vertical clearance of 48·2 m below the Transporter Bridge (54°35'·1N 1°13'·7W) at Middlesbrough. Tees (Newport) Bridge (54°34'·3N 1°15'·7W) at the S end of Billingham Reach is permanently in the down position and has a vertical clearance of 5·8 m. The road bridge 3 cables upstream of Tees (Newport) Bridge has a vertical clearance of 17 m.

Deepest and longest berth
6.98
1 The deepest and longest berths are in the ConocoPhillips Petroleum Terminal (6.118) and in the Corus Redcar Ore Terminal (6.119).

  Caution. All depths are subject to silting. The Harbour Master should be consulted for the latest information.

Tidal levels
6.99
1 River Tees entrance: mean spring range about 4·6 m; mean neap range about 2·3 m.

  Middlesbrough Dock entrance (54°35'N 1°13'W): mean spring range about 4·8 m; mean neap range about 2·4 m.

  See *Admiralty Tide Tables Volume 1.*

Maximum size of vessel handled
6.100
1 305 m LOA, 47·5 m beam and 17·0 m draught. These figures depend on the prevailing conditions and masters of vessels in excess of 16·15 m draught should consult the Harbour Master prior to entry.

Arrival information

Vessel traffic service
6.101
1 Tees Port Control, a Port Operations and Information Service with full radar surveillance, is maintained for the control of shipping in Tees Bay, the approaches to Hartlepool and seawards for 12 miles. See *Admiralty List of Radio Signals Volume 6 (1).*

Notice of ETA required
6.102

1   Vessels over 300 gt should notify the VTS at least 24 hours in advance and all vessels over 20 m in length should contact the VTS at least 6 hours prior to ETA.

Outer anchorage
6.103

1   Vessels may anchor to E or SE of Tees Fairway Light Buoy (54°40′·9N 1°06′·5W). Vessels are likely to drag anchor in wind speeds above Force 8 from any direction, in wind speeds above Force 6 from NNW through N to SE, and where the swell exceeds 4 m. In such conditions vessels are advised not to anchor. If conditions dictate, Masters of anchored vessels will be advised to weigh by Tees VTS or HM Coastguard if serious risk of damage to submarine pipelines exists.

2

3

pipelines. See chart for details.

Pilotage and tugs
6.104

1   **Pilotage** is compulsory for vessels navigating in Tees Approach Channel inward of Tees North Light Buoy (54°40′·4N 1°07′·2W) and in River Tees itself as far as No 23 Light Buoy (54°35′·7N 1°10′·9W) as follows:

Vessels over 95 m LOA,
Vessels exceeding 4000 gt,
Vessels exceeding 4000 dwt,
Vessels over 20 m LOA carrying dangerous goods in bulk,
Vessels requiring the services of a tug.

2   Pilotage is compulsory for vessels greater than 80 m LOA navigating in River Tees between No 23 Light Buoy and the inner limit of Tees and Hartlepool Port Authority (6.92).

3   The pilot boards either 2 miles NNE or 1 mile E of Tees Fairway Light Buoy. The pilot should be contacted by VHF 2 hours prior to arrival.

Tugs are available.

Traffic regulations
6.105

1   Vessels over 20 m in length entering Tees Approach Channel or leaving the berth must confirm to the VTS that:

The vessel is seaworthy in every respect.
All secondary power or mechanical systems are in operation and are immediately available in the event of any failure of a primary system, and all main propulsion units, including thrusters, have been tested in both directions.

2   The steering is under direct manual control and not by any device or equipment designed to function in place of the steersman.

Anchors are cleared away ready for use.

Traffic control is operated when a vessel over 200 m LOA is underway within the river to allow the vessel to negotiate the channel without hindrance from other traffic. Such vessels can only enter the channel with the approval of the VTS.

3   A limited traffic control is operated for vessels carrying certain dangerous cargoes to ensure a clear passage or carefully controlled passing of other traffic, the latter being controlled by the VTS.

No vessel may navigate in the Tees Approach Channel or River Tees in visibility of less than 1000 m, except with the permission of the Harbour Master.

4   All vessels over 20 m in length must enter Tees Approach Channel from N of a line joining Tees North Light Buoy and Tees South Light Buoy (54°40′·3N 1°07′·0W), except with the permission of the Harbour Master.

Harbour

General layout
6.106

1   There are riverside berths on both banks between Redcar, 1½ miles inside the entrance, and Billingham 7 miles from the entrance. The larger and deeper berths are to be found between Redcar and Tees Dock, a tidal dock on the SE bank of the river.

2   Seaton-on-Tees Channel, leads W from the river 1 mile inside the entrance. The channel, which is marked by light

Teesport from N (6.106)
(Original dated 2000)

(Photograph – Air Images)

buoys (lateral), leads to Seaton Port. The intakes of a nuclear power station situated on the N bank of the channel are marked by beacons.

Hazards
6.107

1 **Dredging.** Port Authority vessels are engaged continually in dredging and hydrographic survey work. These vessels display the signals prescribed by *The International Regulations for Preventing Collisions at Sea (1972)*.

2 **Fishing.** An important prawn fishing area lies offshore. See 1.18.

Traffic signals
6.108

1 **River Tees.** International Port Traffic Signals Nos 2 and 5 are exhibited from South Gare and Tees Dock radar towers in order to control traffic in the approach channel and in the main channel. These signals apply to all vessels over 20 m LOA. See *The Mariner's Handbook*.

When the approach channel is closed by restricted visibility, the normal fog signal at South Gare Light changes to Horn (2) 30s.

Tidal streams
6.109

1 **Off River Tees entrance** the tidal streams run as follows:

Time from HW Tees	Remarks
−0305	SE-going stream commences
+0310	NW-going stream commences

2 The spring rate in each direction has been reported to reach 2 kn.

There may be turbulence during the out-going stream from the river, especially with E and NE gales.

In River Tees entrance the tidal streams run as follows:

Time from HW Tees	Remarks
−0520	In-going stream commences
−0040	Out-going stream commences

3 The spring rate in each direction is 2 to 3 kn.

The streams run in the direction of the channel but set towards the outer banks at bends. There is turbulence during the out-going stream off the entrance to ConocoPhillips Inset Dock (6.118), about 1½ miles SW of South Gare Lighthouse, where River Tees stream is met by that from Seaton-on-Tees Channel.

4 With freshets the duration and rate of the out-going stream is increased and the in-going stream correspondingly reduced.

Climate information
6.110

1 See 1.142 and 1.150.

Directions for entering harbour
(continued from 6.52)

Principal marks
6.111

1 **Landmarks:**
Church spire (54°37′·0N 1°04′·9W).
Two gasholders (54°37′·4N 1°07′·7W). A blast-furnace is located 1½ cables E.

Building (34°38′·1N 1°10′·8W), a nuclear power station.
Church tower (54°41′·7N 1°10′·9W).

2 **Major lights:**
The Heugh Light (54°41′·8N 1°10′·6W) (6.50).
South Gare Breakwater Light (white round tower, 13 m in height, on breakwater head) (54°38′·8N 1°08′·2W).

Other aid to navigation
6.112

1 **Racon:**
Tees Fairway Light Buoy (54°41′N 1°06′W).
For details see *Admiralty List of Radio Signals Volume 2*.

Tees Bay to River Tees entrance
6.113

1 **River Tees Leading Lights:**
Front light (red metal framework tower, white bands) (54°37′·2N 1°10′·2W).
Rear light (metal framework tower) (560 m SSW of front light).

The alignment (210°) of these lights leads through Tees Approach Channel to the harbour entrance, passing:

2 Through the prohibited anchorage area (6.103) centred on Tees Fairway Light Buoy (safe water) (54°40′·9N 1°06′·5W). Vessels should invariably pass WNW of the buoy, guarding against the cross set. Thence:

3 Between Tees North Light Buoy (starboard hand) and Tees South Light Buoy (port hand) (54°40′·3N 1°07′·1W) which mark the start of the dredged channel (6.96). The channel is 244 m wide and marked by light buoys (lateral; numbers in sequence from seaward). A wreck with a depth of 12·2 m lies 3 cables NW of Tees North Light Buoy. Thence:

4 WNW of South Gare Breakwater (54°38′·8N 1°08′·2W) with a light (6.111) at its head. The breakwater extends 5 cables N from the N extremity of Tod Point. Traffic signals (6.108) are exhibited from a radar tower standing close S of a brick building, 80 m S of the lighthouse. Thence:

5 To a position ESE of North Gare Breakwater (54°38′·9N 1°09′·5W) which extends only to the LW line and lies 4½ cables W of the channel.

Caution. Depending upon the severity of the conditions, it may be possible to enter River Tees in bad weather between half flood and HW. However, with onshore gales great care is necessary. An appreciable ground swell builds up during NE gales.

River Tees entrance to Tees Dock
6.114

1 From a position about 8½ cables within the entrance, the track follows River Tees in a generally SSW direction for 2 miles to Tees Dock. The channel which is dredged (6.96) and marked on both sides by light buoys (lateral) passes:

2 NW of the seaward extremity of a half-tide training wall (54°38′·0N 1°09′·2W) which runs along the E side of River Tees enclosing a small bight in which lie Bran Sands. At this point the river curves to the S away from the alignment of the leading lights but the continuation of this alignment leads to ConocoPhillips Inset Dock (6.118). Thence:

3 ESE of the entrance to Seaton-on-Tees Channel (6.106) (54°37′·8N 1°09′·7W), thence:

W of Corus Redcar Ore Terminal (6.119) (54°37'·44N 1°09'·22W), and:

E of two tanker berths (54°37'·3N 1°09'·6W) at Norsea Oil Terminal (6.118), thence:

4 NW of Tees Dock (6.119) (54°36'·3N 1°09'·5W), and:

SE of a curved basin (54°36'·5N 1°09'·9W) in which there are several tanker berths (6.118). A turning circle with a diameter of 460 m lies between the basin and the entrance to Tees Dock on the opposite bank. More tanker berths line the W bank of the river for a distance of about 7 cables upstream of the basin.

River Tees above Tees Dock
6.115

1 Above Tees Dock the channel, which is about 150 m wide and marked by light buoys (lateral), leads SW for about 2½ miles to a position off the entrance to Middlehaven, formerly Middlesbrough Dock. Several wharves line the S bank of the river on this reach.

2 From the entrance to Middlehaven, Middlesbrough Reach (54°35'·15N 1°14'·02W) extends 1½ miles WNW to Bamlett's Bight where the river bends sharply S and leads into Billingham Reach. Middlesbrough Reach, which is marked by light buoys (lateral), is crossed by the Transporter Bridge (6.97).

3 Billingham Reach continues S for 1 mile and leads into New Cut, which in turn runs 1 mile WSW to Tees Barrage, located close upstream of the upper limit of the port authority. Neither of the two reaches is marked by buoys and beyond Billingham Reach regular dredging is not carried out. New Cut is crossed by two road bridges (6.97).

Basins and berths
6.116

1 There are numerous berths along the length of River Tees on both banks. The major berths lie close to the river entrance as far upriver as Tees Dock.

Seaton Port
6.117

1 Seaton Port (54°38'·0N 1°11'·5W) is the site of the Teesside Environmental Reclamation and Recycling Centre (TERRC), a facility primarily for the decommissioning of offshore structures and ships. The port occupies a basin with a depth of 6·5 m that contains two quays, the largest being 320 m in length. The basin is entered through a 120 m wide opening and it can be converted into a drydock. A deepwater quay of 312 m in length is located outside the basin.

West bank
6.118

1 Conoco–Phillips Petroleum operates eight tanker berths in Conoco–Phillips Inset Dock and the adjacent Norsea Oil Terminal. Four of the berths are 295 m long with an alongside depth 18·2 m.

Simon Storage has two berths handling chemical tankers up to 35 000 dwt; depths alongside are 9·7 m and 10·4 m.

2 Vopak has three berths for tankers up to 45 000 dwt, the largest berth being 179 m long with an alongside depth 11·0 m.

BASF has two berths for chemical tankers with an alongside depth of 7·2 m.

North Tees Terminal has five tanker berths, the largest being 271 m long with an alongside depth of 12·7 m.

East bank
6.119

1 Corus Redcar Ore Terminal; one berth, 306 m long, depth 17·3 m.

Northumbrian Water RSTC Berth, depth 5·7 m.

Riverside RoRo Terminal, depth 10·4 m.

Excelerate LNG Jetty, depth 13·3 m.

Teesport Container Terminal 1; length of jetty 300 m, depth alongside 7·5 to 8·5 m.

2 Tees Dock; five berths handling general cargo, steel and potash, two container ship berths at Teesport Container Terminal 2 and two RoRo terminals. Depth alongside at all berths is 10·9 m except at No 1 RoRo Terminal which has 8·8 m. Tees Dock can handle vessels up to 50 000 dwt.

Port services

Repairs
6.120

1 Repairs of all kinds can be carried out. There is a small shipyard with two dry docks, the larger being 175 m in length and 22 m wide.

Other facilities
6.121

1 Ship Sanitation Certificates issued (1.92); reception of oily waste; customs; hospitals at Middlesbrough.

Supplies
6.122

1 All types of oil fuel at Teesport or by barge; fresh water at quays or by water boat; provisions and stores.

Communications
6.123

1 Durham Tees Valley Airport is located about 20 miles from Teesport.

Harbour regulations
6.124

1 Vessels on River Tees must comply with the Tees and Hartlepool Harbour Byelaws 1977 and the Tees and Hartlepool Port Authority General Directions.

Copies of these regulations are supplied to all vessels over 20 m LOA which visit River Tees.

RIVER TEES TO WHITBY

General information

Chart 134
Route
6.125

1 From a position in the vicinity of Tees Fairway Light Buoy (54°41'N 1°06'W) the route leads 21 miles ESE to a position NNE of Whitby.

Topography
6.126

1 Except for the rocky ledges off Redcar (54°37'N 1°04'W) the coast is fronted by sandy beaches as far as Saltburn, 5 miles ESE. Thence the coast is an almost continuous line of cliffs, varying in height between 30 and 180 m, to Sandsend Ness, 10 miles ESE. These cliffs are cut away by alum works, now discontinued, and broken by deep ravines at Skinningrove, 6½ miles ESE of Redcar, Staithes 4 miles farther ESE and Runswick, a farther 2 miles ESE. This stretch of coast is subject to heavy landslips and fringed by an irregular ledge of rocks which dry out for about 3 cables. Whitby lies 2 miles ESE of Sandsend Ness and there is a broad sandy beach between the two.

Rescue
6.127
1   There are Coastal Rescue Teams at Redcar (54°37′N 1°05′W), Skinningrove (54°34′N 0°54′W), Staithes (54°33′N 0°47′W), Kettle Ness (54°32′N 0°43′W) and Whitby. See 1.67.

2   An all-weather lifeboat is stationed at Whitby. Inshore lifeboats are stationed at Whitby, Redcar (two boats) and Staithes (6.145). See 1.72.

Tidal streams
6.128
1   The tidal streams generally follow the coastal direction and rates up to 1½ kn can be experienced. Tidal streams are given on the chart and in *Admiralty Tidal Stream Atlas: North Sea, Northwestern Part.*

Directions
(continued from 6.52)

Principal marks
6.129
1   **Landmarks:**
      For marks in the Tees and Hartlepool area see 6.80 and 6.111.
      Coatham Church (spire) (54°37′N 1°05′W).
      Chimneys (54°34′N 0°54′W) close N of Skinningrove village.
      Radio mast (red obstruction lights) (54°34′N 0°51′W).
      Pair of chimneys (54°33′N 0°49′W) at Boulby.
      Hotel (54°29′N 0°37′W) at Whitby.

2   **Major lights:**
      The Heugh Light (54°41′·8N 1°10′·6W) (6.50).
      South Gare Breakwater Light (54°38′·8N 1°08′·2W) (6.111).
      Whitby High Light (white 8-sided tower and dwellings, 13 m in height) (54°28′·7N 0°34′·1W).

Other aid to navigation
6.130
1   **Racon:**
      Tees Fairway Light Buoy (54°41′N 1°06′W).
      For details see *Admiralty List of Radio Signals Volume 2.*

Tees Fairway Light Buoy to Whitby
6.131
1   From a position in the vicinity of Tees Fairway Light Buoy (54°41′N 1°06′W) the route leads ESE to a position NNE of Whitby, passing:

2   NNE of Salt Scar Light Buoy (N cardinal) (54°38′·1N 1°00′·1W), which is moored 1½ miles ENE of Salt Scar and West Scar, two detached rocky ledges lying up to 8 cables offshore. Other ledges lie to the S and SW of Salt Scar. Thence:
      NNE of The High (54°36′·9N 1°00′·6W), a rocky shoal. A submarine pipeline extends 9 cables NE from the shore to an outfall near The High. Submarine cables run NE from the shore close N of the landward end of this outfall. Thence:

3   NNE of Hunt Cliff (54°35′·3N 0°56′·2W), which is dark red and nearly perpendicular. A ridge extends SSW to Warsett Hill lying close SW of the cliff. Saltburn Scar, which marks the change from a sandy coast to one fronted by rocky ledges is immediately W of Hunt Cliff. Thence:

4   NNE of Redcliff, which is dark red and one of the boldest features on the coast, thence:
      NNE of Cowbar Nab (54°33′·6N 0°47′·4W), a prominent point; noting a light buoy (special) (54°34′·5N 0°48′·3W) marking an outfall off Boulby. Old Nab (54°33′·5N 0°46′·5W), a low black cliff, lies E of Cowbar Nab. Thence:

5   NNE of Kettle Ness (54°31′·9N 0°42′·6W), a precipitous reddish point, excavated by an alum works. A cone shaped hill is close by. Thence:
      NNE of Sandsend Ness (54°30′·7N 0°40′·4W), an abrupt point with a disused alum works and fringed by rocky ledges. Keldhowe Steel, a rocky ledge to the NW of Sandsend Ness extends 4 cables offshore. Thence:

6   NNE of Whitby Light Buoy (N cardinal) (54°30′·3N 0°36′·6W) 7 cables off the entrance to Whitby Harbour. A number of dangerous wrecks lie within the 20 m depth contour between Kettle Ness and Whitby.

7   **Caution.** Because of the irregularity of the coast between Hunt Cliff and Whitby, vessels are advised to remain to seaward of the 20 m depth contour.

Clearing bearings
6.132
1   The line of bearing 295° of The Heugh Light (6.50) passes 8 cables NE of Salt Scar Light Buoy.
      The line of bearing 285° of Hunt Cliff, just open N of Cowbar Nab, passes NE of Kettle Ness and Keldhowe Steel.

2   The line of bearing 145° of North Cheek (54°27′N 0°31′W) (6.155) and open E of Whitby High Lighthouse passes NE of Whitby Light Buoy and Whitby Rock (6.139). At night the line of bearing 150° or more of Whitby High Lighthouse, which is within the white sector of the light, also passes NE of Whitby Light Buoy.

Useful marks
6.133
1   Redcar Church (tower) (54°37′N 1°04′W).
      Eston Nab radio masts (54°33′N 1°07′W).
      Saint Mark's Church (tower) (54°36′N 1°01′W), Marske-by-the-Sea.
2   Church (tower) (54°35′N 0°59′W), Saltburn-by-the-Sea.
      Captain Cook's Monument (322 m) (54°29′N 1°05′W) on Easby Moor (Chart 1191).
      Lythe Church (spire) (54°30′N 0°41′W).
      (Directions continue for coastal passage S at 6.154)

Whitby

Chart 1612 plan of Whitby Harbour
General information
6.134
1   **Position.** Whitby Harbour (54°29′·65N 0°36′·77W) stands at the mouth of River Esk.
      Function. Whitby, population about 14 000, is a small commercial and fishing port and also a centre for recreational craft.

Abbey   *Marina*

Whitby Harbour from N (6.134)
(Original dated 2000)

(Photograph - Air Images)

2   **Topography.** To the W of Whitby the coast is sandy, while to the E it is formed by a rocky ledge covered in kelp. The coast is backed by a steep bank.

River Esk rises about 16 miles above Whitby and descends down through hilly country. After prolonged rain the river is subject to sudden and heavy freshets which scour the harbour but in dry periods the stream is hardly perceptible.

Approach and entry. The harbour is approached from N and entered between W Pier Extension and E Pier Extension; lights are exhibited from the heads of both pier extensions. In order to avoid off-lying dangers, vessels arriving from SE should pass to seaward of Whitby Light Buoy (N cardinal) (54°30′·3N 0°36′·6W) before making the final approach.

Port Authority. The port is operated by Scarborough Borough Council (6.156). Correspondence should be addressed to The Harbour Master, Whitby Harbour Office, Endeavour Wharf, Whitby, YO21 1DN.

Website: www.yorkshireports.co.uk

Limiting conditions
6.135

1   **Controlling depths.** The channel within the harbour is maintained at a depth of 1·4 m. However, occasional and rapid silting is liable to occur and the Harbour Master should be consulted for the latest information.

2   **Deepest and longest berth** is Endeavour Wharf (6.141).

Tidal levels: Mean spring range about 4·8 m; mean neap range about 2·4 m. See *Admiralty Tide Tables Volume 1*.

Maximum size of vessel handled is length 85 m, beam 14 m and about 3000 dwt. Maximum draught is 5·0 m to 6·5 m depending on tide. Vessels with larger dimensions

may be accepted subject to equipment levels and handling characteristics.

3   **Local weather and sea state.** No attempt should be made to enter Whitby Harbour in gales from the N to E, when the sea breaks a long way offshore and renders the approach dangerous.

In N gales, Lower Harbour is unusable and Upper Harbour (6.137) acts as a place of refuge.

Arrival information
6.136

1   **Port operations.** Vessels enter the port 2 hours either side of HW. See *Admiralty List of Radio Signals Volume 6 (1)* for further information.

2   **Notice of ETA required.** ETA and requests for a pilot should be sent 12 hours prior to arrival. See 1.45 also.

3   **Outer anchorage** may be obtained in Whitby Road, about 7 cables NNW of the harbour entrance. Holding is good but the anchorage is exposed. Even in W or SW gales it is reported to be uncomfortable.

4   **Pilotage** is compulsory for vessels over 37 m in length. The pilot boards in the vicinity of Whitby Light Buoy, weather permitting.

Regulations concerning entry. The following regulations apply:

Port radio should be contacted prior to entering harbour.

Maximum speed between the entrance and Scotch Head (54°29′·4N 0°36′·8W) is 8 kn; elsewhere in the port it is 5 kn. A safe speed that avoids damage to other craft may be appreciably less than the maximum.

No craft should attempt to transit the bridge when a cargo vessel under pilotage is entering or leaving.

All craft must give way to a cargo vessel under pilotage. When directed they should hold their position or remain alongside until the cargo vessel has passed.

Harbour
6.137

1 **General layout.** The harbour is divided into Upper and Lower Harbours, which are separated by a passage, 21 m wide, spanned by a swing bridge. As far as possible a channel 27 m wide with a depth of 1·4 m is maintained from the inner pierheads through the swing bridge to Upper Harbour.

2 There are several riverside berths, mainly on the W bank (6.141), which require ships to take the ground at LW. The bottom of both harbours is gravel, mud and shale.

There is a marina at the S end of Upper Harbour. Close S of the marina a concrete covered power cable, which dries, forms a weir across the river.

Traffic signals. A green light is exhibited from the lighthouse on West Pierhead (6.138) when a piloted vessel is entering harbour at night.

3 **Bridge signals.** The bridge operates 2 hours either side of HW and contact with bridge control can be made by VHF R/T. For further details see *Admiralty List of Radio Signals Volume 6 (1)*.

4 Green lights exhibited from the bridge indicate it is open and red lights that it is closed. A vessel requiring the swing bridge to be opened may sound three long blasts on her whistle.

5 **Tidal streams** are generally weak in Whitby Road. However, it is reported that in W'ly gales the SE-going stream can achieve a rate of 3 kn and closer inshore in the vicinity of Whitby Light Buoy it can be as much as 5 kn. The corresponding NW-going stream is likely to be negligible at this time.

6 In the vicinity of Whitby Light Buoy the tide turns about 2 hours after local high and low water. Consequently, when approaching the harbour entrance around HW, the SE-going flood stream can be running strongly across the entrance.

With freshets in River Esk, the ebb stream may reach 5 kn in the entrance to the harbour.

Directions for entering harbour
6.138

1 **Principal marks:**
  Lighthouse (yellow round stone tower, 22 m in height, standing on West Pierhead) (54°29'·6N 0°36'·8W).
  Metropole Hotel (54°29'·4N 0°37'·5W).
2 Sneaton Castle (flagstaff) (54°29'·0N 0°38'·5W).
  Saint Mary's Church (tower and flagstaff) (54°29'·3N 0°36'·6W).
  Whitby Abbey (ruins) (54°29'·3N 0°36'·4W).
  TV mast (54°29'·4N 0°36'·3W).
  Major light:
  Whitby High Light (54°28'·7N 0°34'·1W) (6.129).

6.139

1 **Whitby Harbour Outer Leading Marks and Light:**
  Front mark (black and white pole, white triangular topmark) (54°29'·4N 0°36'·7W).
  Rear mark (white disc, black stripe) (20 m S of front mark).
  Light (close SW of Saint Mary's Church) (105 m S of front mark).

TV Mast

Whitby Abbey from NE (6.138)
(Original dated 2000)

(Photograph - Air Images)

2 The alignment (169°) of the two marks and the light, or, at night the line of bearing 169° of the light seen between the two extension pierhead lights, leads through Whitby Road to the harbour entrance, passing (with positions from the harbour entrance):

3 W of Whitby Light Buoy (N cardinal) (7 cables N), thence

E of Upgang Rocks (1 mile WNW), an area of foul ground inside the 5 m depth contour over which the swell breaks heavily. The rocks are covered in kelp and dry close inshore. Thence:

4 W of Whitby Rock (3 cables NE). The Scar, a rocky ledge, lies inshore of the rock and both are covered in kelp. The rocks dry and the swell breaks heavily over them. Thence:

5 To the harbour entrance, which lies between West Pier Extension, from which a light (green wooden tower, 7 m in height) is exhibited and East Pier Extension from which a light (red wooden tower, 7 m in height) is exhibited at night, thence:

6 Between the inner pierheads (¾ cable S). A disused lighthouse (6.138) stands on West Inner Pierhead and a second similar lighthouse (13 m in height) stands on East Inner Pierhead.

6.140

1 **Whitby Harbour Inner Leading Light Beacons.** The alignment (029°) astern of leading lights, which stand on the elbow of East Inner Pier close S of the disused lighthouse, leads through Lower Harbour to Fish Quay (6.141):

2 Front light (white triangle, standing on pier coping) (54°29'·5N 0°36'·7W).
  Rear light (white disc, black stripe) (close NE of front beacon).

3 **Clearing bearings.** The following clearing bearings, which are shown on the chart, may assist in the approach to the harbour entrance:

The alignment (147°) of the light structure on the head of West Extension Pier with the E extremity of the ruins of Whitby Abbey passes 2 cables NE of the 5 m depth contour containing Upgang Rocks.

4 The alignment (176°) of the disused lighthouse on East Pier with the Mortuary Chapel Spire, which stands above trees in Esk Vale, and the W extremity of a prominent house in the town passes W of Whitby Rock and The Scar.

Berths

6.141

1   **Lower Harbour:** Fish Quay on W bank, primarily for fishing vessels, 213 m long, depth alongside 2·0 m.

Upper Harbour: Endeavour Wharf on W bank, 213 m long giving two berths, depth alongside 2·0 m. Eskside Wharf on E bank, depth alongside 1·5 m.

Port services

6.142

1   **Repairs:** repairs can be undertaken; floating dock with lifting capacity of 500 tonnes; small shipyard.

Other facilities: hospital with helicopter landing site (54°29′N 0°37′W); customs.

Supplies: marine diesel by road tanker; fresh water at quays; provisions and limited stores.

Anchorages and minor harbours

Chart 2567
Redcar

6.143

1   **General information.** Redcar (54°37′N 1°04′W), used by fishing vessels, is situated 3 miles SE of South Gare Breakwater (6.113). Coatham adjoins the NW side of Redcar.

Landmarks:

Coatham Church (spire) (54°37′N 1°05′W).
Redcar Church (tower) (54°37′N 1°03′W).

2   **Directions for entering harbour.** Lade Way Leading Lights:

Front Light (metal column, 5 m in height on promenade) (54°37′·1N 1°03′·9W).
Rear Light (Brick building, 8 m in height) (43 m WSW of front light).

The alignment (247°) of these leading lights leads to Redcar Sands, passing between the rocky ledges of High Stone and Sandy Batt.

3   Luff Way Leading Lights:

Front Light (metal column, 5 m in height on esplanade) (54°37′·1N 1°03′·7W).
Rear Light (metal column, 8 m in height) (115 m S of front light).

The alignment (197°) of these leading lights leads to Redcar Sands.

Chart 134
Skinningrove Wick

6.144

1   Anchorage can be obtained for small vessels in Skinningrove Wick (54°35′N 0°53′W) in depths of 9 to 11 m, clay. The position is indicated on the chart.

Staithes Harbour

6.145

1   Staithes (54°34′N 0°47′W) is a small fishing village close to Cowbar Nab (6.131). The harbour, which dries, is formed by two breakwaters; the E breakwater head is marked by a beacon (diamond topmark). The entrance, 61 m wide, faces NE and has depths of 4·6 m at HW springs.

Chart 1612 plan of Runswick Bay
Port Mulgrave

6.146

1   Port Mulgrave (54°33′N 0°46′W), which dries, is formed by two breakwaters and has a depth of 5·2 m alongside at HW springs.

Runswick Bay

6.147

1   **General information.** Runswick Bay (54°32′N 0°44′W) lies between Kettle Ness (6.131) and a point 1 mile W. The village of Runswick is on the W side of the bay and there is usually a good landing close S of the village.

The bay is encumbered by drying rocky ledges. In onshore winds a sea breaks across the entrance, where depths are slightly less than in the centre of the bay.

2   **Anchorage** for small vessels can be obtained 5½ cables ENE of the jetty as indicated on the chart.

Chart 134
Sandsend Road

6.148

1   **Anchorage** can be obtained in Sandsend Road (54°30′N 0°39′W) in depths of 11 m, sand over clay, between Sandsend Ness (6.131) and Upgang Rocks (6.139).

WHITBY TO SCARBOROUGH

General information

Chart 129, 134
Route

6.149

1   From a position NE of Whitby (54°29′N 0°37′W) the coastal route runs 4 miles SE thence SSE 12 miles to a position ENE of Scarborough.

Topography

6.150

1   The coast between Whitby and Scarborough is cliffy, fringed by rocky ledges and relatively steep-to.

Depths

6.151

1   Depths in an area shown on the chart, extending up to 2 miles off the coast between South Cheek (6.155) and Scarborough, are from old leadline surveys. Uncharted shoals and other hazards may exist in this area.

Rescue

6.152

1   There are Coastal Rescue Teams at Robin Hood's Bay (54°26′N 0°32′W), Ravenscar (54°24′N 0°29′W), Burniston (54°20′N 0°25′W) and Scarborough; see 1.67.

An all-weather lifeboat and an inshore lifeboat are stationed at Scarborough. See 1.72.

Tidal streams

6.153

1   Tidal streams are given on the chart and in *Admiralty Tidal Stream Atlas: North Sea, Northwestern Part.*

Directions
(continued from 6.133)

Principal marks

6.154

1   **Landmarks:**

For marks in Whitby see 6.138.
Radio mast (54°24′N 0°30′W).
Scarborough Castle (ruined keep) (54°17′·3N 0°23′·4W).

2   **Major lights:**

Flamborough Head Light (54°07′N 0°05′W) (6.169).
Whitby High Light (54°28′·7N 0°34′·1W) (6.129).

Whitby to Scarborough
6.155

1   From a position NE of Whitby the route leads 4 miles SE thence 12 miles SSE to a position ENE of Scarborough, passing:

> NE of Saltwick Nab (54°29'·3N 0°35'·3W), a dark rocky promontory owned by the National Trust. Black Nab, a dark rocky islet, lies 5 cables SE, thence:

2
> NE of Whitby High Light (54°28'·7N 0°34'·1W) (6.129), thence:

> NE of North Cheek (54°26'·5N 0°31'·4W), a bold headland, in an area of high, dark cliffs with occasional red tinges, thence:

3
> ENE of South Cheek with the village of Ravenscar close SW. Robin Hood's Bay lies between North and South Cheek. The coast is formed by a cliff and grassy bank, broken by the occasional deep gully, backed by cultivated ground rising like an amphitheatre. The shore of the bay is encumbered by ledges up to 5 cables offshore. Thence:

4
> ENE of Hayburn Wyke (54°21'·6N 0°26'·4W), an indentation at the mouth of a wooded valley where the coast decreases in elevation. Cloughton Wyke, a similar feature, is 1¼ miles farther SSE. Thence:

> ENE of Long Nab (54°19'·9N 0°25'·1W). Thence:

5
> ENE of Scalby Ness (54°18'·3N 0°24'·5W), which is encumbered by rocks. An outfall, marked by a light buoy (port hand), runs 8 cables ENE from Scalby Ness, thence:

> To a position ENE of Scarborough Rock (54°17'·3N 0°23'·1W), a headland at the N entry point to Scarborough Bay (6.156). The town of Scarborough encompasses the point but lies mainly to its SW.

(Directions continue at 6.169)

Scarborough

Chart 1612 plans of Scarborough Bay and Scarborough Harbour

General information
6.156

1   **Position.** Scarborough (54°16'·89N 0°23'·42W) is situated at the NW corner of Scarborough Bay.

Function. Scarborough is a small fishing and recreational harbour. Vessels take the bottom at LW.

The population of Scarborough is about 53 600.

2   **Topography.** Scarborough Bay lies between Scarborough Rock and White Nab, a cliffy point, 1 mile S. The bottom of the bay is smooth and depths are regular. The town at the N end of the bay rises in the form of an amphitheatre and is fronted by South Sands; the S part of the bay is bordered by grassy slopes fronted by rocky ledges.

Port Authority. Scarborough Borough Council, Harbour Department, 18 West Pier, Scarborough YO11 1PD.

Limiting conditions
6.157

1   **Controlling depths.** Inner Harbour, which is dredged in its W part to chart datum and in its E part to 1·5 m, is entered through a channel 10 m wide with a least charted depth of 0·1 m. Outer Harbour and its entrance channel dry. Both harbours are subject to silting and the Harbour Master should be consulted for the latest information on depths.

Tidal levels: see *Admiralty Tide Tables Volume 1*. Mean spring range about 4·8 m; mean neap range about 2·3 m.

2   **Maximum size of vessel handled.** Length 80 m; draught 4·66 m at HW springs.

Caution. The bottom of both harbours is mud, sand and clay with stones and boulders. Tidal scour and dredging may expose these stones such that they are dangerous to vessels. Vessels using the harbour should be capable of taking ground on a hard bottom.

3   **Local weather and sea state.** Scarborough Bay is open to the E and the harbour should not be attempted in strong NE to SSE winds when the entrance channel can be affected by silting (6.157), nor should the approach be made across broken water in Scarborough Bay in bad weather. Strong NNW winds also send a heavy swell into the bay.

Arrival information
6.158

1   **Outer anchorage**, indicated on the chart, may be obtained 5 cables ESE of Vincent's Pier Lighthouse (54°16'·9N 0°23'·4W) in 8 m, sand over blue clay. Anchoring is prohibited in the fairway leading to the harbour entrance.

Pilotage is compulsory for vessels over 37 m in length, and for fishing vessels over 45·5 m in length. The pilot normally boards 1 mile E of Vincent's Pier Lighthouse (6.160).

Harbour
6.159

1   **General layout.** The harbour is formed by four piers which divide it into two independent harbours, InnerHarbour, the larger of the two, and Outer Harbour.

Tidal signal. The lighthouse on Vincent's Pier shows its light when there is more than 3·7 m on the bar.

2   **Tidal streams** are barely perceptible in Scarborough Bay. Off East Pier the N-going stream runs with some strength from 1 hour before HW to 2 hours after LW; during SE winds it sets constantly past the harbour entrance.

Directions for entering harbour
6.160

1   **Landmarks:**

> Scarborough Castle (54°17'·3N 0°23'·4W) (6.154).
> Saint Mary's Church (tower and flagstaff) (54°17'·2N 0°23'·6W).
> Vincent's Pier Lighthouse (white round tower, 15 m in height) (54°16'·9N 0°23'·4W).
> War Memorial (54°16'·1N 0°24'·3W) on N slope of Oliver's Mount.

2   **Approach.** From a position E of Scarborough, the alignment (273°) of the two N towers of the Grand Hotel (54°16'·8N 0°23'·9W) leads to a position S of the harbour (54°16'·9N 0°23'·4W), from whence either entrance may be approached, passing:

> N of Ramsdale Scar (54°16'·7N 0°23'·6W), a foul rocky area SSW of the harbour entrance, thence:

3
> To Outer Harbour entrance, 8 m wide, lying between Vincent's Pier head and East Pier head on which stands a light (mast, 4 m in height), alternatively;

> To the channel close W of Vincent's Pier which leads to Inner Harbour entrance, 29 m wide, lying between Old Pier head and West Pier head. Lights are shown from both pierheads.

4   **Caution.** Navigation close to East Pier and Scarborough Rock should be avoided if a heavy swell is running from N or E.

The harbour should be entered between half–flood and first quarter ebb taking into account the tidal signals.

In the three winter months the entrance to Outer Harbour is closed by a boom. Access to Outer Harbour is then between Vincent's Pier and Old Pier at the site of the drawbridge.

Berths
6.161
1   **Inner Harbour:**
North Wharf, 152 m long.
West Pier, used by fishing vessels.
Yacht pontoons occupy the NE half of the harbour. The pontoon area has been dredged to a depth of 1·5 m.
    Outer Harbour:
Outer Harbour, which dries 2 to 5 m, is used as a small craft haven.

Port services
6.162
1   **Repairs** to engine and deck; grid for vessels up to 43 m in length.
    Other facilities: hospital; helicopter landing site at the hospital; customs.
    Supplies: marine diesel at SE end of West Pier; fresh water at quays; provisions.

SCARBOROUGH TO FLAMBOROUGH HEAD

General information
Chart 129
Route
6.163
1   From a position ENE of Scarborough the coastal route leads 15 miles SE to a position E of Flamborough Head.

Topography
6.164
1   From White Nab (6.156), the S entrance point to Scarborough Bay, to Old Horse Rocks, 3 miles SE, the coast is fronted by foul ground extending up to 5 cables offshore. Thence the coast is steep–to as far as Filey Brigg, which juts out 1 mile to seaward and lies 2 miles farther SE. Filey Bay is S of Filey Brigg and curves from S to SE for 3½ miles to King and Queen Rocks. The shore of the bay is cliffy, backed by a steep grassy bank and fronted by a broad sandy beach. Between King and Queen Rocks and Flamborough Head, 6 miles ESE, the coast consists of precipitous cliffs.

Exercise area
6.165
1   Submarines exercise in an area NE of Flamborough Head, which is shown on the chart. See 1.21.

Historic wreck
6.166
1   A restricted area with a radius of 300 m centred on 54°11'·5N 00°13'·5W has been established to protect a historic wreck. See 1.60.

Rescue
6.167
1   There are Coastal Rescue Teams at Filey, Speeton (54°10'N 0°14'W) and Flamborough Head; see 1.67.
2   An all–weather lifeboat and an inshore lifeboat are stationed at Filey. See 1.72.

Tidal streams
6.168
1   Within Filey Bay the tidal streams are barely perceptible, but the NW–going stream runs in an E direction along the S side of Filey Brigg at a rate of ½ kn. Between Brigg End and Filey Brigg Light Buoy (6.170) there might be turbulence; the spring rate is 1¾ kn.
2   In the vicinity of Flamborough Head the streams are stronger closer inshore and although the stream is rectilinear, there is no slack water. There might be turbulence close inshore off Flamborough Head and eddies occur both sides of the head.

Tidal streams are given on the chart and in *Admiralty Tidal Stream Atlas: North Sea, Northwestern Part.*

Directions
(continued from 6.155)

Principal marks
6.169
1   **Landmarks:**
Scarborough Castle (54°17'·3N 0°23'·4W) (6.154).
War Memorial (54°16'·1N 0°24'·3W) (6.160).
Radio mast (54°11'N 0°26'W).
Flamborough Head Lighthouse (white round tower, 27 m in height) (54°07'·0N 0°05'·0W) near the summit of the head.
Disused Lighthouse (2½ cables NW of Flamborough Head Lighthouse).
2   **Major light:**
Flamborough Head Light (above).

Scarborough to Flamborough Head
6.170
1   From a position ENE of Scarborough the coastal route leads 15 miles SE to a position E of Flamborough Head, passing:
2   NE of a light buoy (special, can) (54°16'·3N 0°20'·9W) marking a diffuser at the seaward end of an outfall extending 1 mile NE from White Nab (6.156), thence:
    NE of Yons Nab (54°14'·5N 0°20'·3W). Cayton Bay lies between Yons and White Nab. Two submarine cables run NE from the bay. Thence:
3   NE of Filey Brigg, a chain of ill–defined rocky ledges extending 4½ cables ESE of Carr Nase, a well defined point. High Brigg, the central ledge, is 2 m high and Brigg End is the E extremity of the brigg. Filey Brigg Light Buoy (E cardinal) is moored 4½ cables ESE of Brigg End. Thence:
4   NE of King and Queen Rocks (54°09'·6N 0°13'·4W). Filey Bay (6.172) with the town of Filey, a seaside resort, at its NW end lies between the rocks and Brigg End. Carr Nase affords shelter to the bay from the N. Thence:

Disused Lighthouse   *Light*   *Selwicks Bay*

Flamborough Head from S (6.170)
(Original dated 2000)

(Photograph - Air Images)

5   To a position E of Flamborough Head (54°06′·9N 0°04′·6W) which is a perpendicular cliff of white chalk. Flamborough Steel, a rocky ledge extends 2 cables SE of the head. Flamborough Head is bold and well–lit and is a common point of landfall and departure. The N side of the head is a breeding place for seabirds, especially gannets, which are far more common to the N than the S of the head.

6   **Caution.** Flamborough Head Light might be obscured within 1½ miles of the coast up to 8 miles to the N, and in the N part of Bridlington Bay (6.175). The exact distance at which the cliffs screen the light depends on the state of the tide and height of eye of the observer.

Useful marks
6.171

1   Saint Oswald's Church (tower) (54°13′N 0°17′W) in Filey.
    Radio mast (54°09′N 0°15′W) (Chart 1882 plan of Filey Bay).
    Radio mast (54°08′N 0°19′W).
    (Directions continue for coastal passage S at 6.181)

Anchorage and boat landings

Chart 1882 plan of Filey Bay
Filey Bay
6.172

1   **Anchorage** can be obtained 7 cables E of Filey in depths of 5 m, clay covered with sand. The anchorage in Filey Bay affords fair protection with winds from SSW clockwise to NNE. Submarine cables, the N of which is disused, run SE from the shore to the S of the anchorage and the Feshes, a stony patch, lies to the N.

Chart 129
Boat landings
6.173

1   **North Landing**, 1¼ miles NW of Flamborough Head, is a small inlet which is sometimes used as a landing place by small fishing vessels.
    Selwicks Bay, close N of Flamborough Head Lighthouse, can be used at HW as a landing in offshore winds.

FLAMBOROUGH HEAD
TO RIVER HUMBER

General information

Charts 121, 107
Route
6.174

1   From a position E of Flamborough Head (54°07′N 0°04′W) the route leads about 29 miles SSE to a position NE of Humber Light Float (starboard hand) (53°39′N 0°21′E).

Topography
6.175

1   From Flamborough Head the coast runs W then curves round to the SSE forming Bridlington Bay. The bay is 8 miles across with the town of Bridlington at its head. S of the bay the coast continues to run SSE for 30 miles, terminating at Spurn Head (7.24), the N entrance point of River Humber.

2   Initially the coast is formed of rocky cliffs but these soon give way to clay. These dark clay cliffs then extend as far as Kilnsea (53°37′N 0°08′E), 2½ miles N of Spurn Head and then become sandhills as the coast curves SW to Spurn Head. The background to the coast is low and there are few identifiable features.

3   The coast S of Bridlington is being eroded at an estimated rate of 1·7 m a year. This amounts to about 1½ km in the last 1000 years, sweeping away villages, churches and landmarks.

Depths
6.176

1   The 20 m depth contour, which is close E of Flamborough Head, passes 1 mile E of Smithic Shoal (54°04′N 0°07′W), thence 5 miles offshore as far as Withernsea (53°43′N 0°02′E) where it trends to the SE. Apart from a few charted wrecks, there are no dangers outside this depth contour.

Submarine pipelines
6.177

1   Several submarine pipelines extend NE and ENE from the coast in the vicinity of the gas terminal at Easington (53°40′N 0°07′E). See 1.41.

Firing range
6.178

1 There is a firing danger area 1½ miles SE of Hornsea (53°55′N 0°10′W), as shown on the chart.

Rescue
6.179

1 MRCC Humber is based at Bridlington. There are Coastal Rescue Teams at Bridlington, Hornsea, Withernsea (53°44′N 0°02′E) and Easington (53°37′N 0°11′W). See 1.67.

An all-weather lifeboat is stationed at Bridlington. Inshore lifeboats are stationed at Flamborough (South Landing), Bridlington and Withernsea. See 1.72.

Natural conditions
6.180

1 **Tidal streams** near the shore from close S of Bridlington to Spurn Head run parallel to the coast. The spring rate in each direction increases from about 1 kn near Bridlington to 2 to 3 kn off Spurn Head. There are ripples or overfalls over the rough bottom 5 miles NNE of Spurn Head. There is little change farther to seaward where the stream is more or less rotary anti-clockwise, with a spring rate in each direction of 1½ kn.

2 Tidal stream information is given on the charts and in *Admiralty Tidal Stream Atlas: North Sea, Southern Part*.

Climate information. See 1.142 and 1.151.

Directions
(continued from 6.171)

Principal marks
6.181

1 **Landmarks:**
Flamborough Head Lighthouse (54°07′·0N 0°05′·0W) (6.169).
Disused Lighthouse (2½ cables NW of Flamborough Head Lighthouse).
Priory Church (tower) (54°05′·7N 0°12′·1W).
Holy Trinity Church (spire) (54°05′·2N 0°11′·1W).
Block of flats (54°04′·9N 0°11′·6W).

2 Lighthouse (disused, white octagonal tower, 39 m in height) (53°44′N 0°02′E).
Radio mast (53°39′N 0°06′E).
Spurn Head Lighthouse (disused) (53°35′N 0°07′E) (black round tower, white band, 39 m in height), a second disused lighthouse is close W.

3 **Offshore mark:**
Meteorological mast (lattice structure, 89 m in height) (53°38′·24N 0°15′·73E). Lights are exhibited from the mast.

4 **Major light:**
Flamborough Head Light (above).

Other aid to navigation
6.182

1 **Racon:**
Humber Light Float (53°38′·7N 0°21′·2E).
For details see *Admiralty List of Radio Signals Volume 2*.

Flamborough Head to Humber Light Float
6.183

1 From a position E of Flamborough Head (54°07′N 0°04′W) the coastal route leads SSE to a position NE of Humber Light Float, passing:

2 ENE of North Smithic Shoal and South Smithic Shoal, (centre 54°05′N 0°06′W), which run SW into one another and extend from North Smithic Light Buoy (N cardinal) 5 miles SW to SW Smithic Light Buoy (W cardinal). The two shoals lie on the approach to Bridlington Bay (6.185). Thence:

3 ENE of Hornsea Gap (53°54′N 0°10′W), a break in the coastal cliffs which are 9 to 12 m high. The coast in this vicinity is being eroded; thence:
ENE of a foul area (centre 53°52′N 0°03′W), thence:
WSW of Rough Gas Field (53°50′N 0°28′E).

4 The route continues SSE, passing (with positions from Withernsea (53°44′N 0°02′E)):
ENE of Withernsea, a gap in the cliffs marked by a disused lighthouse (6.181), thence:
ENE of an outfall (1½ miles SE) which extends 6 cables NE from the coast and which is marked by a light buoy (special), thence:

5 ENE of Dimlington High Land (4 miles SSE), where the cliffs rise to an elevation of 40 m. Wrecks, least depth 3·4 m and marked by a light buoy (E cardinal), lie 2 miles NNE of Dimlington High Land. Thence:

6 To a position NE of Humber Light Float (starboard hand) (53°38′·71N 0°21′·23E).

Useful marks
6.184

1 Ulrome Church (tower) (54°00′N 0°14′W) standing amid trees.
Skipsea Church (tower) (53°59′N 0°13′W) standing amid trees.
Mappleton Church (spire) (53°53′N 0°08′W).
Pile (lighted) (53°49′N 0°03′W), a gas storage site.

2 Hilston Tower (53°47′N 0°03′W) of red bricks.
Tunstall Church (spire) (53°46′N 0°01′W).
Withernsea Church (tower) (53°44′N 0°02′E).
Easington Church (tower) (53°39′N 0°07′E).
Kilnsea Church (53°37′N 0°08′E) tower.
(Directions continue for River Humber at 7.20 and for passage SE at 8.12)

Bridlington

Chart 1882 plans of Bridlington Bay and Bridlington
General information
6.185

1 **Position.** Bridlington (54°04′·79N 0°11′·22W) lies at the head of Bridlington Bay.

Function. The small harbour is used only by fishing boats and recreational craft. The town is a holiday resort, with a population of about 31 300.

2 **Topography.** Bridlington Bay (6.175) is a roadstead which lies SW of Flamborough Head with North Smithic Shoal and South Smithic Shoal (6.183) across its approaches. The two shoals are limestone with a surface covering of sand. Depths within the bay are regular but it is too shallow for deep-draught vessels.

3 Initially the coast is composed of cliffs fronted by rocky ledges but about 3½ miles W of the head the cliffs change from rock to clay and reduce in elevation. Bridlington and the coast to the S of it are fronted by broad sands.

4 **Approach and entry.** Bridlington is approached from Bridlington Bay passing to the N of North Smithic Shoal or SW of South Smithic Shoal (6.183) as appropriate.

Seasonal buoyage. Buoys (special) are laid in the approaches to the harbour between March and October.

Port Authority. Bridlington Piers and Harbour Commissioners, Gummers Wharf, West End, Bridlington, East Yorkshire YO15 3AN.

Fish Quay
Bridlington Harbour from ESE (6.185)
(Original dated 2000)

(Photograph – Air Images)

Limiting conditions
6.186

1   **Controlling depths.** The harbour dries. Alongside South Pier (6.188) there is a depth of about 5·0 m at HW springs.

Tidal levels: see *Admiralty Tide Tables Volume 1.* Mean spring range about 5·0 m; mean neap range about 2·4 m.

Maximum size of vessel handled is length 45 m and draught 3·9 m.

Arrival information
6.187

1   **Port radio.** Vessels approaching the harbour may call the duty watchkeeper on VHF. For details, see *Admiralty List of Radio Signals Volume 6 (1).*

2   **Outer anchorage** may be obtained in any part of Bridlington Bay (6.175) between South Smithic Shoal and the coast. Anchorage may be obtained in 10 m, is shown on the chart 1¾ miles SW of Flamborough Lighthouse. This anchorage is protected from the NNE, but vessels should not remain in the bay in E winds unless well provided with ground tackle when some protection is obtained from North Smithic Shoal and South Smithic Shoal.

3   A temporary anchorage for small vessels in good holding ground may be found 4½ cables ESE of Bridlington North Pierhead.

Caution. In N gales a heavy steep sea may be experienced over North Smithic Shoal until well within the lee of Flamborough Head. In these circumstances a vessel seeking shelter in Bridlington Bay should not attempt to pass S of North Smithic Light Buoy (6.190).

4   **Pilotage,** which is not compulsory, is undertaken by the Harbour Master on request by VHF.

Harbour
6.188

1   **General layout.** The harbour is enclosed by two piers, North Pier which runs 1 cable S from the shore and South Pier extending 2 cables E from the shore. The harbour bottom is clay covered with sand and silt.

Within the harbour there are berths for about 40 trawlers and accommodation for recreational craft.

2   **Tidal signals** (Diagram 6.188.1) are exhibited by day from the E end of Fish Quay, close to South Pierhead.

Signal	*Meaning*
	Depth of 2·7m or more in entrance.

Day tidal signals (6.188.1)

3   At night, tidal signals (Diagram 6.188.2) are exhibited from the North Pierhead Light (6.190).

Signal	*Meaning*
●	Depth of 2·7m or more in entrance. Harbour clear.
●	Depth less than 2·7m in the entrance.

Night tidal signals (6.188.2)

4   **Tidal streams** off the entrance to the harbour appear to be affected by eddies and begin about 1½ hours earlier than the streams S of Bridlington.

Climate information: see 1.142 and 1.151.

Directions for entering harbour
6.189

1   **Principal marks:**
    Flamborough Head Lighthouse (54°07'·0N 0°05'·0W) (6.169).
    Priory Church (tower) (54°05'·7N 0°12'·1).
    Holy Trinity Church (spire) (54°05'·2N 0°11'·1W).
    Block of flats (54°04'·9N 0°11'·6W).

Major light:
    Flamborough Head Light (above).

6.190

1   **North-east approach.** From a position E of Flamborough Head (54°07'N 0°04'W) the route leads 6 miles WSW then N to the harbour entrance, passing (with positions from South Landing (54°06'N 0°07'W)):
    NNW of North Smithic Light Buoy (N cardinal) (2 miles E), thence:
    SSE of Flamborough Head (6.170) (1½ miles ENE), thence:

2   NNW of North Smithic Shoal (6.183) (1½ miles ESE), thence:
    SSE of South Landing and close to the anchorage (6.187). South Landing is a break in the cliffs used by fishermen during N winds. There is a prominent road down a ravine from the cliffs above. Thence:
    SSE of a light buoy (special) (8 cables SSW) marking the end of an outfall pipe, thence:
    NNW of South Smithic Shoal (6.183) (2½ miles S), thence:

3   SSE of the harbour entrance (2¾ miles WSW), thence:
    NNW of the light buoy (special) (3 miles SW), marking the seaward end of an outfall extending 9 cables from the coast, thence:
    To the harbour entrance, which is 27 m wide and faces S. It lies between North Pierhead, on which there is a light (column, 9 m in height), and South Pierhead.

4   When entering the harbour the entrance should be opened up well to the S to avoid The Canch, a sandspit which dries ¾ cable S of North Pierhead.

Cautions. Depths in the vicinity of The Canch are subject to frequent change. For the latest information contact the Harbour Master.

5   A number of yacht racing marks (special) are laid between South Smithic Shoal and the shore during the summer months.

6.191

1   **South-east approach.** From a position SSE of South West Smithic Light Buoy, the alignment (332°) of Christ Church (spire) (54°05′·1N 0°11′·6W) with Priory Church (tower) (6.189) leads to the harbour entrance, passing (with positions from the harbour entrance):

2   Close WSW of SW Smithic Light Buoy (W cardinal) (2½ miles SSE), which lies on this alignment, thence:

        ENE of the light buoy (special) (6.190) (9 cables SSE), thence:

        To the harbour entrance (6.190).

    These marks may be difficult to distinguish from the SE.

3   **Clearing bearings:**

        The line of bearing 241° of four white square houses at Wilsthorpe (54°03′·5N 0°13′·0W), which are prominent from seaward, passes SE of Flamborough Steel (6.170) and close NW of North Smithic Light Buoy and leads through the N channel.

        The line of bearing 325° of Flamborough Head Lighthouse passes NE of North Smithic Shoal.

4   **Useful marks:**

        Sewerby Hall (54°06′N 0°09′W), standing amid trees.
        New Spa Theatre (54°04′·8N 0°11′·8W).

Port services

6.192

1   **Repairs** can be effected on craft up to 50 tonnes. There is a boat hoist of 70 tonnes and two slipways.

    Other facilities: hospital; helicopter landing site.

    Supplies: marine diesel at South Pier; fresh water; provisions.

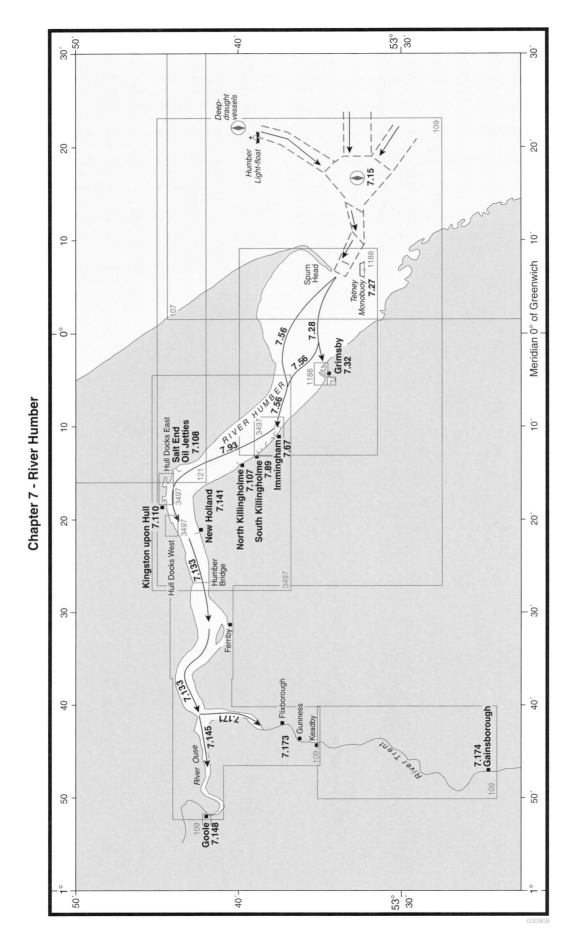

CHAPTER 7

RIVER HUMBER

GENERAL INFORMATION

Charts 107, 109
Scope of the chapter
7.1

1 River Humber is formed by the confluence of Rivers Ouse and Trent, 34 miles from the sea. It also acts as the common outlet for numerous other streams which drain the greater part of Yorkshire and the Midlands. At its head the river is 5 cables wide but increases to 6 miles at its entrance point between Spurn Head (53°34′N 0°07′E) and Donna Nook, a low point on the S side of the estuary. Both sides of the estuary are bordered by extensive flats which dry up to 2 miles offshore in places. The navigable channels are narrowed by numerous shoals.

2 River Humber is mainly confined between low embankments from which water has been progressively excluded by the process of silting or "warping" as it is known locally.

3 The important ports on River Humber, all operated by Associated British Ports, are Grimsby (7.32), Immingham (7.67) Kingston upon Hull or simply Hull (7.110) and Goole (7.148). There are oil terminals at Immingham, Killingholme (7.89) Saltend (7.108) and Tetney Monobuoy (7.27).

4 In 2008 the ports of Immingham and Grimsby handled 65 m tonnes of cargo, the largest quantity of cargo handled by any port in the United Kingdom.

Local knowledge
7.2

1 The low, flat shores of the River Humber offer few marks. In clear weather, due to good channel marking, navigation should not be too difficult. However, tidal streams are strong, the channel is constantly changing and buoys are moved accordingly. Above Humber Bridge the changes are so frequent that only local charts published by Associated British Ports are available. Local knowledge is essential.

For further information relating to local charts and buoyage see *www.humber.com*.

Pilotage
7.3

1 Humber Pilotage and VTS Operations Centre is situated on Spurn Head (53°34′N 0°07′E). The Humber Pilotage limits encompass the approaches to River Humber from seaward of Humber Light Float (53°38′·7N 0°21′·2E) to Goole on River Ouse and Gainsborough on River Trent. Pilotage is compulsory for vessels of 60 m and over in length and all vessels carrying dangerous substances in ...bulk when proceeding to and from the inner anchorages (7.10a, 7.66 and 7.109) for the purpose of anchoring. Vessels which are exempt from compulsory pilotage,... VTS Humber and should give at least 12 hours notice of requirement. Pilot boarding and disembarkation positions are as follows:

Deep-draught vessels (53°39′·8N 0°22′·0E). This position, 1¼ miles NNE of Humber Light Float, is used by vessels defined as Very Large Ships (7.6) both for embarkation and disembarkation. Such vessels may also be boarded in the Deep Water Anchorage (7.10).

3 **PB1 (Papa Bravo 1)** (53°33′·3N 0°15′·0E). This position, about 5 cables SE of Spurn Light Float, is the main boarding position for all inbound vessels except Very Large Ships (7.6) and other large or complex vessels.

PB2 (Papa Bravo 2) (53°34′·4N 0°16′·5E). This position, in the vicinity of S Binks Light Buoy, is the boarding position for large or complex vessels inbound via New Sand Hole TSS.

4 **PB3 (Papa Bravo 3)** (53°33′·2N 0°18′·0E). This position, in the vicinity of Inner Sea Reach Light Buoy, is the boarding position for large or complex vessels inbound via Inner Sea Reach TSS.

River Trent and River Ouse (53°44′·1N 0°20′·4W). Vessels, which are exempt compulsory pilotage on River Humber but which require a pilot for Rivers Trent or Ouse, embark the pilot in Hull Roads off Riverside Quay, Albert Dock.

5 **Outward** (53°32′·5N 0°15′·0E). All vessels, except Very Large Ships (7.6), disembark the pilot about 1 mile E of Haile Sand Light Buoy.

6 For further information see *Admiralty List of Radio Signals Volume 6 (1)*.

Vessel traffic service
7.4

1 Humber VTS is maintained for the control of shipping in Rivers Humber, Ouse and Trent. Subsidiary port radio stations are maintained by the ports, oil terminals and jetties within the scheme for the passing of berthing information. Radar surveillance of shipping is provided from the seaward limits of the VTS area as far upriver as Humber Bridge (53°42′N 0°27′W).

2 Participation in the scheme is mandatory for all vessels over 50 gt and any vessel carrying dangerous substances.

For further information see *Admiralty List of Radio Signals Volume 6 (1)*.

Notice of ETA required
7.5

1 Vessels are required to report their ETA at Spurn Light Float (53°34′N 0°14′E) not less than 24 hours in advance, or, 1 hour after departure from their last port of call if the passage time is less than 24 hours. Amendments to ETA must be reported. Vessels are required to call VTS Humber on VHF, when 2½ hours from Alpha Lightbuoy (7.23) and maintain VHF watch within the VTS area. For details of reporting points see *Admiralty List of Radio Signals Volume 6 (1)*.

Traffic regulations
7.6

1 **Humber Passage Plan**, a booklet, has been prepared by Associated British Ports in order to facilitate the safe movement of Very Large Ships bound to and from Tetney Monobuoy (7.27), the various terminals at Immingham and Killingholme, and Saltend Jetties (7.108). Very Large Ships are defined as vessels of 40 000 dwt and over, vessels with a draught of 11 m and over, and gas carriers of 20 000 m³ capacity and over.

2 As a general rule, a Very Large Ship will require two pilots to be in attendance. Vessels transiting the Sunk Dredged Channel are required to have a minimum UKC of 1 m. However, a UKC of 2 m should be allowed for in the

TSS east of Spurn Head due to sea and swell conditions and turning manoeuveres.

The Humber Passage Plan can be found on the website www.humber.com.

3   **The Humber Navigation Byelaws 1990** apply from Spurn Light Float throughout River Humber, River Trent to Gainsborough and River Ouse to Goole. It should be noted that nothing in these byelaws shall affect the operation of *The International Regulations for Preventing Collisions at Sea (1972)*, including the requirement to make sound signals in restricted visibility as prescribed in Rule 35.

The byelaws state:

4   A vessel shall navigate with due care, reducing speed when necessary to avoid damage to other vessels, especially vessels engaged in underwater operations. When passing any jetty with vessels alongside, or vessels engaged in berthing or unberthing, speed must be reduced to less than 5 kn.

A vessel must not cross the fairway in such a manner as to cause inconvenience or danger to other vessels.

5   A vessel not confined to the fairway by reason of its draught shall not impede any other vessel which is confined to the fairway by reason of draught.

A vessel navigating against the tidal stream shall on approaching bends, fairways or bridges, reduce speed or stop as necessary so as to allow any other vessel navigating with the tidal stream to pass clear. This rule does not apply if the former vessel is restricted in her ability to manoeuvre and showing the appropriate signals or if she can only navigate safely within the fairway.

6   A vessel turning round shall give four short blasts on the whistle followed by one short blast if turning to starboard or two short blasts if turning to port.

A vessel about to get underway from alongside a jetty, lock, or another vessel, shall sound a prolonged blast on the whistle.

The master of a vessel underway shall ensure that the hatches and covers of the vessel, if any, are in place and secured.

7   Masters shall report immediately to Humber VTS any incident of collision, grounding, obstruction of navigation fairway, fire, defect or pollution.

8   **The Humber Serious Marine Emergency Plan** lays down the actions to be taken in the event of an emergency. In the event of a pollution incident, the plan will activate the Humber oil spill contingency plan called "Humber Clean". For details see *Admiralty List of Radio Signals Volume 6 (1)*.

Dangerous substances
7.7

1   **The Dangerous Substances in Harbour Areas Regulations 1987** require vessels carrying dangerous substances into the River Humber and its approaches to:

Give 24 hours notice of the entry of dangerous substances into the harbour area but when this is not possible to give notice before the vessel commences navigation in the Humber.

2   Display a red flag by day and, only when a vessel is at anchor or berthed alongside, an all-round red light at night. The red light is not to be exhibited when a vessel is underway.

Maintain a continuous VHF watch when underway or at anchor.

Be in a state of readiness to be moved at any time, tidal conditions permitting.

Possess the appropriate and valid certificate of fitness.

3   Report incidents involving the escape of dangerous substances to Humber VTS immediately.

Give notice to VTS Humber of dangerous or polluting cargoes at least 2 hours prior to ETD at the time when the pilot is ordered.

7.8

1   All seagoing vessels carrying a dangerous substance in bulk, or in ballast and not gas-free, are prohibited from entry into or exit from the Humber in visibility of 5 cables or less without the express permission of the Harbour Master.

7.9

1   All vessels are to keep a safe distance from any vessel displaying a red flag or an all-round red light. No vessel is to berth alongside a vessel which displays the foregoing signals unless permission has been granted by Humber VTS.

Outer anchorages
7.10

1   **Humber Deep Water Anchorage.** Large vessels awaiting a pilot should anchor in the deep-water anchorage centred 3½ miles SE of Humber Light Float. The limits of the anchorage are marked by four light buoys (cardinal). It contains four designated anchor berths each with a swinging radius of 5 cables and ten berths for smaller vessels with a swinging radius of 2¾ cables.

2   **Caution.** Local experience indicates that on occasions the actual tidal stream considerably exceeds the predicted rate (see 1.102). Vessels anchoring in this area when there are strong tidal streams should keep well clear of other anchored vessels and of the buoys. Vessels anchored in this area have been known to drag anchor in a N direction at a rate of 2 kn towards and over the gas pipelines which are situated about 4 miles N. See 1.41.

Depending upon circumstances, it may be preferable to stem the tide to N of Humber Light Float rather than go to anchor.   ✱ WK 12/10 (SEE ~~FRONT~~ SIDE)

1   **Bull Anchorage.** 1½ miles SW of Spurn Head · ∨ (53°34′N... _____ ......_____ ~~____ ____ _____~~ designated anchorage berths each with a swinging radius of 1 cable. The limits of the anchorage are shown on Chart 1188. Depths in the anchorage range between about 5 m and 13 m.

Vessels should enter or depart the anchorage either between Bull Light Float and Hobo Light Buoy or between No 4 Light Buoy and Bull Sand Light Buoy.

2   **Haile Anchorage,** inset within the SW limit of ⌐ Bull... _____ ___ ___ ___ ___ ⌐ swinging radius of 1 cable, which are used by vessels carrying explosives. Subject to the agreement of the Harbour Master, it may also be used for tank washing and gas-freeing and for the taking of bunkers and the transfer of slops. The S corner of Haile Anchorage is marked by No 2C Light Buoy (port hand).

3   **Hawke Anchorage,** 3 miles WNW of Spurn ⌐ Head is a... _____ ___ ___ ___ ___ ___ ⌐ berths each with a swinging radius of 1 cable and is used by smaller vessels.

The limits of the anchorage are shown on Chart 1188. Depths in the anchorage range between about 3m and 9 m.

Advice about anchoring for vessels arriving off the Humber can be obtained from VTS Humber (7.4). Masters are reminded to report their positions to VTS Humber upon completion of anchoring.

Rescue
7.11
1   MRCC Humber is based at Bridlington (6.185). Within the Humber there are Coastal Rescue Teams at Hull, Cleethorpes (53°33′N 0°01′W) and Donna Nook (53°28′N 0°09′E). See 1.67.

An all-weather lifeboat is stationed at Spurn Head (53°34′N 0°07′E) and an inshore lifeboat at Cleethorpes. See 1.72.

Natural conditions
7.12
1   **Tidal streams** 10 miles to the E of Spurn Head are not affected by the river streams and are given on the chart and in *Admiralty Tidal Stream Atlas: North Sea, Southern Portion.* As the entrance to River Humber is approached the direction of the S-going stream becomes more W and that of the N-going stream more E. The in-going spring rate is 3¾ kn and the out-going 4¼ kn at a position 5 cables SSW of Spurn Head.

2   At the entrance to the river the in-going stream runs very strongly across Chequer Shoal (53°33′N 0°11′E) in the direction of the channel and, still following the direction of the channel, around Spurn Head: the pattern is reversed on the out-going stream. It has been reported that eddies occur between Chequer Shoal and Spurn Point which can have an adverse effect on the handling of small craft. On the S side of the channel in the vicinity of the entrance, the streams are weaker.

3   Within the river the tidal streams are rapid and irregular. In some instances the tidal stream at springs sets in a different direction from the tidal stream at neaps.

Caution. Mariners are advised that the flood stream sets strongly to the N in the Bull Channel (53°35′N 0°03′E) which can carry vessels out of the fairway. It is reported (1994) that vessels have frequently tended to collide with No 5 Gate Buoy which marks the N side of the channel.

4   During and after periods of heavy rain both the duration and rates of the out-going streams are increased and the in-going correspondingly reduced; these changes are small at the river entrance but increase farther upstream. Off Immingham the out-going stream may continue to run for an hour after the time at which the in-going stream would normally begin. It is also reported that off Immingham the streams begin earlier with N winds and later with S winds.

5   Details of the tidal streams in the estuary and the river are given on the charts.

Flow
7.13
1   **Fresh water and salt water streams.** The quantity of fresh water increases as the river is ascended. Upriver the out-going stream on the surface is observed to be considerably stronger and of longer duration than the in-going stream. It seems probable therefore that the fresh water runs out mostly on the surface, while the salt water enters below the surface. Conversely, the in-going stream of salt water on the surface is weaker and of shorter duration than the in-going stream below the surface. This phenomenon means that a deep-draught vessel may not be affected by the tidal stream exactly in accordance with the tidal stream data given on the chart.

2   It should be noted that off Albert Dock in the port of Hull, contrary to the foregoing, the in-going stream is stronger than the out-going stream. See 7.96.

Local weather
7.14
1   At the entrance to River Humber the highest seas occur when NW gales coincide with an in-going tidal stream.
Climate information: see 1.142 and 1.152.

APPROACHES TO RIVER HUMBER

General information
Chart 107, 109, 1188
Routes
7.15
1   Deep-draught vessels approaching River Humber from Dover Strait should follow the route recommended at 2.15 and should embark the pilot 1¼ miles NNE of Humber Light Float. See 7.3.

2   From seaward three Traffic Separation Schemes, from NE, E and SE, converge in an outer Precautionary Area centred 5 miles ESE of Spurn Head (53°34′N 0°07′E). A single TSS then leads W and NW into the Humber. Two additional Precautionary Areas exist; one centred 4 cables SSW of No 3 Chequer Light Buoy (53°33′·1N 0°10′·6E), the other centred 6 cables S of Spurn Point Beacon (53°34′·4N 0°06′·5E).

3   **North-east approach.** From the vicinity of Humber Light Float (53°38′·71N 0°21′·23E), the NE TSS leads 1½ miles SSW and 6 miles SW through New Sand Hole and through the outer precautionary area. Thence the route follows the traffic lane 2 miles W and 2½ miles WNW to a position S of Spurn Head.

4   **East approach.** From the vicinity of Outer Sea Reach Light Buoy (safe water) (53°33′N, 0°23′E), the TSS leads W for 3 miles into a precautionary area, and thence W and WNW in the TSS to a position S of Spurn Head. TSS

South-east approach. From the vicinity of Outer Rosse Reach Light Buoy (safe water) (53°29′·89N 0°20′·79E) TSS leads NW for 3 miles into a precautionary area and thence W and WNW in the TSS to a position S of Spurn Head.

Topography
7.16
1   The shores of River Humber are low-lying and fronted by extensive sands.

Depths
7.17
1   The main approach channel leads through New Sand Hole (53°36′N 0°19′E), a deep and narrow depression with depths ranging from 15 m to 43 m.

2   For deep-draught vessels on passage between Humber Light Float and a position S of Spurn Head, there is a shoal patch with depths of less than 8 m which encroaches up to 4 cables into the inbound traffic lane in the vicinity of Alpha Light Buoy (53°32′·8N 0°13′·2E).

3   Depths are constantly changing and the charts and the Harbour Authority should be consulted for the latest information.

Traffic regulations
7.18
1   The Traffic Separation Schemes described in 7.15 are IMO-adopted and Rule 10 of *The International Regulations for Preventing Collisions at Sea (1972)* applies.

2   On occasions it will be necessary for a departing deep-draught vessel, which is constrained by its draught, to navigate against the traffic flow in that part of the TSS between Spurn Point and Spurn Light Float. Vessels requiring to do this must obtain prior permission from VTS

Humber, which will warn other shipping whilst the transit is being carried out.

Exercise area
7.19

1   A firing practice area is situated between Haile Sand (53°30′N 0°08′E) and Saltfleet Overfalls, 7 miles SE. The area, which is marked by DZ light buoys (special) and beacons (port hand), extends 6 miles to seaward. A floating target (yellow) is moored 2¼ miles E of Donna Nook (53°29′N 0°10′E). See the note on the chart.

<h2 style="text-align:center">Directions</h2>
(continued from 6.184)

Principal marks
7.20

1   **Landmarks:**
Radio masts (red lights) and flares at Easington Gas Terminal (53°40′N 0°07′E).
Spurn Head Lighthouse (disused) (53°35′N 0°07′E) (black round tower, white band, 39 m in height), a second disused lighthouse is close W.
Hydraulic tower (53°35′N 0°04′W) at Grimsby.

2   **Offshore mark:**
Meteorological mast (steel lattice structure on base pile, 82 m in height) (53°38′·2N 0°15′·7E). Lights are exhibited from the mast.

Other aids to navigation
7.21

1   **Racons:**
Humber Light Float (53°38′·7N 0°21′·2E).
Spurn Light Float (53°34′N 0°14′E).
For details see *Admiralty List of Radio Signals Volume 2.*

Approach from the north-east — Humber Light Float to Spurn Light Float
7.22

1   From the pilot boarding position for deep-draught vessels (53°39′·8N 0°22′·0E), the track leads initially SSW, passing (with positions from Humber Light Float):
ESE of Humber Light Float (starboard hand) where the TSS (7.15) is joined, and:
WNW of North New Sand Light Buoy (N cardinal) (8 cables ESE), marking the N limit of the DW anchorage (7.10), thence:
ESE of Outer Binks Light Buoy (starboard hand) (1½ miles SSW).

2   Course is adjusted SW and passes:
NW of Mid New Sand Light Buoy (W cardinal) (2 miles S) moored at the W limit of the DW anchorage. An obstruction and two wrecks lie within 1 mile SW of the buoy. Thence:

3   Between N Binks Light Buoy (starboard hand) (3¼ miles SSW) and N Haile Light Buoy (port hand), 8 cables SE, thence:
NW of the extremity of a coastal bank (4¼ miles SSW) which extends NE from Donna Nook (7.1), and:

4   SE of a series of detached shoals (4 miles SW), thence:
Between S Binks Light Buoy (starboard hand) (4¾ miles SW) and S Haile Light Buoy (port hand), 8 cables SE, and into the outer Precautionary Area.

5   The route continues SW, passing (with positions from Spurn Head (53°34′N 0°07′E)):

SE of Outer Binks (centre 3 miles ENE), an extensive shoal, thence:

6   To a position close S of Spurn Light Float (E cardinal) (4½ miles ESE), moored on the edge of shoals extending SSE of Outer Binks.

Caution. Depths offshore are irregular, and shoals, particularly those outside the main channel, are subject to change. Only those channels which are buoyed should be used.

Approach from east — Outer Sea Reach Light Buoy to Spurn Light Float
7.23

1   From the vicinity of Outer Sea Reach Light Buoy, the W-bound traffic lane leads W for about 3 miles to the seaward Precautionary Area, passing (with positions from Spurn Light Float (53°34′N 0°14′E)):

2   N of Outer Sea Reach Light Buoy (safe water) (5 miles ESE), which marks the E end of a traffic separation zone thence:
To a position close N of Inner Sea Reach Light Buoy (safe water) (2½ miles ESE), which marks the W end of a traffic separation zone, and into the Precautionary Area.

3   Thence the route continues W, to a position close S of Spurn Light Float (7.22) to join the approach from NE. See 7.25.

Approach from south-east — Outer Rosse Reach Light Buoy to Spurn Light Float
7.24

1   From the vicinity of Outer Rosse Reach Light Buoy, the NW-bound traffic lane leads NW for about 2½ miles to the seaward Precautionary Area, passing (with positions from Spurn Light Float (53°34′N 0°14′E)):
NE of Outer Rosse Reach Light Buoy (safe water) (5 miles SE), which marks the SE end of a traffic separation zone, thence:

2   NE of a firing practice area (7.19), thence:
To a position between Inner Rosse Reach Light Buoy (safe water) (3 miles SE), which marks the NW end of a traffic separation zone, and Hotspur Light Buoy (special) (3 miles ESE), and into the Precautionary Area.

3   Thence the route continues NW to a position close S of Spurn Light Float (7.22) to join the approach from NE. See 7.25.

Spurn Light Float to No 3 Chequer Light Buoy
7.25

1   From a position close S of Spurn Light Float the line of bearing 260° of Haile Sand Fort Light (mast, 6 m in height) (53°32′·1N 0°02′·0E) leads through the in-bound traffic lane for 2 miles to a position S of No 3 Chequer Light Buoy, passing (with positions from Spurn Head (7.24)):

2   N of Alpha Light Buoy (safe water) (4¼ miles ESE) marking the E end of a traffic separation zone, thence:
N of Haile Sand Flat (4½ miles SE), which extends 4 miles NNE of Donna Nook and is marked at its NE extremity by No 2 Haile Sand Light Buoy (port hand), thence:

3   S of Chequer Shoal (3 miles ESE), a patch of stony ground marked at its E extremity by SE Chequer Light Float (S cardinal) (3¾ miles ESE), thence:
N of Bravo Light Buoy (safe water) (3¼ miles ESE) marking the W end of a traffic separation zone,

thence into a Precautionary Area S of No 3 Chequer Light Buoy (S cardinal) (2¾ miles ESE).

No 3 Chequer Light Buoy to Spurn Head
7.26
1   From a position S of No 3 Chequer Light Buoy, the inbound traffic lane leads 3 miles WNW to a position SW of Spurn Head (53°34′N 0°07′E) passing (with positions from Spurn Head):

2   SSW of No 3 Chequer Light Buoy (S cardinal) (2¾ miles ESE), thence:

NNE of Charlie Light Buoy (safe water) (2½ miles SE), which marks the SE end of a traffic separation zone, thence:

3   SSW of The Binks (1½ miles E), an irregular shoal running E from Spurn Head, thence:

Between Delta Light Buoy (safe water) (1 mile SE), which marks the NW end of a traffic separation zone, and No 3A Binks Light Buoy (starboard hand) (7 cables SE) and into a Precautionary Area S of Spurn Head, thence:

4   NNE of the E end of Bull Anchorage (7.10), the E extremity of which is marked by Hobo Light Buoy (port hand) (1¼ miles S), thence:

5   To a position about 3½ cables SW of Spurn Head, which consists of sandhills 6 m to 9 m high and terminates in Spurn Point, an indistinct feature from where a light (green cone on metal tripod) is exhibited. Spurn Head Lighthouse (disused) (7.20) stands 5 cables NE of the head. Spurn Point is a National Nature Reserve (1.61).

(Directions continue for Bull Channel at 7.30 and Hawke Channel at 7.62)

Tetney Terminal

Monobuoy
7.27
1   Tetney Monobuoy (53°32′·35N 0°06′·76E), a lighted mooring buoy with moorings extending 2½ cables, lies in an open roadstead. In 2008 the terminal was used by 101 vessels. It is used by large tankers drawing up to 15·5 m for discharging oil. A submarine pipeline runs 3 miles SW from the buoy to the shore at Tetney Haven Oil Terminal. The inner end of the pipeline is marked by beacons. When the buoy is not in use a floating hose, marked by quick flashing lights, extends up to 290 m from the buoy.

2   Tankers berthing at the monobuoy should have a UKC of 2 m. Vessels berth at HW, the approach to the monobuoy being made from the vicinity of No 3 Chequer Light Buoy (7.24).

3   Other vessels should give a wide berth to tankers secured to the buoy or manoeuvring in its vicinity.

The terminal has a port radio; see *Admiralty List of Radio Signals Volume 6 (1)*.

SPURN HEAD TO GRIMSBY

General information
Chart 1188
Route
7.28
1   From a position about 3½ cables SW of Spurn Head (53°34′N 0°07′E) (7.24) the route leads 3 miles WNW through Bull Channel to the approaches to Grimsby.

Tidal streams
7.29
1   The tidal streams in Bull Channel are rectilinear and tend to run in the direction of the fairway.

See tidal stream data on chart.

Directions
(continued from 7.24)

Landmarks
7.30
1   Spurn Head Lighthouse (53°35′N 0°07′E) (7.20).
Water tower (53°34′N 0°02′W) at Cleethorpes.
Building (53°34′·6N 0°03′·6W) at Grimsby.
Hydraulic tower (53°35′N 0°04′W) at Grimsby.
Three chimneys (53°35′N 0°06′W).

Disused Lighthouse

Pilot Jetty   *Operations Centre*   *The Binks*

Spurn Head from SW (7.26)
(Original dated 2000)

(Photograph – Air Images)

Spurn Head to Grimsby

7.31

1   From a position about 3½ cables SW of Spurn Head (53°34′N 0°07′E) the track leads WNW through Bull Channel, which is marked by buoys (lateral) to the approaches to Grimsby, passing (with positions from Spurn Head (7.24)):

2   NNE of Bull Light Float (N cardinal) (1¼ miles SW), thence:

3   SSW of Hawke Light Float (E cardinal) (6 cables WNW) marking the entrance to Hawke Channel (7.62). Grimsby Middle and Middle Shoal divide the Hawke and Sunk Dredged Channels to the N from Bull Channel and Grimsby Road (7.63) to the S. The shoals run 6 miles to the WNW and are subject to great change. Hawke Anchorage (7.10) lies over and adjacent to Grimsby Middle. Thence:

NNE of Bull Sand Fort (1½ miles WSW), standing centrally on Bull Sand and marked by light buoys (N and S cardinal). The depths and configuration of the sand change continuously. Thence:

4   NNE of No 4A Clee Ness Light Float (port hand) moored off the NE extremity of Clee Ness Sand, an extensive flat which dries up to 1½ miles offshore. A light (red beacon) is exhibited from an iron pier at the seaside resort of Cleethorpes.

5   Thence the line of bearing 265° of the hydraulic tower at Grimsby (7.30) leads to a position in the channel close N of No 4B Light Buoy (port hand) (4 miles WNW) from where a direct approach to Grimsby can be made.

(Directions continue at 7.63 and for Grimsby at 7.49)

GRIMSBY

General information

Chart 1188
Position
7.32

1   Grimsby Harbour (53°35′·10N 0°03′·96W) lies on the S bank of River Humber, 6 miles W of Spurn Head (7.24).

Function
7.33

1   It is a medium–sized commercial and fishing port. The port specialises in short sea trade to Europe and the Baltic; principal cargoes include cars, forestry products and frozen food including fish. The population is about 91 000.

Approach and entry
7.34

1   Grimsby is approached through Bull Channel (7.31) and an approach fairway lying to the SE of Grimsby Road. It is entered through one of two entrance locks, depending on the vessel's berth.

Traffic
7.35

1   In 2008 the port was used by 777 vessels totalling 2·2 million dwt.

Port Authority
7.36

1   Associated British Ports, Port Office, Cleethorpe Road, Grimsby, DN31 3LL.

Website: www.abports.co.uk
Alternative website: www.humber.com

Limiting conditions

Controlling depths
7.37

1   Least depth in the fairway approach is 0·7 m (2007). The docks and entrance are subject to constant dredging and depths are liable to change. The Dock Master should be consulted for the latest information.

Deepest and longest berth
7.38

1   Royal Dock (7.51).

Tidal levels
7.39

1   See *Admiralty Tide Tables Volume 1*. Mean spring range about 6·0 m; mean neap range about 3·1 m.

Maximum size of vessel handled
7.40

1   The Commercial Docks (7.46) can accommodate vessels up to 145 m in length, 20·6 m beam and 6·4 m draught (spring tides), 5·8 m draught (neap tides). Vessels over 81·7 m in length have to canal through the entrance lock.

The Fish Docks can accommodate vessels up to 73 m in length, 12·8 m beam and 5·5 m draught. Larger vessels have to canal through the entrance lock.

Local weather and sea state
7.41

1   Winds from the NNE cause the highest tides at Grimsby and those from the NNW the most sea, but the swell seldom prevents opening of the lock gates.

Approaching the locks can be difficult in strong E or W winds.

Arrival information

Port radio
7.42

1   See 7.4. A local port radio service is maintained. See *Admiralty List of Radio Signals Volume 6 (1)*.

Notice of ETA required
7.43

1   See 7.5. The Dock Master requires 2 hours notice of ETA.

Outer anchorage
7.44

1   See 7.10.

Pilotage and tugs
7.45

1   **Pilotage** in River Humber see 7.3. Pilotage within the docks is undertaken by private pilots.

Tugs are available but require 24 hours' notice.

Harbour

General layout
7.46

1   The harbour consists of two enclosed dock comp~~l~~ Fish Docks on the E side and Comme~~~~ comprising Royal Dock, Union Dock~~ on the W side. Each co~~~~

Traffic sign~~~~
7.47

1   **Royal** ~~~~
International~~~~

Development

7.46a Grimsby Riverside Terminal is under construction NE of West Jetty (53°35′·16N 0°04′·1W) construction area is centred on 53°35′·16N 04~~~~ Mariners should navigate with caution in the ~~v~~ity works.

Hydraulic Tower

Grimsby Harbour from NE (7.46)

(Original dated 2000)

(Photograph - Air Images)

Handbook, are exhibited from a mast close W of the entrance lock to Royal Dock.

Fish Dock. Main signals No 2 and No 4 are exhibited from a mast on the W side of the entrance lock to Fish Dock.

Tidal streams
7.48

1   Both the in-going and out-going streams circulate round Royal Dock Tidal Basin (7.50) and, except at HW neaps, set SE across Royal Dock lock entrance.

Directions for entering harbour
(continued from 7.31)

Principal marks
7.49

1   **Landmarks:**
   Water tower (53°34′N 0°02′W) at Cleethorpes.
   Hydraulic tower (53°35′N 0°04′W) at the entrance to
      Royal Dock.
   Three chimneys (53°35′N 0°06′W).

Approach
7.50

2   From a position in Bull Channel close N of No 4B Light Buoy (port hand) (53°35′·1N 0°00′·1E) the route leads W for 2½ miles through the fairway, which is about 3½ cables wide, to the harbour entrance, passing (with positions from the harbour entrance):

3   S of Lower Burcom Light Float (port hand) (1½ miles ENE), marking the SW side of the channel to Immingham, thence:
   To the harbour entrance.

4   **Royal Dock entrance lock** is approached through a tidal basin. The entrance to the basin is 76 m wide and lies between W Pierhead on which stands a light (brown metal column, 7 m in height) and a dolphin (lighted) standing at the N edge of a mud flat which extends offshore from the point that separates the two docks. The alignment (221°) of two beacons (cross topmark) situated on the W side of Royal Dock entrance lock indicates the extent of the shoal water on the W side of Tidal Basin. The entrance lock is 85 m long and 21·3 m wide and has a depth over the sill of 8·2 m at MHWS and 6·8 m at MHWN. The lock normally operates from 3½ hours before HW to 2½ hours after HW, depending on draught. Both lock gates are normally open from 1½ hours before HW until HW. Flood gates are closed at Royal Dock and Fish Dock entrances if the depth over the outer sills exceed 8·5 m.

5   **Fish Dock entrance lock** (1½ cables S) is approached between E Pierhead Light (brown metal column, 7 m in height) and W Pierhead Light (brown wooden mast, 7 m in height). Middle Pierhead on which stands a light (brown wooden mast, 7 m in height) is a short landing pier on the W side of the lock entrance. The lock, which is 21·4 m long and 13·0 m wide, has a depth over the sill of 8·2 m MHWS and 6·8 m at MHWN.

Basins and berths

Commercial Docks
7.51

1   Royal Dock; 1219 m of quayage; dredged depth 6·8 m; two RoRo berths.
   Alexandra Dock; dredged depth 6·6 m; two RoRo berths.

Fish Docks
7.52

1   No1 Fish Dock contains a fish market complex and a base for the servicing of offshore wind farms; No 2 Fish Dock contains a marina.

Port services

Repairs
7.53

1   There are three slipways in No 3 Fish Dock; the largest can handle vessels up to 1200 tonnes.

Other facilities
7.54

1   Reception of oily waste, noxious and harmful substances; Ship Sanitation Certificates issued (1.92); hospital with helicopter landing site; divers.

Supplies
7.55

1   Marine diesel in Fish Docks; water at the quays; provisions and stores.

SPURN HEAD TO IMMINGHAM

General information

Chart 1188
Route
7.56

1   From a position about 3½ cables SW of Spurn Head (53°34′N 0°07′E) (7.24) there are two routes to Immingham, one N and the other S of Middle Shoal. The N route, which is the deeper, leads WNW firstly through Hawke Channel and then W through Sunk Dredged Channel for a total distance of 7½ miles. The S route leads 2¾ miles WNW through Bull Channel then 1 mile W to the fairway off Grimsby, thence WNW 3½ miles to the S of Grimsby Middle and Middle Shoal. The two routes join W of Middle Shoal and the combined route then leads 3½ miles WNW to a position off the entrance lock at Immingham.

Depths
7.57

1   On the N route, Sunk Dredged Channel is dredged continuously. The latest available depth will be announced by VTS Humber in their regular river broadcasts but is normally more than 9·5 m. Mariners requiring immediate information about depths should contact VTS Humber directly. See *Admiralty List of Radio Signals Volume 6 (1)*.

    On the S route, depths are in excess of 6 m (2007) but the latest information should be obtained from the Port Authority.

Traffic regulations
7.58

1   **Sunk Dredged Channel.** Vessels intending to navigate Sunk Dredged Channel must ascertain in advance that the channel is clear by calling Humber VTS before passing Spurn Light Float inbound or before passing No 9A Light Float (53°38′·0N 0°09′·3W) outbound. Except with the permission of the Harbour Master, the master of a vessel shall not navigate his vessel in the Sunk Dredged Channel in the opposite direction to a vessel already navigating within the channel, or overtake any vessel navigating in the same direction.

2   **Passage S of Grimsby Middle.** Inward-bound vessels must keep strictly to the N side of the channel and outward-bound vessels strictly to the S side.

    Passing Immingham Jetties. Mariners are warned against the dangers of overtaking off Immingham Oil Terminal (7.83). The main channel is very narrow at this

point and the wash from overtaking vessels which pass close to tankers moored at the Terminal may endanger the security of their cargo handling operations. Vessels must not approach nearer than 150 metres to the face of the berths. See also 7.6.

3   All vessels requiring tugs for berthing at Immingham or South Killingholme must have their tugs secured before the vessel passes No 10 Upper Burcom Light Float (53°37′·5N 0°08′·7W). Immingham Oil Terminal must not be passed until the tugs have been made fast.

4   **Prohibited anchorages** are established in the fairway to Grimsby and in the channel NE of Burcom Sand (53°36′N 0°04′W) between No 6 Lower Burcom Light Float and No 8 Middle Burcom Light Buoy. Anchoring is also prohibited within 200 m of the three outfalls extending 1½ miles NE from the coast between Grimsby and Stallingborough Flat (53°37′N 0°08′W).

    These prohibited areas are shown on the chart.

Measured distance
7.59

1   A measured distance for use of small vessels is charted close W of Hawkin's Point (53°38′N 0°03′W), marked by three pairs of beacons (black pole, black circular topmark, 12 m in height).

        Running track 112°/292°.
        Distance 1854·1 m between each pair of beacons.

Tidal streams
7.60

1   The tidal streams set strongly in Hawke and Sunk Dredged Channels. Variations of set and rate in Hawke Channel are very pronounced.

    The tidal streams in the channel SW of Grimsby Middle are rectilinear and tend to follow the direction of the channel.

2   Off Immingham the in-going stream sets strongly across Holme Ridge (7.64) to the channel W of Foul Holme Spit.

    See tidal stream data on chart.

Directions

Principal marks
7.61

1   **Landmarks:**
        See 7.49 for marks at Grimsby.
        Four chimneys and flare (53°36′N 0°08′W).
        Three chimneys and two pylons (power station) (53°36′N 0°09′W).
        See 7.81 for marks at Immingham.

North of Middle Shoal — Hawke and Sunk Dredged Channels
(Continued from 7.24)
7.62

1   From a position between Spurn Head (53°34′N 0°07′E) (7.24) and Hawke Light Float (E cardinal) (5 cables WNW of Spurn Head), the route leads WNW through Hawke Channel thence W through Sunk Dredged Channel to a position in mid-channel 5 cables W of the inner end of Sunk Dredged Channel. Both channels are marked by pairs of light buoys (lateral). Sunk Dredged Channel is 213 m wide. See 7.57.

2   Hawkin's Point (53°38′N 0°03′W) is the S point of Sunk Island and lies 6¾ miles WNW of Spurn Head. Between the two is a bay, which lies to the N of Hawke and Sunk Dredged Channels. The whole bay dries, with Trinity Sand to the E and Sunk Sand to the W.

South of Middle Shoal - alternative route
(Continued from 7.31)
7.63

1 From a position in mid-channel between Grimsby Middle and No 4A Clee Ness Light Float (53°35'·0N 0°01'·7E), the route leads WNW through a buoyed channel to a position 5 cables W of the inner end of Sunk Dredged Channel (7.62), passing (with positions from Grimsby Harbour entrance (53°35'·1N 0°04'·0W)):

2 NNE of entrance of the fairway (1¾ miles E) to Grimsby, thence:

SSW of Grimsby Middle (3 miles ENE), marked at its W extremity by No 7 Middle Light Float (S cardinal), thence:

3 NNE of No 8 Middle Burcom Light Buoy (port hand) (1 mile NNW) moored on the N side of Burcom Sand, an offshore bank which dries. Two outfalls marked by light buoys (special) lie 6 cables ESE and 7 cables WNW of the buoy. Thence:

4 To a position in mid-channel 5 cables W of the inner end of Sunk Dredged Channel.

Middle Shoal to Immingham
7.64

1 From a position in mid-channel 5 cables W of the inner end of Sunk Dredged Channel, the route leads 3½ miles WNW through the channel, which is buoyed, to a position NE of the entrance lock to Immingham Dock, passing (with positions from the lock entrance):

SSW of the measured distance (7.59) (3 miles E), thence:

2 NNE of a light beacon (port hand) (2½ miles ESE) marking the end of Humber Power Intake (7.58) E of Stallingborough Flat, thence:

NNE of No 10 Upper Burcom Light Float (port hand) (1½ miles ESE). A light beacon (special), which marks an underwater turbine, is located a ½ cable WSW of the light float. An underwater power cable extends from the device to a jetty on the S bank. Thence:

SSW of Holme Ridge (1 mile ENE), and:

NNE of Immingham Oil Terminal (7.83) (7 cables E),thence:

To a position NE of the entrance lock to Immingham Dock (7.84).

Directional lights
7.65

1 **Immingham Bulk Terminal.** The fixed white sector (290½°-291½°) of a directional light (on building) (53°38'·4N 0°12'·0W) at Immingham Bulk Terminal leads vessels to the various berths at Immingham.

Killingholme. The fixed white sector (291½°-292½°) of a directional light (red tower) (53°38'·8N 0°13'·1W) at Killingholme leads inbound vessels clear of the berths at Immingham until in the vicinity of No 11 Holme Light Buoy (starboard hand) (53°38'·2N 0°10'·2W) whence course can be adjusted to proceed farther upriver.

2 Both the above lights are shown throughout 24 hours.

*(Directions continue for Immingham at 7.81
and Kingston upon Hull at 7.97)*

Anchorage
7.66

1 Subject to the permission of the Harbour Master, very large tankers may anchor and carry out bunkering operations in the vicinity of No 9 Holm Ridge Light Buoy

(53°37'·9N 0°08'·3W). A tug or tugs must be secured to the vessel during the operations.

IMMINGHAM

General information
Chart 3497 plan of Immingham
Position
7.67

1 The port of Immingham (53°38'·00N 0°11'·00W) lies on the SW bank of River Humber, 5½ miles NW of Grimsby.

Function
7.68

1 Immingham, population about 12 300, is the centre of the Humberside chemical and oil refining industries. The port mainly handles liquid and dry bulk commodities but also has a substantial general cargo trade.

Traffic
7.69

1 In 2008 the port was visited by 6109 vessels totalling 88·5 million dwt.

Port Authority
7.70

1 Associated British Ports, Port Office, Cleethorpe Road, Grimsby, DN31 3LL.

Website: www.abports.co.uk
Alternative website: www.humber.com

Limiting conditions
Controlling depths
7.71

1 The least depth on passage between the pilot boarding station for deep-draught vessels (7.3) and the terminals at Immingham is in Sunk Dredged Channel where a minimum depth of 9·5 m is normally available. See 7.57.

Deepest and longest berth
7.72

1 Humber International Terminal (7.87).

Tidal levels
7.73

1 See *Admiralty Tide Tables Volume 1*. Mean spring range about 6·4 m; mean neap range about 3·2 m.

Maximum size of vessel handled
7.74

Berth	Length	Draught	Remarks
Immingham Dock	198 m	10·36 m	26·2 m beam
Eastern and Western Jetties	213 m	10·40 m	30 000 dwt
Immingham Oil Terminal	366 m	13·1 m	300 000 dwt part-laden
Immingham Outer Harbour	240 m	9·5 m	18 500 dwt
Immingham Bulk Terminal	303 m	14·0 m	200 000 dwt part-laden
Humber International Terminal	295 m	14·0 m	200 000 dwt part-laden
Immingham Gas Terminal	280 m	11·0 m	50 000 dwt

Draughts in the above table are based upon a water density of 1017 g/cm^3.

Arrival information

Vessel traffic service
7.75
1   See 7.4.

Outer anchorages
7.76
1   See 7.10

Pilotage and tugs
7.77
1   **Pilotage.** See 7.3

Tugs are available at Immingham. See 7.58.

Harbour

General layout
7.78
1   There are a number of jetties and terminals at Immingham, which together extend over a distance of 2 miles along the SW bank of River Humber. In addition there is an enclosed dock. From SE to NW, the river berths are Immingham Oil Terminal (7.83), Eastern and Western Jetties (7.84), which lie either side of the entrance to the enclosed dock, Immingham Outer Harbour (7.85), Immingham Bulk Terminal (7.86), Humber International Terminal (7.87) and finally Immingham Gas Terminal (7.88).

Traffic signals
7.79
1   **Vessels manoeuvring.** Synchronised traffic lights are exhibited, day and night, from Tower A, a signal tower at the entrance to Immingham Dock, and Tower B, a signal mast at the head of the approach arm to the Oil Terminal, as follows:

Signal	Meaning
White light, 2 flashes, each 2 seconds duration, every 10 seconds	A vessel is arriving at or leaving Immingham Dock, East Jetty or West Jetty or manoeuvring at the Bulk Terminal
White light 1 flash of 6 seconds every 15 seconds	Vessel manoeuvring off Immingham Oil Terminal Jetty

2   **Entrance lock.** Signals No 2 and No 5 of the International Port Traffic Signals are shown from Tower A to regulate traffic entering or leaving Immingham Dock. Instructions for approaching the lock or berthing at Eastern or Western Jetties are given on VHF radio.

For International Port Traffic Signals see *The Mariner's Handbook.*

Tidal streams
7.80
1   Off Immingham the spring rate for the in-going stream is 3½ kn and for the out-going stream 4½ kn. The rates off the jetties and terminals are similar but can reach 4 kn and 7 kn respectively at times.

2   In the close approach to the lock between the elbows of Eastern and Western Jetties, the stream is much weaker than in the channel off the jetties. The line of this division is often indicated by ripples and it is usually nearer the lock entrance at HW than at LW. In addition, there may be a NW-going eddy on the lock entrance side of the divide on the ebb tide between +0100 and +0520 HW Immingham.

3   The division between the weak streams in the close approach to the lock and the entirely slack water at the lock entrance occurs on the line between the outer masonry piers and the pile jetties.

4   When entering with a strong tidal stream running, the stern of a vessel tends to be pushed down tide as its bows enter slack water. If entry speed is high then a collision with the opposite jetty is possible. In these conditions vessels are advised to proceed at low speed close in to Western Jetty during the in-going stream and Eastern Jetty during the out-going stream.

5   It should be noted that the times of entry and departure from the lock are regulated by the port authority and that entry and departure is not permitted when the tidal stream is flowing strongly. Vessels entering without tug assistance should do so only at slack water.

Directions for entering harbour
(continued from 7.65)

Principal marks
7.81
1   **Landmarks:**
    Chimney (53°37′N 0°11′W).
    Silo (53°37′·4N 0°11′·7W).
    Coke silos (53°37′·6N 0°11′·8W).
    Flare (53°38′·8N 0°15′·4W).

Approach
7.82
1   There is direct access to the riverside berths from River Humber.

2   From River Humber the access to Immingham Dock is through an entrance lock, which is approached between Eastern and Western Jetties (7.84). The entrance lock has a length of 256 m, width 27·4 m and there is a depth over the inner sill of 11·3 m at MHWS and 9·7 m at MHWN. The lock has three pairs of gates, which can divide it into an outer part, 96 m long and an inner part, 160 m long.

3   The alignment (216°) of a pair of lights in line (mast structure) in position 53°37′·5N 0°11′·6W assists vessels in entering and leaving the locks. The lights are aligned alongside the E side of the lock which is the side normally used for making fast.

Depths in the entrance to Immingham Dock vary. The Dock Master should be consulted for the latest information.

Basins and berths

Immingham Oil Terminal
7.83
1   Immingham Oil Terminal Jetty lies 7 cables E of the entrance to Immingham Dock. The shore arm of the jetty extends 5 cables NE with three T-headed tanker berths and associated dolphins and mooring dolphins running WNW and ESE. The berths and dolphins exhibit lights at their extremities. A 200 m long inner jetty for product tankers extends WNW from the shore arm, 3½ cables from the shore.

2   A barge passage, which is for authorised vessels only, passes beneath the shore arm, 2½ cables from the shore. The passage is marked by lights (lateral) and the vertical clearance is 4·5 m.

Immingham Oil Terminal from NE (7.83)

(Original dated 2000)

(Photograph – Air Images)

Western Jetty　　　　　　　　　　　　　　　　　　　　　　*Eastern Jetty*

Immingham Dock and Jetties from NE (7.84)

(Original dated 2000)

(Photograph – Air Images)

Immingham Dock and Jetties
7.84

1　Immingham Dock has 1700 m of quays providing a number of berths. Alongside depths are between 8·3 m and 11·0 m. There are four RoRo berths.

Eastern and Western Jetties, which are on either either side of the approach to the entrance lock, lie parallel to the shore and provide three tanker berths. Eastern Jetty has been extended by a pontoon berth for tugs. Lights mark the SE extremity of the pontoon and the NW extremity of Western Jetty.

Immingham Outer Harbour
7.85

1　Immingham Outer Harbour is a tidal basin whose entrance lies between Western Jetty (7.84) and Immingham

Bulk Terminal (7.86). At its NW end are two RoRo berths on a 260 m long finger-jetty. At its SE end is a small area allocated for barges. There is a dredged depth of 10·0 m over the greater part of the basin, with the exception of the barge berth, which is dredged to 7·0 m.

Immingham Bulk Terminal
7.86

1　Immingham Bulk Terminal, an L-shaped jetty lying 1½ cables offshore and 4 cables NW of the entrance to Immingham Dock, has a seaward face 518 m in length, marked by lights at either end, and a dredged depth alongside of 14·0 m. The terminal handles coal and iron ore.

Gas Terminal   HIT   Bulk Terminal   Immingham Outer Harbour

Humber International Terminal (7.87)
(Original dated 2006)

(Photograph - Associated British Ports)

Humber International Terminal

7.87

1   Humber International Terminal (HIT) lies adjacent to the NW end of Immingham Bulk Terminal. The terminal, consisting of a concrete deck on tubular steel piles, is 520 m in length and has a dredged depth alongside of 14·4 m. The terminal provides two berths for vessels up to 100 000 dwt and is used for the import of coal.

Immingham Gas Terminal

7.88

1   Immingham Gas Terminal, an L-shaped jetty lying 2 cables offshore and close NW of Humber International Terminal (7.87) has a seaward face of 80 m and associated mooring dolphins, all marked by lights. There is a dredged depth alongside of 10·0 m.

Gas Terminal   Oil Jetty
Immingham Gas Terminal (7.88) and
South Killingholme Oil Jetty (7.89) from NE
(Original dated 2000)

(Photograph - Air Images)

South Killingholme Oil Jetty

7.89

1   South Killingholme Oil Jetty (53°38'·85N 0°12'·38W) extends 488 m NE from the S shore. In 2008 the terminal was used by 259 vessels totalling 2·7 million dwt. The L-shaped head has a seaward face of 85 m and associated mooring dolphins, all marked by lights, and a dredged depth of 11·0 m alongside. The jetty can accept ships up to 213 m in length. Power cables, suspended 2 m above water level at lowest point, are strung from the dolphins to the jetty.

Port services

Repairs

7.90

1   Depending upon the berth occupied, many types of repair can be undertaken.

Other facilities

7.91

1   Reception of oily waste, noxious and harmful substances; Ship Sanitation Certificates issued (1.92); customs; hospital at Grimsby; divers.

Supplies

7.92

1   All types of fuel oil; water at the quays; stores and provisions.

IMMINGHAM TO KINGSTON UPON HULL

General information

Chart 3497
Route
7.93

1   From a position in mid-channel off the entrance to Immingham Dock (53°38'N 0°11'W), the route leads 7 miles NNW to a position off the entrance to King George Docks at Hull, thence 2 miles W to a position off the entrance to Albert Dock at the W end of Hull.

Depths

7.94

1   The least depth in the buoyed channel between Immingham and Hull is 6·1 m (2008) in position 53°38'·8N 0°11'·4W. However depths are subject to frequent change and the buoyage is moved as necessary. The Harbour Master Humber should be consulted for the latest information.

Prohibited anchorage areas

7.95

1   Anchoring in the following areas is prohibited:
    The fairway.
    Either side of gas pipelines, indicated by pairs of beacons (yellow diamond topmarks) on each shore,

RIVER OUSE TO GOOLE AND SELBY

Chart 109 plan of Whitton Ness to Goole and Keadby

River Ouse, Faxfleet to Goole

7.145

1   Blacktoft Channel leads into River Ouse from the confluence with River Trent at Faxfleet. From the confluence, the distance to Goole is 7 miles and the channel is marked by light beacons (lateral).

Depths. The river is subject to constant change and no controlling depth can be given.

2   **Vertical clearance.** See 7.136. An overhead power cable with a safe vertical clearance of 42 m crosses the river at Yokefleet No 5 Light Beacon (53°42'·4N 0°44'·8W).

3   **Pilotage.** Local knowledge is essential and vessels should have a qualified pilot on board. See 7.3.

Tidal streams in the river normally run at a rate of 3 to 4 kn but may exceed 6 kn.

River Ouse, Goole to Selby

7.146

1   The river is navigable to Selby (7.170) 16 miles above Goole (7.148). It is marked by light beacons as far as Long Drax (7.169), 8 miles above Goole, and by beacons to Selby. Local chart coverage (7.2) does not extend above Goole.

Pilotage is compulsory above Goole for vessels over 40 m in length. River pilots board and land off Victoria Pier at Goole. The Competent Harbour Authority and Navigation Authority is British Waterways, Naburn Lock, Naburn, York, YO19 4RU, Telephone 01904 728500.

Bridges

7.147

1   Bridges cross River Ouse at the following points:

Skelton Railway Bridge (1 mile above Goole) a swing bridge. When vessels approach the bridge they sound 1 long blast followed by 6 short blasts to request opening. Inbound vessels are recommended to use Eastern Channel and outbound vessels Western Channel.

Sandhall Lodge and Light

Skelton Railway Bridge from N (7.147)
(Original dated 2001)

(Photograph - ABP Humber Estuary Services)

2   **Boothferry Bridge** (4 miles above Goole) a road swing bridge at Booth. The same signal as for Skelton Railway Bridge is sounded to request opening.

3   **M62 Motorway Bridge**, at Boothferry, has four piers marked by lights on both the upstream and downstream sides and has a vertical clearance of 22.86 m. A light shown from the bridge indicates the main channel.

4   **Selby Road and Rail Bridges**, both swing bridges. The same signal as for Skelton Railway Bridge is sounded to request their opening. Selby Road Bridge must be navigated with caution as its navigational span is only 10·7 m wide and the channel 9·9 m wide. Vessels exceeding 38 m in length and 8 m beam must pass the bridge in daylight at slack water, or against the stream and attended by a tug. Vessels with a beam greater than 9·5 m must obtain prior consent of the Harbour Master.

5   All swing bridges can be contacted on VHF channel 9.

GOOLE

General information

Chart 109 plan of Goole

Position

7.148

1   The Port of Goole (53°42'·01N 0°52'·40W) lies on the W bank of River Ouse close N of the mouth of Dutch River, a tributary.

Function

7.149

1   Goole is a small commercial port, trading principally with European ports and the Baltic. Imports include steel, aluminium, containers and paper products. The port is directly linked to the inland waterway network.

2   The population of Goole is about 18 000.

Traffic

7.150

1   In 2008 the port was used by 1073 vessels totalling 2·8 million dwt.

Port Authority

7.151

1   Associated British Ports, Port Office, East Parade, Goole DN14 5RB.

Website: www.abports.co.uk

Limiting conditions

Controlling depths

7.152

1   Due to the changing nature of the channel there is no fixed controlling depth but vessels drawing up to 5·5 m can reach Goole on ordinary spring tides and up to 4·6 m at ordinary neap tides. Within the docks the water is maintained at a constant level to allow vessels drawing 5·5 m to enter subject to tidal restrictions.

Deepest and longest berth

7.153

1   Largest dock is West Dock (7.162).

Tidal levels

7.154

1   Mean spring range about 5·4 m; mean neap range about 3·0 m. See *Admiralty Tide Tables Volume 1.*

Maximum size of vessel handled
7.155

1   Maximum size of vessel handled is length 100 m, beam 24 m, draught 5·5 m and 4500 dwt. Larger and deeper draught vessels may be accepted after consultation with the Dock Master.

Arrival information

Vessel traffic service
7.156

1   See 7.4.

Outer anchorages
7.157

1   See 7.10

Lay-by berth. There is a lay-by berth at Blacktoft, 6 miles downstream from Goole.

Pilotage and tugs
7.158

1   **Pilotage.**See 7.3.

Tugs are available between Hull and Goole and small tugs are available within the docks.

Harbour

General layout
7.159

1   Goole Docks consist of a number of interconnected docks which can be entered from either River Ouse or the Inland Waterways (7.175).

Traffic signals
7.160

1   **Ocean Lock.** International Port Traffic Signals Nos 2 and 5 are shown from a signal mast at the entrance to Ocean Lock to control traffic into the lock (see *The Mariner's Handbook*).

2   A flashing white light indicates that a vessel is leaving Ocean Lock and entering the tideway. When exhibited, no other vessel shall pass into the area bounded on the N by an imaginary line drawn 090° from the signal mast, and on the S by an imaginary line drawn 270° from Upper East Goole Light Beacon No 29 on the E bank of Goole Reach.

3   **Victoria Lock.** Signals (Diagram 7.160) are shown from a flagstaff and the lights from a lamp standard.

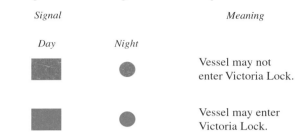

Signal		Meaning
Day	*Night*	
■	●	Vessel may not enter Victoria Lock.
■	●	Vessel may enter Victoria Lock.

Victoria Lock traffic signals (7.160)

Directions for entering harbour
7.161

1   Goole Docks are entered from River Ouse via two locks of the following dimensions:

    Ocean Lock: length 104 m; width 24·4 m; depth over sill at MHWN 6·1 m.

    Victoria Lock: constructed in two sections, total length 145 m; width 14·2 m; depth over sill at MHWN 6·0 m.

2   The locks are operated from approximately 2½ hours before HW to 1½ hours after HW at Goole. Ocean Lock is manned throughout 24 hours and can be operated for small craft and barge traffic at any time; an additional charge is made for this service.

Basins and berths
7.162

1   The nine interconnected docks provide about 3 miles of quays. The largest dock is West Dock which has a length varying between 280 m and 320 m, width varying between 78 m and 88 m, and 740 m of quays. There is a RoRo ramp capable of loads up to 450 tonnes at the SW corner of Railway Dock.

Ocean Lock   *Victoria Lock*

Goole Docks from E (7.162)
(Original dated 2000)

(Photograph - Air Images)

Submarine cable

7.163

1 A high-voltage submarine cable crosses Gutway between Ship Dock and Railway Dock. Mariners are advised against dropping or dredging anchors in the vicinity.

Port services

Repairs

7.164

1 Limited repairs can be carried out.

Other facilities

7.165

1 Reception of oily waste, noxious and harmful substances; hospitals; Ship Sanitation Certificates issued (1.92).

Supplies

7.166

1 All types of fuel oil by road tanker or barge; fresh water; stores and provisions.

Communications

7.167

1 An inland waterway, The Aire and Calder Navigation, (7.175) is entered from South Dock at Goole.

Minor ports

Howdendyke

7.168

1 Howdendyke (53°43'·86N 0°51'·09W), 2½ miles upstream from Goole, provides four berths on jetties with a total length of 186 m. In 2008 the port was used by 130 vessels totalling 246 000 dwt. Vessels up to 3000 dwt, length 88 m, beam 14 m and draught 5·0 m at spring tides or 3·0 m at neap tides can be accommodated. Vessels of greater length can be accommodated on some tides by arrangement. At LW vessels take bottom, which is soft mud. Fresh water is available by road tanker.

Howdendyke E Jetties from SW (7.168)

(Original dated 2001)

(Photograph - ABP Humber Estuary Services)

Long Drax

7.169

1 Long Drax, 8 miles upstream from Goole, has a lay-by berth.

Selby

7.170

1 Selby (53°47'·00N 1°04'·00W) is a small commercial port. There is a quay with a length of 74 m and the port

M62

Howdendyke W Jetty from S (7.168)

(Original dated 2001)

(Photograph - ABP Humber Estuary Services)

has accommodated vessels up to 84 m LOA and draught 6·0 m. However, vessels over 61 m LOA should consult the Port Authority prior to entry.

RIVER TRENT TO GAINSBOROUGH

Chart 109 plans of Whitton Ness to Goole and Keadby and Keadby to Gainsborough

General information

7.171

1 **Route.** From Trent Falls (53°42'N 0°41'W) close S of the confluence of Rivers Trent and Ouse, the route follows River Trent in a generally S direction for 21 miles to Gainsborough. The river is tidal as far as Gainsborough.

Depths. The river is subject to constant change and no controlling depth can be given.

Pilotage. Local knowledge is essential and vessels taking passage in the river should have a qualified pilot on board. See 7.3.

Vertical clearance. See 7.136. At Garthorpe (53°40'·1N 0°41'·4W), River Trent is spanned by power cables with a safe vertical clearance of 39 m.

Tidal streams run at a rate of 3 to 4 kn in the lower reaches of the river but may exceed 6 kn. A bore occurs in River Trent at equinoctial spring tides.

Directions

7.172

1 As far as Keadby, 8 miles above Trent Falls the river is marked by navigation lights and beacons but owing to the constant changes in the channel no directions can be given.

Trent Ports and wharves

7.173

1 There are a number of wharves along the banks of the river as far as Keadby. Although small, these busy wharves are capable of handling vessels between 90 and 100 m in length, draught up to 5·5 m at springs and 3·1 m at neaps and up to about 4500 dwt. In 2008 they were used by 1234 vessels totalling 2·6 million dwt. Principal imports include steel, timber and dry bulks.

From N to S these wharves are:

2 King's Ferry Wharf, Burton Stather, (53°39'·33N 0°41'·65W), one berth.

Flixborough Wharf (53°37'·16N 0°42'·18W), two berths.

3 Neap House Wharves (53°36'N 0°42'W), three berths.

Wharton Grove Wharves (53°36′·39N 0°42′·84W), eight berths on a total quay length of 580 m.

Keadby Wharf (53°35′·39N 0°44′·23W), one berth.

Gunness Wharves (53°35′·22N 0°43′·84W), three berths either side of Keadby Bridge.

King's Ferry Wharf from NW (7.173)

(Original dated 2001)

(Photograph - ABP Humber Estuary Services)

Flixborough Wharf from W (7.173)

(Original dated 2001)

(Photograph - ABP Humber Estuary Services)

Gainsborough

7.174

1   The inland port of Gainsborough (53°24′·32N 0°47′·33W) is 62 miles from the sea. The port has six berths and is capable of taking vessels up to 58 m in length and a draught of 4 m depending on the tide. Vessels bound for Gainsborough have to pass under Keadby Bridge with a vertical clearance of 4·3 m. Fuel is available from barge or road tanker, water is supplied at the quays.

INLAND WATERWAYS

General information

7.175

1   There is access to the Inland Waterways from River Ouse at Goole and Selby and from River Trent at Keadby (7.172). The two major waterways concerned are Aire and Calder Navigation, entered at Goole, and South Yorkshire Navigation, entered at Keadby. The two waterways are linked by New Junction Canal and give access to Leeds, Castleford, Wakefield, Doncaster, Rotherham and Mexborough. Aire and Calder Navigation carries about 2½ million tonnes of cargo a year, mainly coal and some grain.

2   The maximum dimensions in metres for vessels entering the waterways at Goole are:

Port	Length	Beam	Draught	Air-draught
Aire and Calder				
Leeds	62·5	6·1	2·5	3·7
Wakefield	42·6	5·4	1·98	3·7
South Yorkshire				
Mexborough	71·0	6·1	2·5	3·7
Rotherham	61·0	6·0	2·5	3·7

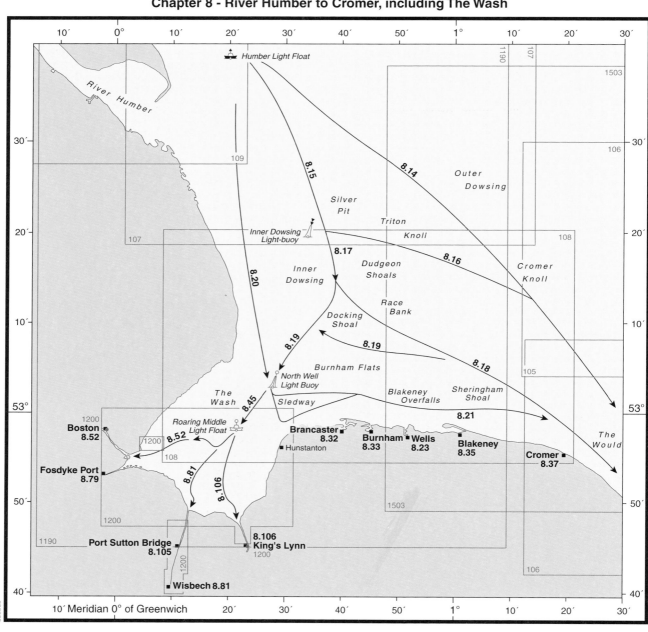

Chapter 8 - River Humber to Cromer, including The Wash

Humber Light Float

River Humber

109

8.15

8.14

Outer
Dowsing

Silver
Pit

Triton
Knoll

Inner Dowsing
Light-buoy

8.17

8.16

107

108

Dudgeon
Shoals

Cromer
Knoll

Inner
Dowsing

8.20

Race
Bank

Docking
Shoal

8.19

8.19

8.18

Burnham Flats

North Well
Light Buoy

105

The
Wash

Sledway

Blakeney
Overfalls

Sheringham
Shoal

8.45

8.21

Boston
8.52

1200

Roaring Middle
Light Float

8.52

Brancaster
8.32

Burnham
8.33

Wells
8.23

Blakeney
8.35

The
Would

1200

108

Hunstanton

Cromer
8.37

Fosdyke Port
8.79

8.81

8.106

1503

1200

1190

Port Sutton Bridge
8.105

8.106
King's Lynn
1200

106

1200

Wisbech 8.81

10´ Meridian 0° of Greenwich

1190

107

109

1503

1190

107

108

106

606030

192

RIVER HUMBER TO CROMER INCLUDING THE WASH

GENERAL INFORMATION

Charts 1190, 1503
Scope of the chapter
8.1

1   In this chapter the coastal passages from Humber Light Float (53°38'·7N 0°21'·2E) SE to Cromer (8.37) and from Humber Light Float S to The Wash (8.39) are described, together with the ports of Boston (8.52), Wisbech (8.81), Port Sutton Bridge (8.105) and King's Lynn (8.106). Inshore routes from Outer Rosse Reach Light Buoy (52°29'·9N 0°20'·8E) to the Wash and from the Wash to Cromer are also described.

2   The principal route into The Wash from SE passes between Race Bank and Docking Shoal and is the reverse of the route described at 8.18.

Topography
8.2

1   The deep bight between the entrance to River Humber and Cromer (52°56'N 1°18'E), about 53 miles SE, is for the most part encumbered with numerous and dangerous sands; some fringe the coast but others lie a considerable distance offshore. The Wash (8.39) roughly square in shape, is the upper part of this bight and lies to the SW of a line between Gibraltar Point (53°06'N 0°20'E) (8.39) and Gore Point (8.39) 10 miles SE.

2   From Donna Nook (53°29'N 0°10'E), the S entrance point of River Humber, to Gibraltar Point, 23 miles SSE, the coast is composed of sandhills. The flat which fronts this part of the coast, apart from some shoals, shelves gradually to the 10 m depth contour, which lies 8 miles E of Donna Nook. At its S end the flat merges with the shoals forming the bar to Boston Deep (8.47).

3   From Gore Point to Wells (8.23), 12 miles E, the coast is again composed of sandhills, thence it is embanked and fronted by marshes but towards Cromer (8.37) it begins to rise and form cliffs of a moderate height.

Exercise area
8.3

1   A firing practice area is situated E of Donna Nook (53°29'N 0°10'E); see 7.19.

Local conditions
8.4

1   The tidal streams are strong and the spring range of the tide is up to 6 m. The weather is frequently misty. The sands and shoals in The Wash, which form an almost continuous chain within the 5 m depth contour, are subject to constant change. These conditions, associated with a low featureless coastline, render navigation difficult and care is necessary. Sounding is important and the state of the tide should always be considered.

HUMBER TO CROMER

General information

Charts 107, 108
Routes
8.5

1   From the vicinity of the Humber Light Float (53°39'N 0°20'E) to Cromer, 53 miles SE, the principal through route is via Outer Dowsing Channel. This route and the alternatives, all of which eventually join it, are described below.

2   There is also an inshore route for vessels of light draught which leads S from the Humber to the entrance to The Wash thence E to Cromer. This route is also described.

Depths
8.6

1   In Outer Dowsing Channel there is a least charted depth in mid-channel of 10·1 m in position 53°25'·6N 0°59'·9E.
The other routes are of shallower depth and the charts should be consulted for the latest information.

Hazards
8.7

1   **Oil and Gas Fields.** A number of production platforms and wells, whose positions are best seen on the chart, lie close to some of these routes. Gas pipelines, also shown on the chart, cross some routes. See 1.41.

2   **Wrecks.** The charts show numerous wrecks throughout the area. These are not mentioned in the directions but care may be necessary to avoid them, depending on draught.
Fishing vessels operate in large numbers in the vicinity of the banks described in this chapter.

Wind farms

Harbours
8.9

1   Along the Norfolk coast between Gore Point (52°59'N 0°33'E) and Cromer, 28 miles to the E, there are a number of small harbours. During strong onshore winds from the E through N to W their harbour entrances become a mass of broken water and the marks difficult to see. The situation worsens when the SE or out-going stream begins or if there is a swell following a previous onshore gale. In these conditions the harbours are not accessible.

Rescue
8.10

1   There are Coastal Rescue Teams at Mablethorpe (53°20′N 0°15′E), Chapel Saint Leonards (53°13′N 0°20′E), Skegness (53°08′N 0°20′E), Wrangle (53°00′N 0°06′E), Sutton Bridge (52°46′N 0°12′E), Wells (52°58′N 0°51′E), Cley next the Sea (52°58′N 1°03′E), Sheringham (52°57′N 1°13′E) and Cromer (52°56′N 1°18′E); see 1.67.

2   All-weather lifeboats are stationed at Skegness, Wells, and Cromer. Inshore lifeboats are stationed at Mablethorpe, Skegness, Wells, Sheringham and Cromer; see 1.72.

Natural conditions
8.11

1   **Tidal streams** are given in *Admiralty Tidal Stream Atlas: North Sea, Southern Part* and in the tables on the charts. Throughout the area the streams change their direction quickly when they are weak, but only at 10°–15° per hour from 2 hours before until 2 hours after the times of their greatest strength.

    Closer inshore spring rates reach 3 kn and there might be ripples or overfalls near the shoals off the coast.

2   **Climate information.** See 1.142, 1.152 and 1.155.

Directions
(continued from 6.184)

Principal marks
8.12

1   **Landmarks:**
      See 7.20 for marks in the approaches to River Humber.
      Building (53°20′N 0°16′E) at Mablethorpe.

Conspicuous building, Mablethorpe from ENE (8.12)
(Original dated 2000)

(Photograph – Air Images)

      Building (pyramid) (53°11′N 0°21′E).
      Meteorological mast (lighted; 87 m in height) 53°18′·8N 0°44′·9E. See 8.8.
      Meteorological mast (lighted; 87 m in height) (53°09′·5N 0°38′·9E) on Docking Shoal. See 8.8.
      Gasometer (53°08′N 0°20′E) at Skegness.

2   Blakeney Church (tower) (52°57′N 1°02′E), a turret on NE angle, 33 m in height.
      Cromer Church (tower) (52°56′N 1°18′E) with battlements.
      Two radio masts (52°55′N 1°21′E).

3   **Major lights:**
      B1D Dowsing (Amethyst offshore platform) (53°34′N 0°53′E).
      Cromer Light (white octagonal tower, 18 m in height) (52°55′N 1°19′E).

Other aids to navigation
8.13

1   **Racon:**
      Humber Light Float (53°38′·7N 0°21′·2E).
      N Outer Dowsing Light Buoy (53°33′·5N 0°59′·6E).
      Inner Dowsing Light Buoy (53°19′N 0°35′E).
      Dudgeon Light Buoy (53°17′N 1°17′E).
      North Well Light Buoy (53°03′N 0°28′E).
      Cromer Light (52°55′N 1°19′E).

2   **AIS:**
      N Outer Dowsing Light Buoy - as above.
      ~~Cromer Light - as above.~~
    ✱ WK 01/11
    For details see *Admiralty List of Radio Signals Volume 2.*

Outer Dowsing Channel
8.14

1   From a position about 5 miles NE of the Humber Light Float (53°38′·7N 0°21′·2E), the route leads SE for 30 miles to a position at the SE end of Outer Dowsing Channel. Thence the track leads SSE for 29 miles to a position 3½ miles NE of Cromer. The track passes:
      SW of the Amethyst Gas Field (53°37′N 0°44′E), thence:

2   Across the N end of Silver Pit (53°36′N 0°44′E), a deep submarine valley lying N/S across the approach to River Humber. At its edges the depths change rapidly, though this change is less marked at its N and S extremities. The edge of the deep is usually marked by tide ripples and these and the change in depths are useful guides. Thence:

3   SW of B1D Dowsing platform (53°34′N 0°53′E) (8.12) located near the NW end of Outer Dowsing Channel, thence:
      NE of Triton Knoll (53°24′N 0°53′E) (8.16), and:
      SW of Outer Dowsing Shoal, which extends 13½ miles SSE from its NW extremity. N Outer Dowsing Light Buoy (N cardinal) (53°34′N 1°00′E) and Mid Outer Dowsing Light Buoy (starboard hand) mark the NW extremity and SW side of the shoal respectively.
    Thence the track leads SSE, passing:

4   ENE of East Dudgeon Shoals (53°18′N 0°59′E) marked on their NE side by E Dudgeon Light Buoy (E cardinal), thence:
      ENE of two light buoys (cardinal) (53°17′N 1°06′E) marking a wellhead, thence:
      WSW of Cromer Knoll (53°18′N 1°18′E), a shoal which extends 4 miles NNW. Dudgeon Light Buoy (W cardinal) (8.13) lies 5 cables W of the S
      ...extremity of the shoal, thence:
      ENE of Sheringham Shoal Offshore Wind Farm (53°08′·1N 1°08′·7E) (8.8).
      ENE of Sheringham Shoal (53°03′N 1°11′E), a thin isolated shoal running 5 miles E/W. It is marked at its E extremity by E Sheringham Light Buoy (E cardinal) and at its W extremity by W Sheringham Light Buoy (W cardinal). Thence:

5   To a position NE of Cromer (52°56′N 1°18′E).
    (Directions for coastal route continue at 9.21)

    ✱ WK 12/10

Humber to Inner Dowsing Light Buoy
8.15

1   From a position about 5 miles NE of Humber Light Float (53°38'·7N 0°21'·2E), the route leads SSE for 18 miles to a position 7 miles NNE of Inner Dowsing Light Buoy (E cardinal) (8.13) (53°19'·1N 0°34'·8E), passing (with positions from Inner Dowsing Light Buoy):

2   ENE of Humber DW anchorage (19 miles NNW), marked at its E extremity by Outer Sand Light Buoy (E cardinal), thence:

        WSW of C1D platform (20 miles N), thence:

        WSW of a light buoy (special) (13½ miles N), thence:

3   ENE of Protector Overfalls (7 miles NW) marked by Protector Light Buoy (port hand), thence:

        ENE of several detached patches (4 miles NNW), which have a least charted depth of 7·5 m, thence:

        To a position 7 miles NNE of Inner Dowsing Light Buoy.

Inner Dowsing Light Buoy to Cromer passing between Triton Knoll and Dudgeon Shoal
8.16

1   From a position about 7 miles NNE of Inner Dowsing Light Buoy (E cardinal) (8.13) (53°19'·1N 0°34'·8E), the route leads ESE for 18 miles to a position about 5½ miles WNW of Dudgeon Light Buoy (W cardinal) (8.13), thence SSE to a position NE of Cromer, passing:

2   NNE of North Ridge (53°24'N 0°49'E) and Dudgeon Shoal (53°17'N 0°55'E). North Ridge is marked at its W extremity by West Ridge Light Buoy (W cardinal) and extends 9 miles ESE into Dudgeon Shoal. At LW there are conspicuous overfalls when there is a strong tidal stream running across the ridge. A meteorological mast (8.12) stands 3 cables SE of West Ridge Light Buoy. Thence:

3   SSW of Triton Knoll (53°24'N 0°53'E), consisting of many detached patches extending 10 miles WNW/ESE. The Knoll is indicated by tide rips. Thence:

4   NNE of East Dudgeon Shoals (53°18'N 0°59'E), marked on its NE side by E Dudgeon Light Buoy (E cardinal), thence:

        SSW of the detached patches (53°22'N 1°02'E) extending ESE from Triton Knoll, thence:

        NNE of two light buoys (cardinal) (53°17'N 1°06'E) marking a wellhead, thence:

5   To a position WNW of Dudgeon Light Buoy (8.13) (53°16'·6N 1°16'·8E) at the SE end of Outer Dowsing Channel whence the track described at 8.14 is joined.

   Under certain tidal conditions this route might be preferable to the route described in 8.14. *Admiralty Tidal Stream Atlas: North Sea, Southern Part* and the tables on chart 1190 should be consulted.

Inner Dowsing Light Buoy to Docking Shoal
8.17

1   From a position 7 miles NNE of Inner Dowsing Light Buoy (E cardinal) (8.13) (53°19'·1N 0°34'·8E), the route leads 8 miles S to a position NW of Docking Shoal, passing (with positions from Inner Dowsing Light Buoy):

2   E of Inner Dowsing (4 miles SSW), a narrow ridge of sand running 7 miles N/S and marked at its S extremity by S Inner Dowsing Light Buoy (S cardinal), and:

        W of North Ridge (8 miles E) with W Ridge Light Buoy (W cardinal) at its extremity, thence:

        To a position NW of Docking Shoal (7 miles SE) (8.18).

Docking Shoal to Cromer passing between Docking Shoal and Race Bank
8.18

1   From the vicinity of 53°17'N 0°39'E at the NW end of the channel between Docking Shoal and Race Bank, the route leads SE and ESE for 34 miles to a position NE of Cromer, passing:

2   NE of Docking Shoal (53°10'N 0°44'E), an extensive triangular shaped shoal spreading to the S and SE, which is marked at its N point by N Docking Light Buoy (N cardinal) and its SE point by E Docking Light Buoy (port hand). A light buoy (special) marking measuring instruments is moored 1 mile SE of the latter. And:

3   SW of Race Bank (53°13'N 0°51'E), a thin shoal stretching 10½ miles SE which is marked at its NW extremity by N Race Light Buoy (starboard hand) and its SE extremity by S Race Light Buoy (S cardinal), thence:

4   NE of Blakeney Overfalls (52°59'N 0°59'E), a shoal lying parallel to the shore and marked at its E extremity by Blakeney Overfalls Light Buoy (port hand). A light buoy (special) marking measuring instruments is moored 8 cables NNE of Blakeney Overfalls Light Buoy.

   Thence the track leads ESE, passing:

        SSW of Sheringham Shoal (8.14) (53°03'N 1°11'E) marked by light buoys (W and E cardinal), thence:

5   To a position NE of Cromer (11 miles ESE).

        (Directions continue for coastal route at 9.21)

Docking Shoal to The Wash
8.19

1   From a position NW of Docking Shoal the route leads 5½ miles S to a position E of Scott Patch, thence 11 miles SSW to North Well Light Buoy (53°03'·0N 0°27'·9E) at the entrance to The Wash, passing (with positions from Gibraltar Point (53°06'N 0°20'E)):

2   W of Docking Shoal (centre 53°10'N 0°44'E) and N Docking Light Buoy (N cardinal) (8.18), thence:

        E and SE of Scott Patch (11½ miles NE) marked by Scott Patch Light Buoy (E cardinal), thence:

        WNW of a meteorological mast (8.12) (12 miles ENE) situated near the NW entrance to a side channel (see below) lying between Docking Shoal and Burnham Flats, thence;

3   WNW of Burnham Flats (12 miles E), an extensive shoal extending 6 miles S and 9 miles ESE. Burnham Ridge, consisting of a number of sand waves, fronts Burnham Flats to the W and lies S of Burnham Flats Light Buoy (W cardinal) which is moored off the N extremity of the flats. There might be less water than charted on the ridge. Thence:

4   ESE of Lynn Knock (4½ miles ESE), which consists of unstable sandwaves and is subject to heavy overfalls during spring tides. The E side of Lynn Knock is marked by Lynn Knock Light Buoy (starboard hand). Thence:

5   WNW of Woolpack (10 miles ESE) (8.21). Woolpack Light Buoy (port hand) is moored WSW of Woolpack and at the W end of Sledway (8.21). Three shoals lie in the channel to the W and SW

of Sledway. These shoals are formed of sandwaves and are liable to change. Thence:

6 To the vicinity of North Well Light Buoy (safe water) (5½ miles SE) which is moored at the NE end of The Well, a deep extending into The Wash. A light buoy (special) marking instruments is moored 6 cables NE. Two unmarked dangerous wrecks lie 1½ miles NNE and 9 cables NNW of North Well Light Buoy.

7 **Alternative route into Wash from SE.** A channel whose W end is in position 53°09′N 0°38′E, lies between Docking Shoal to the N and Burnham Flats to the S. From a position NE of Cromer, the track leads 33 miles WNW to join the route described above, passing SSW of Sheringham Shoal (8.14) and NNE of Blakeney Overfalls (8.18). Local knowledge is required.

(Directions continue for The Wash at 8.43)

Humber to The Wash, inshore route
8.20

1 From a position 5 cables SW of Outer Rosse Reach Light Buoy (safe water) (53°29′·89N 0°20′·79E) vessels with local knowledge may proceed S for 27 miles to North Well Light Buoy (safe water) (53°03′·0N 0°27′·9E) passing:

2 E of the firing practice area at Donna Nook (53°28′N 0°15′E) (7.19). Saltfleet, Theddlethorpe and Trusthorpe Overfalls, forming practically one shoal, lie to the S of the area in a line 7 miles long running parallel to the coast. Trusthorpe Overfalls lie to seaward of Mablethorpe, a seaside resort, made conspicuous by the building (8.12). Thence:

3 Clear of Protector Overfalls (53°25′N 0°25′E) (8.15).

The route continues S, passing (with positions from Ingoldmells Point (53°11′N 0°21′E)):

E of a light buoy (special) (3½ miles N) marking measuring instruments, thence:

4 W of Inner Dowsing Overfalls (8½ miles NE), a group of detached patches lying SW of Inner Dowsing Light Buoy (E cardinal) (8.13) and to the W of Inner Dowsing (8.17). There are considerable overfalls on these patches. Thence:

5 Clear of Inner Dowsing Wind Farm development area (8.8) (3¼ miles E), and:

E of Ingoldmells Point, which stands at the extremity of a long run of sand hills and coast protected by groynes. A buoy (special), marking an outfall, lies 1½ miles E of the point. Thence:

6 E of a light buoy (special) (2½ miles SE) marking measuring instruments, thence:

Clear of Lynn Wind Farm development area (8.8) (5 miles SE), and:

7 E of Skegness Middle (4 miles S), which lies off Skegness, a seaside resort. The shoal lies to the N of a group of shoals which dry and run roughly parallel to the coast off Gibraltar Point. These shoals from E to W are Outer Dogs Head, Outer Knock and Inner Knock. Thence:

8 E of Lynn Knock (4½ miles ESE) (8.19) and Lynn Knock Light Buoy (starboard hand), thence:

To the vicinity of North Well Light Buoy (safe water) (8.19).

(Directions continue for The Wash at 8.43)

The Wash to Cromer, inshore route
8.21

1 Vessels of a suitable draught and with local knowledge can use the inshore route which leads 34 miles E from the vicinity of North Well Light Buoy (53°03′N 0°28′E) through Sledway to a position NE of Cromer, passing (with positions from Scolt Head (52°59′N 0°42′E)):

2 S of Woolpack (5 miles NW), a shoal patch to the N of Sledway. Woolpack Light Buoy (port hand) is moored 1½ miles WSW of Woolpack and also marks the W end of Sledway. Thence:

3 N of Middle Bank (6 miles E), which extends E into Gore Middle, both of which dry and lie to the S of Sledway, thence:

N of Scolt Head, a remarkable long sandhill and the N point on this coast, thence:

4 N of Bridgirdle (2½ miles NE) a spit which dries with Stiffkey Overfalls, a tongue of shoal water, to its E. Bridgirdle Light Buoy (port hand) is moored N of Bridgirdle and on the NW edge of Stiffkey Overfalls. Thence:

5 N of Wells Harbour (6 miles E) (8.23). Wells Harbour Light Buoy (port hand) is moored to the N of the harbour entrance. The coast between Wells and the entrance to Burnham Harbour (3½ miles W) is lined by sandhills covered with coarse grass known as Holkham Meals. Thence:

6 S of Knock (8 miles ENE) and Blakeney Overfalls (10 miles ENE) (8.18).

The route continues E, passing (with positions from Cromer (52°56′N 1°18′E)):

7 N of Blakeney Point (12 miles WNW), with Blakeney Harbour (8.35) to the S. The coast between Blakeney and Wells is embanked and fronted by marshes with The High Sand and West Sand extending 1¼ miles offshore. The background is well wooded. Thence:

N of a light buoy (special) (8 miles WNW) moored close inshore and marking measuring instruments, thence:

8 N of Pollard (7½ miles WNW), an isolated shoal, thence:

S of Sheringham Shoal (8 miles NW) (8.14), thence:

9 N of a light buoy (port hand) (2½ miles NW) marking the N extremity of a foul area containing the remains of a collapsed rig, thence:

To a position NE of Cromer (8.37).

10 **Alternative channel.** As an alternative to Sledway, vessels of suitable draught may use The Bays (52°59′N 0°32′E), a narrow, shallow and uneven passage lying between Gore Middle and Middle Bank to the N and the sandbanks off Gore Point to the S. Once clear SE of Gore Middle, the route leads 6 miles ENE passing WNW of Bridgirdle before rejoining the route above.

(Directions continue for coastal passage ESE at 9.21)

Useful marks
8.22

1 Saint Clement's Church (tower) (53°24′N 0°12′E).
Tower (53°23′N 0°13′E) black, 8 m in height.
Radio mast (red obstruction lights) (53°19′N 0°16′E).
Ingoldmells Church (tower) (53°12′N 0°20′E).
Addlethorpe Church (tower) (53°12′N 0°19′E).
Thornham Church (tower) (52°58′N 0°35′E) in ruins.
Titchwell Church (spire) (52°58′N 0°37′E) among trees.

2 Brancaster Church (52°58′N 0°38′E), a square tower among trees.
Brancaster Harbour Light (on club house) (52°58′N 0°38′E).
Lifeboat house (white, red roof) (52°58′N 0°51′E).

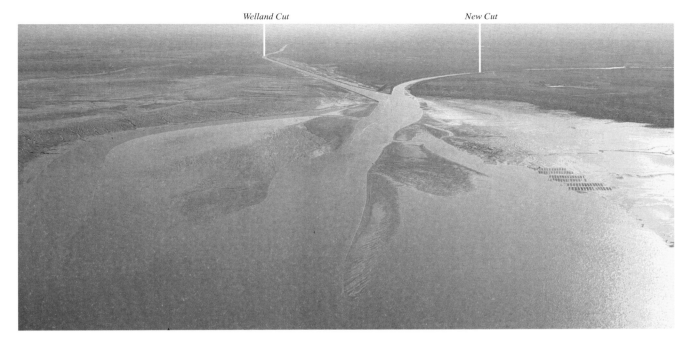

Welland Cut   *New Cut*

New Cut and Welland Cut from ENE (8.71)
(Original dated 2000)

(Photograph - Air Images)

The track is marked by fixed white leading lights and by light beacons with fixed red lights on the S side of the channel and fixed green lights on the N side. Details of the leading lights are noted on the chart.

Basins and berths

Boston Dock
8.73

1   The dock has 730 m of quay providing up to seven berths in depths of 7·6 m at springs and 5·4 m at neaps. There is a RoRo berth and two ramps at E end of the dock.

Riverside berths
8.74

Riverside Quay which dries out on a bottom of soft mud, extends 700 m upstream of the dock entrance and provides seven berths.

Witham Wharf cement berth on S bank (disused 2003).

Port services

Repairs
8.75

1   Minor engine repairs only.

Other facilities
8.76

1   Hospital with helicopter landing site adjacent; SSCECs and extensions issued (1.92).

Supplies
8.77

1   Fuel oils by road tanker; fresh water; stores and provisions.

River Witham above Boston

General information
8.78

1   River Witham Navigation is entered through Grand Sluice Lock, 1 mile upstream of Boston Dock. The lock is 22·7 m in length and 4·6 m in width; craft of 1·4 m draught with a height of no more than 2·3 m can use the Navigation. The sluice is the upper limit of the tidal river and, in dry weather, silting may occur below the sluice.

River Welland

Fosdyke
8.79

1   **General information.** Fosdyke (52°52′·32N 0°02′·31W) is 6 miles SW of the entrance to River Welland and is used mainly by recreational craft.

2   **Vertical clearance.** Within the river mouth there is a power cable with a safe overhead clearance of 23 m, 8 cables downriver of Fosdyke Bridge. Fosdyke Bridge has a vertical clearance of 1·3 m.

3   **Directions.** The entrance to River Welland is formed by Welland Cut, a narrow channel protected by training walls, which leads SW across tidal flats. The cut is entered close W of Welland Light Beacon (52°56′·1N 0°05′·3E) (8.71) and it is marked by a series of light beacons (lateral), as well as a number of radar reflectors which stand at 5 cable intervals on the SE training wall. Beyond the cut, the channel leads a further two miles SW through the mouth of River Welland to Fosdyke. It is marked by light beacons (lateral).

4   **Local knowledge** is essential for passage through the cut.

Tidal streams. Within Welland Cut, the in-going stream begins at –0345 HW Immingham and the out-going stream at +0100 HW Immingham.

Berth. A tidal platform 20 m long and 10 m wide is located on the N bank just upriver of Fosdyke Bridge. It is used for the inspection and maintenance of a barge whose purpose is to transport revetment stone to various locations in the Wash.

Chart 1190
Spalding
8.80

1   **General information.** Spalding lies 6 miles above Fosdyke Bridge (52°52'N 0°02'W) and vessels with a draught of 2·1 m can reach the town at spring tides. At Fulney, 1 mile below Spalding there is a lock which is 33·5 m long and 9 m wide.

WISBECH AND APPROACHES

General information

Chart 1200
Position
8.81

1   Wisbech (52°40'·37N 0°09'·35E) stands on both banks of River Nene.

Function
8.82

1   It is a small commercial port which imports timber and construction materials and exports steel scrap. The population of the town is about 25 000.

Port limits
8.83 ✳1

1   ~~The limits of the port include Wisbech Channel as far offshore as Bar Flat (8.97) and are shown on the chart.~~

Traffic
8.84

1   In 2008 the port was used by 39 vessels totalling 78 621 dwt.

Port Authority
8.85

1   Port of Wisbech Authority, Harbour Office, Crab Marsh, Wisbech, Cambridgeshire, PE13 3JJ.

Limiting conditions

Controlling depths
8.86

1   Wisbech Channel has a least charted depth of 0·7 m (2006). However the channel is tortuous and both the line and depths are liable to change. The Harbour Master should be consulted for the latest information.

The depths alongside the berths within the harbour at LW are between 0·3 m and 1·8 m and vessels take the bottom, soft mud.

Vertical clearance
8.87

1   Overhead power cables cross River Nene above Sutton Bridge in two places as shown on the chart. Least safe vertical clearance is 30 m.

Tidal levels
8.88

1   See *Admiralty Tide Tables Volume 1*. Wisbech Cut, (52°48'N 0°13'E) mean spring range not available; mean neap range about 2·9 m.

✳1 1   Pilotage is compulsory for all commercial vessels. The pilot boards in position 52°54'·43N 0°14'·79E; in bad weather, the pilot boards S of Holbeach RAF No 4 Light Buoy (52°52'·58N 0°13'·08E). See *Admiralty List of Radio Signals Volume 6 (1)*.

Maximum size of vessel handled
8.89

1   The port is capable of accommodating vessels up to 83 m long, 11·5 m beam and about 2000 dwt. Maximum arrival draught is 4·9 m at HW springs. In all other cases, the maximum draught is 2 m less than the predicted tide for inbound vessels and 2·4 m less than the predicted tide for outbound vessels.

Local weather and sea state
8.90

1   It is reported that a heavy swell can occur on Outer Westmark Knock (53°52'N 0°14'E) during and after NE gales.

The tidal streams and current at Wisbech and Port Sutton (8.95) can be very strong. Head and stern moorings should be doubled and checked frequently.

Arrival information

Notice of ETA required
8.91

1   See 1.46.

Outer anchorage
8.92

1   An outer anchorage area, the limits of which are shown on the chart, is centred 8 cables NNE of Nene Roads Light Buoy (52°54'·4N 0°15'·4E).

Vessels should report to Wisbech or Sutton Bridge pilots upon arrival at the anchorage. See *Admiralty List of Radio Signals Volume 6 (1)*.

Pilotage
8.93

1   Pilotage is compulsory for all vessels over 20 m LOA. The pilot boards from a cutter marked "Pilots" in the outer anchorage area (8.92). In bad weather, the pilot boards S of Holbeach RAF No 4 Light Buoy (52°52'·5N 0°13'·1E), as shown on the chart. The cutter is on station from 3 hours before HW until HW when vessels are expected. See *Admiralty List of Radio Signals Volume 6 (1)*.

Harbour

Bridge signals
8.94

1   Cross Keys Bridge (52°46'·0N 0°11'·7E) at Sutton Bridge is a revolving iron structure with an opening 21 m wide. Signals, exhibited in both directions, control river traffic and are shown in Diagram 8.94.

Signal	Meaning
●	Bridge closed.
○	Preparatory signal for opening bridge.
●	Bridge open.

Bridge signals (8.94)

2   The E and W dolphins of the bridge are illuminated.

3   Vessels in transit are required to give position reports to the swing bridge by VHF. The sound signal Morse Code "B" may also be used to request a bridge opening.

Tidal streams
8.95

1 Tidal streams in Wisbech Cut, at Sutton Bridge and at Wisbech are as follows:

Time from HW Immingham	*Remarks*
Wisbech Cut	
−0400	In-going stream begins
HW	Out-going stream begins
Sutton Bridge	
−0300	In-going stream begins
+0030	Out-going stream begins
Wisbech	
−0200	In-going stream begins
+0130	Out-going stream begins

2 The streams are reported to be strong at springs with rates up to 6 kn. At neaps, with freshets in the river, the in-going stream does not reach Wisbech. The in-going stream normally runs for 4 hours at Sutton Bridge and at springs, for 3 hours at Wisbech. It should be noted that fresh to strong S winds cause tidal heights to be lower than predicted.

Directions for entering harbour
(continued from 8.46)

Principal marks
8.96

1 **Landmarks:**

Trial Bank (52°50′·5N 0°14′·6E), an artificial island, elevation 10 m, light beacon 3 m in height.

Mound (52°49′·1N 0°17′·2E) 8 m in elevation, causeway to shore.

Two lighthouses (disused) (52°48′·5N 0°12′·7E) near entrance to Wisbech Cut.

Trial Bank from NE (8.96)
(Original dated 2000)

(Photograph - Air Images)

Roaring Middle Light Float to Wisbech Channel
8.97

1 From the vicinity of Roaring Middle Light Float (safe water) (52°58′·6N 0°21′·1E), the track leads 5½ miles SW to the entrance to Wisbech Channel, passing (with positions from Wisbech Channel entrance (52°54′N 0°16E)):

SE of Freeman Channel entrance (52°57′·8N 0°15′·1E) (8.70) and Roger Sand (8.70) to the S of the channel, thence:

2 NW of Roaring Middle (52°54′·9N 0°17′·7E), a shoal which dries, marked on its W side by No 2 Light Buoy (port hand) and No 4 Buoy (port hand), thence:

3 SE of Gat Channel entrance (8.49) (52°56′·2N 0°15′·0E), lying between Roger Sand and Gat Sand, thence:

Clear, depending upon draught, of a small shoal patch (52°55′·1N 0°16′·4E) with a depth of 4·7 m, thence:

SE of a light buoy (special) (52°55′·1N 0°14′·5E) marking measuring instruments, thence:

4 To the entrance to Wisbech Channel marked by Nene Roads Light Buoy (safe water) (52°54′·4N 0°15′·4E) moored on Bar Flat.

Wisbech Channel
8.98

1 Wisbech Channel runs in a generally S direction for 6 miles between extensive drying sands which front the coast. The sand to the W of the channel is Old South and, to the E, Outer Westmark Knock and Inner Westmark Knock.

2 The channel is marked by light buoys and light beacons. A stranded wreck and a tide gauge are located close W of RAF No 4 Light Buoy (E cardinal) (52°52′·5N 0°13′·1E) (8.40) and there are yacht moorings in this vicinity also.

Frequent changes occur in the channel and navigation marks are liable to be moved without prior notice.

River Nene and Wisbech Cut
8.99

1 From its entrance which is formed by Wisbech Cut, River Nene leads 9 miles S to Wisbech. The entrance to the cut is marked by Big Tom Light Beacon (port hand) (52°49′·6N 0°13′·1E) and Big Annie Light Buoy (starboard hand) about 1 cable WNW. Big Tom Light Beacon stands very close E of the seaward end of a detached training wall on the E side of the entrance. The wall is 5 cables in length and is further marked by two additional light beacons (port hand), at its middle and at its inner end. Within the entrance, the banks of River Nene are marked by several light beacons (lateral).

Berths
8.100

1 Quays are situated on the E bank of the river either side of Horse Shoe Corner (52°40′·6N 0°09′·1E) and total 800 m, providing five principal berths. The swinging basin is on the E bank just downstream of Horse Shoe Corner.

Port services

Repairs
8.101

1 There is a patent slipway for vessels up to 120 tonnes displacement and a 75 tonne boat hoist. Minor engine repairs only.

Other facilities
8.102

Hospital with helicopter landing site; facilities for disposal of galley waste; Ship Sanitation Certificates issued (1.92).

Supplies
8.103

1 Fuel by road tanker; fresh water; stores and provisions.

Communications
8.104

1 Wisbech is connected by River Nene and canals to Peterborough and Northampton and thence to Grand Union Canal.

Port Sutton Bridge
8.105

1   **General information.** Port Sutton Bridge (52°46′·58N 0°12′·05E) is 3 miles from the entrance to River Nene. The wharf is capable of receiving vessels up to 120 m in length, draught 6·3 m and 5000 dwt. Depending upon draught and tidal height vessels may take the bottom, which is soft mud. In 2008 the port was used by 249 vessels totalling 583 404 dwt.

2   **Port Authority.** Port of Wisbech Authority, Harbour Office, Crab Marsh, Wisbech, Cambridgeshire, PE13 3JJ.

    Port Operator. Port Sutton Bridge, West Bank, Sutton Bridge, Spalding, Lincolnshire, PE12 9QR.

    Pilotage is compulsory See *Admiralty List of Radio Signals Volume 6 (1)*.

    Directions for entering harbour. See 8.96 to 8.99.

    Berths. The wharf is 350 m in length, providing four berths. Depths alongside are 9·3 m at HW springs, 5·25 m at HW neaps and 2·9 m at LW springs. A swinging basin lies 1½ cables SSW of the wharf.

3   **Other facilities:** facilities for disposal of galley waste.

    Supplies: fuel by road tanker; fresh water; provisions.

KING'S LYNN AND APPROACHES

General information

Chart 1200
Position
8.106

1   King's Lynn (52°45′·51N 0°23′·42E) lies 2 miles SSE of the entrance to Lynn Cut, which is the artificially straightened mouth of River Great Ouse with embankments up to 3·5 m high.

Function
8.107

1   King's Lynn is a small commercial port which handles steel, timber, fuel, agricultural products and aggregates. Grain is exported from the port. The population is about 41 300.

Topography
8.108

1   The town lies on flat ground but fine wooded country rises behind it.

Port limits
8.109

1   The port limits, which are shown on the chart, extend over the SE half of The Wash, adjoining those of Wisbech (8.83) and Boston (8.54).

Approach and entry
8.110

1   King's Lynn is approached from The Wash through Bull Dog Channel (8.129) which leads to Lynn Cut. There are a number of side channels but these are only suitable for small craft and local knowledge is required.

Traffic
8.111

1   In 2008 the port was visited by 358 vessels and 777 312 tonnes of cargo was handled.

Port Authority
8.112

1   Harbour Authority: King's Lynn Conservancy Board, Harbour Office, Common Staith, King's Lynn PE30 1LL.

    Dock Authority: Associated British Ports, St Ann's Fort, King's Lynn, PE30 1QS.

Limiting conditions
Controlling depths
8.113

1   The approach to King's Lynn is navigable by seagoing vessels from 2 hours before to 2 hours after HW. Lynn Cut carries sufficient water to ensure it does not dry completely but in some places the bed level is 2·0 m above chart datum.

2   Within the harbour there is sufficient water to ensure it does not dry completely but in some places the bed level is 2·0 m above chart datum. Vessels on Riverside and South Quays take bottom at LW.

Vertical clearance
8.114

1   Power cables with a safe overhead clearance of 45 m cross the river 1 mile N of the town.

Deepest and longest berths
8.115

1   For vessels remaining afloat at all times: Alexandra Dock (8.135).

    For vessels taking bottom at LW: Riverside Quay (8.133).

Tidal levels
8.116

    See *Admiralty Tide Tables Volume 1*. Mean spring range about 5·8 m; mean neap range about 3·2 m.

Maximum size of vessel handled
8.117

1   The port can accommodate vessels up to 140 m LOA and 20 m beam on Riverside Quay and 120 m LOA and 13·85 m beam in the enclosed docks. The allowable draught is dependent upon the state of tide: at springs, the maximum draught for Riverside Quay is 5·8 m and for the Docks is 5·5 m; at neaps, the maximum draught is about 3·4 m. See 8.123.

Arrival information
Port operations
8.118

1   For the Harbour Authority's channel approach chart and for navigational and safety warnings see *www.portauthoritykingslynn.fsnet.co.uk*.

Port radio
8.119

1   There is a port radio station. See *Admiralty List of Radio Signals Volume 6 (1)*.

Notice of ETA required
8.120

1   Notice of 24 hours is required with amendments up to 4 hours in advance of HW.

Outer anchorage
8.121

1   There is a triangular anchorage area S of Roaring Middle Light Float (52°58′·6N 0°21′·1E) (8.45) as shown on the chart.

Bentinck Dock   *Silo*

Alexandra Dock

King's Lynn from W (8.124)

(Original dated 2000)

(Photograph - Air Images)

Pilotage and tugs
8.122

1   **Pilotage** is compulsory for vessels over 35 m in length. Requests for Pilots are to be made 24 hours in advance. For further details see *Admiralty List of Radio Signals Volume 6 (1)*.

There are two pilot cutters, each painted blue with white superstructure and orange wheelhouse tops. When vessels are expected, the pilot cutter will be on station close W of Sunk Light Buoy (52°56'·3N 0°23'·4E) from 2 hours before HW until it is too late for the vessel concerned to reach King's Lynn.

2   **Tugs** are available. The attendance of a tug is compulsory for tankers over 73 m in length and other vessels over that length not fitted with bow thrusters or suitable manoeuvring aids.

Regulations concerning entry
8.123

1   All vessels entering and departing the port must have sufficient under-keel clearance, being guided by local notices to mariners. All vessels over 100 m LOA must be notified to the harbour office for consideration regarding draughts, prior to being fixed for the port.

2   Vessels berthing on Riverside Quay are required to use a minimum of three headlines, three sternlines and backsprings. The main engine is to be used for shifting berth.

Harbour

General layout
8.124

1   There are two enclosed docks, Alexandra Dock entered through a lock on the E bank of the river and Bentinck Dock, entered from Alexandra Dock. Riverside berths, at which vessels take ground at LW, lie on the E bank

extending up to 1½ cables N and between 3 and 5 cables S of Alexandra Dock entrance.

Fisher Fleet, a tidal basin used by fishing vessels, lies 1½ cables N of Alexandra Dock.

Traffic signals
8.125

1   Signals (Diagram 8.125) are shown from a flagstaff on the S side of Alexandra Dock.

Day	Night	Meaning
■	●	Vessel may enter dock.
■	●	Vessels leaving dock. Vessels in river keep clear.
No flag or light.	Lock closed.	

Dock signals (8.125)

In addition to the above, an amber flashing light is displayed day and night when a vessel is leaving the dock.

Tidal streams
8.126

1   In the approaches, the tidal streams follow channels which lie in a SSW/NNE direction but set across other channels, especially when the sandbanks are covered. See tables on the chart. Off King's Lynn the streams set as follows:

Time from HW Immingham	Remarks
–0300	In-going stream begins
+0130	Out-going stream begins

2 The tidal streams off King's Lynn are fairly strong. The times of HW can be affected by the influence of the wind.

Directions for entering harbour
(continued from 8.46)

Principal marks
8.127

1 **Landmarks:**
Trial Bank (52°50'·5N 0°14'·6E) (8.96).
Mound (52°49'·1N 0°17'·2E) (8.96).
Pylons (52°46'·4N 0°22'·8E) for an overhead power cable spanning the river (8.114).

Roaring Middle Light Float to Bull Dog Channel
8.128

1 From the vicinity of Roaring Middle Light Float (52°58'·6N 0°21'·1E) the route leads 2½ miles SSE to Bull Dog Channel, the main approach channel to Lynn Cut, passing (with positions from Snettisham Scalp (52°52'·4N 0°26'·8E)):

2 WSW of Sunk Sand (5 miles N), and:
WSW of a light buoy (special) (5 miles NNW) marking measuring instruments, thence:
ENE of Seal Sand Light Buoy (N cardinal) (5½ miles NW) moored N of Seal Sand and NE of Roaring Middle sandflat, thence:

3 WSW of Sunk Light Buoy (W cardinal) (4½ miles NNW) moored W of South Sunk Sand and at the entrance to Bull Dog Channel.

Bull Dog Channel to Lynn Cut
8.129

1 From Sunk Light Buoy (52°56'·3N 0°23'·4E) the route leads 9 miles in a generally S direction to the entrance to Lynn Cut. The narrow channel is marked by light buoys (lateral), which are moved frequently as the channel itself changes, and passes:
E of Old Bell Middle (52°54'N 0°22'E) and Blackguard Sand (52°53'N 0°23'E), two shoals which dry. Bull Dog Beacon (starboard hand) on the edge of Old Bell Middle is equipped with a tide gauge. And:
W of Stylemans Middle (52°53'N 0°23'E), a shoal which dries, thence:
Through Pandora Sand (52°51'N 0°22'E), a tidal flat.

2 For the final 2½ miles of the approach channel a training wall, marked at its N end by West Stones Light Beacon (N cardinal) and at its S end by West Bank Light Beacon (yellow pile, tide gauge, 10 m in height) (52°47'·4N 0°22'·0E), lies to the W of the channel. It should be noted that this training wall, which is marked by light beacons (special), does not necessarily mark the edge of the channel. A shorter training wall extends 1 mile NNW on the E side of the channel. Both training walls dry.

3 **Caution.** Vessels which are constrained by their draught keep to the deepest water. Therefore mariners are advised that they may encounter vessels on either side of the channel, especially when rounding bends.

Lynn Cut and River Great Ouse to King's Lynn
8.130

1 From the S end of the approach channel, the route continues SSE through Lynn Cut and River Great Ouse to King's Lynn. At its outer end Lynn Cut is 161 m wide at HW reducing to 111 m wide at LW; at its inner end the cut is 148 m wide at HW and 140 m wide at LW. The entrance

to Alexandra Dock is 2 miles SSE of West Bank Light Beacon. The entrance lock is 15·2 m wide and has a depth over the sill at HW springs of 7·6 m, and 5·4 m at HW neaps. The lock is open from 1 hour before HW and closed shortly after HW. Bentinck Dock is entered from Alexandra Dock through a passage 96 m long and 15·2 m wide, which is spanned by two swing bridges.

2 **Caution.** A small passenger ferry crosses the river 1½ cables S of the entrance to Alexandra Dock. The ferry landings are marked by light beacons.

Useful marks
8.131

1 Silo (52°45'·7N 0°23'·8E).
Saint Nicholas Church (Spire) (52°45'·4N 0°23'·8E).
Saint Margaret's Church (towers and flagstaff) (52°45'·1N 0°23'·7E).

Side channels

General information
8.132

1 Old Lynn Channel (52°54'N 0°16'E), Teetotal Channel (52°54'N 0°19'E), Daseley's Sled (52°54'N 0°22E'), and Cork Hole (52°54'N 0°24'E) are unmarked channels leading towards King's Lynn. They are either no longer in use or may be used only by small craft with local knowledge.

Basins and berths

Riverside berths
8.133

1 Riverside Quay, 220 m long (approx.); depth 2·5 m (1997) but subject to change.
South Quay, 396 m long, dries at LW.
Boal Quay, not used by commercial vessels, is 122 m long, and dries at LW.

Fisher Fleet
8.134

1 Fish Landing Stage, 120 m long; dries at LW.

Enclosed docks
8.135

1 Alexandra Dock; 350 m of quayside, RoRo berth.
Bentinck Dock; 800 m of quayside.

Port services

Repairs
8.136

1 Limited repairs to both hull and engine can be carried out.

Other facilities
8.137

1 Reception of oily waste; hospital with helicopter landing site; Ship Sanitation Certificates issued (1.92); customs.

Supplies
8.138

1 Fuel by road tanker; fresh water; stores and provisions.

Communications
8.139

1 King's Lynn is connected by river and canal to Cambridge.
London (Stansted) Airport 1 hour 45 minutes; Norwich Airport 40 minutes.

NOTES

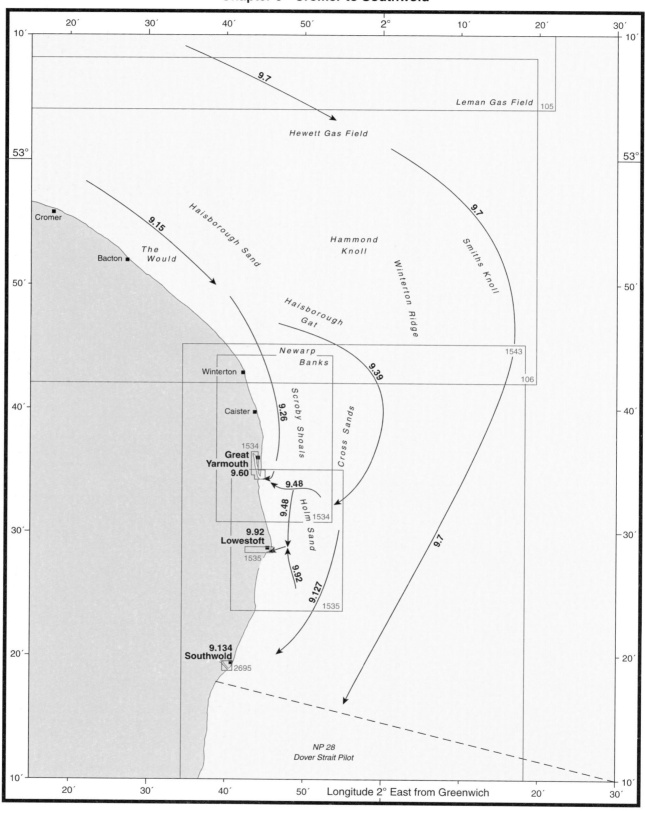

CHAPTER 9

CROMER TO SOUTHWOLD

GENERAL INFORMATION

Charts 1503, 1504
Scope of the chapter
9.1

1   In this chapter the continuation of the offshore passage from Outer Dowsing Channel ESE between Hewett Ridges and Leman Bank, thence E of Smith's Knoll and finally SSW to Southwold (9.134) is described at 9.12. Also described is the coastal passage SE from Cromer through The Would (9.23) and Haisborough Gat (9.40).

The chapter describes the ports of Great Yarmouth (9.60) and Lowestoft (9.92) and their approaches.

Topography
9.2

1   From Cromer (52°56′N 1°18′E) the coast curves gently to the SE, thence S and finally SSW from Lowestoft to Southwold, which is 43 miles from Cromer following the line of the coast.

2   The coastal and offshore waters are generally shallow with depths of less than 40 m. Between Winterton Ness, 17 miles SE of Cromer, and Lowestoft, 15 miles farther S, shallow banks front the coast. There are also off-lying banks, some with depths of less than 3 m over them. These off-lying banks are described in Chapter 2.

Transfer of cargo
9.3

1   Transfer of liquid cargo between tankers takes place occasionally about 11 miles ESE of Southwold. Vessels engaged in such transfers might be at anchor or otherwise unable to manoeuvre and should be given a wide berth.

Tidal streams
9.4

1   In coastal waters the streams follow the line of the coast and of the channels between the banks. Offshore the streams are more or less rotary, but when strongest they follow the line of the channel.

Details of the tidal streams are given on the charts and in *Admiralty Tidal Stream Atlas: North Sea, Southern Part.*

Gas fields and pipelines
9.5

1   A number of gas fields, most of them connected to the shore by pipelines, lie within the area described in this chapter. For general information relating to platforms and pipelines associated with gas fields see 1.25 and 1.41.

The general disposition of oil and gas fields is shown on Diagram 2.22.

Dumping grounds
9.6

1   See 2.4.

CROMER TO SOUTHWOLD—
OFFSHORE ROUTE

General information

Charts 1503, 106, 1543
Route
9.7

1   From a position about 15 miles N of Cromer (52°56′N 1°18′E), the offshore route leads 40 miles ESE passing between Leman Bank and Hewett Ridges to the N end of Smith's Knoll and thence 45 miles S passing E of Smith's Knoll to a position ESE of Southwold.

From a position at the N end of Smith's Knoll vessels may also proceed SE across the North Sea to the ports of Northern Europe (see *NP55 North Sea (East) Pilot*).

2   An alternative route over The Middle Ground (52°50′N 2°09′E) leads SE between Haisborough Sand (52°55′N 1°42′E), Hammond Knoll (52°52′N 1°55′E) and Winterton Ridge (52°50′N 2°01′E) to SW and Smiths Knoll (52°53′N 2°12′E) to NE. This route is not described.

Depths
9.8

1   Depths along the route passing N of Smith's Knoll are greater than 20 m.

Gas pipelines
9.9

1   Numerous gas pipelines run into Bacton Gas Terminal (52°52′N 1°28′E) from offshore production platforms in the North Sea and from Balgzand in The Netherlands (52°53′N 4°43′E) and Zeebrugge (51°20′N 3°10′E) in Belgium. Vessels should not anchor or trawl near these pipelines, see 1.41.

Rescue
9.10

1   See 9.19.

Tidal streams
9.11

1   The spring rate in each direction is about 2½ kn. Details of the tidal streams are given on the charts and in *Admiralty Tidal Stream Atlas: North Sea, Southern Part.*

Directions
(continued from 8.14)

Major lights
9.12

1   Cromer Light (52°56′N 1°19′E) (8.12).
Lowestoft Light (white round tower, 16 m in height) (52°29′·2N 1°45′·4E).
Southwold Light (white round tower standing in the middle of the town, 31 m in height) (52°19′·6N 1°40′·9E).

Other aids to navigation
9.13

1   **Racon:**
Cromer Light (52°55′N 1°19′E).
N Haisbro' Light Buoy (53°00′N 1°32′E).
Smith's Knoll Light Buoy (52°44′N 2°18′E).
For details see *Admiralty List of Radio Signals Volume 2.*

2   **AIS transponder:**
    Cromer Light. - as above.
    ~~Lowestoft Light (52°29′·2N 1°45′·4E).~~
    ~~Southwold Light (52°19′·6N 1°40′·9E).~~

✳ wks 01/11

Cromer to Southwold, offshore route
9.14

1   From a position about 15 miles N of Cromer (52°56′N 1°18′E), the route leads ESE to a position N of Smith's Knoll, passing:
    SSW of Inner Cromer Knoll (53°13′N 1°26′E), which is 5½ miles SE of Cromer Knoll (8.14), thence:
    SSW of Haddock Bank (53°17′N 1°35′E), which runs NW/SE over a distance of 15 miles, thence:

2   SSW of Leman Bank (53°08′N 1°56′E), a thin bank stretching 23 miles NW/SE along the N side of the channel. Lying parallel to Leman Bank and to its NE there are a number of similar banks (2.14). Thence:
    Clear of North Hewett Gas Field (53°06′N 1°46′E), Hewett Gas Field (5 miles S) and Della Gas Field (5 miles ESE), thence:

3   NNE of Hewett Ridges (52°57′N 2°04′E), consisting of two banks. The N bank extends along the S side of the channel. Thence:
    NNE and ENE of Smith's Knoll (52°53′N 2°13′E). The channel narrows to 3 miles between the N end of Smith's Knoll and the SE end of Leman Bank. The knoll is a narrow ridge 16 miles long which parallels the Norfolk coast. Thence:

4   Clear of Camelot Gas Field (52°57′N 2°09′E), situated close to the N end of Smith's Knoll and S of Leman Gas Field, about 6 miles N.
    Thence course is adjusted S, passing:
    E of Smith's Knoll Light Buoy (S cardinal) (9.13) (52°44′N 2°18′E), which is moored off the S end of Smith's Knoll, thence:
    To a position ESE of Southwold (9.134).
    (Directions for passage S to Thames Estuary and Dover Strait are given in the Dover Strait Pilot)

CROMER TO WINTERTON NESS

General information

Chart 106
Route
9.15

1   From a position NE of Cromer (52°56′N 1°19′E), the inshore route leads 18 miles SE through The Would to a position NE of Winterton Ness.

Topography
9.16

1   The coast between Cromer and Winterton Ness is subject to extensive landslips and fringed by a submarine forest. The coast is composed of cliffs as far as Happisburgh, 10 miles SE of Cromer, where it changes to sandhills which run to Winterton Ness. Initially the sandhills have an elevation of 9 to 12 m but they gradually decline to the SE.

2   Between Hempstead and Waxham (5½ miles and 3½ miles NW of Winterton Ness) coast defences, consisting of large artificial reefs of stone positioned about 1½ cables offshore, have been constructed. They have a height of about 1·7 m above MHWS and are marked by lit and unlit beacons. Leading lights have been established for the

Happisburgh Lifeboat Station, which is located at Sea Palling (52°47′·35N 1°36′·28E).

3   Between Waxham and Winterton Ness the coast is protected by a number of groynes and artifical reefs (9.23), marked by beacons (black conical topmarks) at their heads.

Depths
9.17

1   At the NW end of The Would there are charted depths of 16 m. Thereafter depending on the precise track followed depths in excess of 20 m can be maintained in The Would.

Submarine pipelines
9.18

1   See 9.9.

Rescue
9.19

1   There are Coastal Rescue Teams at Mundesley (52°53′N 1°27′E), Happisburgh (52°49′N 1°32′E) and Winterton-on-Sea; see 1.67.
    Inshore lifeboats are stationed at Mundesley, Happisburgh and Sea Palling; see 1.72.

Tidal streams
9.20

1   The spring rate in each direction is about 2½ kn. Details of the tidal streams are given on the charts and in *Admiralty Tidal Stream Atlas: North Sea, Southern Part.*

Directions
(continued from 8.14, 8.18 and 8.21)

Principal marks
9.21

1   **Landmarks:**
    Cromer Church tower (52°56′N 1°18′E).
    Radio masts (52°55′N 1°21′E).
    Radome (52°54′N 1°24′E) at Trimingham.

Radome at Trimingham from NNE (9.21)
(Original dated 2000)
(Photograph - Air Images)

    Water tower (52°53′N 1°26′E) at Mundesley.
    Two radio masts (red obstruction lights) (52°51′N 1°28′E).
    Happisburgh Church tower (52°49′N 1°32′E).
    Happisburgh Lighthouse (white tower, three red bands, 26 m in height) (52°49′N 1°32′E).

2   Winterton-on-Sea Church (52°43′N 1°41′E), visible above sandhills. Ten wind turbines stand about 7 cables WSW.
  Major light:
    Cromer Light (52°56′N 1°19′E) (8.12).

Happisburgh Church Tower from E (9.21)
(Original dated 2005)

(Photograph - MV Confidante)

Happisburgh Lighthouse from E (9.21)
(Original dated 2005)

(Photograph - MV Confidante)

Winterton-on-Sea Church from NE (9.21)
(Original dated 2005)

(Photograph - MV Confidante)

Other aid to navigation
9.22

1 **Racon:**

wk
3⁹/₁₀

North Haisbro Light Buoy (52°00′N 1°32′E)
~~Winterton Church tower (52°43′N 1°41′E).~~
→ ~~Newarp Light Buoy (52°48′N 1°56′E)~~   ✣ VALID
For details see *Admiralty List of Radio Signals Volume 2.*

Cromer to Winterton Ness
9.23

1 The Would, a channel about 7 miles wide, lies between the Norfolk coast and Haisborough Sand.

From a position NE of Cromer (52°56′N 1°18′E) (8.37), the route leads SE through The Would to a position NE of Winterton Ness, passing (with positions from Happisburgh Lighthouse (9.21) (52°49′N 1°32′E)):

2 SW of Haisborough Sand (8½ miles NE), which is 10 miles long and 1 mile wide lying parallel to the Norfolk coast. It is marked to the NW by N Haisbro' Light Buoy (N cardinal), to the SE by S Haisbro' Light Buoy (S cardinal) and to the W by Mid Haisbro' Light Buoy (starboard hand). The shoal has three drying patches (1995) close NE, E and ESE of the Mid Haisbro' Light Buoy. Except at slack water their positions are indicated by tidal eddies and even a slight sea or moderate swell breaks on the shallower parts of the shoal. There are a number of foul patches on the S part of the shoal. There are strong eddies on and around the bank, especially to the NW (52°59′·5N 1°34′·5E). Thence:

3 NE of a buoy (port hand) which marks the seaward end of an outfall extending 9 cables NE from Mundesley, (5¼ miles NW), thence:

NE of Bacton Gas Terminal (3¾ miles NW). The buildings of the Gas Terminal, which are brightly illuminated at night, stand 5 cables NW of the prominent church in Bacton. Thence:

4 NE of Sea Palling, a village (3 miles SE). A row of nine artificial reefs, the extremities of which are marked by a light beacon, stands close inshore. The entire shoreline between Happisborough and Winterton Ness is protected from erosion by groynes which are marked by beacons. Thence:

Artificial Reefs off Sea Palling from N (9.23)
(Original dated 2005)

(Photograph - MV Confidante)

5 To a position NE of Winterton Ness (7½ miles SE). Winterton-on-Sea, situated behind sandhills and close to a nature reserve (1.61), is 1¼ miles SSE of the ness. Winterton Old Lighthouse (white

Winterton Old Lighthouse from SE (9.23)
(Original dated 2002)

(Photograph - Crown Copyright)

round tower, black band near top), which is disused, stands on a hill 3½ cables SE of Winterton Church (9.21).

(Directions continue for offshore approach to Great Yarmouth and Lowestoft at 9.45 and for inshore route at 9.33)

Anchorage and landing

Overstrand
9.24

1   Overstrand (52°55′N 1°21′E), which stands back from the cliff with a wooded background, has a long tarmac ramp used by fishing boats.

The Would
9.25

1   The Would (9.23) offers an anchorage in offshore winds, off the coast between Bacton (52°52′N 1°28′E) and Winterton Ness (11 miles SE), avoiding the numerous wrecks, pipelines and cables shown on the chart. Haisborough Sand offers some protection from E winds; N and NW winds cause the greatest sea.

WINTERTON NESS TO GREAT YARMOUTH - INSHORE ROUTE

General information

Charts 106, 1534
Routes
9.26

1   The inshore route to Great Yarmouth from N leading to Caister Road and Yarmouth Road is described below. An offshore route, which leads to Holm Channel, the principal approach from seaward to the ports of Great Yarmouth and Lowestoft, is given at 9.39.

2   **Caution.** Changes in the sandbanks and channels are frequent. No channel should be used unless it is buoyed, even if the charted depths appear sufficient; experience has shown that changes in channels which are not buoyed are more frequent than elsewhere.

Due to these rapid changes, buoyage might be altered before the relevant Notice to Mariners has been published.

Topography
9.27

1   From Winterton Ness (52°44′N 1°41′E) the coast runs 5½ miles SSE to Caister Point. The coast is sandy and backed by sandhills and sandy cliffs, up to 17 m in height. South of Caister Point the coast runs 4½ miles S to the entrance to Great Yarmouth. This stretch of coast is low and sandy.

2   A chain of sandbanks, lying up to 5 miles offshore, extends 15 miles S from a position 3½ miles NNE of Caister Point (52°39′N 1°44′E). These banks enclose the inner channel and the roads off Great Yarmouth and Lowestoft. The depths over these natural breakwaters are less than 5 m and they dry in several locations. The banks are also subject to great changes.

Depths
9.28

1   The approach from the N passes between Cockle Shoal and the N end of North Scroby Shoal, where there is a sandwave field (1.94) in depths of less than 10 m. In mid-channel between Hemsby Light Buoy (52°41′·8N 1°46′·2E) and N Scroby Light Buoy, 5 cables SSE, there was a least depth of 7·6 m m (2009) but depths are continually changing.

Wind farm
9.29

1   Scroby Sands Wind Farm is located on Middle Scroby Shoal within a rectangular area about 2 miles long and 8 cables wide centred on 52°38′·6N 1°47′·3E. It comprises

Lowestoft   Great Yarmouth   Britannia Pier

Scroby Sands Wind Farm from N (9.29)
(Original dated 2004)

(Photograph - Mike Page)

30 wind turbines; those at the four corners and additionally two at the middle of the rectangle exhibit lights (special) and are equipped with red obstruction lights and radar reflectors. All the wind turbines are interconnected by submarine cables.

2   The wind farm is located in shoal water where the depths are liable to frequent change. Mariners in small craft are advised not to sail through the wind farm area.

Submarine cables
9.30
1   Submarine cables are laid across Yarmouth Road from the SW corner of Scroby Sand Wind Farm (9.29) to the mainland as shown on the chart. Mariners are advised to avoid anchoring or fishing in the vicinity of these cables. See 1.41.

Rescue
9.31
1   Coastal Rescue Teams are based at Winterton and Gorleston; see 1.67.

An all-weather lifeboat and an inshore lifeboat are stationed at Great Yarmouth. Caister Volunteer Rescue Service maintains an all-weather lifeboat and an inshore lifeboat at Caister. See 1.72.

Tidal streams
9.32
1   Off the coast between Winterton Ness and Great Yarmouth the S-going tidal stream is strong at local HW and the N-going stream at local LW. Ripples or overfalls form when the streams cross shoals or other bottom inequalities and are more pronounced at LW when the strong N-going stream is running. When N gales oppose the N-going stream the sea breaks heavily over the shoals.

2   The tidal streams generally run in the direction of the coast and through channels aligned with the coast. They set across the shoals and channels not so aligned, the S-going stream setting towards the shoals on the SW side of the channels and the N-going stream towards the shoals on the NE sides. In particular the S-going stream sets onto the Scroby Shoals (9.36) and the N-going stream onto the Caister and Cockle Shoals (9.35).

3   For details see tables on the charts and *Admiralty Tidal Stream Atlas: North Sea, Southern Part.*

Directions
(continued from 9.23)

Principal marks
9.33
1   **Landmarks:**
    Newarp Light Buoy (52°48′N 1°56′E)
    Winterton Church tower (52°42′·9N 1°41′·2E) (9.21).
    Water Tower (52°39′·5N 1°42′·9E) of stone; taller radio mast close NNW.
    Caister Lifeboat House (52°38′·7N 1°44′·2E).

2   Nelson's Monument (52°35′·3N 1°44′·0E).
    Chimney of South Denes Power Station (52°35′·0N 1°44′·1E).

3   **Offshore mark:**
    Wind monitoring mast (52°40′·1N 1°47′·1E), 50 m in height. Lights are exhibited from the mast.

4   **Major light:**
    Lowestoft Light (52°29′·2N 1°45′·4E) (9.12) (Chart 1535).

Caister water tower from ENE (9.33)
(Original dated 2002)

(Photograph - Crown Copyright)

Caister Lifeboat Station from E (9.33)
(Original dated 2005)

(Photograph - MV Confidante)

Nelson's Monument from E (9.33)
(Original dated 2002)

(Photograph - Crown Copyright)

Other aids to navigation
9.34
1   **Racon:**
    ✳ wk 39/10 ~~Winterton Church tower (52°43′N 1°41′E).~~
    Cross Sand Light Buoy (52°37′N 1°59′E).
    For details see *Admiralty List of Radio Signals Volume 2.*

Winterton Ness to North Scroby
9.35
1   From a position at the SE end of The Would and NE of Winterton Ness, the route leads about 6 miles S to Caister

Outfall Beacon

South Denes Power Station from ENE (9.33)

(Original dated 2005)

(Photograph – MV Confidante)

North Scroby wind monitoring mast from SW (9.33)

(Original dated 2002)

(Photograph – Crown Copyright)

Road (52°41′·5N 1°45′·3E), passing (with positions from Winterton Church (52°48′N 1°56′E)):

W of Winterton Shoal (4½ miles NE), thence:

W of Winterton Overfalls (3½ miles ENE) which are usually marked by pronounced rippling and over which there can be breakers in bad weather, and:

E of Cockle Light Buoy (E cardinal) (1¾ miles NE) marking the N extremity of Cockle Shoal, thence:

2 Between Cockle Shoal (2½ miles ESE) and the N end of North Scroby (3¾ miles ESE). The fairway is marked by Hemsby Light Buoy (port hand) and N Scroby Light Buoy (N cardinal).

3 **Caution.** There are usually heavy tide rips over Cockle Shoal.

North Scroby to Great Yarmouth
9.36

1 From the N end of Caister Road (52°41′·5N 1°46′·0E), the route leads about 7 miles S through Caister and Yarmouth Road to a position E of the entrance to Great Yarmouth, passing (with positions from Caister Point (52°39′N 1°44′E)):

2 E of Caister Shoal (1½ miles NNE), which runs N/S over a distance of 4½ miles and forms the W side of Caister Road. The sea breaks heavily over the shoal which is marked on its E side by N Caister Light Buoy (port hand) and Mid Caister Light Buoy (port hand). And:

3 W of the Scroby shoals, which lie parallel to the coast and stretch about 6 miles S of Cockle Shoal. They consist of North (2½ miles NE), Middle (2½ miles ESE) and South Scroby (3 miles SSE) and form the E side of Caister Road and Yarmouth Road. The sea breaks heavily over both North and Middle Scroby, and Middle and South Scroby have extensive drying patches. There are tide rips over South Scroby. The shoals are marked by light buoys to their N and W and a conspicuous mast (9.33) stands between North and Middle Scroby. Scroby Sands Wind Farm (9.29) stands on Middle Scroby. Scroby shoals are continually altering and should not be approached on their unmarked side without local knowledge. Thence:

4 E of Yarmouth Outfall Light Buoy (port hand) (1½ miles SSE), marking the seaward extremity of an outfall, thence:

5 E of Britannia Pier (2¼ miles S), which is on the seafront at Great Yarmouth and has a large pavilion. Lights are exhibited from the head of Britannia Pier, which dries at MLWS. The Jetty and Wellington Pier, the latter with a large pavilion, lie 4 and 5 cables S of Britannia Pier. Lights are exhibited from both their heads. Thence:

Britannia Pier from NE (9.36)

(Original dated 2002)

(Photograph – Crown Copyright)

6 E of an obstruction (3½ miles S), with a least depth of 4·5 m. It lies at the seaward extremity of an outfall extending 3½ cables NE from South Denes Power station. The outfall is marked by a red occulting sector light (217°-227°) exhibited from the power station chimney. Another outfall marked by a light beacon (red triangular beacon on concrete plinth) stands 3 cables SSW. And:

7 W of the W extremity of Corton Sand.

Corton Sand extends about 2½ miles along the NE side of Holm Channel (9.56). It is shallow and dries; the sea breaks over the centre of the shoal.

Thence the track leads to a position off the entrance to Great Yarmouth.

(Directions continue for Great Yarmouth at 9.82)

Side channels
9.37

1 **Hemsby Hole** (52°42′·3N 1°43′·1E) leads from Cockle Gatway in the N to Yarmouth Road, and lies between Cockle and Caister Shoals and the coast. Depths of over 10 m can be maintained in the greater part of the channel but at the S end as it enters Yarmouth Road it passes over a ridge where depths are less than 3 m and constantly changing. Hemsby Hole is not marked by buoys and should not be attempted without local knowledge. Moreover, the sea breaks heavily onto Caister Shoal and the W side of it is steep-to.

2 **Barley Picle**, (52°40′N 1°50′E) which is not buoyed, lies between the Scroby shoals (9.36) and Cross Sand (9.47). It provided an approach to Great Yarmouth through a channel between the Scroby shoals and Corton Sand (9.36) but this channel has silted and Barley Picle is effectively closed to the W by these shoals.

Anchorages
9.38

1 Anchorage can be obtained in any part of Caister and Yarmouth Roads (9.36), depth 10 to 24 m, sand, shells, stones and shingle but clear of the spoil ground, submarine power cables and other charted obstructions. The roads are exposed to E winds which cause a short choppy sea. In these conditions it is best to anchor off the shallower parts of the off-lying sandbanks, indicated by the heavier breakers, in particular close W of the S part of Scroby Shoals. In the latter position no direct sea is experienced but some swell finds its way round the ends of the bank.

2 Gorleston Road (9.57), SE of the entrance to Great Yarmouth provides good anchorage, depth 10 to 20 m, sand but is only partially sheltered from E winds by the off-lying sandbanks.

Masters should ensure that they do not anchor in the approaches to Great Yarmouth harbour. In favourable conditions suitable anchorage can be obtained off the coast between Britannia Pier (9.36) and the N port limit, 9 cables S.

3 Small craft will find the best anchorage W of Caister Shoal.

WINTERTON NESS TO OUTER APPROACH TO GREAT YARMOUTH AND LOWESTOFT

General information

Charts 106, 1543
Route
9.39

1 From a position NE of Winterton Ness (52°44′N 1°41′E) the route leads about 7 miles ESE through Haisborough Gat and thence 16 miles SSW to a position E of Holm Channel, the principal approach from seaward to the ports of Great Yarmouth and Lowestoft.

Topography
9.40

1 Haisborough Gat is 2 miles wide and the continuation SE of The Would (9.23). It lies between a series of banks, principally Hammond Knoll (9.47) and Winterton Ridge (9.47) to the NE and Newarp Banks (9.47) to the SW.

Once clear of the Gat, the route lies to seaward of the coastal shoals and banks.

For a description of the coast S of Winterton Ness see 9.27.

Depths
9.41

1 Depending on the precise track followed, depths in excess of 20 m can be maintained in Haisborough Gat and to its SSW.

Submarine cables
9.42

1 Two cables run NE and E across Haisborough Gat from Winterton-on-Sea, 1 mile SE of Winterton Ness. Several disused cables have landings here also.

Rescue
9.43

1 See 9.31.

Tidal streams
9.44

1 The spring rate in each direction is about 2½ kn, although rates close to banks may be higher. Details of the tidal streams are given on the charts and in *Admiralty Tidal Stream Atlas: North Sea, Southern Part.*

Directions
(continued from 9.23)

Principal marks
9.45

1 **Landmarks:**
 Winterton Church tower (52°42′·9N 1°41′·2W) (9.21).
 Water tower at Caister (52°39′·5N 1°42′·9E) (9.33).
2 **Major light:**
 Lowestoft Light (52°29′·2N 1°45′·4E) (9.12).

Other aids to navigation
9.46

1 **Racon:**
 ✳ wk 39/10 ~~Winterton Church tower (52°43′N 1°41′E).~~
 Newarp Light Buoy (52°48′N 1°56′E).
 Cross Sand Light Buoy (52°37′N 1°59′E).
 For details see *Admiralty List of Radio Signals Volume 2.*

Winterton Ness to Holm Channel
9.47

1 From a position NE of Winterton Ness (52°44′N 1°41′E) the route leads ESE through Haisborough Gat thence SSW to a position E of Holm Channel, passing:
 SSW of S Haisbro Light Buoy (S cardinal) (52°51′N 1°48′E), marking the S extremity of Haisborough Sand (9.23), thence:
2 SSW of Haisborough Tail (52°53′N 1°51′E), which is 2½ miles E of Haisborough Sand and parallel to the latter's SE end. Depths between the two shoals are uneven. Thence:
 NNE of Winterton Shoal (52°46′N 1°47′E), marked by tidal eddies, and:
3 SSW of Hammond Knoll (52°53′N 1°55′E) parallel to and 2 miles E of Haisborough Tail. Hammond Knoll Light Buoy (W cardinal) is moored 1¾ miles SE of the shoal and E Hammond Light Buoy (E cardinal) is moored 2 miles E of the shoal and 1 mile NNW of Winterton Ridge (below). Thence:
4 SSW of Newarp Light Buoy (safe water) (52°48′N 1°56′E) (9.46), thence:

NNE of Newarp Banks (52°46′N 1°55′E), a series of shoals running NW/SE for over 4 miles, thence:

5   SSW of Winterton Ridge (52°49′N 2°02′E), which extends over 4 miles NNW/SSE. S Winterton Ridge Light Buoy (S cardinal) marks the SE end of the shoal. Thence:

SSW of Hearty Knoll (52°46′N 2°08′E), which runs NNW/SSE along the NE side of the Gat at its SE end.

6   Thence course is adjusted SSW, passing:

ESE of Cross Sand, which as defined by the 20 m depth contour extends 12 miles S from Newarp Banks to merge with the SE extremity of Corton Sand (9.36). It has three shallow areas, respectively North Cross Sand (52°43′N 1°52′E), Middle Cross Sand (52°40′N 1°53′E) and South Cross Sand (52°37′N 1°51′E), which may be indicated by tide rips. NE Cross Sand Light Buoy (E cardinal) is moored NE of North Cross Sand, E Cross Sand Light Buoy (port hand) to E of Middle Cross Sand and S Corton Light Buoy (S cardinal) to SSW of South Cross Sand. The sands are continually altering and should not be approached without local knowledge. Thence:

7   Clear of Cross Sand Light Buoy (safe water) (9.46) (52°37′N 1°59′E), 4 miles E of the S end of Middle Cross Sand, thence:

8   To a position NE of Holm Sand (52°30′N 1°48′E). The sea breaks over the shoal in all but the calmest weather and it has an extensive drying area. Holm Channel (9.56), the principal approach channel to Great Yarmouth and Lowestoft, is entered NE of Holm Sand. ~~Corton~~ Light Buoy (E cardinal) is moored at the SE entrance to Holm Channel.

9   **Caution.** Considerable dredging activity takes place in a large area, indicated on Chart 1543, to E of Cross Sand. The dredgers move slowly and might reverse their course without notice.

(Directions continue for the offshore approach to Great Yarmouth and Lowestoft at 9.54 and coastal passage S at 9.131)

OUTER APPROACH TO GREAT YARMOUTH AND LOWESTOFT

General information

Chart 1535, 1534
Routes
9.48

1   The principal approach to Great Yarmouth is from SE through Holm Channel and Gorleston Road. From Gorleston Road, the port of Lowestoft may be approached from N via Corton Road and Lowestoft North Road.

2   These routes are described below.

Lowestoft can also be approached from S through Stanford Channel. This route is described at 9.117.

Caution. Changes in the sandbanks and channels are frequent. No channel should be used unless it is buoyed, even if the charted depths appear sufficient. Experience has shown that changes in channels which are not buoyed are more frequent than elsewhere.

3   Due to these rapid changes, buoyage may be altered before the relevant Notice to Mariners has been published.

Topography
9.49

1   From the entrance to Great Yarmouth Haven (52°34′N 1°44′E), the coast runs 5½ miles SSE to Lowestoft Ness, the most eastern extremity of the United Kingdom. The entrance to Lowestoft Harbour is 6 cables SSW of Lowestoft Ness. The coast as far as Corton village, 3½ miles S of Great Yarmouth Haven, consists of cliffs up to 17 m high composed of sand gravel and red loam. To the S of Corton the shore is low-lying and sandy but that part of Lowestoft to N of Lake Lothing is situated on elevated ground and is conspicuous from seaward.

2   The 5 m depth contour lies close to the coast between Lowestoft Ness and Great Yarmouth Haven.

Offshore the chain of sandbanks (9.27) continues to the S, protecting the seaward side of the various roads which lead to Great Yarmouth and Lowestoft.

Depths
9.50

1   1   Depths are subject to change and the Port Authority should be consulted for the latest information.

~~of the channel depths in excess of 8 m may be found. Depths are subject to change and the port authority should be consulted for the latest information.~~

Depths are greater than 10 m in Gorleston Road, Corton Road and North Lowestoft Road to a position 1½ miles NE of the entrance to Lowestoft Harbour.

Movement reporting
9.51

1   Vessels on passage which pass close to Lowestoft are recommended to obtain details of vessel traffic movements from the Port Operations Service, as vessels leaving the port have very limited vision until clear of the piers. See *Admiralty List of Radio Signals Volume 6 (1)*.

Rescue
9.52

1   There is a Coastal Rescue Team at Lowestoft; see 1.67.

An all-weather lifeboat is stationed in the Outer Harbour at Lowestoft; see 1.72.

Tidal streams
9.53

1   In Corton Road and North Lowestoft Road the tidal streams probably run in the direction of the coast. East of Holm and Newcome Sands the tidal streams appear to be deflected E by the shoals in the vicinity. For details see information on the chart.

2   For tidal streams off and in the entrance to Lowestoft see 9.112.

Directions
(continued from 9.47)

Principal marks
9.54

1   **Landmarks:**

For marks at Great Yarmouth see 9.33.
Corton Church tower (52°31′·3N 1°44′·4E).

2   Building (St Peter Court Flats) (52°28′·9N 1°45′·2E).
Wind turbine (52°28′·8N 1°45′·7E).
Silo (52°28′·4N 1°44′·5E).

    Major light:

Lowestoft Light (52°29′·2N 1°45′·4E) (white round tower, 16 m in height).

Corton Church Tower from E (9.54)
(Original dated 2005)

(Photograph - MV Confidante)

Wind Turbine at Lowestoft from E (9.54)
(Original dated 2005)

(Photograph - MV Confidante)

Other aid to navigation
9.55

1   **Racon:**

Cross Sand Light Buoy (52°37′N 1°59′E) (Chart 1543).

✳ w/k 01/11   **AIS:**

Lowestoft Light (52°29′·2N 1°45′·4E).

For further details see *Admiralty List of Radio Signals Volume 2.*

Holm Channel
9.56 *1*   From the vicinity of Holm Approach Light Buoy (E cardinal) (52°30′·9N 1°50′·2E), the route leads 4¾ miles NW through...

Holm Channel to Gorleston Road from where a direct approach can be made to Great Yarmouth. Holm Channel is marked by light buoys and lies between Corton Sand (9.36) to NE and Holm Sand (9.47) to SW. The sea breaks over the shoals on either side of Holm Channel. See caution 9.48.

(Directions for Great Yarmouth continue at 9.82)

Gorleston Road to Lowestoft
9.57

1   From Gorleston Road the route leads 5 miles S through Corton Road and Lowestoft North Road to a position NE of the entrance to Lowestoft, passing (with positions from Corton Church (52°31′·3N 1°44′·4E)):

2   W of Holm Sand (3 miles SE) (9.47) which extends 6½ miles S to a position SE of the entrance to Lowestoft. Holm Sand is marked on its W side by NW Holm, W Holm and SW Holm Light Buoys (all starboard hand). NW Holm and W Holm Light Buoys also mark the E side of the fairway through Corton Road and Lowestoft North Road. Thence:

3   To a position E of Lowestoft Ness (2½ miles SSE) (9.49) and NE of the entrance to Lowestoft. An obstruction marked by two light buoys (E and S cardinal) lies 3 cables E of the Ness.

4   **Caution.** Along the coast there are numerous groynes, which are a danger to craft close inshore. Most are marked by beacons (triangular topmarks but can-shaped topmarks closer to Lowestoft).

Useful marks:
9.58

1   St Margaret's Church Spire (52°29′·2N 1°44′·5E). Monument (52°29′·3N 1°45′·3E).

(Directions continue for Lowestoft at 9.118)

Anchorages
9.59

1   **Corton Road** affords good anchorage between Holm Sand (9.47) and the coast with blue clay and mud, in depths of about 8 to 12 m.

2   **Lowestoft North Road** affords anchorage between Holm Sand (9.47) and the coast, sand and gravel, in depths of

Building   *Lighthouse*   *St. Margaret's Church Spire*   *Monument*

Landmarks at Lowestoft from ENE (9.54)
(Original dated 2002)

(Photograph - Crown Copyright)

about 10 to 13 m. This anchorage is exposed to E winds which cause a short, choppy sea in some respects worse than the sea outside the sandbanks. A number of disused submarine cables running in an E direction from Lowestoft Ness cross the S part of Lowestoft North Road.

GREAT YARMOUTH

General information

Chart 1534 plans of Great Yarmouth Haven and Outer Harbour
Position
9.60

1   Great Yarmouth (52°34′·49N 1°44′·80E) stands on a narrow strip of land between the E bank of River Yare and the sea. Two lifting bridges at the N end of Great Yarmouth Haven connect the town with the suburbs of Cobholm and Southtown on the W bank and thence with Gorleston-on-Sea to the W and S of the river mouth.

Function
9.61

1   Great Yarmouth Haven, situated in the lower reach of River Yare, is a small commercial port and the principal base for the offshore oil and gas field industry in the southern part of the North Sea.

The population of Great Yarmouth Borough is about 89 100.

Topography
9.62

1   To N of the mouth of River Yare, the coast is low and sandy but S of the entrance there are low cliffs (9.49).

Traffic
9.63

1   In 2008 the port was used by 331 vessels totalling 1 057 576 dwt.

Port Authority
9.64

1   Great Yarmouth Port Company Ltd., 20–21 South Quay, Great Yarmouth NR30 2RE.

        Website: www.eastportuk.co.uk

Limiting conditions

Controlling depth
9.65

1   For depths in the approach from N between Cockle Shoal and North Scroby Shoal see 9.28; in the approach from SE via Holm Channel see 9.50; in the approach from S via Stanford Channel there is a least depth of 6·3 m (2009).

Outer Harbour has a project depth of 10 m.

2   Controlling depth in the approach and entrance to River Yare is 4·4 m, but depths are subject to change. Temporary shoaling can occur after strong E winds when depths may be 1 m less than expected.

The Haven has a least depth in the fairway of 4·1 m. Depths are maintained by regular dredging and the Harbour Master should be consulted for the latest depths.

Vertical clearance
9.66

1   When closed, Haven Bridge (9.84) has a vertical clearance of 1·8 m.

When closed, the fixed spans of Breydon Bridge (9.91) provide a vertical clearance of about 4·0 m.

Deepest and longest berth
9.67

1   North Quay in Outer Harbour (9.86).

Tidal levels
9.68

1   Mean spring range about 2·0 m; mean neap range about 1·2 m. See *Admiralty Tide Tables Volume 1.*

Maximum size of vessel handled
9.69

1   Large vessels intending to use the port should consult the Harbour Master prior to arrival.

The maximum size of vessel projected to be handled in Outer Harbour is 180 m LOA and with a draught of about 9·5 m.

Great Yarmouth Haven has accommodated vessels up to 138 m LOA but it should be noted that the river is only about 90 m wide and there is no turning basin but see 9.77. Vessels with a draught up to 6·2 m can berth alongside but may take bottom at MLWS.

Local weather and sea state
9.70

1   During strong SE winds, heavy seas may be experienced in the entrance.

Arrival information

Port operations
9.71

1   The port is normally open at all times but vessels with limited manoeuvrability should plan to enter at HW or LW slack periods on account of strong tidal streams (9.81).

2   A Port Operations Service is maintained. See *Admiralty List of Radio Signals Volume 6 (1)*. It is necessary to book a mooring crew.

Notice of ETA required
9.72

1   At least 24 hours, or, immediately upon departure from last port or offshore installation. Confirmation of ETA is required at 8 hours and 2 hours prior to arrival.

Outer anchorages
9.73

1   See 9.38.

Spare
9.74

~~remains closed to navigation.~~
~~Vessels should keep well to seaward of any vessels engaged in completion operations in the close vicinity of Outer Harbour. Port Operations should be contacted for further information if required.~~

Submarine cables and pipelines
9.75

1   A gas pipeline (1.41) crosses the haven at its S end. Warning notices (yellow diamonds, black letters) indicate landing places.

Submarine power cables cross the river 1 mile N of Brush Bend; beacons mark the landing places.

Pilotage and tugs
9.76

1   **Pilotage** is compulsory for all vessels of 40 m in length and over, except warships, vessels exempt by law and vessels changing berth within River Yare. However if local

220

2   knowledge is limited, a pilot is recommended for shifting or swinging within the port.

2   Pilots embark in Great Yarmouth and Lowestoft Outer boarding position (52°32′·0N 1°51′·9E) or at Great Yarmouth Inner boarding position (52°34′·8N 1°46′·0E) for those vessels bound for the Outer Harbour. Vessels bound for berths within the River Yare embark pilots at Great Yarmouth and Lowestoft Outer boarding position (see above) or Great Yarmouth River Port boarding position (52°34′·3N 1°45′·2E). The pilot boats have a black hull and orange superstructure.

Due to strong tidal streams in the river (9.81), it is customary for pilots to steer vessels. Anchors should be ready for immediate use.

3   **Tugs** are available. 24 hours notice is required.

Traffic regulations
9.77

1   **Speed.** All vessels should maintain a slow speed in the harbour. The maximum permitted speed of 7 kn is not necessarily a safe speed and a slower speed may be appropriate.

Designated swinging areas. Brush Bend maximum 100 m; Berth 3 maximum 92 m; Atlas Berth maximum 85m.

Vessels may be swung in other areas dependent upon vessel's length, draught and other traffic movements. Fenders should be prepared and Port Operations should be contacted prior to any swing.

Harbour

General layout
9.78

1   **Outer Harbour,** a new development, lies on the seaward side of the South Denes peninsula adjacent to the mouth of River Yare. The harbour basin is rectangular and enclosed by N and S breakwaters. The entrance is 210 m wide and the basin has a project depth of 10 m. Lights (lateral) are exhibited from the breakwater heads.

2   **Great Yarmouth Haven** lies along the banks of River Yare. From its entrance, the track leads 2½ cables W and then turns abruptly N at Brush Lighthouse to open up the haven itself. There are riverside berths on either bank for a distance of 2 miles up to Haven Bridge. Most of the commercial quays have the berth number displayed.

Traffic signals
9.79

1   **Outer Harbour.** Signals Nos 1, 2 and 5 of the International Port Traffic Signals are exhibited from the root of the north breakwater.

River Port. Signals Nos 1, 2, 3 and 5 of the International Port Traffic Signals are exhibited from the E end of ~~Gorleston Pier~~. Signals Nos 1, 2, 3 and 5 are also exhibited on the S side of Brush Bend for vessels proceeding down river. When signal No 2 is exhibited vessels should not approach Brush Bend.

For further details see *The Mariners' Handbook.*

Bridge traffic signals
9.80

1   Three red lights disposed vertically, are exhibited from Haven Bridge (9.84) and Breydon Bridge (9.91) downstream or upstream as appropriate, to prohibit traffic passing through the bridge from that direction. These lights are only switched on 5 minutes before the bridge is due to open.

Vessels should contact the Bridge Master on VHF Channel 12 prior to passing through the bridge.

Tidal streams
9.81

1   One mile NE of the haven entrance tidal streams set as follows:

Time from HW Dover	Remarks
+0600	S-going stream begins.
–0020	N-going stream begins. Spring rate in each direction 2¼ kn.

2   Off Brush Quay the tidal streams set as follows:

Time from HW Dover	Remarks
+0545 (Local LW +2 hours)	In-going stream begins. It rarely exceeds 2 kn except at Haven Bridge where it can reach 3 kn.
–0030 (Local HW +1½ hours)	Out-going stream begins. Normal rate 4 kn, but can reach 6 kn.

3   The streams begin later upriver.

The S-going stream outside the harbour entrance runs past North Pier and turns NW passing Gorleston Pier as the in-going stream. The main part of the stream runs W to Brush Bend but a part forms an eddy current running E along North Pier. In these conditions inbound vessels must take care to avoid being set onto North Pier, as the NW-going eddy current acts strongly on the port bow deflecting the vessels towards North Pier.

4   The out-going stream runs past North Pier and turns N with the N-going stream. The latter does not set so sharply across the entrance as the eddy on the in-going stream. However at Gorleston Pier part of the stream sets SE before joining the N-going stream. Inbound vessels may then round Gorleston Pier stemming this stream. In mid-channel inbound vessels may find the bow deflected to port towards Gorleston Pier by this set.

5   During and after heavy rain the duration and rate of the out-going stream is increased and the in-going stream correspondingly reduced. Under these circumstances the out-going stream may attain 6 kn off Brush Quay and there may be a continuous out-going stream for 18 hours.

6   Slack water normally occurs at local HW+1½ and LW+2 hours. Prolonged strong winds or heavy rainfall may cause these times to vary and also alter the tidal range by more than 1 m. The following can be expected:

	HW slack	LW slack	Tidal height
N wind	later	earlier	increased
S wind	earlier	later	decreased
Heavy rain	earlier	later	increased

Directions for entering harbour
(continued from 9.36 and 9.56)

Principal marks
9.82

1   Landmarks:

Nelson's Monument (52°35′·3N 1°44′·0E) (9.33).
Chimney at power station (52°35′·0N 1°44′·1E) (9.33).
Brush Lighthouse (disused) (52°34′·3N 1°43′·9E); red round brick tower, 21 m in height.

River Yare entrance to Brush Quay
9.83

1   From the vicinity of the Great Yarmouth River Port pilot boarding position (52°34′·3N 1°45′·2E) the track leads

Outer Harbour
9.82a

1   The Outer Harbour (9.78) is entered between two breakwaters with lights at the breakwater heads. The chart is sufficient guide.

Great Yarmouth Inner Harbour Entrance (9.83)
(Original dated 2005)

(Photograph - MV Confidante)

about 5 cables W to the river mouth which is about 70 m wide. The track passes (with positions from Brush Lighthouse (disused) (54°34′·3N 1°43′·9E)):

S of the entrance to the Outer Harbour (9.78) (6 cables NE), thence:

S of a light (green metal column with ladder, 7 m in height) (52°34′·38N 1°44′·38E) standing on the S side of the Outer Harbour S breakwater.

S of North Pierhead (3 cables ENE) which projects 150 m E from the coast and from which a light (green metal column with ladder, 7 m in height) is exhibited, thence:

2   N of Gorleston Pierhead (2 cables E) which extends from the coast at Gorleston-on-Sea. A light is exhibited from a square building on the pierhead; the upper half is composed of red brick but the lower half is painted white and illuminated to assist mariners at night and in reduced visibility. Thence:

3   S of a training wall (1½ cables ENE) which lies on the N side of the channel. Five sets of lights (starboard hand) are exhibited from the training wall. And:

4   N of Gorleston Pier (1 cable E) a stone embankment which is marked by seven sets of lights (port hand). At Brush Bend on which stands a conspicuous lighthouse (disused) (9.82) the embankment curves sharply to the N. Tugs may be required to assist the turn and anchors should be ready. On completion of the turn there is a direct approach to the riverside berths lying to the N.

River Yare and Great Yarmouth Haven
9.84

1   From a position E of Brush Lighthouse, River Yare runs 2 miles N to Haven Bridge. This part of the river forms the haven, which has a generally uniform width of about 80 m.

Haven Bridge is a double bascule bridge with a width of 26·8 m when open. Lights mark the navigation span. Advance application is required for the bridge to be opened.

Useful marks
9.85

1   Church (tower) (52°36′·2N 1°43′·8E).
Church (tower) (52°34′·7N 1°43′·5E).

Berths

Outer Harbour
9.86

1   North Quay is projected to be 400 m in length with a project depth of 10 m alongside. It is intended to comprise two berths which are equipped for the short sea container trade.

On the W side of the harbour a berth of projected length 200 m is intended for RoRo vessels.

Great Yarmouth Haven
9.87

1   Apart from those berths used in offshore support activities, the main berths from the S are:

Berth	Length (m)	Least Depth (m)
East Bank		
3, 4A, 4B	250	3·7
5A, 5B, 5C (East Quay)	270	4·6
7A, 7B (Ocean Terminal)	145	4·6
8, 9	250	4·5
13, 14	317	3·4

Berth	Length (m)	Least Depth (m)
West Bank		
25, 26 (Southtown)	160	2·6

2   Berthing is not normally permitted between Brush Lighthouse and the pilot station at Mission Quay.

Port services

Repairs
9.88

1   Repairs of all types can be carried out.

The dry dock has a length of 85 m, width of 13 m and depth over sill 4·4 m at MSL.

Other facilities
9.89

1   Domestic waste disposal; Ship Sanitation Certificates issued (1.92); customs; hospitals, one with helicopter landing site; reception of oily waste.

Supplies
9.90

1   All types of fuel from facilities on either bank; water at most berths; stores and provisions.

Inland waterways

General information

9.91

1   River Yare is joined by River Bure close N of Haven Bridge (9.84). Thence it runs 3½ miles WSW under Breydon Bridge and through Breydon Water to be joined by River Waveney. The three rivers provide over 120 miles of inland navigation and access to Norwich, Coltishall, Beccles and Lowestoft (9.125).

   The opening span of Breydon Bridge has a width of 23 m. When closed vessels should use the fixed span immediately on the starboard side of the centre span. See 9.66.

LOWESTOFT AND SOUTH APPROACH

General information

Chart 1535
Position
9.92

1   The port of Lowestoft (52°28'·31N 1°45'·38E) is situated on the banks of Lake Lothing and the harbour entrance is 6 miles S of Great Yarmouth.

Function
9.93

1   The port of Lowestoft (52°28'·31N 1°45'·38E) is a commercial and fishing port. It is also a base for supply ships servicing the offshore oil and gas industry and for vessels servicing offshore wind farms. Drilling rig structures and wind turbines are fabricated in the port area and in addition there are ship repair facilities (9.122). The port is a recreational centre and has several marinas.

2   The population of Lowestoft is about 67 000.

Traffic
9.94

1   In 2008 the port was visited by 975 vessels of all types, except fishing vessels; cargo handled at the port totalled 160 000 tonnes.

Port Authority
9.95

1   Associated British Ports, Port Office, North Quay Cargo Terminal, Commercial Road, Lowestoft NR32 2TE.

   Website: www.abports.co.uk

Limiting conditions

Controlling depths
9.96

1   A maintained channel, depth 4·7 m, leads from the harbour entrance to a position 7 cables W of the lifting bridge (9.119). The channel is liable to silting, but this is soon cleared by dredgers. Farther W the channel progressively reduces in depth to 1·5 m at the W end of Lake Lothing (9.109).

Vertical clearance
9.97

1   When closed, Lowestoft Harbour Bridge (9.103) has a vertical clearance of 1·7 m, Carlton Swing Bridge (9.126) a vertical clearance of 4·1 m and Mutford Road Bridge (9.126) 1·6 m.

Deepest and longest berth
9.98

1   Deepest Berth: Hamilton Quay (9.121).
   Longest Berth: North Quay Cargo Terminal (9.121).

Tidal levels
9.99

1   See *Admiralty Tide Tables Volume 1*. Mean spring range about 1·9; mean neap range about 1·1 m. There are tide gauges in Bridge Channel (9.119).

Abmormal water levels
9.100

1   Winds from the ENE through S to SW depress the sea level, while winds from the other directions raise it. A wind from the ESE force 3 to 4 can depress the sea level by about 0·1 m and a NW wind force 3 to 4 can raise it by a similar amount. It is reported that strong winds and gales can raise or depress sea levels by as much as 1·2 m.

2   Such changes in sea level have several consequences. At neaps sea level may rise continuously during the normal period of the falling tide or at springs the normal in-going and out-going streams may be nearly cancelled. There may also be seiches of considerable range. During strong N gales the rising tide may be interrupted frequently by falls and the falling tide by rises.

3   In these circumstances the tidal streams at the entrance and in the harbour are equally affected and may change from in-going to out-going and the reverse, at frequent intervals, attaining a rate of up to 4 kn at the bridge in extreme conditions. See 9.112.

Maximum size of vessel handled
9.101

1   The port can accept vessels up to 100 m in length and draught 6·0 m at MHWS.

Arrival information

Port radio
9.102

1   A port radio station is maintained. For details see *Admiralty List of Radio Signals Volume 6 (1)*.

Bridge
9.103

1   Lowestoft Harbour Bridge (9.11 demand for commercial shipp discouraged from passage during 1230–1300, and 1700–1745 daily. opening times for small craft is pub mariners. Inbound small craft awa can secure to a 35 m long pont Trawl Dock.

2   For details of bridge signals s

Notice of ETA required
9.104

1   Twenty-four hours notice of E' should confirm ETA 3 hours and stating preferred pilot boarding po

Outer anchorages
9.105

1   A recommended anchorage in dep 21 m lies 4 miles SSE of the hark exposed to E winds. For anchorages N of Lowestoft see 9.59.

After Paragraph 9.103 2 line 1 Insert:

Caution. The bascule bridge structure imposes restraints upon vessels transiting the Bridge Channel. In the fully raised position parts of the bridge structure are within a few centimetres horizontally of the coping edge. Contact with the bridge leaves could damage a vessel, the bridge structure or its control systems. If it is not certain whether a risk exists the Harbour Master should be consulted.

Harbour Master Lowestoft
(SDD 201 1000 142241)

[34/11]

Pilotage and tugs

9.106 Pilotage is compulsory for the following vessels:

1 ~~Pil~~ All vessels or tows of 60 m LOA or over.

' All vessels or tows over 20 m LOA carrying dangerous or noxious liquid substances in bulk.

' All vessels or tows over 20 m LOA carrying explosives.

All vessels or tows over 30 m LOA carrying more than 12 passengers.

' All vessels of less than 60 m in length, deemed to be a potential hazard to navigation.

2 The following categories of vessel are exempt from compulsory pilotage:

HM vessels and foreign naval vessels.

Vessels not calling at Lowestoft and in transit through the area of pilotage jurisdiction.

3 Pilots board as follows:

Great Yarmouth and Lowestoft Outer (52°32'·0N 1°51'·9E). Sea pilotage is available from this position for vessels wishing to use Holm Channel to approach the port.

Lowestoft South (52°26'·7N 1°48'·3E). Pilotage is available from this position for vessels wishing to use Stanford Channel, particularly when approaching from S or E.

4 Lowestoft Inner (52°29'·8N 1°47'·0E). Pilotage is available from this position for any vessel wishing to enter Lowestoft. This position will be used in all cases where the sea conditions do not permit safe boarding at the Outer or South boarding positions.

5 Vessels waiting for a pilot should not approach closer than these limits. The pilot vessel has a dark hull, orange upperworks with "PILOT" painted on each side. See *Admiralty List of Radio Signals Volume 6 (1)*.

Tugs: Three tugs are available.

Local knowledge

9.107

1 In view of the continually changing nature of the shoals in the approaches to Lowestoft, especially from the S, local knowledge is essential. For first time visitors the services of a pilot are recommended. See caution 9.48.

Speed

9.108

1 The maximum speed for vessels is 4 kn. Because the harbour is narrow vessels are required to proceed at the minimum safe speed to avoid interaction with moored vessels and pontoons. This applies especially to large displacement vessels underway at LW.

Harbour

General layout

9.109

1 The harbour is entirely artificial and consists of Outer and Inner Harbours. On the N side of Outer Harbour, Trawl, Waveney and Hamilton Docks are used mainly by support vessels for the North Sea oil and gas fields, support vessels for offshore wind farms, fishing vessels and recreational craft. North Pier, which forms the seaward side of Waveney and Hamilton Docks, is used for the construction of offshore platform modules. These can be conspicuous when viewed from seaward.

On the S side of Outer Harbour there is an enclosed yacht basin and marina.

2 Inner Harbour formed by Lake Lothing, is used by commercial vessels and offshore support vessels. It is approached from Outer Harbour via Bridge Channel which is spanned by a double leaf bascule bridge (9.119).

Traffic signals

9.110

1 International Port Traffic Signals Nos 2 and 5 (see *The Mariner's Handbook*) are used for the control of shipping in the entrance to the harbour. They are shown from the light tower on Gorleston Pier.

2 **Note.** In the interests of safety, all vessels must observe these international port signals and navigate with the understanding that the Port Control, and departing vessels in Outer Harbour, have extremely limited vision to the N of the entrance piers.

3 International Port Traffic Signals Nos 2 and 5 also shown from the E arm of the Yacht Basin entrance and from the W entrance to Waveney Dock. These signal lights are only visible from inside the basins and are used to control vessels exiting the basins. There are no signal lights to control vessels entering the basins. Vessels should therefore proceed with caution when entering and leaving the basins and should report their movements to the port radio station.

Bridge signals

9.111

1 Navigation in Bridge Channel is controlled by Lowestoft Port Control. A fixed red light (E and W of the bridge) is displayed prior to and during bridge lift operations. Once open, a fixed green light indicates it is clear for vessels to proceed. If the fixed red light remains illuminated, vessels should remain clear of other vessels using the channel and await instructions on VHF. Large vessels may not approach within 150 m of the bridge unless so directed.

Tidal streams

9.112

1 In the entrance to Lowestoft Harbour the tidal streams are strong and complex. See also 9.100.

The tidal streams set as follows:

Time from HW Dover	Remarks
Outside the entrance	
–0645	S-going stream begins
–0030	N-going stream begins. Spring rate in each direction 2½ kn.
Across the entrance	
–0645	S-going stream begins.
–0215	N-going stream begins. However within 90 m of the entrance the S-going stream runs strongly for 3 hours, then is much reduced or even forms a N-going eddy advancing the start of the N-going stream from as early as –0315 Dover.
In the entrance (Bridge Channel)	
+0430	In-going stream begins.
–0130	Out-going stream begins. At springs the in-going rate is 2 kn for 3 hours, after which it is much weaker; the out-going rate is 1 kn. At neaps both rates are ½ kn.

Trawl Dock　　　　　　　　*Lake Lothing*

Waveney Dock　　　　　*Hamilton Dock*

Lowestoft Harbour from ENE (9.111)

(Original dated 2000)

(Photograph - Air Images)

2　　**Caution.** The table given above is a guide to expected streams. Actual tidal streams at the entrance to Lowestoft may vary and will be affected by weather conditions

9.113

1　　After HW Lowestoft, the N-going stream produces a strong N set across the harbour entrance, which is met by the out-going stream. Together these run NE along North Pier extension. In these conditions a vessel entering will have the out-going stream on her starboard bow, while the N-going stream is on her port quarter, resulting in a tendency to sheer towards Gorleston Pier as the entrance is approached.

2　　When the S-going stream and in-going streams are running, a SW stream results along North Pier extension and into the harbour or across Gorleston Pier, and a vessel will tend to be swept onto Gorleston Pier as the entrance is approached.

Directions for entering harbour

Principal marks
9.114

1　　**Landmarks:**
　　　　Building (St Peter Court Flats) (52°28'·9N 1°45'·2E).
　　　　Wind turbine (52°28'·8N 1°45'·7E).
　　　　Silo (52°28'·4N 1°44'·5E).
　　　　Water tower (52°26'·9N 1°43'·5E).
　　　　Kessingland Church (tower) (52°25'·0N 1°42'·9E).

Pakefield - Conspicuous water tower from E (9.114)

(Original dated 2002)

(Photograph - Crown Copyright)

　　Major light:
　　　　Lowestoft Light (52°29'·2N 1°45'·4E) (9.12).

Other aid to navigation

Spare
9.115

General
9.116

1　　To minimise the effects of the tidal streams at the harbour entrance (9.112), it is recommended that vessels enter harbour on the in-going stream and depart on the out-going stream. The optimum time to enter Lowestoft is 1 hour before local HW, when the tidal streams across the entrance should be weak. Whether approaching from the N or S, the approach should be made as slowly as possible until about 100 m off the entrance when speed should be increased and the appropriate wheel applied to maintain the centreline of the entrance.

2 Entry is feasible during E gales just after LW as the offshore sandbanks make an excellent breakwater. Entry is not advisable for large or low powered vessels during SE gales.

South Approach via Stanford Channel
9.117

1 Stanford Channel, marked by light buoys (lateral), lies between Holm Sand (9.47) and Newcome Sand, the latter a shoal patch running roughly N/S. The N part of the shoal, 1 mile SSE of the harbour entrance, dries.

2 From a position ENE of Newcome Sand Light Buoy (port hand) (52°26′N 1°47′E), the route leads 2½ miles NNW following Stanford Channel to a position NE of the harbour entrance. The track passes WSW of S Holm Light Buoy (S cardinal) (52°27′N 1°47′E) marking the S extremity of Holm Sand.

See caution 9.48.

Approach to harbour entrance
(Continued from 9.58 and 9.117)
9.118

1 From a position about 1 mile NE of the harbour entrance

1 cable ESE of the harbour entrance whence direct approach to the entrance can be made, passing (with positions from the harbour entrance):

2 SE of a pair of light buoys (E and S cardinal), marking an obstruction with a depth of 4·7 m (7½ cables NE), thence:

NW of an unmarked wreck (6 cables NE) with a depth of 4·0 m, thence:

NW of a detached shoal patch (5 cables NE) with depths of less than 5 m. N Newcome Light Buoy (port hand) is moored close to the E extremity of the patch. Thence:

3 NW of Lowestoft Bank (4½ cables ESE), which connects to the N part of Newcome Sand (9.117) and to the coastal bank which extends from the shore S of the harbour entrance. Lowestoft Bank has depths of less than 2 m. Thence:

4 To the harbour entrance which is 45 m wide and lies between North and Gorleston Piers. North Pier and its extension runs 3 cables SW from the NE corner of the harbour. Gorleston Pier extends 2 cables E from the shore along the S side of the harbour. Similar lights (white tower on small pavilion, 9 m in height, floodlit) are exhibited from the pierheads.

5 **Caution.** A wall on North Pier, 3 m high, partially prevents small boats leaving Waveney Dock from seeing or being seen.

Harbour entrance to Inner Harbour
9.119

1 From the harbour entrance the route follows the dredged channel, which is 40 m wide, in a generally WNW direction 2½ cables through Outer Harbour to the bascule

bridge thence into Inner Harbour, passing (with positions from the bridge):

SSW of the entrance to Waveney Dock (2 cables E) which leads to Hamilton Dock, thence:

S of the entrance to Trawl Dock (1 cable E), thence:

2 To Bridge Channel which is 22·7 m wide and lies between Inner N and Inner S Piers and leads to Inner Harbour. Lowestoft Harbour Bridge, a bascule bridge, is only opened on demand for commercial shipping; see 9.103.

Useful marks
9.120

1 Saint Margaret's Church Spire (52°29′·2N 1°44′·5E).
Water tower (52°27′·3N 1°43′·7E).
Pakefield Church tower (52°27′·2N 1°44′·1E).

Pakefield Church and water tower
(52° 27·3′N, 1° 43·7′E) from E (9.120)
(Original dated 2002)

(Photograph – Crown Copyright)

Basins and berths
9.121

1 **Outer Harbour.** Hamilton Quay Berth 1, E face, has a length of 60 m and a dredged depth alongside of 5·0 m.

Inner Harbour. There are about 2000 m of quays mainly on the N side of Lake Lothing. North Quay Cargo Terminal, about 5 cables W of the bridge, has a length of 500 m and dredged depth of 3·7 m. Silo Quay, about 3 cables W of the bridge, is 200 m in length with a dredged depth of 4·0 m alongside and is used for the export of grain. CEFAS Quay, a berth for research vessels, 2 cables W of the bridge has been dredged to 6 m but is liable to silting.

Port services

Repairs
9.122

1 The local shipyards can undertake repairs of all types. There are several slipways and the largest is capable of taking vessels up to 55 m in length and 800 tonnes displacement.

There is a dry dock, length 76 m, width 14·5 m and depths below chart datum of 2·2 m at the blocks at the entrance and 1·8 m at the head.

Other facilities
9.123

1 Limited salvage capability; reception of oily waste, noxious and harmful substances; Ship Sanitation Certificates issued (1.92); hospital.

Supplies
9.124

1   Fuel is available by road tanker at most berths; fresh water at most quays; stores and provisions available locally.

Inland waterways

General information
9.125

1   Lowestoft and Norwich Navigation passes from Lake Lothing to Oulton Broad (52°28′·5N 1°42′·5E) and provides access for small craft via Rivers Waveney and Yare to Norwich. Beyond Mutford Lock, *The International Regulations for Preventing Collisions at Sea (1972)* are replaced by The Broads Authority regulations.

Mutford Lock and bridges
9.126

1   The lock, with safe usable dimensions of 22 m in length and 6·5 m in width, has a depth of 2 m plus tidal variations and should be used by craft suitable for the depth of Oulton Broad. Visiting craft with a draught exceeding 1·7 m should seek advice from Mutford Lock staff and consider Oulton Broad tide which is approximately 3 hours after Lowestoft with a mean range of 0·7 m.

2   Mutford Road Bridge, adjacent to the lock, has a vertical clearance of 1·6 m and it is therefore essential for all craft requiring an opening to make an advance booking and to be prepared to wait. Such bookings will automatically include Carlton Swing Bridge located close E. VHF is monitored by Mutford Lock Control and Oulton Broad Yacht Station between 0800 and 1800 from April to October and between 0800 and 1100 from November to March. See *Admiralty List of Radio Signals Volume 6 (1).*
  There is a waiting pontoon on the S bank between Carlton Swing Bridge and Mutford Lock.

3   Craft entering with an air draught of more than about 6·8 m are confined to River Waveney by fixed bridges.

HOLM CHANNEL
TO SOUTHWOLD

General information

Chart 1543
Route
9.127

1   From a position NE of Holm Sand (52°30′N 1°48′E) the coastal route leads 14 miles SSW to a position ESE of Southwold.

Topography
9.128

1   South of Lowestoft the offshore banks merge with the coastal bank and close the shore in the vicinity of Benacre Ness (9.133), 5 miles S of Lowestoft. Thence the 5 m depth contour lies 3 to 4 cables to seaward and parallel to the shore.

2   The coast generally consists of low cliffs interspersed with beaches. For about 2 miles to the S of Benacre Ness the coast is eroding and after HW springs or storms debris such as tree trunks may be encountered offshore.

Rescue
9.129

1   There is a Coastal Rescue Team at Southwold; see 1.67. An inshore lifeboat is stationed at Southwold; see 1.72.

Tidal streams
9.130

1   Details of the tidal streams are given on the charts.

Directions
(continued from 9.47)

Principal marks
9.131

1   **Landmarks:**
  For marks at Lowestoft see 9.114.
  Kessingland Church (tower) (52°25′·0N 1°42′·9E).

Kessingland Church from E (9.131)
(Original dated 2002)

(Photograph – Crown Copyright)

  Covehithe Church (tower) (52°23′N 1°42′E).
  Southwold Church (tower) (52°20′N 1°41′E).
  Water tower (3 cables W of Church tower) at Southwold.

2   **Major light:**
  Lowestoft Light (52°29′·2N 1°45′·4E) (9.12).
  Southwold Light (52°19′·6N 1°40′·9E) (9.12).

Other aid to navigation

1   **Spare**
9.132

Holm Sand to Southwold
9.133

1   From a position NE of Holm Sand (52°30′N 1°48′E), the route leads SSW to a position ESE of Southwold, passing (with positions from Benacre Ness (52°24′N 1°44′E)):
  ESE of Holm Sand (6 miles NNE) (9.47) and ESE of E Newcome Light Buoy (port hand) (5¾ miles NNE) thence:

2   ESE of Newcome Sand (3½ miles NNE) (9.117), thence:
  ESE of Barnard (1 mile NNE), an irregular shoal which is steep-to on its seaward side and is marked on its E side by E Barnard Light Buoy (E cardinal), thence:

3   ESE of Benacre Ness, a low indefinite point, with a well-wooded and slightly undulating background, thence:
  ESE of a light buoy (special) (2 miles SSW) moored close inshore and marking instruments, thence:

Clear of a light buoy (special) (5½ miles SSE) marking instruments, thence:

To a position ESE of Southwold.

(Directions for coastal passage S continue in Dover Strait Pilot.)

Southwold

Charts 2695 plan of Southwold Harbour, 1543
General information
9.134

1   Southwold (52°18'·80N 1°40'·51E), a seaside resort, stands on a hill and is almost surrounded at HW by a combination of River Blyth, Buss Creek and the sea. The harbour, which is located at the mouth of River Blyth about 5 cables SSW of the town, is used mainly by small fishing boats and recreational craft. Southwold Harbour is administered by Waveney District Council, Town Hall, Lowestoft. The population is about 4000.

A pleasure pier with a fendered T-head extends 1 cable offshore in the N part of the town. The pier carries several prominent white buildings and lights (galvanised metal post) are exhibited.

Limiting conditions
9.135

1   **Controlling depths.** The harbour is approached over a bar which has a least charted depth of about 0·5 m. Within the harbour there is a minimum charted depth in the channel of 1·4 m.

2   **Tidal levels:** see *Admiralty Tide Tables Volume 1*. Mean spring range about 1·9 m; mean neap range about 1·2 m.

Local weather and sea state. There is a confused sea in the entrance with an onshore wind and an out-going stream. If the wind is strong onshore then it is dangerous to cross the bar. Entry at LW with a strong out-going stream is also very difficult.

Arrival information
9.136

1   **Local knowledge.** No pilot is available. Because of the changing nature of the bar, the Harbour Master should be consulted before attempting to enter the harbour. The Harbour Master can usually be contacted by VHF 2½ hours either side of HW.

Anchorage, shown on chart 1543, is available 8 cables ESE of the entrance to Southwold Harbour.

Harbour
9.137

1   **General layout.** The harbour lies at the mouth of River Blyth and its entrance is protected by two piers (9.139). Within the entrance, the harbour is up to 64 m wide between The Quay on the N bank and S pier. The Quay, which is in a poor state of repair and exposed to any swell, has depths ranging from 1·6 to 3·4 m. Most craft berth at upstream pontoons and jetties near the Harbour Master's office at Blackshore Quay.

Traffic signals International Port Traffic Signals Nos 2 and 3 are exhibited from the N pierhead. See *The Mariner's Handbook.*

A daytime signal consisting of two red flags displayed at the N pierhead signifies that the port is closed.

2   **Tidal streams** are slack for a short period in the harbour entrance about 30 minutes after local HW. The spring out-going stream can attain a rate of 4 to 5 kn. The stream scours the N bank of the harbour in the vicinity of The Quay displacing the channel to that side.

Directions for entering harbour
9.138

1   **Landmarks:**
Southwold Church (52°19'·7N 1°40'·7E).
Water tower (52°19'·6N 1°40'·3E).
Pier (52°19'·2N 1°41'·2E) (9.134).
Southwold Light (52°19'·6N 1°40'·9E) (9.12).

Southwold Harbour from S (9.134)

(Original dated 2000)

(Photograph - Air Images)

navigate within Mortimer's Deep after obtaining prior clearance from Forth Navigation Service.

Movement of Selected Vessels bound to or from Grangemouth Docks

11. **Hen & Chickens Buoy** Vessels shall not navigate within the fairway west of the Hen & Chickens Buoy, Longitude 03°38′·00 West without the express permission of the harbour master and when such a vessel is underway in the fairway no other vessel shall proceed in the opposite direction to the said vessel within that section of the fairway.

> (**Note:** *For the purposes of the Direction, a selected vessel is a vessel of more than 80 metres LOA which carries, in bulk, goods classified in the IMDG Code as being of Classes 2, 3.1, or 3.2. A vessel of more than 80 metres LOA which has residues in empty tanks or cargo holds which have been used for the carriage of such Classes (as above) and have not been cleaned, purged, gas freed or ventilated as appropriate, is also a selected vessel*):

(a) Vessels are prohibited, except in the case of emergencies, from anchoring in the fairway west of Hen & Chickens Buoy.

(b) **Docking** Vessels will normally be locked into and out of the docks singly unless expressly permitted otherwise by the harbour master.

(c) When a vessel is manoeuvring in the docks, no other vessel shall proceed underway within the docks without the express permission of the harbour master.

Anchorages

13. The master of any vessel intending to anchor within the port shall inform the Forth Navigation Service of his intention to anchor and shall, if required by the Duty Officer, anchor his vessel in one of the anchorages detailed in the Appendix hereto and shall not move from such anchorage unless clearance to do so has been given by the Duty Officer.

(This note is not part of the Forth Byelaws.)

The Appendix to the Byelaws is not included in this volume; the anchorages are shown on the charts and mentioned in the text where appropriate. There are also a number of areas where anchoring is prohibited, which are also shown on the charts and mentioned in the text.

Passage Plan

16. On a vessel served with an authorised pilot, the embarked pilot upon arrival onboard and following any action to establish the navigational safety of the ship, will advise the vessel's master of his Pilotage Passage Plan. He will also advise the vessel's master of any changes made necessary to the vessel's Port Passage Plan by local circumstances. Before proceeding with the passage, the master and pilot shall agree the Pilotage Passage Plan for the voyage into the port and such agreement shall be reported to Forth Navigation Service (FNS).

On a vessel not embarking an authorised pilot but navigating or intending to navigate within the Port (including those vessels having a valid PEC holder navigating the vessel for the passage in the port) the master and/or the PEC holder shall prepare a Port Passage Plan in respect of the vessel's voyage and before proceeding with the voyage shall:

a) confirm to FNS that a Port Passage Plan has been prepared and is in use;

b) provide the relevant details of the Port Passage Plan to FNS.

The master of a vessel which is navigating or intending to navigate in the Forth, in preparing his Port Passage Plan, shall use appropriate and properly corrected navigational charts and consider and take full account of correct regulations and advice promulgated by Forth Ports PLC including:

> Forth Byelaws
> Forth General Directions
> Tide Tables
> Notices to Mariners
> Any information provided by VTS of current circumstances in the port.

Speed Restrictions

17. Forth Ports PLC, in exercise of their powers under Section 3 of the Forth Ports Order 1980 and having carried out the consultations required by that section, has given the following general direction to vessels navigating in the port.

Without prejudice to any other obligation to navigate with due care and at a moderate speed, merchant and other private power-driven vessels when navigating within the waters of the port shall (except for such purpose and subject to such conditions as may be specified in a licence in writing given by the Chief Harbour Master) observe the following speed restrictions when West of meridian 3°16′W:

a) When East of the Forth Railway Bridge:
  i) Vessels of 100 metres or more in length overall
    – 12 knots over the ground
  ii) Vessels of less than 100 metres in length overall
    – 15 knots over the ground

b) When West of the Forth Railway Bridge:
  All vessels – 12 knots over the ground

c) The imposition of a strict speed limit of 10 knots over the ground when passing within 5 cables of a ship lying alongside Crombie Jetty or Hound Point Terminal, or when passing within 5 cables of a vessel at anchor moored to a buoy.

APPENDIX II

The Territorial Waters Order in Council 1964

AT THE COURT AT BUCKINGHAM PALACE

The 25th day of September 1964

Present,

THE QUEEN'S MOST EXCELLENT MAJESTY IN COUNCIL

Her Majesty, by virtue and in exercise of all the powers enabling Her in that behalf, is pleased, by and with the advice of Her Privy Council, to order, and it is hereby ordered, as follows:

1. This Order may be cited as the Territorial Waters Order in Council 1964 and shall come into operation on 30th September 1964.

2.-(1) Except as otherwise provided in Articles 3 and 4 of this Order, the baseline from which the breadth of the territorial sea adjacent to the United Kingdom, the Channel Islands and the Isle of Man is measured shall be the low-water line along the coast, including the coast of all islands comprised in those territories.

(2) For the purpose of this Article a low-tide elevation which lies wholly or partly within the breadth of sea which would be territorial sea if all low-tide elevations were disregarded for the purpose of the measurement of the breadth thereof and if Article 3 of this Order were omitted shall be treated as an island.

3.-(1) The baseline from which the breadth of the territorial sea is measured between Cape Wrath and the Mull of Kintyre shall consist of the series of straight lines drawn so as to join successively, in the order in which they are there set out, the points identified by the co-ordinates of latitude and longitude in the first column of the Schedule to this Order, each being a point situate on the low-water line and on or adjacent to the feature, if any, named in the second column of that Schedule opposite to the co-ordinates of latitude and longitude of the point in the first column.

(2) The provisions of paragraph (1) of this Article shall be without prejudice to the operation of Article 2 of this Order in relation to any island or low-tide elevation which for the purpose of that Article is treated as if it were an island, being an island or low-tide elevation which lies to seaward of the baseline specified in paragraph (1) of this Article.

4. In the case of the sea adjacent to a bay, the baseline from which the breadth of the territorial sea is measured shall, subject to the provisions of Article 3 of this Order—

  (a) if the bay has only one mouth and the distance between the low-water lines of the natural entrance points of the bay does not exceed 24 miles, be a straight line joining the said low-water lines;

  (b) if, because of the presence of islands, the bay has more than one mouth and the distances between the low-water lines of the natural entrance points of each mouth added together do not exceed 24 miles, be a series of straight lines across each of the mouths drawn so as to join the said low-water lines;

  (c) If neither paragraph (a) nor (b) of this Article applies, be a straight line 24 miles in length drawn from low-water line to low-water line within the bay in such a manner as to enclose the maximum area of water that is possible with a line of that length.

5.-(1) In this Order—

  the expression "bay" means an indentation of the coast such that its area is not less than that of the semi-circle whose diameter is a line drawn across the mouth of the indentation, and for the purposes of this definition the area of an indentation shall be taken to be the area bounded by the low-water line around the shore of the indentation and the straight line joining the low-water lines of its natural entrance points, and where, because of the presence of islands, an indentation has more than one mouth the length of the diameter of the semi-circle referred to shall be the sum of the lengths of the straight lines drawn across each of the mouths, and in calculating the area of an indentation the area of any islands lying within it shall be treated as part of the area of the indentation;

  the expression "island" means a naturally formed area of land surrounded by water which is above water at mean high-water spring tides; and

  the expression "low-tide elevation" means a naturally formed area of drying land surrounded by water which is below water at mean high-water spring tides.

(2) For the purpose of this Order, permanent harbour works which form an integral part of a harbour system shall be treated as forming part of the coast.

(3) The Interpretation Act 1889(a) shall apply to the interpretation of this Order as it applies to the interpretation of an Act of Parliament.

6. This Order shall be published in the *London Gazette*, the *Edinburgh Gazette* and the *Belfast Gazette*.

W.G. AGNEW

(a) 52 & 53 Vict.c.63.

EXPLANATORY NOTE

(This Note is not part of the Order, but it is intended to indicate its general purport).

This Order establishes the baseline from which the breadth of the territorial sea adjacent to the United Kingdom, the Channel Islands and the Isle of Man is measured. This, generally, is the low-water line round the coast, including the coast of all islands, but between Cape Wrath and the Mull of Kintyre a series of straight lines joining specified points lying generally on the seaward side of the islands lying off the coast are used, and where there are well defined bays elsewhere lines not exceeding 24 miles in length drawn across the bays are used.

TERRITORIAL SEA (AMENDMENT) ORDER 1998

For the schedule to the Territorial Waters Order in Council 1964 **(a)** there shall be substituted the schedule set out below:

SCHEDULE

POINTS BETWEEN CAPE WRATH AND LAGGAN JOINED BY GEODESICS TO FORM BASELINES

	Latitude North			Longitude West			Name of Feature
	°	′	″	°	′	″	
1.	58	37	40	5	00	13	Cape Wrath
2.	58	31	12	6	15	41	Lith–Sgeir
3.	58	30	44	6	16	55	Gealltuig
4.	58	29	09	6	20	17	Dell Rock
5.	58	18	28	6	47	45	Tiumpan Head
6.	58	17	36	6	52	43	Màs Sgeir
7.	58	17	09	6	55	20	Old Hill
8.	58	14	30	7	02	06	Gallan Head
9.	58	14	01	7	02	57	Islet SW of Gallan Head
10.	58	10	39	7	06	54	Eilean Molach
11.	57	59	08	7	17	42	Gasker
12.	57	41	19	7	43	13	Haskeir Eagach
13.	57	32	22	7	43	58	Huskeiran
14.	57	14	33	7	27	44	Rubha Ardvule
15.	57	00	50	7	31	42	Greuab Head
16.	56	58	07	7	33	24	Doirlinn Head
17.	56	56	57	7	34	17	Aird a' Chaolais
18.	56	56	05	7	34	55	Biruaslum
19.	56	49	21	7	39	32	Guarsay Mor
20.	56	48	00	7	39	57	Sron an Duin
21.	56	47	07	7	39	36	Skate Point
22.	56	19	17	7	07	02	Skerryvore
23.	56	07	58	6	38	00	Dubh Artach
24.	55	41	36	6	32	02	Frenchman's Rocks
25.	55	40	24	6	30	59	Orsay Island
26.	55	35	24	6	20	18	Mull of Oa
27.	55	17	57	5	47	54	Mull of Kintyre
28.	54	58	29	5	11	07	Laggan

The positions of points 1 to 28 are defined by co-ordinates of latitude and longitude on the Ordnance Survey of Great Britain (1936) Datum (OSGB 36).

The Territorial Waters (Amendment) Order 1996 **(b)** is hereby revoked.

N. H. Nicholls
Clerk of the Privy Council

EXPLANATORY NOTE

(This note is not part of the Order)

The Order amends the Schedule to the Territorial Waters Order in Council 1964 by adding a new baseline between Mull of Kintyre and Laggan, as well as making minor changes to points 5, 9 and 22, which result from the publication of a new, larger scale chart of the area.

(**a**) 1965 III, p.6452A; revised Schedules were substituted by the Territorial Waters (Amendment) Order in Council 1979 and the Territorial Sea (Amendment) Order 1996.

(**b**) SI 1996/1628

TERRITORIAL SEA ACT 1987

Be it enacted by the Queen's Most Excellent Majesty, by and with the advice and consent of the Lords Spiritual and Temporal, and Commons, in this present Parliament assembled, and by the authority of the same, as follows:

1.-(1) Subject to the provisions of this Act—
    (a) the breadth of the territorial sea adjacent to the United Kingdom for all purposes be 12 nautical miles; and
    (b) the baselines from which the breadth of that territorial sea is to be measured shall for all purposes be those established by Her Majesty by Order in Council.

(2) Her Majesty may, for the purpose of implementing any international agreement or otherwise, by Order in Council provide that any part of the territorial sea adjacent to the United Kingdom shall extend to such line other than that provided for by subsection (1) above as may be specified in the Order.

(3) In any legal proceedings a certificate issued by or under the authority of the Secretary of State stating the location of any baseline established under subsection (1) above shall be conclusive of what is stated in the certificate.

(4) As from the coming into force of this section the Territorial Waters Order in Council 1964 and the Territorial Waters (Amendment) Order in Council 1979 shall have effect for all purposes as if they were Orders in Council made by virtue of subsection (1)(b) above: and subsection (5) below shall apply to those Orders as it applies to any other instrument.

(5) Subject to the provisions of this Act, any enactment or instrument which (whether passed or made before or after the coming into force of this section) contains a reference (however worded) to the territorial sea adjacent to, or to any part of, the United Kingdom shall be construed in accordance with this section and with any provision made, or having effect as if made, under this section.

(6) Without prejudice to the operation of subsection (5) above in relation to a reference to the baselines from which the breadth of the territorial sea adjacent to the United Kingdom is measured, nothing in that subsection shall require any reference in any enactment or instrument to a specified distance to be construed as a reference to a distance equal to the breadth of that territorial sea.

(7) In this section "nautical miles" means international nautical miles of 1,852 metres.

2.-(1) Except in so far as Her Majesty may by Order of Council otherwise provide, nothing in section 1 above shall affect the operation of any enactment contained in a local Act passed before the date on which that section comes into force.

(2) Nothing in section 1 above, or in any Order in Council under that section or subsection (1) above, shall affect the operation of so much of any enactment passed or instrument made before the date on which that section comes into force as for the time being settles the limits within which any harbour authority or port health authority has jurisdiction or is able to exercise any power.

(3) Where any area which is not part of the territorial sea adjacent to the United Kingdom becomes part of that sea by virtue of section 1 above or an Order in Council under that section, subsection (2) of section 1 of the Continental Shelf Act 1964 (vesting and exercise of rights with respect to coal) shall continue, on and after the date on which section 1 above of that Order comes into force, to have effect with respect to coal in that area as if the area were not part of the territorial sea.

(4) Nothing in section 1 above, or in any Order in Council under that section, shall affect—
    (a) any regulations made under section 6 of the Petroleum (Production) Act 1934 before the date on which that section or Order comes into force; or
    (b) any licences granted under the said Act of 1934 before that date or granted on or after that date in pursuance of regulations made under that section before that date.

(5) In this section—
"coal" has the same meaning as in the Coal Industry Nationalisation Act 1946; "harbour authority" means a harbour authority within the meaning of the Harbours Act 1964 or the Harbours Act (Northern Ireland) 1970; and "port health authority" means a port health authority for the purposes of the Public Health (Control of Disease) Act 1984.

3.-(1) The enactments mentioned in Schedule 1 to this Act shall have effect with the amendments there specified (being minor amendments and amendments consequential on the provisions of this Act).

(2) Her Majesty may by Order in Council—
    (a) make, in relation to any enactment passed or instrument made before the date on which section 1 above comes into force, any amendment corresponding to any of those made by Schedule 1 to this Act;
    (b) amend subsection (1) of section 36 of the Wildlife and Countryside Act 1981 (marine nature reserves) so as to include such other parts of the territorial sea adjacent to Great Britain as may be specified in the Order in the waters and parts of the sea which, by virtue of paragraph 6 of Schedule 1 to this Act, may be designated under that section;
    (c) amend paragraph 1 of Article 20 of the Nature Conservation and Amenity Lands (North Ireland) Order 1985 (marine nature reserves) so as to include such other parts of the territorial sea adjacent to Northern Ireland as may be specified in the Order in the waters and parts of the sea which, by virtue of paragraph 9 of Schedule 1 to this Act, may be designated under that Article.

(3) Her Majesty may by Order in Council make such modifications of the effect of any Order in Council under section 1(7) of the Continental Shelf Act 1964 (designated areas) as appear to Her to be necessary or expedient in consequence of any provision made by or under this Act.

(4) The enactments mentioned in Schedule 2 to this Act are hereby repealed to the extent specified in the third column of that Schedule.

4.-(1) This Act may be cited as the Territorial Sea Act 1987.

(2) This Act shall come into force on such day as Her Majesty may by Order in Council appoint, and different days may be so appointed for different provisions and for different purposes.

(3) This Act extends to Northern Ireland.

(4) Her Majesty may by Order in Council direct that any of the provisions of this Act shall extend, with such exceptions, adaptations and modifications (if any) as may be specified in the Order, to any of the Channel Islands or to the Isle of Man.

INDEX

Names without a paragraph number are for gazetteer purposes only

NOTES

NOTES

NOTES

NOTES

PREVIOUS EDITIONS

North Sea Pilot Volume II

First published 1857
Second Edition 1868
Third Edition 1875
Fourth Edition 1885
Fifth Edition 1895
Sixth Edition 1905
Seventh Edition 1914
Eighth Edition 1923
Ninth Edition 1935
Tenth Edition 1949
Eleventh Edition 1959
Twelfth Edition 1960

North Sea Pilot Volume III

First Edition 1858
Second Edition 1869
Third Edition 1874
Fourth Edition 1882
Fifth Edition 1889
Sixth Edition 1897
Seventh Edition 1905
Eighth Edition 1914
Ninth Edition 1922
Tenth Edition 1933
Eleventh Edition 1948

North Sea (West) Pilot

First Edition 1973
Second Edition 1991
Third Edition 1995
Fourth Edition 1997
Fifth Edition 2000
Sixth Edition 2003
Seventh Edition 2006

Produced in the United Kingdom
by UKHO